D0860285

UNIVERSITY CASEBOOK SERIES

ARBITRATION

SECOND EDITION

by

ALAN SCOTT RAU
Robert F. Windfohr & Anne Burnett Windfohr Professor of Law
The University of Texas at Austin School of Law

EDWARD F. SHERMAN
Professor of Law
Tulane University School of Law

SCOTT R. PEPPET
Associate Professor of Law
University of Colorado School of Law

This edition is the successor to John S. Murray, Alan Scott Rau, & Edward F. Sherman, Processes of Dispute Resolution: The Role of Lawyers, first published in 1989 (2nd Edition 1996)

NEW YORK, NEW YORK

FOUNDATION PRESS

2002

Reprinted in part from Rau, Sherman & Peppet, Processes of Dispute Resolution, Third Edition © 2002
By Foundation Press

395 Hudson Street
New York, NY 10014
Phone Toll Free 1–877–888–1330
Fax (212) 367–6799
fdpress.com

Printed in the United States of America

ISBN 1–58778–089–5

TEXT IS PRINTED ON 10% POST CONSUMER RECYCLED PAPER

PREFACE

This paperback dealing with arbitration was originally written as a chapter of our coursebook, Processes of Dispute Resolution: The Role of Lawyers, which is designed for a course on the full range of alternative dispute resolution procedures. With a growing interest in commercial arbitration, and a growing number of law school courses and seminars focusing specifically on that process, we thought it might be useful to reprint it separately, for use by instructors who wish to focus only on arbitration.

The teaching of arbitration must, of course, reflect at several points an awareness of the issues raised by the use of "alternative" processes generally. Alternative methods of dispute resolution have become part of the processing of a wide range of disputes in our society. Hundreds of thousands of disputes are voluntarily submitted to mediation each year through community dispute resolution centers, other non-profit institutions, and a growing host of entrepreneurial providers. In a sizable number of state and federal courts, dispute resolution procedures are invoked as part of the litigation process. Private companies and governmental agencies have adopted "system designs" incorporating ADR procedures to prevent, or to resolve, the inevitable disputes that arise in their operations. Delivery of mediation and arbitration services has moved to videoconferencing and cyberspace, as experimentation with different forms continues. And arbitration has also expanded from such traditional fields as labor and construction to a wide range of contractual services such as investments, banking, health care, and employment. It is obvious that lawyers today must have a grounding in ADR in order to provide adequate advice and representation in many areas of the law.

Most law schools now offer courses in ADR. Still, stereotypes persist, and habits that developed over many decades change slowly. Within the first few months of law school, law students are often socialized to believe that the most prestigious role for a lawyer finds its principal outlet in the courtroom. Litigation is the standard; negotiation, mediation and arbitration are invisible processes. Our aim in this book is to bring litigation into perspective—to encourage students to see it as a system of dispute resolution, one with its own virtues and failings, but not an inevitable or the only process for resolving legal disputes. We want students to see that the many alternative processes of dispute resolution are not distinct from litigation, nor mutually exclusive, but usefully complementary processes. The contemporary lawyer needs to develop an ability to work effectively with all available processes, separately, in series, and even simultaneously.

The reasons for the great expansion of ADR in the last couple of decades are varied. They stem in part from the inadequacies of litigation as a dispute resolution mechanism. Parties have expressed dissatisfaction with a court system that imposes heavy costs in terms of time and money and that lacks flexibility in providing solutions. But there are other important dimensions of ADR than an anti-litigation bias that account for its new popularity, such as its potential for reducing the adversariness of the trial system and accomplishing both a more efficient and a more satisfactory resolution of disputes. We will examine in this book both the philosophical wellsprings of the ADR movement and the countervailing objections of its critics.

As the title to our book indicates, our focus is on process. At times, this is theoretical and policy-oriented. We think an understanding of the underlying philosophy, history, strengths, and weaknesses of each alternative dispute resolution process is necessary for a lawyer to appreciate how and when it can be used in helping clients resolve their disputes. But we place equal importance on practical application. Thus, we attempt to provide a comprehensive overview of the legal procedures and doctrines that a lawyer will need to know in order to use the techniques effectively. These legal aspects are sometimes highly technical—as in the litigation procedures that influence negotiated settlement, the law governing arbitration practice, and the formalities of court-administered ADR—and we believe these materials provide a solid introduction to their use. We have included extensive citations to cases and other sources so that these materials will also be a helpful reference book for students once they are in practice.

We place particular stress on the role of "the law" in each alternative process, on the lawyer's role in choosing processes and implementing strategies, and on the lawyering skills needed to use the processes effectively. The skills component to the course can be substantial, depending on the specific objectives of the instructor. We believe that the more students practice ADR skills and become comfortable with ADR procedures, the better equipped they will be to serve their clients' interests.

A note on form: We have substantially edited most cases and selections to delete unnecessary material. Deletions of text due to our editing are indicated by spaced asterisks. Citations in the text, and footnotes from the text, have usually been omitted without indication. Where footnotes to selections do appear, however, we have retained the number they have in the original material. A reader desiring to use the opinion as a research tool can, of course, go to the official case reporters.

We have benefited from the helpful comments and critiques of many colleagues and students who have used the prior editions of this book. We are also extremely grateful to those whose conscientious and able research and administrative assistance made completion of this book possible—in particular Christina Garcia, Chris Piazzola, Sandy Schmieder, Shawn Stigler, Mary Pace, Jonae Harrison, Janice Sayas, Pat Smith, and Pat Floyd.

A.S.R.

E.F.S.

S.R.P.

January, 2002

*

ACKNOWLEDGMENTS

The following authors and publishers gave us permission to reprint excerpts from copyrighted material; we gratefully acknowledge their assistance.

CHAPTER I

Drawing by Lorenz; copyright © 1991 The New Yorker Magazine, Inc.

Landes & Posner, Adjudication as a Private Good, 8 J. Legal Stud. 235, 235-40, 245-47 (1979). Copyright © 1979 by the University of Chicago. All rights reserved.

Fuller , Collective Bargaining and the Arbitrator, 1963 Wisc L Rev. 3, 11-12, 17.

Sperber, Overlooking Negotiating Tools, 20 Les Nouvelles 81 (June 1985).

Galanter, Justice in Many Rooms: Courts, Private Ordering, and Indigenous Law, 19 J. Pluralism & Unofficial L. 1, 17-18, 25 (1981).

Mentschikoff, The Significance of Arbitration-A Preliminary Inquiry, 17 Law & Contemporary Problems 698, 709 (1952). Copyright © 1952 Duke University School of Law.

Craver , The Judicial Enforcement of Public Sector Interest Arbitration, 21 B.C.L.Rev., 557, 558 n.8 (1980). Reprinted by permission of Boston College, Office of the Law Reviews.

Jones, Three Centuries of Commercial Arbitration on New York: A Brief Survey, 1956 Wash. U.L.Q. 193, 209-10, 218-19.

Mentschikoff, Commercial Arbitration, 61 Colum. L. Rev. 846, 848-54 (1961). Copyright © 1961 by the Directors of the Columbia Law Review Association Inc. All rights reserved. This article originally appeared at 61 Colum. L. Rev. 846 (1961). Reprinted by permission.

Craig, Park, & Paulsson, International Chamber of Commerce Arbitration 638, 29-30, 744 (3rd Ed. 2000).

Tang, Arbitration—A Method Used in China to Settle Foreign Trade and Economic Disputes, 4 Pace L. Rev. 519, 533-34 (1984).

Hays, Labor Arbitration: A Dissenting View 112-13 (1966).

Getman, Labor Arbitration and Dispute Resolution, 88 Yale L.J. 916, 928-30 (1979). Reprinted by permission of The Yale Law Journal Company and

William S. Hein Company from The Yale Law Journal, Vol. 88, pages 916-949.

Moller, Rolph, & Ebener, Private Dispute Resolution in the Banking Industry 12-13 (RAND 1993). RAND, MR-259-ICJ.

Terry, The Technical and Conceptual Flaws of Medical Malpractice Arbitration, 30 St. Louis U.L.J. 571, 572-73, 586 (1986). Reprinted with permission.

Henderson, Contractual Problems in the Enforcement of Agreements to Arbitrate Medical Malpractice, 58 Va.L.Rev. 947, 994 (1972). Reprinted by permission of Fred B. Rothman & Co.

St. Antoine, Judicial Review of Labor Arbitration Awards: A Second Look at Enterprise Wheel and its Progeny, 75 Mich. L. Rev. 1137, 1140, 1142 (1977).

Rau , Contracting Out of the Arbitration Act, 8 American Review of International Arbitration 225 (1997).

Rau, On Integrity in Private Judging, 14 Arbitration International 115, 146-150, 230-31 (1998).

Rau, Integrity of Private Judging 38 So. Tex. L. Rev. 485, 526-27 (1997). Reprinted by permission of South Texas College School of Law.

Hart & Sacks, The Legal Process 310 (1994).

Stein, The Selection of Arbitrators, N.Y.U Eighth Annual Conference on Labor 291, 293 (1955).

Raffaele, Lawyers in Labor Arbitration, 37 Arb.J. No.3 (Sept. 1982).

Roth, When to Ignore the Rules of Evidence in Arbitration, 9 Litigation 20 (Winter 1983). Copyright © 1983 American Bar Association. Reprinted with permission from Vol. 9, No.2, Litigation. All rights reserved.

Allison, The Context, Properties, and Constitutionality of Nonconsensual Arbitration,1990 Journal of Dispute Resolution 1, 6, 15. Reprinted by permission from the Journal of Dispute Resolution and the Curators of the University of Missouri-Columbia. For more information, contact: Editor-in Chief, Journal of Dispute Resolution, University of Missouri School of Law, Columbia, Missouri 65211.

Summers, Public Sector Bargaining: Problems of Governmental Decision-making, 44 U Cinn. L. Rev. 672 (1975). Reprinted with permission.

Raiffa, The Art and Science of Negotiation 118 (1982). Reprinted by permission of the publisher from THE ART AND SCIENCE OF NEGOTIATION: HOW TO RESOLVE CONFLICTS AND GET THE BEST OUT OF BARGAINING by Howard Raiffa, The Belknap Press of Harvard University Press, Copyright © 1982 by the President and Fellows of Harvard College.

Fuller, Collective Bargaining and the Arbitrator, Proceedings, Fifteenth Annual Meeting, National Academy of Arbitrators 8, 29-33, 37-48 (1962). Reprinted with permission. Chapter 2, pages 8, 29-33, and 37-48 and 34-41 from Collective Bargaining and the Arbitrator's Role (Proceedings of the 15th Annual Meeting National Academy of Arbitrators), by Lon L. Fuller. Copyright © 1962, by The Bureau of National Affairs, Inc. Washington, D.C. 20037.

Panel Discussion, Proceedings, 33rd Annual Meeting, National Academy of Arbitrators 232 (1981). Reprinted with permission, Chapter 7, pages 224-239 from Decision Thinking of Arbitrators and Judges, (Proceedings of the 33rd Annual Meeting National Academy of Arbitrators) by Rolf Valtin. Copyright © 1981, by The Bureau of National Affairs, Inc. Washington, DC 20037.

Folberg & Taylor, Mediations 277-78 (1984). Reprinted by permission of Jossey-Bass, Inc.

Christensen, Private Justice: California's General Reference Procedure, 1982 American Bar Foundation Research J. 79, 81-82, 103.

Note, The California Rent-A-Judge Experiment: Constitutional and Policy Considerations of Pay-As-You-Go Courts, 94 Harv. L. Rev.. 1592, 1601-02, 1607-08 (1981). Copyright © 1981 by the Harvard law Review Association.

*

SUMMARY OF CONTENTS

*

TABLE OF CONTENTS

*

TABLE OF CASES

Principal cases are in bold type. Non-principal cases are in roman type. References are to Pages.

*

ARBITRATION

*

Snow White and the Wicked Queen submit the fairness question to binding arbitration.

• •

ARBITRATION

A. THE PROCESS OF PRIVATE ADJUDICATION

1. INTRODUCTION

William M. Landes & Richard A. Posner, Adjudication as a Private Good

8 J. Legal Stud. 235, 235–40 (1979).

Adjudication is normally regarded as a governmental function and judges as public officials. Even economists who assign a highly limited role to government consider the provision of judicial services as indisputably apt function of government; this was, for example, Adam Smith's view. Few economists (and few lawyers) realize that the provision of judicial services precedes the formation of the state; that many formally public courts long had important characteristics of private institutions (for example, until 1825 English judges were paid out of litigants' fees as well as general tax revenues); and that even today much adjudication is private (commercial arbitration being an important example).

* * *

1. *Introduction.* A court system (public or private) produces two types of service. One is dispute resolution—determining whether a rule has been violated. The other is rule formulation—creating rules of law as a by-product of the dispute-settlement process. When a court resolves a dispute, its resolution, especially if embodied in a written opinion, provides information regarding the likely outcome of similar disputes in the future. This is the system of precedent, which is so important in the Anglo–American legal system.

* * *

The two judicial services are in principle severable and in practice often are severed. Jury verdicts resolve disputes but do not create precedents. Legislatures create rules of law but do not resolve disputes. In the Anglo–American legal system rule formation is a function shared by legislatures and (especially appellate) courts; elsewhere judicial law making tends to be less important.

2. *Dispute Resolution.* Imagine a purely private market in judicial services. People would offer their services as judges, and disputants would select the judge whom they mutually found most acceptable. The most popular judges would charge the highest fees, and competition among judges would yield the optimum amount and quality of judicial services at minimum social cost. This competitive process would produce judges who were not only competent but also impartial—would thus fulfill the ideals of procedural justice—because a judge who was not regarded as impartial could not get disputes submitted to him for resolution: one party would always refuse.

A voluntary system of dispute resolution does not presuppose that the dispute has arisen from a consensual relationship (landlord-tenant, employer-employee, seller-buyer, etc.) in which the method of dispute resolution is agreed on before the dispute arose. All that is necessary is that when a dispute does arise the parties to it choose a judge to resolve it. Even if they are complete strangers, as in the typical accident case, the parties can still choose a judge to determine liability.

Although dispute resolution could thus be provided (for criminal as well as civil cases) in a market that would operate free from any obvious elements of monopoly, externality, or other sources of "market failure," it may not be efficient to banish public intervention entirely. Public intervention may be required (1) to ensure compliance with the (private) judge's decision and (2) to compel submission of the dispute to adjudication in the first place. The first of these public functions is straightforward, and no more compromises the private nature of the adjudication system described above than the law of trespass compromises the private property rights system. The second function, compelling submission of the dispute to judge, is more complex. If A accuses B of breach of contract, the next step in a system of private adjudication is for the parties to select a judge. But suppose B, knowing that any impartial judge would convict him, drags his feet in agreeing to select a judge who will hear the case, rejecting name after name submitted by A for his consideration. Although a sanction for this kind of foot-dragging (a sanction analogous to the remedies that the National Labor Relations Board provides for refusals to bargain collectively in good faith) is conceivable, there may be serious difficulty in determining when the bargaining over the choice of the judge is in bad faith—it is not bad faith, for example, to reject a series of unreasonable suggestions by the other side.

Two ways of overcoming the submission problem come immediately to mind. The first is for the parties to agree on the judge (or on the method of selecting him) before the dispute arises, as is done in contracts with arbitration clauses. This solution is available, however, only where the dispute arises from a preexisting voluntary relationship between the parties; the typical tort or crime does not. * * *

Another type of private solution to the problem of enforcement and the selection of a private judge is available when both parties to the dispute are members of the same (private) group or association. The group can expel any member who unreasonably refuses to submit to an impartial adjudication (perhaps by a judge selected by the group) or to abide by the judge's decision. To the extent that membership in the group confers a value over and above alternative opportunities, members will have incentives to bargain in good faith over the selection of the judge and to abide by his decision. In these circumstances dispute resolution can operate effectively without public intervention.

* * *

3. *Rule Production.* Private production of rules or precedents involves two problems. First, because of the difficulty of establishing property rights in a precedent, private judges may have little incentive to produce precedents. They will strive for a fair result between the parties in order to preserve a reputation for impartiality, but why should they make any effort to explain the result in a way that would provide guidance for future parties? To do so would be to confer an external, an uncompensated, benefit not only on future parties but also on competing judges. If anything, judges might deliberately avoid explaining their results because the demand for their services would be reduced by rules that, by clarifying the meaning of the law, reduced the incidence of disputes. Yet, despite all this, private judges just might produce precedents. We said earlier that competitive private judges would strive for a reputation for competence and

impartiality. One method of obtaining such a reputation is to give reasons for a decision that convince the disputants and the public that the judge is competent and impartial. Competition could lead private judges to issue formal or informal "opinions" declaring their interpretation of the law, and these opinions—though intended simply as advertising—would function as precedents, as under a public judicial system. * * *

The second problem with a free market in precedent production is that of inconsistent precedents which could destroy the value of a precedent system in guiding behavior. If there are many judges, there is likely to be a bewildering profusion of precedents and no obvious method of harmonizing them. An individual contemplating some activity will have difficulty discovering its legal consequences because they will depend on who decides any dispute arising out of the activity.

* * *

[A] system of voluntary adjudication is strongly biased against the creation of precise rules of any sort. Any rule that clearly indicates how a judge is likely to decide a case will assure that no disputes subject to the rule are submitted to that judge since one party will know that it will lose. Judges will tend to promulgate vague standards which give each party to a dispute a fighting chance.

2. Arbitration and Dispute Resolution

The traditional model of arbitration is precisely that of the "private tribunal"—private individuals, chosen voluntarily by the parties to a dispute in preference to the "official" courts, and given power to hear and "judge" their "case." The materials that follow explore the ramifications of this model, which is still the prevalent one. "Arbitration," however, cannot be so easily pigeon-holed, and in recent years the term has come to serve for a broad spectrum of dispute resolution processes. We will see later in this section how other models of arbitration have altered our conventional view of the process. Arbitration, for example, is sometimes imposed by law as a *mandatory,* non-consensual form of dispute resolution (See Section E.1 infra), and it has also been used to resolve kinds of disputes different from the traditional sort of "cases" which might otherwise have found their way into the judicial system.

There are many reasons why parties may choose arbitration as a more "efficient" means of dispute settlement than adjudication. To begin with, it seems likely that a dispute processed through arbitration will be disposed of more quickly than if the parties had made their way through the court system to a final judgment. In the commercial arbitration cases administered by the American Arbitration Association in 1999, an average of 114 days elapsed between the date the case was assigned to an arbitrator and the date the file was closed (by award or otherwise); the median processing time was 101 days. Arbitration tends to be a speedier process in part because it allows the parties to bypass long queues at the courthouse door and to schedule hearings at their own convenience. In addition, as we will see, arbitration procedure is relatively "informal"; pre-trial procedures, pleading, motion practice, and discovery are substantially streamlined or in many cases completely eliminated. And the arbitrator's decision is likely to be final: There is no delay imposed by any appeal process, and court review is highly restricted. It is not surprising, therefore, that surveys of practicing attorneys indicate that arbitration is overwhelmingly considered a speedier means of dispute resolution than either jury trial or bench trial; see Stipanowich, Rethinking American Arbitration, 63 Ind.L.J. 425, 460 (1988). Any savings in time and in related pre-and post-trial work are also likely to be reflected in savings in expense—for example, in lawyers' fees—although there can be no assurance that this will always be the case.

There may be other benefits as well. Taking a dispute out of the courtroom and into the relative informality of arbitration may reduce the enmity and heightened contentiousness which so often accompany litigation, and which work against a future cooperative relationship. The privacy of the process may also contribute to a lessening of hostility and confrontation. An arbitration hearing (unlike a trial) is not open to the public, and unless the result later becomes the subject of a court proceeding it is not a matter of public record.

Finally, the parties themselves are able to choose their "judges." They are free, therefore, to avail themselves of decision-makers with expert knowledge of the subject matter in dispute. The arbitrator may have a similar background to the parties, or be engaged in the same business; he is likely, then, to be familiar with the presuppositions and understandings of the trade. The usefulness of such expertise is particularly apparent when a contract dispute hinges on interpretation of the agreement—which in turn may depend on the content of trade custom and usage—or when the dispute is over whether goods sold meet the necessary technical standards. In such cases arbitration avoids the task (which may in some cases be insuperable) of educating judge or jury as to the content of these industry norms. In short, "the evidence from arbitration is that a single qualified lay judge is superior to six or twelve randomly selected laymen—on reflection, a not implausible suggestion."[1]

Lon Fuller, Collective Bargaining and the Arbitrator

1963 Wisc.L.Rev. 3, 11–12, 17.

Labor relations have today become a highly complicated and technical field. This field involves complex procedures that vary from industry to industry, from plant to plant, from department to department. It has developed its own vocabulary. Though the terms of this vocabulary often seem simple and familiar, their true meaning can be understood only when they are seen as parts of a larger system of practice, just as the umpire's

1. Landes & Posner, Adjudication as a Private Good, 8 J.Legal Stud. 235, 252 (1979).

"You're out!" can only be fully understood by one who knows the objectives, the rules and the practices of baseball. I might add that many questions of industrial relations are on a level at least equal to that of the infield fly rule. They are not suitable material for light dinner conversation.

In the nature of things few judges can have had any very extensive experience in the field of industrial relations. Arbitrators, on the other hand, are compelled to acquire a knowledge of industrial processes, modes of compensation, complex incentive plans, job classification, shift arrangements, and procedures for layoff and recall.

Naturally not all arbitrators stand on a parity with respect to this knowledge. But there are open to the arbitrator, even the novice, quick methods of education not available to courts. An arbitrator will frequently interrupt the examination of witnesses with a request that the parties educate him to the point where he can understand the testimony being received. This education can proceed informally, with frequent interruptions by the arbitrator, and by informed persons on either side, when a point needs clarification. Sometimes there will be arguments across the table, occasionally even within each of the separate camps. The end result will usually be a clarification that will enable everyone to proceed more intelligently with the case. There is in this informal procedure no infringement whatever of arbitrational due process. On the contrary, the party's chance to have his case understood by the arbitrator is seriously impaired if his representative has to talk into a vacuum, if he addresses his words to uncomprehending ears.

The education that an arbitrator can thus get, say, in a half an hour, might take days if it had to proceed by qualifying experts and subjecting them to direct and cross examination. The courts have themselves recognized the serious obstacle presented by traditional methods of proof in dealing with cases involving a complex technical background.

* * *

Courts have in fact had difficulty with complicated commercial litigation. The problems here are not unlike those encountered in dealing with labor agreements. There are really few outstanding commercial judges in the history of the common law. The greatest of these, Lord Mansfield, used to sit with special juries selected from among experienced merchants and traders. To further his education in commercial practice he used to arrange dinners with his jurors. In Greek mythology it is reported that Minos prepared himself for a posthumous career as judge of shades by first exposing himself to every possible experience of life. It is not only in labor relations that the impracticability of such a program manifests itself.

NOTES AND QUESTIONS

1. Consider the possible use of arbitration in the following circumstances, and weigh its advantages and disadvantages from the perspective of dispute settlement:

In 1986, the Hunt brothers of Dallas filed two lawsuits in federal court seeking a total of $13.8 billion against some of the country's biggest banks. The banks were accused of fraud, breach of contract, and banking and antitrust law violations after they refused to restructure about $1.5 billion in debts owed by certain Hunt companies, including Placid Oil Company. In December 1986 the Hunts hired a Houston attorney, Stephen Susman, to take charge of the two lawsuits. Placid Oil was then involved in Chapter 11 bankruptcy proceedings. In a court filing seeking the bankruptcy judge's approval to represent Placid, Susman proposed to charge $600 per hour for his time:

> If the Susman firm is terminated by the Hunts for any reason other than malpractice—or the Hunts drop their lawsuits—the firm can pocket the entire retainer [of $1 million]. A malpractice or fee dispute would be arbitrated by the dean of the University of Texas School of Law, Mr. Susman's alma mater. A decision by the dean is final, the fee agreement says.
>
> The Wall Street Journal, December 30, 1986, p. 4.

2. Later in this chapter we will consider in some detail the conduct of an arbitration proceeding, see Section D, infra. An arbitration, like a trial, entails the adversary presentation of evidence and argument before a neutral third party; as we will see, however, the rules of procedure and of evidence that constrain behavior at "trial" will be noticeably lacking. One federal court has observed that "[t]he present day penchant for arbitration may obscure for many parties who do not have the benefit of hindsight that the arbitration system is an inferior system of justice, structured without due process, rules of evidence, accountability of judgment and rules of law." Stroh Container Company v. Delphi Industries, Inc., 783 F.2d 743, 751 n. 12 (8th Cir.1986). As we proceed through this chapter, you should continue to ask if it is appropriate to consider arbitration as an "inferior system of justice." In what sense may this be true? Is the process merely another, somewhat streamlined, form of "trial"? Is there a danger that the pervasive influence of the judicial model may make it difficult for us to assess arbitration on its own terms? And in any event, isn't it clear that "whether to accept rougher justice in exchange for cost savings" is always "a question for contracting parties themselves"? Nagel v. ADM Investor Services Inc., 65 F.Supp.2d 740, 745 (N.D.Ill.1999).

3. Lawyers are quick to perceive the advantages that inhere in the expeditious, "businesslike," expert settlement of a controversy provided by arbitration. These are largely advantages of "efficiency." However, whether arbitration ultimately turns out to be a blessing or a curse may in fact depend upon the tactical position of the particular client. Rapid resolution of a dispute may in theory benefit everyone; nevertheless the party against whom a claim is being asserted will probably find that there are offsetting advantages in delaying the ultimate reckoning. The larger of the disputants may also prefer to exploit the fact that its smaller opponent does not have the financial resources for an extended struggle. In addition, a party for whom the stakes and risk of loss are high may for that reason become less interested in "informality"—and more reluctant to chance a decision without having taken every possible advantage of the full panoply of legal procedures, including the ability to play out his hand to the bitter end. Similarly, a party who is aware that his case is a weak one may not always find a knowledgeable arbiter to be desirable; he may prefer instead to take his chances with a decision maker who is somewhat less expert and considerably more malleable. The General Counsel of Refac Technology Development Corporation has in fact written this about his company's patent litigation strategy:

> [I]f patent validity or infringement is questionable, why take a chance with an arbitration expert who will know exactly how weak the patent is and how dubious infringement is? It makes sense to take one's chance with a judge inexperienced in the technical and legal aspects involved. If the infringer is much bigger than the patentee or an entire industry has copied the patent, a jury trial would be much more beneficial than arbitration because of the sympathy and deep-pocket doctrine that can be played to the hilt.

Sperber, Overlooked Negotiating Tools, 20 Les Nouvelles 81 (June 1985).

4. The newly-appointed curator of drawings at the Getty Museum in Los Angeles came to believe that some of the Museum's expensive and highly-publicized acquisitions were in fact forgeries. "Some of the drawings were so patently bogus that they began to annoy me to look at them," he said. He was, however, instructed by the Museum director not to inform the Getty's trustees about the drawings' dubious authenticity. Over a number of years the relationship between the Museum and the curator worsened: The curator complained that the drawings department was being denied an adequate budget and gallery space—and in his opinion, the Museum "was punishing him and subverting his credibility in order to cast doubt on his forgery claims." He eventually sued the Museum for defamation, and the parties reached a settlement: The curator was to receive a large monetary payment and agreed to resign; the Getty promised to publish an exhaustive catalogue he had written of the Museum's drawings collection, part of which was devoted to the forgery allegations. The catalogue, however, was never published—and the curator was convinced that the Getty's intention was in fact to bury it in order to minimize embarrassment to the Museum. He later filed another suit, in which his allegations of fraud centered on the Getty's failure to publish his catalogue; the case was sent to arbitration.

In the course of the proceedings, the Getty's lawyers filed a motion with the arbitrator to keep the curator from discussing with the press anything discovered during the case: "The Getty argued that arbitration is an inherently confidential proceeding and so [the curator] should not be permitted to say anything to the media, especially about the forgeries." The motion, however, was denied—the arbitrator noting that after all, "*Erin Brockovich* was an arbitration." Peter Landesman, "A Crisis of Fakes," New York Times Magazine, March 18, 2001, at pp. 37, 38–40.

As we will see, arbitration has been used in a number of diverse contexts, to resolve many different types of disputes. However, it has flourished most in situations where parties to a contract have or aspire to have a continuing future relationship in which they will regularly deal with each other. The paradigm is the relationship between management and union in the administration of a collective bargaining agreement, or, perhaps, the relationship between a buyer and a seller of fabric in the textile industry. In both cases there is a history and a likelihood of continued mutual dependence by which both parties may profit; there also exist non-legal sanctions allowing either party to withdraw from (or seek to adjust) the relationship, or at least to withhold vital future cooperation. All this makes it easier to settle in advance on arbitration as a less disruptive method than litigation for resolving any future disputes. It also tends to induce the parties to comply with arbitration decisions once they are handed down (as does the feeling, in a long-term relation, that "awards are likely to be equalized over the long run and that erroneous awards can be dealt with through negotiation"[2]). In both cases there is an understandable reluctance to assert officially-defined legal "rights," or to rely on formal, technical arguments or on accusations of misconduct or impropriety—all of which may seem inappropriate in the context of a "family row" and which may hurt the prospects of future collaboration. And in both cases the parties may be more willing in advance to entrust to arbitrators the task of working out the details of their arrangement in accordance with the common values, the "shared norms," of the trade or of the "shop."

William M. Landes & Richard A. Posner, Adjudication as a Private Good

8 J.Legal Stud. 235, 245–47 (1979).

[I]f one party to a dispute expects that an impartial arbitrator would rule against him, he has an incentive to drag his feet in agreeing to the appointment of an arbitrator. Consistently with this point, writers on arbitration agree that the problem of selection makes arbitration a virtually unusable method of dispute resolution where there is no preexisting contractual or other relationship between the disputants. This suggests a clue to the superior ability of primitive compared to advanced societies to function without public institutions of adjudication. Primitive communities tend to be quite small and their members bound together by a variety of mutually advantageous relationships and interactions. Expulsion, outlawry, ostracism, and other forms of boycott or collective refusal to deal are highly effective sanctions in these circumstances. Another way of putting this point is that reputation, a factor recognized in the literature as deterring people from breaking contracts even in the absence of effective legal sanctions, is a more effective deterrent in a small community, where news

2. Getman, Labor Arbitration and Dispute Resolution, 88 Yale L.J. 916, 922–23 (1979).

travels rapidly throughout the entire circle of an individual's business and social acquaintances, than in large, modern, impersonal societies.

Yet even in modern society, certain trade, religious, and other associations correspond, to a degree, to the close-knit, primitive community. For example, securities or commodities exchanges whose members derive substantial benefits from membership can use the threat of expulsion as an effective sanction to induce members to submit to arbitration. So can a religious association in which excommunication is regarded by members as a substantial cost[30]; so can a university. Exchanges, religious associations, and (private) universities are in fact important examples of modern "communities" in which private adjudication (whether called arbitration or something else) is extensively utilized in preference to public adjudication.

In The Matter of the Arbitration Between Mikel and Scharf

Supreme Court, Special Term, Kings County New York, 1980.
105 Misc.2d 548, 432 N.Y.S.2d 602, aff'd, 85 A.D.2d 604, 444 N.Y.S.2d 690 (1981).

■ ARTHUR S. HIRSCH, J.

This is a motion to confirm an arbitration award rendered by a rabbinical court.

[Respondents are the shareholders of a corporation that operates a nursing home. In 1973, the corporation agreed to lease premises from a partnership. Negotiations on behalf of the partnership were conducted primarily by Barad, one of the partners, and the agreed monthly rental was $25,208.

[In 1977 respondents contacted Barad and told him that because of business reverses, they would have to vacate the premises unless there were a substantial reduction in rent. After negotiations, an oral agreement was reached to reduce the monthly rental by $8000, and a writing to this effect was signed by respondents on behalf of the corporation and by Barad on behalf of the landlord.]

During the negotiations, respondents had met with other partners besides Barad, but at no time had they come in contact with petitioner or with his father, who acted as his son's surrogate in the arbitration proceedings and from whom petitioner had received the 6% interest in the partnership. * * *

In November, 1977, respondents received notice from the Union of Orthodox Rabbis to appear before a rabbinical court for a "*Din Torah*" or arbitration of a claim brought against them by petitioner. Respondents testified they refused to appear at first on grounds that they had no

30. The threat of excommunication was, for example, the ultimate sanction for refusal to submit to, or obey the decision of, the medieval English ecclesiastical courts, which had an immense jurisdiction covering matrimonial disputes, perjury, and a variety of other matters as well as strictly religious disputes.

knowledge of petitioner, but did appear after receiving written notice that refusal would result in the court's invoking a "sirov."

The first meeting of the rabbinical court, presided over by the requisite three rabbis, took place on Sunday, May 14, 1978. The respondents appeared with their attorney, who was present as their legal representative and to testify as witness to all meetings between [landlord] and [tenant], at which the attorney was present.

Respondents are persistent in their claim that theirs was a special appearance before the rabbinical tribunal to establish that there was never a business nor contractual relationship between the claimant and themselves, and therefore, a *Din Torah,* or arbitration, would be improper and invalid. Their participation thereafter was to obtain a determination on this limited issue, i.e., whether a *Din Torah* should be convened and not for a determination as to the merits of the claim.

The respondents were required by the court to sign a Hebrew Document entitled a "Mediation Note" which, in effect, is an agreement to voluntarily arbitrate "the dispute existing" between the parties. Respondent Asher Scharf, who has a complete understanding of the Hebrew language, contends that much discussion ensued until it was unequivocally established that the "dispute" referred to in the "Mediation Note" was the question of the propriety of having a *Din Torah* and that he overcame his conceded reluctance to sign the document when he was assured by the court of the limited scope of the dispute. Respondents were summoned and attended two additional meetings. At the insistence of the rabbinical court, respondents' attorney did not attend any meeting after the first. On December 31, 1978, a written judgment of the rabbinical court was rendered, in which respondents were directed, among other things, to pay to petitioner a lump sum of $9,000 and to make monthly payments of 6% of $23,000, representing petitioner's share of the rental due and owing to the [landlord].

Petitioner has moved for an order confirming the award, with respondents opposing and moving to vacate the award on numerous grounds.

Rabbinical Court–Din Torah

As earlier indicated, the customary arbitration proceeding was not utilized by the parties. An accepted, but more unusual forum was selected, that of arbitration by a tribunal of rabbis conducting a *Din Torah.*

The beginnings of Jewish arbitral institutions are traceable to the middle of the second century. Throughout the centuries, thereafter, in every country in which Jews have been domiciled, Jewish judicial authority has existed, via the institute of arbitration conducted by special rabbinical courts. Orthodox Jews, prompted by their religious, national feelings, accepted Jewish judicial authority, by resorting to the arbitration procedure of their own free will. This method of arbitration has the imprimatur of our own judicial system, as a useful means of relieving the burdens of the inundated courts dealing with civil matters. Through Talmudic sages, it is learned that special rules or procedures have been provided under which the rabbinical courts function as a *Din Torah* (literally translated as torah judgment), with Judaic or torah law as its basis. * * *

In addition to the procedural rules established by Judaic Law, there are state, civil, procedural rules for arbitration (CPLR, Article 75) to which the rabbinical court, as an arbitration forum, must also adhere.

* * *

Respondents [challenge] the rabbinical court's award, claiming first, the arbitration agreement was entered involuntarily, under duress and is consequently void, [and] second, charging the arbitrators with misconduct * * *.

Involuntary Agreement–Duress

Both parties are members of the orthodox Jewish community. Respondent's denial of the existence of any disputable issue between themselves and petitioner convinced them to refuse to appear for a *Din Torah* and they would not have done so had they not received the threat of a "sirov." Rabbis testifying for respondents stated that a sirov, literally translated as contempt of court, is a prohibitionary decree that subjects the recipient to shame, scorn, ridicule and ostracism by his coreligionists, fellow members of his community. Ostensibly, he is ostracized and scorned. Other Jews refuse to eat or speak with him. He is discredited and dishonored. The respondents maintain that the draconian measures of a sirov are sufficiently threatening so as to compel their compliance with the demand to appear. They claim they would have become outcasts among their friends and coreligionists. However, from other testimony, it appears that the sirov, while most assuredly ominous in its potential power, is honored in its breach. The court cannot, of course, know the actual state of mind of respondents and it may be that their fear of a sirov decree was real. However, it seems more plausible that if respondents believed the consequences so fearful, they would not, at this point, be willing to defy the rabbinical court by refusing to accept the arbitrator's determination. Undoubtedly, pressure was brought to bear to have them participate in the *Din Torah,* but pressure is not duress. Their decision to acquiesce to the rabbinical court's urgings was made without the coercion that would be necessary for the agreement to be void.

Misconduct

CPLR 7511 (subd [b], par. 1, cl [i]) allows for the vacation of an award if the rights of a party are prejudiced by corruption, fraud or misconduct. Courts have used the term misconduct to denote actions of fundamental unfairness, whether intentional or unintentional.

Respondents charge misconduct by the rabbinical tribunal in their refusal to permit respondents to have legal representation and, further, to hear testimony or accept material documents offered by respondents' attorney, as witness to the lease negotiations. This, they contend, violated their due process rights. Respondents appeared at the first meeting with their attorney, Abraham Bernstein. From the beginning, it became apparent the tribunal would not tolerate the presence of an attorney at a *Din Torah.* Petitioner's father strenuously objected, claiming he had no attorney to represent petitioner. At first, attorney Bernstein was not permitted to speak, but later was allowed to make a short statement in which he attempted to establish the fact that a lease was executed between the corporation tenant and the landlord partnership without personal involvement of the parties and when he offered to submit the lease and other documents for the perusal of the court, the papers were returned to him. Thereafter, he interjected himself wherever possible to explain respondents' position regarding the lack of legal connection between the parties. For the most part, the court refused to acknowledge him, quelling his attempts to speak or take part in the proceedings. He was not permitted to ask questions of petitioner or his father, who at all times acted as representative and voice of petitioner.

* * *

Biblical law requires that parties appear before a magistrate in person and not by proxy (*Deuteronomy* 19:17). For many years, this supported a Jewish judicial prejudice against proxies, including attorneys and even interpreters, it being determined essential that argument be heard directly from the mouths of litigants or witnesses. There was a tradition, however, that the high priest, when sued in court, could appoint an attorney to represent him (*Talmud Yerushalmi,* Sanhedrin 2:1, 19d). It may be this tradition that precipitated the admittance of defense attorneys into rabbinical courts. Where the parties were present to give testimony, thus permitting Judges to perceive their demeanor and evaluate their credibility, legal counsel was no longer considered to be anathema. The rabbinical court in the instant matter obviously did not abide by this accepted legal concept.

The tribunal's proclivity for conducting their court under outdated concepts resulted in inadvertent violations. Respondents were denied due process. The right of counsel, which is a constitutional right, is further enunciated in Article 75 of the CPLR, and is an unwaivable right. Consequently, respondent's participation without counsel, after receiving the court's warning to appear alone, did not have a negative effect on their inherent right to legal representation, the deprivation of which is sufficient to vitiate the award.

Respondent Asher Scharf's unrebutted testimony indicated that at a session he attended, one of the three rabbi arbitrators called him out to talk with him privately. The rabbi argued for a cash settlement, to be paid by respondent on the grounds that petitioner was a poor student. Scharf testified the rabbi asked, "Well, what does a few thousand dollars mean to you?"

Under Judaic law (*Deuteronomy* 1:17), a Judge must judge impartially in favoring the rich or the poor. In an interpretation of this portion of the Torah, the foremost authority, Rashi, in *Commentary Rashi,* states that the version should be understood as follows: A judge "should not say: 'This is a poor man and his fellow (opponent) is rich and he will consequently obtain some support in a respectable fashion.' "

To ensure fairness, it is axiomatic and imperative that an arbitrator's impartiality be above suspicion. The rabbinical court was obviously prejudiced against respondents because of their affluence and considered the financial status of the parties above the issues. Such conduct, forbidden by the Torah, the law under which the rabbinical court has jurisdiction, constitutes another instance in which the tribunal deviated from its own *Din Torah* precepts.

The procedural format of the sessions was haphazard; no prescribed order was followed. A rabbinical court normally operates in a set manner, with presentation of claims, counterclaims, testimony of witnesses and cross-examinations conducted in a fairly orderly manner. This is not to say that any formal hearings are required. However, it appears that no semblance of administrative court proceeding, formal or informal, was followed by this rabbinical court. Witnesses were not called, real evidence was not accepted and no recognizable and required *Din Torah* procedure was followed. Under these highly unusual and chaotic conditions, a fair award could not be given.

* * *

Despite the established and well-grounded precedent that courts rarely set aside an arbitration award, in this instance the court finds it obligatory to vacate the award of the rabbinical court for the reasons enunciated above. A new arbitration proceeding will not be scheduled, as the court is convinced that no legal dispute exists between these particular parties.

NOTES AND QUESTIONS

1. Closely-knit Jewish communities throughout the Western world developed—out of necessity—a long-standing proscription against submitting intragroup disputes to hostile or uncomprehending secular courts. See Congregation B'Nai Sholom v. Martin, 382 Mich. 659, 173 N.W.2d 504 (1969). At the same time such communities developed their own systems of dispute resolution. With assimilation into the wider society, the role of these autonomous tribunals has naturally declined; even today, however, a practice of rabbinical "arbitration" still persists in Jewish communities. The majority of cases heard in this country by Jewish courts seem to concern divorce matters. See, e.g., Avitzur v. Avitzur, 58 N.Y.2d 108, 459 N.Y.S.2d 572, 446 N.E.2d 136 (1983). For the modern history of Jewish tribunals, see Note, Rabbinical Courts: Modern Day Solomons, 6 Col.J.Law & Soc.Prob. 48 (1970); Israel Goldstein, Jewish Justice and Conciliation (1981); James Yaffe, So Sue Me! The Story of a Community Court (1972).

2. In a business or employment dispute, it is usually understood by the parties that a Jewish rabbinical tribunal "may seek to compromise the parties' claims, and is not bound to decide strictly in accordance with the governing rules of Jewish law, but may more carefully weigh the equities of the situation." See Kingsbridge Center of Israel v. Turk, 98 A.D.2d 664, 469 N.Y.S.2d 732, 734 (1983). Is that what the tribunal attempted to do in the principal case?

3. Professor Marc Galanter has written that "[j]ust as health is not found primarily in hospitals or knowledge in schools, so justice is not primarily to be found in official justice-dispensing institutions. People experience justice (and injustice) not only (or usually) in forums sponsored by the state but at the primary institutional locations of their activity—home, neighborhood, workplace, business deal and so on * * *." This social ordering, found in a variety of institutional settings (such as universities, sports leagues, housing developments, and hospitals) he refers to as "indigenous law." He notes that although

> indigenous law may have the virtues of being familiar, understandable and independent of professionals, it is not always the expression of harmonious egalitarianism. It often reflects narrow and parochial concerns; it is often based on relations of domination; its coerciveness may be harsh and indiscriminate; protections that are available in public forums may be absent.

Galanter, Justice in Many Rooms: Courts, Private Ordering, and Indigenous Law, 19 J. Pluralism & Unofficial L. 1, 17–18, 25 (1981).

4. For further discussion of court review of "arbitration" awards, see Section C.4.a infra.

3. ARBITRATION AND THE APPLICATION OF "RULES"

The Landes and Posner excerpt at the beginning of this chapter introduces another recurrent theme in these materials. Many writers suggest that arbitration, as a voluntary and private process, may not proceed by formulating, applying, and communicating general principles of decision, or "rules." A number of related points form an essential backdrop for this discussion.

First of all—particularly outside the field of labor arbitration—arbitrators (unlike judges) commonly do not write reasoned opinions attempting to explain and justify their decisions. In fact the American Arbitration Association, which administers much commercial arbitration, actively discourages arbitrators from doing so. In addition, we do not in any event expect that an arbitrator will decide a case the way a judge does. We do not expect that he will necessarily "follow the law"—or indeed apply or develop any body of general rules as a guide to his decision. An arbitrator, it is said, "may do justice as he sees it, applying his own sense of law and equity to the facts as he finds them to be and making an award reflecting the spirit rather than the letter of the agreement."[1] Furthermore, a decision by any particular arbitrator will not necessarily control the result of later cases involving

1. In the Matter of the Arbitration Between Silverman and Benmor Coats, Inc., 61 N.Y.2d 299, 308, 473 N.Y.S.2d 774, 779, 461 N.E.2d 1261, 1266 (1984).

other parties—or, indeed, have any precedential value at all for later arbitrators. And finally, an arbitrator's decision is not subject to later review and correction by a court to insure that general rules of law have been complied with. The highly restricted role courts play in passing on the decisions of arbitrators, and the implications of a system in which elaborate reasoned awards are rare, are discussed in some detail in Section C.4 infra.

What are some of the implications of a system of private justice in which cases are "decided," but without the use or communication of consistent rules of decision? When cases are diverted into a private forum, operating without a formal system of precedent, any judicial function of shaping future activity may be neglected. In addition, it may be more difficult for private parties to predict the future results of cases heard in these private tribunals. Information disseminated by courts in the form of precedents is used every day by private actors in routine decisions concerning which claims they should assert, and under what circumstances they should settle those claims. With no certainty as to the rule a particular arbitrator would apply—and with no consistent application of rules across the entire community of "competing" arbitrators, purporting independently to decide particular cases without reference to each other or to generally accepted rules—any firm basis on which to build future conduct is undermined:

> You cannot say today that a check need not contain an unconditional promise or order to pay to be negotiable and tomorrow that it must. You cannot say today that F.O.B. means free on board and tomorrow that it means only that the seller must get the goods as far as his shipping room. And so on. Mankind needs an irreducible minimum of certainty in order to operate efficiently. That irreducible minimum would seem to be better handled by the courts than by arbitration even though in the particular case the result would have been better decided in arbitration.[2]

However, unless the parties to an arbitration are "repeat players"—with a stake in the rules applied that extends beyond the result in the particular case—creating and promulgating "rules" of decision could from their point of view serve only to confer a benefit on *other* people, at the cost of increasing the duration and the expense of their own proceedings.

Of course, much of the above discussion has to be qualified. Any dichotomy between an ad hoc, particularistic system of private arbitration and a rule-and precedent-bound judiciary can easily be overstated. All first-year law students know that such a characterization can grotesquely exaggerate the predictability of court decisions and the meaningfulness of rules of decision in predicting or explaining the results of litigation. And even in the absence of a formal system of precedent, criteria of decision can be agreed on, developed, and communicated in other ways: by private

2. Mentschikoff, The Significance of Arbitration—A Preliminary Inquiry, 17 Law & Contemporary Problems 698, 709 (1952).

associations, through past practice and the evolution of trade custom, and particularly through the pre-existing contractual relations of the parties. Lawyers who are experienced in arbitration tend to feel that they are able to predict the results of arbitration with some certainty, at least in part because these sources supply rules of decision likely to be consistently applied. It is, of course, a separate question whether the rules so applied will be consonant with officially-declared public values, or whether the arbitration process may implicate important public policy concerns which should be reserved to the official court system. This is a subject which is explored further in later sections.

In addition, the arbitration of disputes arising under collective bargaining agreements has come to evolve certain unique characteristics, distinguishing it from other forms of private dispute resolution. It does appear to be the general practice for *labor* arbitrators to write explanations and justifications—sometimes elaborate ones—for their decisions; these decisions are often publicly reported, cited to later arbitrators, and relied on in later cases. "An extensive survey of labor arbitration disclosed that 77 percent of the 238 responding arbitrators believed that precedents, even under *other* contracts, should be given 'some weight.' "[3] As we will see, there has developed a "common-law" of labor arbitration. In addition, the growth of labor arbitration over the last 50 years to a central place in the settlement of labor disputes has been accompanied by the development of the profession of "labor arbitrator." In the commercial area it may be unusual for an arbitrator to decide more than one or two cases a year, but for many labor arbitrators arbitration constitutes a primary source of their livelihood. One may suspect that Landes and Posner's point concerning the advertising value of reasoned opinions may have particular relevance here.

4. "RIGHTS" ARBITRATION AND "INTEREST" ARBITRATION

> "Interest" arbitration is distinguished from the more familiar grievance or "rights" arbitration by the fact that in the former situation the designated neutral is employed to determine the actual contract terms which will bind the parties during the life of their new agreement, while in the latter situation the arbitrator is only empowered to decide disputes concerning the interpretation and application of the terms of an already existing contract. The grievance arbiter is generally precluded from adding to or modifying the terms of the contract in dispute.[4]

The distinction between "rights" and "interest" arbitration is a familiar one. You will often see reference to it, particularly in relation to the arbitration of labor-management disputes. The paradigm of a "rights" arbitration is a hearing on the grievance of an employee alleging that he has been discharged "without just cause." The paradigm of an "interest" arbitration is a hearing held at the expiration of a collective bargaining

3. Frank Elkouri & Edna A. Elkouri, How Arbitration Works (4th ed. 1985) 418.

4. Craver, The Judicial Enforcement of Public Sector Interest Arbitration, 21 B.C.L.Rev. 557, 558 n. 8 (1980).

agreement, after negotiations over a union's demand for higher wage rates in a "new" contract have failed. While "interest" arbitration remains an unusual and infrequent device in comparison to other forms of arbitration, it is quite commonly resorted to in resolving disputes over the terms of employment of public employees. Public employees, such as police or school teachers, are usually forbidden to engage in strikes; economic pressure, and the usual tests of economic strength used in the private sector to determine contract terms after a bargaining impasse, are therefore limited in the public interest. "Interest" arbitration to determine the terms of a new contract when bargaining fails provides a common alternative mechanism. In many cases, in fact, state statutes impose this as a *mandatory* means of settlement. See Section E.1 infra. Such legislation in effect gives to public employee unions the "right" to resort to the arbitration mechanism to determine the future terms of employment.

Now compare the following three cases. Are these examples of "rights" or of "interest" arbitration? What precisely are the differences, if any, between them?

(a) A law firm entered into a lease of space in an office building. The term of the lease was ten years. At the firm's request, a clause was added to the lease by which it would have the option to renew the lease for an additional ten years; it provided that "rental for the renewal term shall be in such amount as shall be agreed upon by the parties based on the comparative rental values of similar properties as of the date of the renewal and on comparative business conditions of the two periods." The lease contained a general arbitration clause providing that "all disputes relating to" the lease shall be settled by arbitration. The parties fail to agree on a rental for the renewal term.

(b) A coal supply agreement provided that for a period of ten years a coal company would tender and a power company would purchase specified quantities of coal. There was a base price per ton, and a provision for the calculation of adjustments in base price upon changes in certain labor costs and in "governmental impositions." The agreement also provided:

> Any gross proven inequity that may result in unusual economic conditions not contemplated by the parties at the time of the execution of this Agreement may be corrected by mutual consent. Each party shall in the case of a claim of gross inequity furnish the other with whatever documentary evidence may be necessary to assist in effecting a settlement.

Another clause called for "any unresolved controversy between the parties arising under this Agreement" to be submitted to arbitration. Four years later, after a rapid escalation in the price of coal, the open market price of coal of the same quality was more than three times the current adjusted base price under the agreement. The coal company requested an adjustment in the contract price which the power company adamantly rejected.[5]

5. See Georgia Power Co. v. Cimarron Coal Corp., 526 F.2d 101 (6th Cir.1975).

(c) An agreement between a newspaper and its employees was to last for three years, with a provision that "this contract shall remain in effect until all terms and conditions of employment for a succeeding contract term are resolved either through negotiation or through arbitration." After a bargaining deadlock, the union moved for arbitration. The employer presented to the arbitrator a number of items which it wanted included in the agreement for the new term, including the right to make layoffs on account of automation or the introduction of new processes. The Union also presented a number of issues to the arbitrator, including "wages; mailers brought up to mechanical department [wage] scale; proof room brought up to composing room scale; pension; sick leave; vacations; increased mileage; grievance procedure; jurisdiction of jobs—need for job descriptions; holidays; jury and witness duty; overtime after thirty hours during holiday weeks; night differential; life insurance; option under Blue Cross for eyeglasses; option under Dental Plan for payment for dentures; paid uniforms for pressmen; addition of grandparent and guardian to funeral leave."

As these examples illustrate, it may sometimes be difficult satisfactorily to distinguish an "interest" dispute from one concerning "rights." Moreover, from a broader perspective, even in what are assumed to be "rights" disputes (such as employee grievances) the process of interpretation must necessarily involve considerable flexibility. In complex and long-term relationships there will inevitably be some uncertainty concerning matters inadvertently (or purposely) left open when the contract was entered into, or where past solutions are no longer neatly adapted to changed needs. When the parties participate in this procedure, they are in a very real sense taking part in a process which "involves not only the settlement of the particular dispute but also interstitial rule-making"[6]—a process aimed at creating, refining, and elaborating for the future the rules which will govern their relationship.

The supposed distinction between "rights" and "interest" arbitration may then be—as are most distinctions in the law—a mere question of degree or emphasis. However, this is not to say that it is without analytic utility or practical importance. Parties to a contract who are considering arbitration as a device to handle future disputes must ask themselves a number of questions. The distinction between "rights" and "interest" arbitration forces them to ask some important ones. To what extent is arbitration suitable for establishing the basic structure, the essential parameters of the relationship? What important differences are there between doing this, and asking the arbitrator merely to spell out the implications of a bargain they have hammered out for themselves? Are there reasons to

6. See Feller, A General Theory of the Collective Bargaining Agreement, 61 Calif.L.Rev. 663, 744–45 (1973).

hesitate before confiding this task to arbitrators as a substitute for their own bargaining? A few of the relevant considerations are suggested in the paragraphs that follow.

Assume that the parties know from the outset—either because of a mandatory statutory procedure, or a contractual agreement—that they will later be able to turn to arbitration to determine their future rights. How might this affect the dynamics of the bargaining process? Is it likely that one or the other of them may assume more extreme positions at the bargaining stage, trusting that an arbitrator will later seek out a middle ground? Is there a danger that the parties may use the possibility of arbitration as a crutch, and resort to it too readily rather than face the hard issues themselves? Is it likely that negotiators will resort to the arbitration mechanism to insulate themselves from the dissatisfaction of their own constituencies—union members, or taxpayers—who might personally hold them accountable for inevitable concessions made in negotiation?

If the contract confides to arbitrators the ultimate responsibility for determining the essential rights of the parties in the future, what standards are the arbitrators to use? The possible value choices are far more diverse, the possible criteria of decision far more nebulous, than in cases where an arbitrator acts more "judicially" in deciding whether particular goods are defective or whether certain employee conduct merited discharge.

In Twin City Rapid Transit Co., 7 Lab.Arb. 845 (1947), a collective bargaining agreement between a privately-owned company and an employee union provided that "if at the end of any contract year the parties are unable to agree upon the terms of a renewal contract, the matter shall be submitted to arbitration." In his decision, the arbitrator wrote:

> Arbitration of contract terms * * * calls for a determination, upon considerations of policy, fairness, and expediency, of what the contract rights ought to be. In submitting this case to arbitration, the parties have merely extended their negotiations—they have left it to this board to determine what they should, by negotiation, have agreed upon. We take it that the fundamental inquiry, as to each issue, is: what should the parties themselves, as reasonable men, have voluntarily agreed to?
>
> In answering that question, we think that prime consideration should be given to agreements voluntarily reached in comparable properties in the general area. For example, wages and conditions in Milwaukee, the city of comparable size nearest geographically to Minneapolis and St. Paul, whose transit company is neither bankrupt, municipally owned, nor municipally supported, might reasonably have had greater weight in the negotiations between the parties than Cleveland or Detroit, both municipally owned and farther distant, or Omaha and Council Bluffs, more distant in miles and smaller in population. Smaller and larger cities, however, and cities in other geographical areas should have secondary consideration, for they disclose trends and, by indicating what other negotiators, under different circumstances, have found reasonable, furnish a guide to what these parties, in view of the

differing circumstances, might have found reasonable. * * * To repeat, our endeavor will be to decide the issues as, upon the evidence, we think reasonable negotiators, regardless of their social or economic theories might have decided them in the give and take process of bargaining. We agree with the company that the interests of stockholders and public must be considered, and consideration of their interests will enter into our considerations as to what the parties should reasonably have agreed on.

NOTES AND QUESTIONS

1. Does the inquiry in *Twin City Rapid Transit* ("what should the parties themselves, as reasonable men, have voluntarily agreed to?") seem meaningful to you in light of your understanding of the negotiation process? Should the arbitrator try to reconstruct the murky totality of the bargaining process, including the various dimensions of bargaining power, when the parties' own negotiations have failed? Can he do so? Or is he necessarily reduced to acting as a "legislator" and mandating what he thinks the "fair" result would be? Presented with all the outstanding bargaining issues with which the arbitrator was faced in case (c) above, how does he go about distinguishing between issues as to which the parties have reached a serious impasse and "throwaway" issues placed on the table for bargaining advantage? Is it feasible to impose criteria in advance on the arbitrator, by statute or contract? Or to structure the process so as to limit the scope of his discretion?

2. Of course, *courts* daily adjudicate grievances and disputes concerning "rights." Do they *also* handle types of disputes which might be characterized as "interest" disputes? In contracts cases, as you remember, the traditional wisdom is that courts "interpret" agreements, but they will not "make a contract for the parties" or enforce arrangements where the parties have merely "agreed to agree." The received learning has it that

> "[b]efore the power of law can be invoked to enforce a promise, it must be sufficiently certain and specific so that what was promised can be ascertained. Otherwise, a court, in intervening, would be imposing its own conception of what the parties should or might have undertaken, rather than confining itself to the implementation of a bargain to which they have mutually committed themselves. * * * [A] mere agreement to agree, in which a material term is left for future negotiations, is unenforceable."

Joseph Martin, Jr. Delicatessen, Inc. v. Schumacher, 52 N.Y.2d 105, 436 N.Y.S.2d 247, 417 N.E.2d 541 (1981).

Is that distinction in contract law the equivalent of the "rights"/"interest" dichotomy?

An economist would say that when courts insist on a certain level of clarity and completeness in the terms of a contract, they are attempting to insure that the deal is "allocatively efficient"—roughly, that it serves to reallocate resources to higher-valued uses—and that they do so by assuring that the deal has been bargained out by the parties themselves, in terms of their own assessments of their own interests. They may also be trying to prevent parties from taking a "free ride" on the public court system by shifting onto the courts the burden of determining contract terms. Do any of the same objections apply to "interest" arbitration?

The reluctance of courts to help in fashioning bargains left incomplete by the parties may be changing. Compare Sun Printing & Publishing Ass'n v. Remington Paper & Power Co., 235 N.Y. 338, 139 N.E. 470 (1923)—a wooden mainstay of the Contracts curriculum—with David Nassif Associates v. United States, 557 F.2d 249 (Ct.Cl.1977), 644 F.2d 4 (Ct.Cl.1981). See also Uniform Commercial Code §§ 2–204(3), 2–305. Or is it fair to say that courts, like arbitrators, have been doing much the same thing all along, under the guise of "interpretation"—but without admitting it?

3. Lon Fuller has suggested that the adjudicative process may not be well-suited to resolve what he calls "polycentric" or "many-centered" disputes, in which the resolution of any one issue may have "complex repercussions" with respect to other aspects of the dispute. See Lon Fuller, The Forms and Limits of Adjudication, 92 Harv.L.Rev. 353 (1978). See also p. 301 infra. Are any of the "interest" disputes we are looking at here "polycentric"? Do Fuller's objections apply to arbitration as well as to the judicial process? How might an "interest" arbitrator proceed so as to minimize the problems that Fuller raises?

4. The arbitrator in an "interest" arbitration may be asked to determine the wages to be paid to employees in a "new" or renewal contract. How relevant in such a determination is the employer's claim of financial hardship or inability to pay? Is the answer in any way dependent on whether the arbitrator suspects the employer's "hardship" is due to managerial inefficiency, or to general conditions in a declining industry?

In one case an arbitrator, granting a union's requested wage increase, rejected the employer's claim by writing that

> The *price of labor* must be viewed like any other commodity which needs to be purchased. If a new truck is needed, the City does not plead poverty and ask to buy the truck for 25% of its established price. It can shop various dealers and makes of truck to get the best possible buy. But in the end the City either pays the asked price or gets along without a new truck.

In re City of Quincy, Illinois and International Association of Machinists, 81 Lab.Arb. 352, 356 (1982).

Compare In re School Board of the City of Detroit and Detroit Federation of Teachers, 93 Lab. Arb. 648 (1989). In this case the arbitrator accepted the union's argument that in terms of comparison with other school districts the salary position of Detroit schoolteachers "is too far down in the ranks, * * * is deteriorating and eroded by inadequate increases and the cost of living"; "the Union's contention that [a] 7% [increase] is necessary to preserve the *status quo ante* is a sound one." Nevertheless the arbitrator ordered a wage increase of only 5%:

> The deficit incurred by the district, coupled with its continued precarious financial position, * * * all make it clear that these are perilous times for the state of education in Detroit. * * * We must be certain that any award involving salaries does not detract from or interfere with the district's educational program. * * * [T]he fact is that Detroit is very much at the margin and the voters might rebuke the District if an excessive wage increase was perceived to capture all available funds, without any consideration of educational enhancement.

5. In the case of a public employer, can the arbitrator weigh the claims of employees against other claims to public funds? Should the arbitrator take into account the employer's ability to pass on any increase in wages to others—to taxpayers or to the customers of a public utility? This may of course entail the exercise of some delicate judgment on matters of social and economic policy. In addition, the arbitrator is a creature of contract, hired and paid by employer and union: Is it appropriate for him in the course of making his decision to weigh the interests of those who are *not* parties to the agreement? See In re Nodak Rural Elect. Coop. and Int'l Bro. of Elect. Workers, 78 Lab.Arb. 1119 (1982) (rural North Dakota electrical cooperative; "This arbitrator grew up on an Iowa farm in the 1930's so he understands the meaning of a depressed farm economy and is sympathetic to the farmer's current conditions. * * * It is not likely that it would be wise for either the company or the union to ignore the condition of the farm economy. After all, the farmers and Nodak employees are dependent on each other. The farmers must be able to pay their bills in order for Nodak employees to retain their jobs and get paid.").

6. Can an existing "interest" arbitration clause be invoked in order to obtain inclusion of a similar clause in a *new* contract? Courts that have answered "no" have reasoned in this way:

> The contract arbitration system could be self-perpetuating; a party, having once agreed to the provision, may find itself locked into that procedure for as long as the bargaining relationship endures. Exertion of economic force to rid oneself of the clause is foreclosed, for the continued inclusion of the term is for resolution by an outsider. Parties may justly fear that the tendency of arbitrators would be to continue including the clause * * *.
>
> [T]he perpetuation of [interest] arbitration clauses in successive contracts may well serve to increase industrial unrest. Under [interest] arbitration, an outsider imposes contract terms, perhaps * * * unguided by any agreed-upon standards. In these circumstances, a disappointed party can readily believe that the arbitrator lacked appreciation of its needs or failed to apply appropriate standards, for example, "fair wages." * * * The result is that a party's dissatisfaction with an award may be aggravated by doubts about its legitimacy. The likelihood that one party will feel aggrieved by a contract arbitration award increases as parties move from contract to contract. The factors which determine the parties' relative strength for strikes and lockouts often changes with the passage of time. * * * Courts cannot bind the parties in

perpetuity to forego use of economic weapons in support of bargaining positions.

NLRB v. Columbus Printing Pressmen & Assistants' Union No. 252, 543 F.2d 1161, 1169–70 (5th Cir.1976).

The *Columbus Printing* court also held that in negotiating the terms of a collective bargaining agreement, a union may not insist on the inclusion of an "interest" arbitration clause; to bargain to an "impasse" on this issue would constitute an "unfair labor practice."

B. Some Frequent Uses of Arbitration

1. Commercial Arbitration

William C. Jones, Three Centuries of Commercial Arbitration in New York: A Brief Survey

1956 Wash.U.L.Q. 193, 209–10, 218–19.

[I]t is commonplace among those who write about arbitration that it has been in use for centuries.

* * *

[E]nough material on arbitration has been uncovered to show fairly conclusively that arbitration was in constant and widespread use throughout the colonial period in New York. * * * Seemingly, arbitration was used primarily in situations where the decision would not be entirely for one side or the other, but where there was, rather, considerable area for negotiation. The settlement of an account resulting from a long course of dealing between two merchants is an example. Land boundaries and the distribution of the proceeds from a privateering expedition are others. Evidently, from the way in which individuals felt it worthwhile to advertise in the newspapers their willingness to arbitrate, there was some social pressure to arbitrate a dispute before taking it to court, and even to submit it to arbitration after the suit was begun. This tends to substantiate a feeling that one function of arbitration was to supply a final stage in the negotiation process between two disputants and that a willingness to negotiate was highly esteemed in the community.

* * *

[T]he existence of the practice of extensive arbitration over so long a period of time in the mercantile community tends to show that, as used by merchants, arbitration is not really a substitute for court adjudication as something that is cheaper or faster or whatever,[112] but is rather a means of dispute settling quite as ancient—for all practical purposes anyway—as

112. Though, interestingly enough, arbitration was presented as such an alternative in the eighteenth century in almost the same language as is used today.

court adjudication, and that it has, traditionally, fulfilled quite a different function. The primary function of arbitration is to provide the merchants fora where mercantile disputes will be settled by merchants. This, in turn, suggests that merchants wish to form, and have for a long time succeeded in forming, a separate, and, to some extent, self-governing community, independent of the larger unit. For law this means that courts may perform, in the commercial field at least, a different function from that which we usually assign to them. In many cases, they may not be the primary fora for adjudication. If this is true, when they are called upon to decide a commercial case in one of these areas, it will be either after another adjudicatory agency has acted or because the other system cannot, or will not, cope with the case. In some areas, courts may almost never get a case. * * * Insofar as this area, in which arbitration is and—most importantly—has always been the primary dispute-settling agency, is an important one (and an area which includes stockbrokers, produce brokers, coffee merchants, etc., seems to be such an area), it cannot really be said that one has studied commercial law, in the sense of the rules that actually guide the settlement of disputes involving commercial matters, if he has studied only the reports of appellate courts and legislation. We cannot even understand the significance of the "law" contained in the reports and statutes until we have studied arbitration decisions. * * *

Having gone so far with hypothesis, one may be forgiven for going a little farther and suggesting that the existence of a sufficient sense of community identity or separateness on the part of merchants to cause them to have a separate adjudicatory system tends to show that there is a mercantile community which is, to a considerable degree, self-governing. This community has existed in this form for centuries. Its existence suggests that there may be others—religious and educational communities come to mind.

Soia Mentschikoff, Commercial Arbitration

61 Col.L.Rev. 846, 848–54 (1961).

The first thing to be noted is that although commonly thought of as a single type phenomenon, both the structure and the process of commercial arbitration are determined by the different institutional contexts in which it arises. There are three major institutional settings in which commercial arbitration appears as a mechanism for the settlement of disputes.

The simplest is when two persons in a contract delineating a business relationship agree to settle any disputes that may arise under the contract by resort to arbitration before named arbitrators or persons to be named at the time of the dispute. In this, which can be called individuated arbitration, the making of all arrangements, including the procedures for arbitration, rests entirely with the parties concerned. Although we do not know, we believe that the chief moving factors here are: (1) a desire for privacy as, for example, in certain crude oil situations where such arrangements exist; (2) the availability of expert deciders; (3) the avoidance of possible legal difficulties with the nature of the transaction itself; and (4) the random acceptance by many businessmen of the idea that arbitration is faster and less expensive than court action.

A second type of arbitration arises within the context of a particular trade association or exchange. The group establishes its own arbitration machinery for the settlement of disputes among its members, either on a voluntary or compulsory basis, and sometimes makes it available to nonmembers doing business in the particular trade. A particular association may also have specialist committees, which are investigatory in character, with the arbitration machinery handling only the private disputes involving nonspecialist categories of cases. * * *

The third setting for commercial arbitration is found in administrative groups, such as the American Arbitration Association, the International Chamber of Commerce, and various local chambers of commerce, which provide rules, facilities, and arbitrators for any persons desiring to settle disputes by arbitration. Many trade associations with insufficient business to warrant separate organizations make special arrangements with one of these groups to process disputes that arise among their members.

* * *

Factors Determining the Need for Arbitration

At this point it is useful to distinguish between those factors that can be said to produce a need for arbitration machinery in commercial groups and those factors that merely make it desirable. The reasons commonly given for arbitration—speed, lower expense, more expert decision, greater privacy—are appealing to all businessmen, and yet not all utilize arbitration. It seems reasonably clear, therefore, that for some trades these factors are of greater importance than for others, and that for some trades there must be countervailing values in not resorting to arbitration. We postulated three factors as being theoretically important in determining whether or not a particular trade needed institutionalized use of arbitration, and incorporated questions relating to these factors in our trade association questionnaire.

The first factor was the nature of the economic function being performed in relation to the movement of the goods by the members of the association. We postulated that persons primarily buying for resale, that is merchants in the original sense of the term, were much more likely to be interested in speed of adjudication, and that since price allowance would be a central remedy for defects in quality or, indeed, for nondelivery, the speed and low cost characteristics of arbitration would be particularly attractive to them, thus leading to the creation of institutionalized machinery. The trade associations in which such merchants constitute all or part of the membership reported as follows: 48 percent use institutionalized machinery, 34 percent make individual arrangements for arbitration, and only 18 percent never arbitrate. These figures are to be contrasted with the reports from those trade associations that stated that their memberships did not include any merchants. In those groups 23 percent reported the existence of institutionalized arbitration, 44 percent reported individual arrangements, and 33 percent reported no arbitration whatever.

The second major factor that we thought would be important in determining the need for arbitration was the participation of the members of the association in foreign trade. Apart from the enhanced possibility of delay inherent in transnational law suits, when the parties to a transaction are governed by different substantive rules of law, resort to the formal legal system poses uncertainty and relative unpredictability of result for at least one of the parties. This uncertainty and unpredictability is increased by the fact that the very rules governing the choice of the applicable law are themselves relatively uncertain and are not uniform among the nations of the world. Faced with such an uncertain formal legal situation, any affected trade group is apt to develop its own set of substantive rules or standards of behavior as the controlling rules for its members. Obviously, when a trade group develops its own rules of law, it requires as deciders of its disputes persons who are acquainted with the standards it has developed. Since this knowledgeability does not reside in the judges of any formal legal system, the drive toward institutionalized private machinery is reinforced.

* * *

The third factor that we thought would bear on the need for arbitration machinery relates to the kind of goods dealt with by the members of the association. One of the major areas of dispute among businessmen centers on the quality of the goods involved. If, therefore, the goods are such as not to be readily susceptible of quality determination by third persons, arbitration or, indeed, inspection, is an unlikely method of settling disputes. If goods are divided into raws, softs, and hards, the differences in their suitability for third party adjudication becomes relatively clear. On the whole, raws are a fungible commodity, one bushel of #1 wheat being very much like another bushel of #1 wheat. On the other hand, hards, which consist of items like refrigerators and automobiles, are not viewed by their producers as essentially fungible, however they may appear to the layman. We did not believe that Ford would like to have General Motors sitting on disputes involving the quality of Ford cars, or vice versa. Moreover, quality differentials in raws can normally be reflected by price differentials, but defects in hard goods frequently affect their usefulness and therefore price differential compensation is not feasible. Thus, the normal sales remedy for raws has come to be price allowance, whereas the normal sales remedy for hard goods has come to be repair or replacement. Raws, involving fungibility and ease of finding an appropriate remedy, are therefore highly susceptible to third party adjudication, whereas hard goods tend to move away from such adjudication. Soft goods, which are an intermediate category and range from textiles to small hardware, we thought would constitute a neutral category.

In our survey of exchanges dealing in grain and livestock, 100 percent of those responding reported the use of institutionalized arbitration. There are, of course, other reasons for such a unanimous response by the exchanges, but the nature of the goods involved is a very important one. The trade association survey showed that of all the reporting associations, dealings in raws, 46 percent had machinery, 29 percent made individual arrangements, and only 25 percent never arbitrated. On the other hand, only 4 percent of those reporting hards as their basic goods had machinery, 46 percent made individual arrangements, and 50 per cent never arbitrated. * * *

To the extent that the factors leading to institutionalized machinery reinforce each other, as, for example, in the case of an association reporting that its members have an import relationship to foreign trade, deal in raws, and consist of merchants, the existence of arbitration machinery rises to approximately 100 percent. When the contrary report is made, that is, that the membership consists of manufacturers of hard goods engaged only in domestic business, the percentage drops off to about 8 percent.

We can thus say that the presence of institutionalized arbitration is a strong index of the existence of a generally self-contained trade association having its own self-regulation machinery and that the forces leading to institutionalized arbitration also, therefore, tend to lead to the creation of self-contained, self-governing trade groups.

Note: The American Arbitration Association

The AAA is a private non-profit organization founded in 1926 "to foster the study of arbitration, to perfect its techniques and procedures under arbitration law, and to advance generally the science of arbitration." It works actively to publicize and promote arbitration. Of far greater importance, however, is its central role in the administration of much of the arbitration that takes place in this country. The parties to a contract will frequently stipulate that disputes which later arise are to be arbitrated under the auspices of the AAA. This means, for one thing, that the proceedings will automatically be governed by AAA rules. In a commercial case, the AAA's "Commercial Arbitration Rules" will resolve questions concerning the method of choosing arbitrators, their powers, time limits for various steps in the proceedings, and the conduct of the hearing. There are also alternative sets of rules available for adoption in particular trades. In the construction industry for example, use of the AAA's Construction Industry Arbitration Rules (recommended by such trade groups as the American Institute of Architects and the American Society of Civil Engineers) has become standard. The AAA also administers a large number of labor arbitrations under its Voluntary Labor Arbitration Rules, and uninsured motorist accident arbitrations under its Accident Claims Arbitration Rules. In all these cases, using contracts that incorporate pre-existing bodies of rules saves the parties the burden, costs, and delay of having to negotiate and spell out an entire code for the conduct of the arbitration.

Over 194,000 arbitration cases were filed with the AAA in 2000. Of these, 17,791 were commercial cases; 4,677 were construction cases; 13,680 were labor cases, and 2,049 were individual employment cases. (By far the largest part of the AAA's arbitration caseload was made up of uninsured-motorist and no-fault insurance cases).[1] The Association maintains a panel of 6000 arbitrators willing to serve in commercial cases (and another panel of more than 3000 arbitrators for construction cases); the parties select their arbitrators from a number of names suggested by AAA administrators, who furnish information concerning the background and experience of the candidates. The AAA itself will appoint the arbitrator to hear the case if the parties cannot agree on a name. In addition, during the course of the proceeding the AAA staff will furnish a variety of administrative services, concerning, for example, notice to the parties, pre-hearing conferences, and the scheduling, location, and conduct of the hearing—all intended to insure that the process runs smoothly and that the chances of a successful later challenge to the award are minimized. Selection of arbitrators and arbitration procedure are discussed in some detail at Section D.1.a., infra.

While the AAA remains the dominant arbitral institution in the United States, it has in recent years been subject to increasing competition for business from a number of more entrepreneurial for-profit rivals, including Judicial Arbitration & Mediation Services, Inc., (JAMS) and National Arbitration Forum (NAF). See Pollock, "Arbitrator Finds Role Dwindling as Rivals Grow," Wall St. J., April 28, 1993 at B1.

NOTES AND QUESTIONS

A survey of textile disputes arbitrated through the AAA found that much textile arbitration was handled by a relatively small group of lawyers: Only five lawyers were counsel to 43 of the 182 parties who submitted to arbitration in one of the years studied. "When asked to compare the predictability of an arbitrator's decision to that of a judge or the verdict of a jury, each of the five lawyers replied without hesitation that the decision of an arbitrator was by far the 'most predictable,' that a judge's decision was 'predictable at some but not all times,' and a jury's decision was 'virtually one of pure chance.' " Bonn, The Predictability of Nonlegalistic Adjudication, 6 Law & Soc'y Rev. 563 (1972). However, the author attributed this predictability largely to the fact that sellers would carefully "screen" or "preselect" cases they took to arbitration. Sellers would pursue arbitration primarily against "buyers who are marginal firms or who have weak or specious claims"; where a buyer had "a strong case, say one based on a legitimate quality claim," and was a good future business prospect, sellers would choose instead to settle the dispute informally.

In another survey of textile arbitration cases the same author found that out of 78 cases, "business relations were resumed" following the arbitration in only 14. Bonn, Arbitration: An Alternative System for Handling Contract Related Disputes, 17 Admin.Sci.Q. 254, 262 (1972). Is this clearly an indication that arbitration may be as "lethal to continuing relations" as litigation? Cf. Galanter, Reading the Landscape of Disputes:

1. American Arbitration Association, *Dispute Resolution Times,* April–June 2001, at pp. 1, 19.

What We Know and Don't Know (And Think We Know) About Our Allegedly Contentious and Litigious Society, 31 U.C.L.A.L.Rev. 4, 25 n. 117 (1983). See also Baruch Bush, Dispute Resolution Alternatives and the Goals of Civil Justice: Jurisdictional Principles for Process Choice, 1984 Wisc.L.Rev. 893, 992–93. Bush suggests that the "informality" of arbitration may well contribute to reducing hostility between the parties—especially in comparison with litigation—in that it limits the amount and intensity of "direct party confrontation" in the form of evidentiary and procedural contentions. He argues, however, that this function is far more likely to be accomplished by a process like mediation that is aimed directly at facilitating mutual understanding and sympathy.

2. International Commercial Arbitration

Many of the same factors inducing parties to choose arbitration as a dispute settlement technique in domestic commercial transactions are likely to be present when the transaction expands across national boundaries. Indeed, as Professor Mentschikoff points out, the involvement of more than one body of law and more than one court system is likely to provide even further impetus to nonjudicial dispute resolution. The time, expense, and procedural complexities of litigating in another country's courts are likely to be considerable. There may not even be any effective protection against parallel litigation proceeding simultaneously in the courts of the United States and of a foreign country. There is likely to be far greater uncertainty with respect to the rules of decision that will govern the dispute in a foreign tribunal, and thus as to the outcome; the rules of "conflict of laws" will not always give a bankable answer even to the question of *which* nation's law will apply to the transaction. In addition, the "foreign" party to the litigation will not only feel disadvantaged by his relative unfamiliarity with the "rules of the game," but may also doubt how fairly and even-handedly he will be treated in comparison to his "local" opponent.

Another troubling cause of unpredictability in international litigation stems from uncertainty as to when and to what extent a judgment obtained in one country will be enforceable in another. A favorable decision against a French supplier in a New York court, for example, may be of little value if the courts of France will not recognize the New York judgment. However, "[c]ompared with ordinary court decisions, arbitration is far ahead as far as enforcement in other countries is concerned."[2] In many countries, enforcement of a foreign arbitral award is simpler and more assured than is enforcement of a foreign judgment—a difference in outcome perhaps explained by the common tendency to regard an arbitral award as "the outcome of contractual relationships, rather than of the exercise of state powers."[3] This favorable treatment of foreign arbitral awards has been

2. Sanders, International Commercial Arbitration—How to Improve its Functioning?, [1980] Arbitration 9.

3. Gardner, Economic and Political Implications of International Commercial Arbitration, in Martin Domke (ed.), International Trade Arbitration 20–21 (1958).

reinforced by international treaty. See the United Nations Convention on the Recognition and Enforcement of Foreign Arbitral Awards, infra Appendix B.

It is therefore not surprising that in international commercial contracts, arbitration clauses "not only predominate but are nowadays almost universal" and are "virtually taken for granted."[4] The Supreme Court has on a number of occasions recognized the unique value of international arbitration in promoting "the orderliness and predictability essential to any international business transaction," and has drawn from it a strong policy favoring international commercial arbitration. See Scherk v. Alberto–Culver Co., 417 U.S. 506, 516, 94 S.Ct. 2449, 41 L.Ed.2d 270 (1974); Mitsubishi v. Soler, infra p. 170. It has been suggested that international arbitrators have been moving towards a "common law of international arbitration"—that they have been developing a "customary law of international contracts"[5] that stresses general norms of conduct suited to international business practices independent of the rules of particular bodies of national law. This is particularly marked in arbitration decisions dealing with such thorny recurring problems in international trade as the effect on contracts of "impossibility" (*force majeure*) or currency fluctuations.

Parties to international transactions often prefer to proceed with arbitration outside of any institutional framework, and to administer the arbitration themselves on an "ad hoc" basis. However, dispensing with the administrative support of organizations like the AAA is not likely to be successful in cases where the level of cooperation and trust between the parties is low and one of them may be dragging his feet in resolving the problem. In addition, where a recognized institution has supervised the arbitration, the institution's reputation may lend credibility to the award should a national court ever come to review the arbitration. There exist a large number of other organizations besides the AAA which compete in the administration of international commercial arbitrations; by far the most important of these is the International Chamber of Commerce (ICC), based in Paris.

It is inevitable that international arbitration will often turn out to be considerably more protracted and expensive than its domestic counterpart. The ICC in particular is often criticized on this account. In ICC proceedings the administrative charges paid to the ICC for its services, and the fees paid to the arbitrators themselves, are calculated on the basis of the amount in dispute between the parties. In a $10 million case these may range from a bare—and unlikely—minimum of $62,550 to a maximum, if three arbitrators are used, of $441,800. The most articulate apologists for ICC arbitration respond to criticisms of excessive expense with a plea that:

4. Kerr, International Arbitration v. Litigation, [1980] J. Business Law 164, 165, 171.

5. W. Laurence Craig, William Park, & Jan Paulsson, International Chamber of Commerce Arbitration 638 (3rd ed. 2000). See also Rene David, Arbitration in International Trade §§ 16 ("Search for an autonomous commercial law"), 17 (1985).

the cost must be evaluated in relation to the alternatives. Certainly, ICC arbitration seems cheaper than abandoning one's rights altogether. Litigation, even in one's own home courts, is not necessarily a less expensive alternative, given the possibility of one or more appeals. More importantly, it simply is not always reasonable to expect that one's home forum will be acceptable to a foreign contracting party. ICC arbitration is too often compared—unrealistically and unfairly—with a perfect world in which there are no administrative difficulties, no judicial prejudice against foreign parties, no language problems, no uncooperative parties, and where the just always prevail at no cost to themselves.[6]

NOTES AND QUESTIONS

1. In many countries the government assumes a far more active role in economic transactions—particularly those involving capital investment and the exploitation and development of national resources—than it does in the United States. The foreign state or one of its instrumentalities will often be a party to such contracts, which are likely to have political and economic implications and symbolic importance far greater than in the case of domestic transactions. This can be a factor which complicates the question of dispute resolution. A foreign state will understandably be reluctant to submit to the jurisdiction of the courts of another sovereign (as, of course, the foreign investor will be reluctant to submit to the courts of the host country.) However, developing countries in particular have long been sensitive to the implications of submitting to *any* forum where the location or the decision-maker is foreign, and such reluctance has been extended to foreign arbitrations as well.

This unwillingness to submit to foreign arbitration is probably most marked in Latin American countries, where historical memory of one-sided international "arbitrations" dominated by European or North American partners is still vivid. A Brazilian writer has recently argued that:

> Functioning as an active element to denationalize (or internationalize) the contract, arbitration by removing a dispute from resolution by local courts applying local law, takes it to a plane where the rules are made by the great international commercial interests, a process from which Third World countries normally are excluded.

Quoted in Nattier, International Commercial Arbitration in Latin America: Enforcement of Arbitral Agreements and Awards, 21 Tex.Int'l L.J. 397, 407 (1986). See also Echeverria & Siqueiros, Arbitration in Latin American Countries, in Sanders (ed.), Arbitration in Settlement of International Commercial Disputes 81, 82 (1989) (the failure of arbitration to take root in Latin America "may only be explained as a consequence of the traditional view that international arbitration was a surrogate for diplomatic interven-

6. W. Laurence Craig et al., supra n.5 at 29–30, 744 ("Calculating ICC Administrative Expenses and Fees of Arbitrators According to the ICC Schedule").

tion by the great powers"). For many years the "Calvo doctrine," incorporated in several Latin American constitutions or statutes, made impossible the litigation or arbitration abroad of state contracts and required foreign investors to consent to the dispute resolution processes of local courts.

In many Latin American countries, in fact, the validity even of agreements between *private* parties to submit disputes to foreign arbitral tribunals has been uncertain. This traditional attitude, however, has gradually been changing. In recent years a number of such countries have enacted modern arbitration laws providing for the enforcement of arbitration agreements and awards, and have become parties to international arbitration treaties such as the New York Convention (see Appendix B), the similar Inter–American Convention on International Commercial Arbitration (see Appendix C), and the Convention on the Settlement of Investment Disputes (the ICSID Convention; see note (2) infra). Brazil's new arbitration law, adopted in 1996, for the first time made pre-dispute arbitration clauses specifically enforceable—although doubts have persisted as to the constitutionality of this legislation. See Wald et al., Some Controversial Aspects of the New Brazilian Arbitration Law, 31 U. Miami Inter–Amer. L. Rev. 223 (2000)(enactment of the new law "signifies a true cultural revolution whose significance is only now being recognized by the judiciary"; "[u]nder the pressures of huge caseloads," Brazilian courts are abandoning their traditional hostility to arbitration and recognizing its increasing importance); Barral & Prazeres, Trends of Arbitration in Brazil, Mealey's Int'l Arb. Rep., Aug. 2000, at p. 22. See also Trevino, The New Mexican Legislation on Commercial Arbitration, 11 J.In'tl Arb. 5 (1994); Siqueiros, Mexican Arbitration—The New Statute, 30 Tex.Int'l L.J. 227 (1995).

2. In December 1985, Walt Disney Productions and the French Government signed a letter of intent for the construction of a new Disneyland, to be located near Paris. France and Spain had both competed vigorously for this project, which French officials estimated would involve long-term American investment of as much as $6.7 billion and the creation of more than 30,000 jobs. The French Government had made commitments to build rail and highway networks linking the site to Paris and to develop an infrastructure, including roads and telephone trunk lines, for the area.

The contract negotiations, however, proved extremely difficult. Political opposition to the project—French Communists denounced it as "the encroachment of an alien civilization next to the city of enlightenment"—figured in the parliamentary elections held throughout France in March 1986. Another major snag was Disney's demand that any disputes which might later arise out of the French Government's undertakings be resolved by arbitration through the International Center for the Settlement of Investment Disputes (ICSID).

ICSID was established by treaty in 1966 to provide a neutral forum for the resolution of disputes between states and foreign investors, and to reduce the fear of political risks that might discourage the flow of private foreign capital to developing countries. ICSID functions under the auspices of the World Bank and is a "public" body, administered by representatives of the various participating governments. Only 57 cases have as yet been referred to the Center; most of these have involved disputes arising out of mining, construction, or joint venture agreements with developing states in sub-Saharan Africa and Latin America. See generally Ibrahim Shihata & Antonio Parra, The Experience of the International Centre for Settlement of Investment Disputes, 14 ICSID Rev.-Foreign Investment L.J. 299 (1999).

Fear was expressed in France that acceding to Disney's demand would create a "precedent" by which all new foreign investments might have to go to arbitration. And one French official was said to have commented that "Disney's request for ICSID was shocking and a bit dumb. France is not a banana republic." International Herald Tribune, March 15, 1986, pp. 1, 15; see also Washington Post, August 21, 1986, p. C8; "The Real Estate Coup at Euro Disneyland," Fortune, April 28, 1986, p. 172.

The agreement between Disney and the French Government was finally signed in March 1987. It did contain a provision for dispute settlement by arbitration—but through the ICC, to take place in France.

3. In concluding commercial contracts with foreign businesses, negotiators from the People's Republic of China invariably try to obtain an agreement that any future disputes will be arbitrated in China by the China International Economic and Trade Arbitration Commission ("CIETAC"). CIETAC today has a caseload that makes it one of the world's busiest arbitration centers. Under CIETAC rules, each party to a dispute selects one arbitrator from the Commission's list of arbitrators; the third and presiding member of the panel is chosen by CIETAC itself and is in most cases an employee of the Commission. Most of the arbitrators on CIETAC's list are Chinese nationals, although more than a fourth of the names on the list are now from foreign countries. Some insight into the nature of an arbitration conducted by CIETAC can be gleaned from this account by a leading official of the organization:

> A foreign buyer ordered 500 cases of goods from a Chinese seller. According to the contract, the goods were to be shipped from a Chinese port to Hong Kong and then transshipped from Hong Kong to the port of destination. Upon arrival at the port of destination, part of the goods were found damaged. The buyer claimed against the seller for compensation of the losses incurred * * * on the grounds that the packing was defective. The seller argued that the packing was not defective because it was the normal packing he used for exporting the goods and no extra or special requirements for packing were specified in the contract. * * * The buyer then applied to [CIETAC] for arbitration. With the consent of both parties, the arbitration tribunal decided the case according to principles of conciliation. It was the opinion of the arbitration tribunal that although no extra or special requirements for packing were specified in the contract, the seller knew that the goods were to be transshipped at Hong Kong, which was different from shipment directly from a Chinese port to the port of destination. The packing should be suitable for that specific transportation. However,

> the nails and the wood used for the packing were not appropriate for the purpose. The arbitration tribunal proposed an appropriate compensation to the buyer for his losses. The seller accepted the arbitration tribunal's proposal but pointed out that the amount claimed by the buyer was too large and asked for a reduction. The arbitration tribunal consulted the buyer and eventually the buyer agreed to reduce his claim by seventy percent. Both parties came to a compromise agreement from which the arbitration tribunal delivered a Conciliatory Statement and closed the case.

Tang, Arbitration—A Method Used by China to Settle Foreign Trade and Economic Disputes, 4 Pace L.Rev. 519, 533–34 (1984). For more recent developments, see also Harpole, How China Organizes Arbitral Tribunals, Disp. Res. J., Jan. 1997 at p. 72; Blay, Party Autonomy in Chinese International Arbitration, 8 Am. Rev. Int'l Arb. 331 (1997); Peerenboom, The Evolving Regulatory Framework for Enforcement of Arbitral Awards in the People's Republic of China, 1 Asian–Pac. L. & Policy J. 12 (2000).

CIETAC acts under the supervision of the China Chamber of International Commerce, which is nominally a non-governmental organization whose mission is to promote foreign investment and trade by promoting links between foreign companies and the Chinese government. Its arbitrators may understandably be reluctant to finally adjudicate the merits of a dispute between a Western trading company and a domestic state unit, since such a decision might well affect the future business relations between the parties. Cf. Chew, A Procedural and Substantive Analysis of the Fairness of Chinese and Soviet Foreign Trade Arbitrations, 21 Tex.Int'l L.J. 291, 330–34 (1986). In addition, a general aversion to formal third-party adjudication and a predilection for conciliation and compromise have long marked Chinese legal culture. See, e.g., Schwartz, On Attitudes Toward Law in China, in Katz (ed.), Government Under Law and the Individual 27–39 (1957). In any event, as this excerpt illustrates, CIETAC will proceed to "decide" a dispute only in those cases where its efforts to induce a voluntary agreement through conciliation have failed. To what extent does this model correspond to the American understanding of the arbitration process? See also the discussion of "Med–Arb" at Section E.3 infra.

4. Fujitsu (Japan's largest computer company) developed and marketed IBM-compatible operating system software, which IBM claimed was in violation of its copyrights. The companies agreed to submit the dispute to two arbitrators (a law professor and a retired computer executive) under AAA auspices. The arbitrators were determined from the outset "to avoid becoming engulfed in an extensive adjudicatory fact-finding process with respect to hundreds of programs previously released by [Fujitsu]." "While this might determine in particular instances whether IBM's intellectual property rights had been violated, it would not directly address and resolve the parties' dispute with respect to [Fujitsu's] ongoing use of IBM programming material in its software development process."

Through their mediation efforts, the parties came instead to agree on the concept of a "coerced license" that was to be administered by these arbitrators into the future. The arbitrators' award allowed the Japanese company to examine IBM programs in a "secured facility" for a period of five to ten years and, "subject to strict and elaborate safeguards," to use such information in its software development; this would provide Fujitsu with a "reasonable opportunity to independently develop and maintain IBM–compatible operating system software." Fujitsu was to "fully and adequately compensate" IBM for such access in amounts to be determined by the arbitrators. In effect the arbitrators' award and subsequent decisions "will constitute the applicable intellectual property law until the end of the Contract Period, notwithstanding copyright decisions of U.S. or Japanese courts * * *." One of the arbitrators later commented that their decisions "will be considerably more detailed than existing copyright law, because there haven't been all that many cases and they haven't got into as many areas as we've gotten into." Wall.St.J., July 1, 1988, p. 4. See also Johnston, The IBM–Fujitsu Arbitration Revisited—A Case Study in Effective ADR, 7 Computer Law. 13 (May 1990).

5. Athletes participating in the Olympic Games are required to sign entry forms in which they agree to settle all Games-related disputes through arbitration before the Court of Arbitration for Sport. The CAS was created in 1984 by the International Olympic Committee, but is now more or less independent, and operates under the general supervision of the International Council of Arbitration for Sport. (The ICAS is composed of twenty "high-level jurists," four of whom are appointed respectively by the IOC, by the Association of National Olympic Committees, and by the International Federations that govern individual sports such as swimming and gymnastics—with the remaining members chosen by those already appointed). The ICAS in turn selects a panel of 150 arbitrators who are supposed to have "legal training and who possess recognized competence with regard to sport": "From the professor of Sports Law, to the lawyer who once won an Olympic wrestling medal, the paths of 'specialization' are diverse." See Kaufmann–Kohler, "Art and Arbitration: What Lessons Can be Drawn from the Resolution of Sports Disputes," 11 Studies in Art Law 123, 128 (1999).

The CAS makes arbitrators available on-site at each Olympics, with a commitment to render awards within 24 hours after the demand for arbitration. (Under its rules, however, the "seat" of every arbitration panel is deemed to be in Lausanne, Switzerland, and the arbitration is to be governed by Swiss law). CAS jurisdiction is by no means limited to the Olympics: It is a permanent body that may decide any "matters of principle relating to sport or matters of pecuniary or other interests brought into play in the practice or the development of sport"; its case load of around 20 arbitrations per year has included disputes involving such matters as substance abuse, eligibility for competition, and the interpretation of endorsement contracts or contracts between athletes and agents or managers. Perhaps the most highly-publicized award, however, was made at the 2000 Sydney games: A 16–year old Romanian gymnast was stripped of her gold medal by the IOC after testing positive for a banned substance—apparently she had been given two over-the-counter cold pills by the team's doctor. It was conceded that neither her intent, nor the effect of the drug, had been to enhance her performance. The CAS arbitration panel, made up of arbitrators from Australia, Switzerland, and the United States, nevertheless upheld the IOC's decision: "A strict liability test must be applied," it said in a brief opinion, "the consequence being automatic disqualification as a matter of law and in fairness to all other athletes."

6. As we have seen, the practice in domestic commercial arbitration is to dispense with reasoned opinions. In contrast, parties in international cases *do* usually expect arbitrators to provide a written opinion that sets out the reasons for their award. The ICC requires its arbitrators to give reasoned awards; under the ICSID treaty, an award may be "annulled" by an ad hoc appellate committee if "the award has failed to state the reasons on which it is based." This expectation of a reasoned opinion in international arbitration reflects in part the pervasive influence of Continental legal systems, where unreasoned awards are often considered contrary to public policy and thus unenforceable. See Rene David, Arbitration in International Trade 319–328 (1985); W. Laurence Craig, William Park & Jan Paulsson, International Chamber of Commerce Arbitration § 19.04 (3rd ed. 2000).

3. Labor Arbitration

A collective bargaining agreement between an employer and the union that represents the firm's employees is likely to be a complex document. It will deal with a large number of subjects, among many other things setting wages and other terms of employment, imposing limits on the employer's right to discharge or discipline employees, and providing for seniority for purposes of layoffs, promotion, and job assignments. It will constitute, in short, an overall framework for employer-employee relations.

Most agreements also spell out a process by which the inevitable questions of interpretation and application arising during the life of the contract will be settled. There are typically a number of steps in this process: At the beginning, for example, there may be informal attempts to adjust a grievance on the shop floor by consultations between the employee's immediate supervisor and the union shop steward; if the dispute is not settled at this stage it will move to successively higher levels. The agreement is likely to make it clear that at all stages work is not to be interrupted because of the dispute but is to continue pending a final settlement, and is likely also to impose strict time limits to insure that a grievance is heard and processed speedily. The final stage in the grievance process, to handle those "cases that are not winnowed out by the process of day-to-day negotiation,"[7] is likely to be binding arbitration. The Department of Labor estimates that more than 96% of all collective bargaining

7. Getman, Labor Arbitration and Dispute Resolution, 88 Yale L.J. 916, 919 (1979).

agreements—covering a total of almost 6½ million workers—provide for arbitration of grievance disputes.[8]

Section 301 of the Labor Management Relations Act of 1947 (the Taft–Hartley Act) granted jurisdiction to federal district courts to hear suits for violation of collective bargaining agreements "in an industry affecting commerce." In Textile Workers Union v. Lincoln Mills, 353 U.S. 448, 77 S.Ct. 912, 1 L.Ed.2d 972 (1957), the Supreme Court held that § 301 was "more than jurisdictional," and that it "authorizes federal courts to fashion a body of federal law for the enforcement of these collective bargaining agreements." "Plainly the agreement to arbitrate grievance disputes is the *quid pro quo* for an agreement not to strike." Federal policy therefore was that promises to arbitrate grievances under collective bargaining agreements should be specifically enforced, and that "industrial peace can be best obtained only in that way."

Federal courts have for the past thirty years engaged in "fashioning" a federal common law dealing with the enforcement of arbitration agreements—to such an extent that it is not an exaggeration to say that the field of "labor law" is now to a large degree the law of labor arbitration. In 1960, in what is still the Supreme Court's most significant pronouncement on the subject, Justice Douglas undertook an evaluation of the purpose and function of labor arbitration and of the central place it occupies in our system of workplace bargaining. Some extracts from his discussion follow.

United Steelworkers of America v. Warrior & Gulf Navigation Co.

Supreme Court of the United States, 1960.
363 U.S. 574, 80 S.Ct. 1347, 4 L.Ed.2d 1409.

■ Opinion of the Court by MR. JUSTICE DOUGLAS.

* * *

The present federal policy is to promote industrial stabilization through the collective bargaining agreement. A major factor in achieving industrial peace is the inclusion of a provision for arbitration of grievances in the collective bargaining agreement.

Thus the run of arbitration cases * * * becomes irrelevant to our problem. There the choice is between the adjudication of cases or controversies in courts with established procedures or even special statutory safeguards on the one hand and the settlement of them in the more informal arbitration tribunal on the other. In the commercial case, arbitration is the substitute for litigation. Here arbitration is the substitute for industrial strife. Since arbitration of labor disputes has quite different functions from arbitration under an ordinary commercial agreement, the

8. U.S. Dept. of Labor, Characteristics of Major Collective Bargaining Agreements 112 (1981).

hostility evinced by courts toward arbitration of commercial agreements has no place here. For arbitration of labor disputes under collective bargaining agreements is part and parcel of the collective bargaining process itself.

* * *

A collective bargaining agreement is an effort to erect a system of industrial self-government. When most parties enter into [a] contractual relationship they do so voluntarily, in the sense that there is no real compulsion to deal with one another, as opposed to dealing with other parties. This is not true of the labor agreement. The choice is generally not between entering or refusing to enter into a relationship, for that in all probability preexists the negotiations. Rather it is between having that relationship governed by an agreed-upon rule of law or leaving each and every matter subject to a temporary resolution dependent solely upon the relative strength, at any given moment, of the contending forces. The mature labor agreement may attempt to regulate all aspects of the complicated relationship, from the most crucial to the most minute over an extended period of time. Because of the compulsion to reach agreement and the breadth of the matters covered, as well as the need for a fairly concise and readable instrument, the product of negotiations (the written document) is, in the words of the late Dean Shulman, "a compilation of diverse provisions: some provide objective criteria almost automatically applicable; some provide more or less specific standards which require reason and judgment in their application; and some do little more than leave problems to future consideration with an expression of hope and good faith." Gaps may be left to be filled in by reference to the practices of the particular industry and of the various shops covered by the agreement. Many of the specific practices which underlie the agreement may be unknown, except in hazy form, even to the negotiators. Courts and arbitration in the context of most commercial contracts are resorted to because there has been a breakdown in the working relationship of the parties; such resort is the unwanted exception. But the grievance machinery under a collective bargaining agreement is at the very heart of the system of industrial self-government. Arbitration is the means of solving the unforeseeable by molding a system of private law for all the problems which may arise and to provide for their solution in a way which will generally accord with the variant needs and desires of the parties. The processing of disputes through the grievance machinery is actually a vehicle by which meaning and content are given to the collective bargaining agreement.

Apart from matters that the parties specifically exclude, all of the questions on which the parties disagree must therefore come within the scope of the grievance and arbitration provisions of the collective agreement. The grievance procedure is, in other words, a part of the continuous collective bargaining process. It, rather than a strike, is the terminal point of a disagreement.

* * *

The labor arbitrator's source of law is not confined to the express provisions of the contract, as the industrial common law—the practices of the industry and the shop—is equally a part of the collective bargaining agreement although not expressed in it. The labor arbitrator is usually chosen because of the parties' confidence in his knowledge of the common law of the shop and their trust in his personal judgment to bring to bear considerations which are not expressed in the contract as criteria for judgment. The parties expect that his judgment of a particular grievance will reflect not only what the contract says but, insofar as the collective bargaining agreement permits, such factors as the effect upon productivity of a particular result, its consequence to the morale of the shop, his judgment whether tensions will be heightened or diminished. For the parties' objective in using the arbitration process is primarily to further their common goal of uninterrupted production under the agreement, to make the agreement serve their specialized needs. The ablest judge cannot be expected to bring the same experience and competence to bear upon the determination of a grievance, because he cannot be similarly informed.

Arbitration of labor disputes serves, then, to give "meaning and content" over time to the vague or ambiguous terms of the collective bargaining agreement. In addition, the very existence of this dispute resolution mechanism itself may affect the dynamic of the parties' relationship. Through the processing of a grievance dispute, for example, useful information may be communicated about the needs and attitudes of one party to the agreement, and about potential trouble spots in the relationship. Another function of labor arbitration was highlighted by Justice Douglas in a formulation which has now attained something of the status of a cliché: In a companion case to *Warrior & Gulf,* Justice Douglas noted that "[t]he processing of even frivolous claims may have therapeutic values of which those who are not a part of the plant environment may be quite unaware."[9]

Just what does it mean to claim that labor arbitration can have a "therapeutic" function? It has been suggested that the ability to participate in the selection of a neutral decisionmaker, and to present one's own story to him in an informal, "non-threatening" atmosphere, may be "empowering" for each of the parties to the dispute.[10] It is important also to bear in mind here that any particular grievance under a collective bargaining agreement is likely to be that of the individual *employee,* who may have been dismissed or whose job classification may have been changed. However, the parties to the bargaining agreement are the employer and the *union;* the union, as the exclusive representative of all the employees in the bargaining unit, is in exclusive control of the administration of the contract

9. United Steelworkers of America v. American Mfg. Co., 363 U.S. 564, 568, 80 S.Ct. 1343, 4 L.Ed.2d 1403 (1960).

10. See, e.g., Abrams, Abrams & Nolan, Arbitral Therapy, 46 Rutgers L.Rev. 1751, 1765, 1767, 1769 (1994).

and controls access to the grievance procedure at every stage. In these circumstances, pursuing even a hopeless claim to arbitration has at least the virtue of giving the employee the assurance that his case has been heard and that he has been taken seriously. Grievance arbitration may thus serve as a "safety valve for troublesome complaints"[11] the employee's presence at the hearing watching management witnesses subjected to "searching and often embarrassing cross-examination" may result in "a kind of catharsis that helps to make even eventual defeat acceptable" to the grievant.[12]

Carrying a case through the arbitration process may have other advantages for the union. It is often more politic for union representatives to "pass the buck" to the arbitrator, who they know will reject the grievance, than to be obliged *themselves* to convince their constituent that he is wrong and that the claim should be dropped. In addition, a union that is found to have "arbitrarily" refused to pursue an employee's grievance to arbitration, or to have "process[ed] it in a perfunctory fashion," may well be open to a suit by the employee for "unfair representation."[13] Nevertheless, the fact remains that the overwhelming proportion of employee grievances are screened or settled without resort to arbitration, just as the overwhelming proportion of lawsuits are settled before trial. It has been estimated that a grievance rate of 10 to 20 per 100 employees per year is "typical" in this country.[14] If any substantial proportion of those cases were to go to arbitration the entire grievance system would collapse.

Awards handed down by labor arbitrators generally reveal considerable sensitivity to those considerations mentioned by Justice Douglas in his paean to labor arbitration in *Warrior & Gulf*—the need to reduce tensions and to foster a good working relationship within the plant setting, the need to pay attention to the "common law of the shop" and to the "customs and practices which the parties have come to consider as settled patterns of conduct."[15] Some selections from recent arbitral awards give a good flavor of how labor arbitrators purport, at least, to see their role in the process. Would you expect to find opinions like these written by "judges"?

(a) The employee had worked for the employer for eight years and had never been disciplined. He was discharged for being disrespectful to the Company President ("If you don't like the way I'm doing the work, do it yourself") in the presence of a number of the company's other employees. The arbitrator held that the employer did not have "proper cause" to

11. Cox, Current Problems in the Law of Grievance Arbitration, 30 Rocky Mt.L.Rev. 247, 261 (1958).

12. Aaron, The Role of the Arbitrator in Ensuring a Fair Hearing, 35 Proc.Nat'l Acad.Arb. 30, 32 (1983).

13. Vaca v. Sipes, 386 U.S. 171, 87 S.Ct. 903, 17 L.Ed.2d 842 (1967); see also Bowen v. U.S. Postal Service, 459 U.S. 212, 103 S.Ct. 588, 74 L.Ed.2d 402 (1983).

14. See Feller, A General Theory of the Collective Bargaining Agreement, 61 Cal. L.Rev. 663, 755 (1973).

15. See In re Standard Bag Corp. and Paper Bag, Novelty, Mounting, Finishing and Display Workers Union, 45 Lab.Arb. 1149 (1965).

discharge the employee and that he should be reinstated, although without recovering back pay or accruing seniority or vacation benefits for the seven months he was off work:

> Since discharge is in essence "capital punishment" in the work place, it is necessary to examine with extreme care all of the evidence before determining whether it is appropriate or not. This would include the facts and circumstances leading to the discharge, the grievant's length of service, the degree of aggravation involved in the offense, whether the conduct was intended or rather an accidental outburst, the grievant's past record and finally whether the events are likely to recur were the grievant to be reinstated. * * *
>
> Management's main argument was that it would be difficult for [the President] to run his operation with employees knowing that they could talk back to the President of the Company and get away with it. However, with this employee having been off work for over seven months without pay, I doubt that any employee will seriously think that he "got away with" very much. Upholding the discharge would be the most severe form of industrial penalty, but giving the grievant his job back without the seven months of back pay is still a very significant penalty. In salary alone that amounts to approximately $6,000.00 of gross earnings. (The grievant did not collect unemployment compensation and has not worked.) * * *
>
> On the day he returns to work, but as a condition precedent to returning to work, the grievant will apologize to [the President] either privately or in front of the employees of Stylemaster. (The presence or lack thereof of other employees to be at the discretion of the Company.)

In re Stylemaster, Inc. and Production Workers Union of Chicago, 79 Lab.Arb. 76 (1982).

(b) A collective bargaining agreement provided that the employer, a grocery chain, would remain closed on January 1 "contingent upon similar limitations being contractually required of other organized food stores and/or being generally observed by major unorganized food competitors in the cities in which the Employer operated." The arbitrator found that the employer violated this agreement by opening on January 1. He then turned to the question of the proper remedy to be granted the Union. The arbitrator denied the Union's request for punitive damages, since he was "of the view that they are bad medicine when administered to a participant in an ongoing, union-management relationship." Although the employer's violation was "clear and unmistakable," "it is always hard to say that a beleaguered competitor, as Kroger undoubtedly considered itself, acted subjectively in bad faith. Moreover, it seems to me that a healing process is what is most needed in the relations between this Company and the Union, and I question whether punitive damages will contribute to that end." Nor, he held, was there any basis for awarding damages to the employees: "I do not mean that it would be impossible to attach a dollar value to a January 1 with family and friends, perhaps in front of the TV set watching a bowl game * * * but I do not find that such a showing was made here."

However, to prevent "unjust enrichment," the arbitrator did award to the union "restitution of any profits that may be attributable to the Company's operations on January 1." In re The Kroger Company and United Food and Commercial Workers, 85 Lab.Arb. 1198 (1985).

(c) The employee had worked for the employer for twenty-two years as a messenger; her job was to pick up and deliver advertising proofs and materials to customers. She was discharged for failing to report to work at the scheduled time: This was apparently "the fourth occurrence of this behavior in the past six months," and four months previously, she had been suspended for three days without pay in a similar incident. The arbitrator held that the discharge should be set aside, and that the employee should be returned to her former position without loss of seniority:

> When [the grievant] was testifying at the Arbitration Hearing my personal observation of her demeanor and appearance indicated that she was emotionally distraught beyond the customary nervous reaction of a witness. I * * * believe that [the grievant] deserved compassionate understanding. * * *
>
> If Grievant performed with reasonable competency essentially the same messenger duties for about twenty-two years and only during the past year * * * did she demonstrate incompetence there must be some reason. It could be possible that Grievant suddenly developed a contemptuous disregard for her supervisor's instructions, It is more likely that some other explanation accounts for her recent erratic work performance. * * *
>
> It was not until the Arbitration Hearing that the [employer's] supervisor learned that [the grievant] lived with her mother who was suffering with Alzheimer's disease and Grievant had to assist her. Grievant, at 43 years of age, is within the age span of 40 to 54 years that physicians believe that the climacteric usually occurs. This aging process, commonly called the change of life, in women sometimes produces sudden emotional changes that usually are temporary but which disrupt normal activities. Such a condition could interfere with a woman's required work activities and responsibilities. * * *
>
> The evidence proves that [the grievant's] work performance during the last year had declined to an unacceptable level. The time she has been suspended from work shall be considered a disciplinary penalty to impress upon her, and other employees, the necessity of conforming to proper standards of conduct. Perhaps this lengthy period [grievant] has been off duty provided an opportunity to regain her health and emotional stability.
>
> It probably would be beneficial to both bargaining unit employees and Management if specific rules for reporting off and obtaining sick leave or vacation days would be set forth in writing and distributed to all

> employees in this department. In the past there seems to have been considerable laxity in enforcement of reporting off and attendance requirements and also some ambiguity as to what attendance standards employees were expected to observe.

In re Pittsburgh Post–Gazette and Pittsburgh Typographical Union, 113 Lab. Arb. 957 (1999).

Note: Compromise Decisions

> POSNER: The arbitration literature says—something that is very difficult to find out independently—that arbitrators are not supposed to compromise. Arbitrators are supposed to decide a dispute as if they were judges.
>
> LEFF: The literature says that for the same reason that signs in subways say, "Don't Smoke," because there is a very strong tendency to smoke and therefore you have to say it over and over again. That reflects the fact that arbitrators compromise a great deal * * *.[16]

Observers often note that arbitrators have a propensity to tailor their decisions so as to make them acceptable to both parties. Such a criticism is heard most vociferously perhaps with respect to labor arbitrators, although it is by no means confined to the labor area. It is often supposed that this is done to insure the future "acceptability" of the arbitrator *himself*. Labor arbitrators are paid, often quite handsomely, for their work; what would be more natural than for this to create an incentive to try to assure themselves of repeat business? This incentive may often result in compromise decisions, "splitting the difference" so as not to appear unduly to favor either of the two parties whose future goodwill must be retained. A similar dynamic might be reflected in a *course* of decisions by the same arbitrator which over time, taken together, appears to show a rough balance between awards favorable to labor and those favorable to management.

As might be expected, this tendency to engage in compromise decisions appears particularly marked in "interest" arbitrations. In such cases the arbitrator is likely to be aware that the stakes riding on his decision are high, that the impact of his decision may be great and felt in all sorts of ways that he cannot be sure of in advance, and that intense dissatisfaction with a "mistaken" award may adversely affect the working relationship of the parties for some time to come. Do you expect that judges are often impelled to take such considerations into account in deciding cases?

Compare the following two excerpts, whose authors appear to take sharply differing views of the propriety of this behavior and of its function within the context of labor-management relations:

> A proportion of arbitration awards, no one knows how large a proportion, is decided not on the basis of the evidence or of the contract or

16. Discussion by Seminar Participants, 8 J.Legal Stud. 323, 345 (1979).

other proper considerations, but in a way calculated to encourage the arbitrator's being hired for other arbitration cases. It makes no difference whether or not a large majority of cases is decided in this way. A system of adjudication in which the judge depends for his livelihood, or for a substantial part of his livelihood or even for substantial supplements to his regular income, on pleasing those who hire him to judge is per se a thoroughly undesirable system. In no proper system of justice should a judge be submitted to such pressures. On the contrary, a judge should be carefully insulated from any pressure of this type.

Paul R. Hays, Labor Arbitration: A Dissenting View 112–13 (1966).

Compare Getman, Labor Arbitration and Dispute Resolution, 88 Yale L.J. 916, 928–930 (1979):

In none of the literature is it suggested that an arbitrator's desire to promote acceptability might affect the process in a way that is basically desirable. However, if, as I contend, economic efficiency is promoted by arbitration partly because through it the parties conclude their negotiations, then it is likely that the desire to maintain acceptability plays a useful role in helping to achieve the resolution that the parties would have achieved had they had the opportunity to negotiate with respect to the issues in dispute. Such a resolution would by definition further the goal of efficiency.

The negotiating process reflects both the relative economic strength and the differing priorities of the parties. * * * Economic strength is necessarily a factor in arbitration because it shapes the language of the collective-bargaining agreement, which is always the starting point, and sometimes the sole basis, for the arbitrator's decision. The parties' priorities are more difficult to ascertain. The arbitrator must pay careful attention to the clues that the parties give concerning how strongly they feel about a particular case. My judgment is that the need to maintain acceptability makes arbitrators more attentive to such clues than judges and more likely than judges would be to utilize them in their decision. Arbitrators whose decisions over time accurately reflect the priorities of the parties are likely to maintain and enhance their acceptability more than arbitrators who take either a more narrowly judicial role or a personally activist role. Thus, the process of selection will tend to produce arbitrators and a body of arbitral precedent that facilitate and extend the process of negotiation. * * *

The careful selection process also motivates arbitrators to try to please both sides, if possible, with their decision. Thus, the split award and the decision in which it is difficult to tell which side has won are frequent in labor relations. Although the parties constantly insist it is contrary to their wishes, this system of giving a little bit to each side permits the process to achieve the results of successful negotiation.

NOTES AND QUESTIONS

1. As Getman suggests, it is almost inevitable that in the course of a hearing an arbitrator will receive some intimation from the parties or their attorneys as to what an "acceptable" settlement will look like, and that he will be influenced by such hints or suggestions. In an extreme case this may even take the form of what is called a "rigged award." The union representative and the management may actually *agree* between themselves as to how a case should be resolved; this understanding is conveyed to the arbitrator, who incorporates it in the final award as "his" decision without openly revealing that it is in fact the result of the parties' compromise. The hearing itself then becomes a mere charade. The practice of the "rigged award" has been often and scathingly condemned as "the crassest infringement of adjudicative integrity," "the most severe criticism which could be made of arbitration," "vicious" and "a shocking distortion of the administration of justice." See Fuller, Collective Bargaining and the Arbitrator, 1963 Wisc.L.Rev. 3, 20 (1963); Eaton, Labor Arbitration in the San Francisco Bay Area, 48 Lab.Arb. 1381, 1389 (1967); Paul R. Hays, Labor Arbitration: A Dissenting View 113, 65 (1966).

Why might the parties want the arbitrator to proceed in this way, when they could simply "settle" the case and withdraw it from the purview of the arbitrator? And just *why* is the arbitrator not entitled to do this? What is wrong with the "rigged award"? Might there be a difference if this practice is used in "interest" arbitration rather than with respect to a "rights" dispute? Finally, if the arbitrator is unwilling merely to rubber-stamp the parties' understanding, how should he proceed? What as a practical matter is he able to do?

2. Some writers have suggested that the "procedures for arbitration that have been developed in the context of labor relations make the technique particularly adaptable to prison problems." To resolve disputes arising out of grievances by prison inmates, "third-party neutrals who have particular expertise in corrections may be chosen by both prisoners and the officials. Furthermore, the parties could stipulate in advance the rules to be followed and the issues to be settled." Goldfarb & Singer, Redressing Prisoners' Grievances, 39 Geo.Wash.L.Rev. 175, 316 (1970); see also Keating, Arbitration of Inmate Grievances, 30 Arb.J. 177 (1975). Do you agree?

4. Arbitration of Consumer Disputes

The Bank of America, the nation's second-largest bank, has 11.5 million checking and savings accounts in California and has issued a total of 7 million credit cards nationwide. In the summer of 1992 the Bank announced that all its contracts with depositors and credit-card holders would henceforth contain arbitration clauses. Under the Bank's new contract, any individual disputes would be decided by arbitration under the commercial rules of the AAA; any complaints brought as class actions would be "referred" to a neutral under California's "rent-a-judge" statute (See p. 305 infra.) Notice of the arbitration clause was sent to the bank's customers as "stuffers" in their monthly statements; cardholders, for example, were told that if they continued to use their cards after receiving the notice, the arbitration provision would apply to all past and future transactions.

During the 1980's a number of California banks, including the Bank of America, had already begun to experiment with using arbitration in other product lines, particularly mid-range commercial loans. This was in reaction to a series of pro-borrower "lender liability" cases which seemed to broaden the scope of the duties owed to a borrower by a bank:

> [The banks] concluded that both their exposure and their transaction costs could be reduced by the adoption of arbitration provisions. First, they believed that their exposure would be both more predictable and better contained with arbitration. In their view, arbitrators generally had a better grasp of underlying contractual issues than juries and were less likely to consider factors outside those presented in the case at issue; for example, the fact that the bank is a large institution able to spread out any losses relative to the individual, who may be forced into extreme hardship. Firms also believed that arbitrators were less likely to award punitive damages. Furthermore, firms anticipated that the fact that disputes would be heard before an arbitrator would, in turn, affect plaintiffs' and plaintiffs' attorneys' calculus in deciding whether to bring suit in the first place; as possible verdicts declined, plaintiffs would be less likely to bring suit.[17]

In the first few years of the program, fewer than 20 disputes between the Bank and its customers went as far as arbitration. And in 1998, the Bank's arbitration mechanism was held on narrow grounds to be unenforceable: The California Court of Appeals held that under the original terms of its customer agreements, the Bank had no right to unilaterally impose this modification on its credit-card holders. (See pp. 111–112 infra). However, the Bank's introduction of arbitration clauses in its customer contracts was closely watched, and its example apparently encouraged other companies to follow its lead. Shortly after the Bank's announcement California's second-largest bank, Wells Fargo, also modified its deposit and credit-card contracts to include a mandatory "Comprehensive Dispute Resolution Program." The Program would apply only to claims of more than $25,000 (the limit for claims that can be brought in municipal court in California), and to both individual and class action suits. Under the Program, if any dispute could not be settled by good-faith negotiation or mediation, the dispute would then be submitted to a "rent-a-judge" process under the auspices of Judicial Arbitration and Mediation Services, Inc. (JAMS), or, if both parties prefer, to a JAMS arbitration. In addition, First USA, the nation's second-largest issuer of credit cards and a unit of Chicago-based Bank One, has also begun to require its customers to

17. Erik Moller, Elizabeth Rolph, & Patricia Ebener, Private Dispute Resolution in the Banking Industry 12–13 (RAND 1993).

arbitrate any disputes under the auspices of the "National Arbitration Forum."

Indeed, the possibilities for the use of arbitration in consumer contracts seem endless. Securities brokers invariably insist that individual investors who wish to open a margin or an option account agree to arbitration, and a substantial and increasing number of brokerage firms require arbitration even for investors wishing to open a cash account. Such a requirement is "never or almost never waived or negotiated."[18] After a customer orders a Gateway computer over the phone, the computer will eventually arrive in a box containing all the necessary equipment—along with a copy of Gateway's "Standard Terms and Conditions," which includes the obligation to arbitrate any disputes. The nation's second largest home-warranty company, Home Buyers Warranty Corp., now requires homeowners to agree to arbitration of any warranty claims.[19] Arbitration clauses can be found in many contracts of insurance.[20] And in 1994, the makers of Honey Nut Cheerios conducted a "sweepstakes" in which individuals with winning "game cards" would be entitled to certain prizes. (The odds were 1 in 10,000 that winners would receive a Sega Genesis Home Entertainment System with a Sega Cartridge—"you will receive either Dr. Robotnik's Mean Bean Machine or Toe Jam & Earl in Panic on Funkatron.") The back of the cereal box contained dense and lengthy rules by which "[a]s a condition of entering this contest," the participant agreed that "any and all disputes, claims and causes of action arising out of or connected with this contest, or any prizes awarded shall be resolved individually, without resort to any form of class action, and exclusively by arbitration under the rules of the American Arbitration Association in Minneapolis, Minnesota."[21]

Note: Medical Malpractice: Disputes Between Doctors and Patients

A dramatic increase in the number and size of medical malpractice claims and awards first entered the public consciousness during the 1970's, under the banner of the "malpractice crisis." The threatened effects of this "crisis" on the health and insurance industries spawned a large variety of legislative responses. These have ranged from tinkering with the formal legal standard of negligence or the statute of limitations in malpractice cases, to more dramatic reforms such as abolishing the collateral source

18. U.S. General Accounting Office, Securities Arbitration: How Investors Fare 28–30 (1992).

19. The arbitration is to be administered by Construction Arbitration Services of Dallas, which will "appoint arbitrators from its panel of persons knowledgeable in residential construction," CAS Rules for the Arbitration of Home Warranty Disputes, R.3. If CAS is for any reason unable to conduct the arbitration, then the AAA will instead administer the arbitration under its own rules. See Home Buyers Warranty Corp., Home Buyers Warranty Booklet, at p. 6. See also Blumenthal, "Shaky Support: Some Home Buyers Find Their Warranties Can Be Nearly Useless," Wall St.J., Nov. 30, 1994 at p. 1.

20. See, e.g., 2 Alan Widiss, Uninsured and Underinsured Motorist Insurance § 26.4 (2d ed. 1992).

21. "Honey Nut Cheerios/Sega Sweepstakes Official Rules"; see also Wall St.J., June 30, 1994, p. 1.

rule or imposing ceilings on recoverable damages or on attorney's contingent fees. Among these legislative "reforms" there inevitably appeared changes in the *process* by which malpractice claims could be asserted, and attempts to divert such claims entirely from the time-honored system of tort litigation.

(a) Some states have imposed preliminary hurdles on malpractice litigation by *requiring* that claims first be submitted to a "medical review" or "professional liability review" panel. (These may sometimes be called "arbitration boards.") Under some statutes, this required panel must consist of three physicians.[22] Another common pattern is for the panel to consist of a physician, an attorney, and a member of the "general public"[23]; still other states simply provide for a "tripartite board" (with one member named by each party and a chairman selected by the other two members or by the court) without specifying the profession or background of the arbitrators. Under the various statutes the fees and expenses of the arbitrators may be shared equally by the parties, may be assessed by the arbitrators as an element of costs, or may in some cases come directly from state funds.

If either party is dissatisfied with the arbitration award, he has the right to demand a trial de novo to be held in the regular state courts. In consequence it is often said that the review panels serve not so much to "decide" disputes, as to provide "an expert opinion" based on evidence submitted to them—that they act "in the nature of a pretrial settlement conference," or that, by giving the parties a preliminary, disinterested evaluation of the merits of a claim, they serve an "advisory" function and help to "promote an early disposition of many cases by a voluntary settlement."[24] Dispute resolution processes that can serve similar functions are quite common and are discussed at length in Chapter IV of Rau, Sherman and Peppet, Processes of Dispute Resolution: The Role of Lawyers. In a number of states, however, decisions of review panels are given somewhat greater clout by being made admissible in any later trial of the malpractice claim.[25]

(b) There has been some experimentation also with the use of *voluntary* agreements to arbitrate malpractice claims between a patient and a medical defendant. As in the case of traditional arbitration, such agreements can be entered into either prior to treatment or as the submission of an existing dispute; where such an agreement is made, the arbitrator's decision will be binding on both parties.

22. See, e.g., Neb.Rev.St. § 44–2841 (each party selects one physician and the two thus chosen select a third; panel also includes attorney who acts in "advisory capacity" and has no vote).

23. See, e.g., Md.Code, Courts & Jud.Proceed. §§ 3–2A–03, 3–2A–04 (state "Health Claims Arbitration Office" circulates lists of arbitrators in each category to the parties, who may strike unacceptable names); Del.Code Tit. 18, §§ 6804, 6805 (each panel consists of two "health care providers," one attorney, and two "lay persons" chosen from a "list of 100 objective and judicious persons of appropriate education and experience" maintained by the Commissioner of Insurance).

24. Prendergast v. Nelson, 199 Neb. 97, 256 N.W.2d 657, 666–67 (1977).

25. E.g., La.S.A.–Rev. Stat. 40:1299.47(H) (report of the "expert opinion" of the panel is "admissible," but not "conclusive").

In a number of states, statutes expressly authorize the arbitration of medical malpractice disputes:[26] These statutes are intended not only to encourage agreements to arbitrate but also to regulate the process; they commonly provide, for example, that notice that an agreement contains an arbitration clause must be printed in conspicuous "bold red type," and that an agreement to arbitrate "may not be made a prerequisite to receipt of care or treatment" by a doctor or hospital.[27] In other jurisdictions, voluntary arbitration agreements between patients and health care providers may also be enforceable under the state's general arbitration statute.

It appears that agreements for binding arbitration are not as yet widespread in the medical setting—although recent surveys do suggest "a dynamic innovation environment," since "organizations that are well positioned to stimulate use of agreements are aware of them, and alert to information that may demonstrate they have value." One California study reveals that while only 9% of physicians and hospitals in the state use arbitration agreements, 60% of the physicians using such agreements have adopted them since 1990—"suggesting that a reasonably persistent diffusion process is underway in the physician community."[28] About a third of the responding physicians and hospitals that did *not* use arbitration agreements attributed their reluctance to the fear that such agreements "set the wrong tone" for the patient,[29] creating "an uncomfortable situation."[30] Other possible reasons for the current lack of physician enthusiasm also might be suggested: For example, the supposed propensity of arbitrators to indulge in compromise decisions might not be attractive to physicians who in malpractice cases "possess a strong interest in vindicating their conduct."[31] And even where claims are subject to an arbitration agreement, defense attorneys will commonly fail to move to dismiss lawsuits filed by patients: Some defense attorneys in fact prefer to keep a case in court despite the existence of an arbitration agreement—apparently "for fear that a physician arbitrator would easily recognize that in that particular case, a deviation in the standard had occurred."[32]

In sharp contrast to the limited use by individual physicians and hospitals, the same California survey revealed that 71% of the state's

26. E.g., Alaska Stat. ch. 55 § 09.55.535; S.H.A.Ill.Comp.Stat. ch. 710 § 15/1; La.S.A.–Rev.Stat. § 9:4232; Ohio Rev. Code Tit. 27, § 2711.22; West's Ann.Cal.Code Civ.Proc. § 1295; see Pietrelli v. Peacock, 13 Cal.App.4th 943, 16 Cal.Rptr.2d 688, 689 (1993) ("The purpose of § 1295 was to encourage and facilitate arbitration of medical malpractice disputes"); cf. N.Y.–McKinney's C.P.L.R. 7550 et seq. (limited to HMO's).

27. West's Ann.Cal.Code Civ.Proc. § 1295(b); Alaska Stat. ch. 55, § 09.55.535(a).

28. Rolph et al., Arbitration Agreements in Health Care: Myths and Reality, 60 Law & Contemp. Probs. 153, 171–72, 180 (1997).

29. Id. at 175.

30. See U.S. General Accounting Office, Medical Malpractice: Few Claims Resolved Through Michigan's Voluntary Arbitration Program 6 (1990).

31. Metzloff, Alternative Dispute Resolution Strategies in Medical Malpractice, 9 Alaska L.Rev. 429, 440 (1992).

32. Whitelaw, Health Care Arbitration in Michigan: An Effective Method of Alternative Dispute Resolution, 72 Mich. Bar J. 1158, 1162 (1993).

HMO's do use binding arbitration agreements with their subscribers. Such arbitration agreements are usually designed by HMO's to apply to contract disputes only—and not to claims alleging medical malpractice. However, an important exception to this finding is the nation's largest HMO, Kaiser Permanente—which *does* require all of its subscribers in California and in three other states to agree to arbitrate any medical malpractice claims, as well as any other disputes arising out of their health care plans. (Over 6 million Kaiser subscribers are subject to mandatory arbitration agreements).

Kaiser's arbitration program was originally designed to be self-administered—with "administrative functions performed by outside counsel retained to defend Kaiser in an adversarial capacity."[33] Kaiser claimed that plaintiffs in its arbitrations tended to win about half of the time—although arbitration was also thought to "reduce the likelihood of excessive awards."[34] However, in 1997 the California Supreme Court refused to compel arbitration against the estate of a deceased plan participant—finding that Kaiser had engaged in fraud both "in the inducement "and "in the application" of the arbitration agreement: An independent statistical analysis of Kaiser arbitrations found that in only 1% of all Kaiser cases was a neutral arbitrator appointed within the 60–day period mandated by the plan; on average it took 863 days to reach a hearing in a Kaiser arbitration. For the court, a fraud claim could be premised on Kaiser's conduct in setting up a self-administered arbitration system "in which delay for its own benefit and convenience was an inherent part"—and yet nevertheless "persist[ing] in its contractual promises of expeditiousness."[35] As a result of such criticisms, Kaiser has since re-designed its arbitration mechanism to provide for independent administration. It has appointed the Law Offices of Sharon Lybeck Hartmann—"a boutique firm specializing in monitoring consent decrees and injunctions and in alternative dispute resolution, primarily in the field of civil rights"—to serve as the "Office of the Independent Administrator," and to write rules of procedure for Kaiser arbitrations, to create a panel of qualified neutrals, and to monitor the progress of the arbitrations "to assure that each case moves as expeditiously as possible." The OIA began administering arbitrations in March 1999; its first annual report can be found at www.slhartmann.com/oia.

33. Engalla v. Permanente Medical Group, Inc., 15 Cal.4th 951, 64 Cal.Rptr.2d 843, 849, 938 P.2d 903 (1997).

34. U.S. General Accounting Office, Medical Malpractice: Alternatives to Litigation 8–9 (1992); see also "Med–Mal Arbitration in California: Murky Results," Legal Times, Sept. 13, 1993 at 10. Cf. Zuckerman et al., Information on Malpractice: A Review of Empirical Research on Major Policy Issues, 49 Law & Contemp.Probs. 85, 103–06 (1986) (summarizing results of empirical studies of medical malpractice arbitration; "a major problem in assessing the attributes of arbitration is that so few cases have been arbitrated," and "controlled comparisons with conventional litigation are difficult to conduct").

35. Engalla v. Permanente Medical Group, Inc., supra n.33 at 853, 858 (held, "there is evidence to support the [plaintiff's] claims that Kaiser fraudulently induced [plaintiff] to enter the arbitration agreement in that it misrepresented the speed of its arbitration program, a misrepresentation on which [plaintiff's] employer relied by selecting Kaiser's health plan for its employees").

Nevertheless a recent report by the California Research Bureau—the research arm of the California Legislature—has been highly critical of both the fairness and efficiency of patient-insurer arbitration. This 2000 report covered 50 health plans, although most of its data came from Kaiser. The Bureau noted that 12% of all Kaiser arbitrations under the OIA were dismissed on summary judgment (by contrast, the summary judgment rate in civil litigation was only 0.6%): This was attributed in part to the fact that it is "easier to file an arbitration claim" than to institute litigation (so that arbitrators see more plaintiffs who probably would never make it to court), and in part to the fact that many Kaiser arbitrations are conducted *pro se* (so that the claimant "may be unable to present evidence correctly or even understand what evidence needs to be presented."). Large malpractice awards are apparently less common in arbitration than in comparable jury trials: Excluding summary judgment, patients were successful in only 35% of the cases arbitrated; 45% of the awards were under $100,000, and only 6% were more than $1 million. The report pointed out that during the selection process, the health plan is likely to have far more information than the claimant with respect to the track record of potential arbitrators, and is therefore "in a good position to make informed decisions": Thirty percent of the Kaiser arbitration claims were decided by eight repeat arbitrators, most of whom were likely to rule in favor of the defense. (None of the arbitrators in cases awarding more than $1 million had a second reported case). As a consequence—"[b]ecause the potential earnings, relative to the costs of preparing a case, are too limited"—lawyers are seldom willing to take such arbitration cases on a contingency basis.[36]

NOTES AND QUESTIONS

1. In this section you have been introduced to a use of arbitration quite different from the models presented in the labor and commercial areas. You can see that the term "arbitration" is commonly applied to describe any number of different processes, developing along different lines and responding to different needs. Indeed, the long-standing acceptability and respectability of "arbitration" make it a useful term to be co-opted by innovators in the dispute resolution field.

Some of the attributes traditionally claimed for arbitration may be present here as well. In consumer arbitration, an arbitrator is typically asked to apply fairly straightforward rules of decision to limited and tractable fact questions; in addition, the stakes are likely to be small and the procedure extremely informal. In such circumstances there are likely to be advantages, at least to the plaintiff, of reduced delay and costs—similar to the advantages often claimed for small claims courts. Studies indicate also that arbitration, at least where it is voluntary in inception and binding in result, may bring similar benefits to medical malpractice claimants in

36. Nieto & Hosel, Arbitration in California Managed Health Care Systems 2, 19 (CRB 2000).

the form of increased speed and reduced expense. See, e.g., Note, Medical Malpractice Arbitration: A Patient's Perspective, 61 Wash.U.L.Q. 123, 153–155 (1983).

However, there are also some significant differences. The usefulness of arbitration may be diluted where the parties do not (as they may in labor and commercial disputes) "have an interest in the pie of continued collaboration." See Henry M. Hart & Albert M. Sacks, The Legal Process 315 (1994). Especially where the parties' autonomy in the choice of the process or in the selection of arbitrators is reduced, the decision-makers are no longer "their" arbitrators, spelling out the meaning of "their" agreement in terms of their probable preferences or past practice. It then becomes more appropriate to view arbitration not as part of the world of "private ordering" but simply as a form of economic regulation. Particularly in the field of medical malpractice such regulation is often responsive to a not-very-well-hidden agenda, as the following excerpt indicates:

> The push for the arbitration of malpractice claims * * * must not be seen as linked to the general interest in alternative dispute resolution mechanisms exhibited over the past two decades. This examination of alternative mechanisms has had as its primary goal the identification of fora and procedures suitable for the resolution of meritorious claims that, for essentially economic reasons, had been excluded from the litigation system. In direct contrast, malpractice claims have always been guaranteed judicial resolution because of the contingency fee system. * * *
>
> There are two primary goals set forth by those propounding the arbitration of malpractice claims: first, to chill attorney interest in what are labelled *vel non* as frivolous or unmeritorious claims; and second, to reduce the size of damage awards in meritorious claims. Neither goal is related to providing a resolution for otherwise unresolvable claims. Both are intimately linked, however, to the widely held belief that the judiciary is unwilling or unable to exercise effective control over juries in civil trials. * * *
>
> Arbitration and pretrial review of medical malpractice claims serve different legislative goals. At the most general level, both are designed to freeze or slow the acceleration of the size of malpractice insurance premiums. The effect of pretrial review, however, is to chill plaintiff interest in pursuing marginal claims, both practically and psychologically, and to encourage settlement by forcing additional plaintiff expenditure without providing for concomitant recovery. Arbitration, on the other hand, is viewed primarily as a constitutionally safe method of avoiding jury determinations of liability and quantum of damages.

Terry, The Technical and Conceptual Flaws of Medical Malpractice Arbitration, 30 St. Louis U.L.J. 571, 572–73, 586 (1986).

2. A Florida statute provides that either party to a medical malpractice suit may request a "medical arbitration panel" to determine damages. An agreement by both parties to participate in arbitration binds both to the panel's decision. In such a case the plaintiff's noneconomic damages will be capped at $250,000 per incident and "calculated on a percentage basis with respect to capacity to enjoy life" (so, for example, a finding that the plaintiff had suffered a "50% reduction in his capacity to enjoy life" would warrant an award of not more than $125,000 in noneconomic damages). No punitive damages may be awarded, but the plaintiff is entitled to attorneys' fees of up to 15% of the award. If the defendant offers to arbitrate but *the plaintiff refuses,* the plaintiff may proceed to trial, although his noneconomic damages at trial will be limited to $350,000 per incident. If, however, it is the *defendant who refuses arbitration,* the plaintiff may proceed to trial without any limitation on damages at all—and in addition is entitled to recover attorneys' fees up to 25% of the award.

What incentives are this statute intended to create? See West's Fla. Stat.Ann. §§ 766.207, 766.209, 766.211, 766.212; University of Miami v. Echarte, 618 So.2d 189 (Fla.1993).

3. One common provision in statutes regulating medical malpractice arbitration is a "cooling off period." The Ohio statute, for example, allows a patient to "withdraw" his consent to arbitrate by written notice within 60 days "after the termination of the physician-patient relationship" (in the case of a hospital, within 60 days after the patient's discharge). Ohio Rev.Code Tit. 27 § 2711.23(B).

What is the point of a statutory "cooling off" period? Is it that a patient may *retroactively* withdraw his consent to arbitrate disputes over treatment already received? The Louisiana statute, however, is explicit that while an arbitration agreement is "voidable" within 30 days after "the date of execution," it is nevertheless "binding" as to acts of malpractice committed "prior to the revocation date." La.S.A.-Rev.Stat. § 9:4233.

4. Another area where there has been recent experimentation with use of the arbitration process has been in disputes between consumers and automobile manufacturers. General Motors and some other manufacturers, for example (including Honda, Nissan, and Volkswagen) have agreed to submit disputes over new-car warranties to the "Auto Line" program administered by the Better Business Bureau. In this program, the consumer's complaint is heard by volunteer arbitrators—"lawyers, professors, accountants, company executives, housewives, trade association personnel"—who have gone through a short training program but who have no necessary background in either the law or in automobile mechanics; they are told to "make common sense adjudications based on their own sense of fairness." General Motors Corp. v. Abrams, 897 F.2d 34, 37 (2d Cir.1990). "In the vast majority of cases both parties represent themselves, and do not find it necessary to involve an attorney." The arbitrators will hear any claims under an automobile warranty, although they will not consider claims for consequential damages such as for personal injury or lost wages. The program is funded by the manufacturer, operates at no cost to the consumer, and is designed to resolve any complaint within 40 days after filing. The manufacturer generally agrees in advance to be bound by the award. The consumer, however, is free either to reject any unfavorable award and pursue a warranty claim in court, or indeed, to bypass the arbitration process entirely. See generally the BBB's web site at http://www.dr.bbb.org/autoline.cfm.

5. As part of the expansion of consumer protection legislation over the last two decades, most states have enacted so-called "lemon laws" aimed at insuring that automobile manufacturers conform the vehicle to any express warranty. These statutes grant additional rights to the consumer by requiring the manufacturer to refund the purchase price or provide the consumer a new replacement vehicle if it cannot correct any defect after a "reasonable number of attempts."

State "lemon laws" also commonly provide that where the manufacturer has set up or participates in a qualified "third party dispute resolution process" to hear warranty claims, then the consumer must first assert any "lemon law" claims through such a process. See Tanner Consumer Protection Act, Cal. Civ. Code § 1793.22 (c), (d). A number of states such as California have "certified" the BBB's AutoLine program as meeting the minimum standards of the state lemon law. A recent survey by California's Department of Consumer Affairs indicated that an "AutoLine" arbitration decision was in the consumer's favor 58% of the time, but that consumers reported they were "satisfied with the arbitration process" in 64% of the cases, and that they "would recommend the arbitration process to others" in 66% of the cases. Apparently a post-arbitration lawsuit was filed by the consumer in only 8% of the cases. 1999 Annual Consumer Satisfaction Survey, "Arbitration Certification Program," available at *http://www.dca.ca.gov/acp/survey_99.htm*. Cf. Harrison v. Nissan Motor Corp., 111 F.3d 343 (3d Cir.1997)(Pennsylvania "lemon law"; held, BBB AutoLine mechanism is not "arbitration" within the Federal Arbitration Act, so circuit court had no appellate jurisdiction under FAA to review a district court's refusal to dismiss the consumer's complaint for failure to "first resort" to the AutoLine program).

In New York, by contrast, consumers have the option of selecting arbitration under AAA auspices as an alternative to any process that the manufacturer sets up or sponsors. A consumer is free to initiate an AAA arbitration under the state "lemon law" even if she has already resorted to the manufacturer's own non-binding process and been denied relief. Most notably, AAA arbitration is made *mandatory* for the manufacturer at the consumer's option. If the consumer elects AAA arbitration and pays a filing fee she will, however, be bound by the result in the same way as the manufacturer. See N.Y.Gen.Bus.Law § 198–a(k), (m).

6. Disputes between attorneys and clients over legal fees constitute the major share of all attorney-client conflict—it has even been said that such disputes constitute "the principal source of public dissatisfaction with the judicial system." Anderson v. Elliott, 555 A.2d 1042, 1049 (Me.1989). Litigation over fees is a highly unsatisfactory method of dispute resolution for the attorney; a suit over unpaid fees virtually guarantees a counterclaim for malpractice, so that "fee suits can be ugly affairs." Charles Wolfram, Modern Legal Ethics § 9.61 at 554 (1986). And litigation may be equally unattractive for the client. In addition to the cost, it may be difficult even to find a local lawyer willing to handle a fee case against another attorney; there is also the risk that in such litigation confidential information that had earlier been revealed to the attorney may become part of the public record. See Model Rules of Professional Conduct, Rule 1.6(b)(2).

As a consequence, a number of states have made binding arbitration of fee disputes mandatory for the attorney at the request of a client. See, e.g., Anderson v. Elliott, supra; In re LiVolsi, 85 N.J. 576, 428 A.2d 1268 (1981). In most other states, state or local bar associations offer programs by which attorney and client can voluntarily enter into binding arbitration after a fee dispute has arisen. These arbitration programs are usually administered by the bar association, and attorneys serve as the arbitrators (although in larger cases, where a panel of three arbitrators is used, it is common for one lay person to sit on the panel along with the attorneys.) See generally Alan Rau, Resolving Disputes Over Attorneys' Fees: The Role of ADR, 46 S.M.U.L.Rev. 2005 (1993).

In addition, lawyers are increasingly experimenting with *pre-dispute* arbitration agreements, entered into with the client at the time the attorney is retained. Such agreements frequently purport to cover not only fee disputes but also later claims of malpractice. See, e.g., McGuire, Cornwell & Blakey v. Grider, 765 F.Supp. 1048 (D.Colo.1991) (agreement bound client to submit to arbitration "any fee disputes * * * and claims by you regarding [the firm's] handling of your matter," although it expressly permitted the firm to "[collect] amounts due to it in other ways, including litigation").

Might such pre-dispute agreements raise ethical problems for the attorney? Is any guidance to be found in Rule 1.8 of the Model Rules of Professional Conduct? In some ethics opinions Rule 1.8 has been thought to make such agreements impermissible unless the client has actually been "counseled by another attorney" before signing: See, e.g., Md. State Bar Comm. on Ethics Dock. 90–12 (1989) ("If the client refuses to seek independent counsel, then the lawyer is prohibited from entering into such a written agreement"). See also D.C. Bar Legal Ethics Comm., Op. 211 (1990)("the lawyer entering into a retainer agreement with a client for arbitration of all disputes, including malpractice, could not adequately explain the tactical considerations of arbitration versus litigation to the lay client—considerations such as lack of formal discovery, lack of a jury trial, and the closed nature of arbitration proceedings"); cf. Op. 218 (1991)(agreement calling for mandatory arbitration of *fee* disputes before the bar association's Attorney–Client Arbitration Board is ethically permissible given that the Board's procedures and rules are "relatively simple to understand" and that counseling is provided by the Board staff). An Ohio opinion concludes that since "it is impractical to expect most clients to 'hire a lawyer to hire a lawyer,'" the practice of requiring clients to prospectively agree to arbitrate legal malpractice disputes should be generally "discouraged"—and that such arbitration should in all cases "be a voluntary decision made by a client after opportunity to consider the facts and circumstances of the dispute." Ohio Bd. Comm. Griev. & Discip. Op. 96–9 (1996),

Other opinions indicate that a lawyer may contractually require arbitration of malpractice claims only if he "fully discloses, in writing and in terms that can be understood by the client, the advantages and disadvantages of arbitration" and "gives the client a reasonable opportunity to seek the advice of independent counsel," State Bar of Ariz. Op. 94–05 (1994); see also Pa. Bar Ass'n Comm. on Legal Ethics & Prof. Resp., Formal Op. 97–140 (1997)(it is not necessary to require that the client actually consult independent counsel "because such would mean that a client would have to consult a lawyer to retain a lawyer, and such could go on indefinitely"). In still other states, by contrast, pre-dispute arbitration clauses for malpractice claims are freely permitted on the ground that they do not limit the attorney's liability at all—but "merely select the forum in which liability will be determined," Calif. State Bar, Ethics Op. 1989–116 (1989); see also Maine Bd. of Bar Overseers Prof. Ethics Comm'n Op. 170 (1999)(the suggestion that someone is necessarily prejudiced by having to proceed to arbitration reflects a "jaundiced view of arbitration"). Is this rationale convincing?

7. Do you expect that resolution of consumer and malpractice claims that is "private"—that is, that uses non-"official" decision makers, does not establish precedent or communicate its decisions in reasoned opinions, and is otherwise withdrawn from public scrutiny—is likely to have the deterrent or accident-reduction effects of tort litigation?

8. Arbitration clauses found in consumer transactions are increasingly being challenged on the ground that they are not enforceable as contracts—because, for example, they are "unconscionable" contracts of adhesion. See the discussion at pp. 103–116 infra; see also p. 186 infra (Magnuson–Moss Act and "public policy").

C. ARBITRATION AND THE COURTS

1. INTRODUCTION

The traditional attitude of judges towards arbitration has been one of considerable hostility, "explained," if at all, by ritual invocation of the phrase that agreements to submit disputes to arbitration "oust the jurisdiction of the courts." Perhaps this rhetorical flourish masked some concern over the diversion from the court system of cases implicating public values, or fear that private tribunals might ignore or undermine the enforcement of "legal" rules. Somewhat more cynically, one might also suppose that it originated in considerations of competition for business, at a time when judge's salaries still depended on fees paid by litigants.

At common law, if the parties did voluntarily submit a dispute to arbitration *and* the arbitrator proceeded to render an award, the award would be considered binding. Barring some exceptional defense such as arbitrator misconduct, the award could be enforced in a separate court action brought by the successful plaintiff. However, purely *executory* agreements to arbitrate had little force. A party could refuse to honor such an agreement and could revoke it at any time; a court would not specifically enforce an agreement to arbitrate existing or future disputes. While damages could in theory be awarded for breach of this contract, how could they possibly be calculated?[1] So a potential "defendant" could deprive the arbitration agreement of any effect simply by giving notice of his objection and refusing to participate in the process. A potential "plaintiff" could, after revocation, simply bring his own lawsuit, and the court would hear the case without regard to the agreement to arbitrate. A readable summary of the situation at common law can be found in Judge Frank's opinion in Kulukundis Shipping Co. S/A v. Amtorg Trading Corp., 126 F.2d 978 (2d Cir.1942).

Beginning with New York in 1920, most states have now passed statutes completely reversing the common law position on arbitration. The Uniform Arbitration Act, on which many modern state statutes have been modeled, was adopted by the National Conference of the Commissioners on Uniform State Laws in 1955.[2] The Federal Arbitration Act (FAA) was enacted in 1925. All of these statutes are quite similar in their broad outlines, although there is considerable variation in detail. The Federal Act, because of its overwhelming importance, is set out in Appendix A, infra. Read the text of the Act carefully: It is deceptively simple for a statute which has grown to assume such pervasive importance. What does the Act do to change the common law attitude towards arbitration? How does it assure the enforceability of agreements to arbitrate?

The situation is further complicated by the fact that even in states with "modern" statutes modeled on the New York or Uniform Act, the statute is usually not interpreted to be exclusive. As a consequence, "common law arbitration" still survives. Thus, even where the arbitration statute has not been complied with—for example, where there has been no written agreement to arbitrate or where the subject matter of the dispute has been specifically excluded from the coverage of the statute—the arbitrator's decision will have the same binding force it would have at common law, as long as consent to arbitrate has not been revoked and the parties have proceeded without objection to an award. See, e.g., L.H. Lacy Co. v. City of Lubbock, 559 S.W.2d 348 (Tex.1977) (arbitration statute did not apply to construction contracts); see generally Sturges and Reckson, Com-

1. See Munson v. Straits of Dover S.S. Co., 102 F. 926 (2d Cir.1900) (plaintiff sought damages, in the form of lawyer's fees and costs incurred in defending a lawsuit, for breach of agreement to arbitrate; held, plaintiff entitled to nominal damages only; judicial process is "theoretically at least, the safest and best devised by the wisdom and experience of mankind.").

2. A revised version of the Uniform Arbitration Act was approved by the NCCUSL at its Annual Meeting in August, 2000. The Revised Uniform Arbitration Act is available at http://www.law.upenn.edu/bll/ulc/ulc_frame.htm.

mon–Law and Statutory Arbitration: Problems Arising From Their Coexistence, 46 Minn.L.Rev. 819 (1962).

Nor have state arbitration statutes frozen the independent *development* of the common law. On the contrary, in a number of places they seem to have aided in its growth. Increasingly, decisions can be found where courts will rely on the "pro-arbitration" policy of the state statute to enforce an arbitration agreement *outside* the statute's substantive scope, and *despite* one party's prior attempt to "revoke." See Olshan Demolishing Co. v. Angleton Independent School District, 684 S.W.2d 179 (Tex.App.—Houston [14th Dist.] 1984) (agreement to arbitrate lacked statutory notice; "[e]ncouraging arbitration will reduce some of the backlog in our trial courts"); Kodak Mining Co. v. Carrs Fork Corp., 669 S.W.2d 917 (Ky.1984) (statute then in force applied only to submission of existing disputes to arbitration).

2. THE FEDERAL ARBITRATION ACT AND STATE LAW

a. PREEMPTION OF STATE LAW

The FAA was enacted before *Erie v. Tompkins* (in 1938) called for a fundamental rethinking of the relationships between state and federal courts. Over the last 50 years, problems of federalism in the enforcement of arbitration agreements have surfaced on a number of occasions. Only recently have some fundamental issues been more or less settled.

Bernhardt v. Polygraphic Co. of America, Inc., 350 U.S. 198, 76 S.Ct. 273, 100 L.Ed. 199 (1956), was a diversity case in federal court. The contract provided that any future disputes would be settled by arbitration; the transaction was assumed *not* to "involve" interstate commerce. At that time, Vermont law made an agreement to arbitrate revocable at any time before an award was actually handed down. In such circumstances, could the federal court enforce the arbitration agreement? The Supreme Court said "no": In the absence of a "transaction involving commerce," *state* law on arbitration was to be applied in federal courts in diversity cases. Arbitration was therefore "substantive" for *Erie* purposes: "The change from a court of law to an arbitration panel may make a radical difference in ultimate result." Furthermore, the Court said, the "procedures" for enforcing arbitration agreements in section 3 of the Federal Act were limited by section 2; applying the FAA, therefore, even in a federal court, is dependent on the existence of "a transaction involving commerce."

It later became settled that the FAA had been enacted as an exercise of Congress' commerce and admiralty powers. The Act thus laid down substantive rules of decision, binding on federal courts even in diversity cases as long as interstate or foreign commerce or maritime matters were involved. In this respect, though, the FAA remains something of an anomaly among federal statutes: Although enacted under Congress' commerce power, of itself it confers no federal question *jurisdiction.* Therefore, an action to enforce an arbitration agreement under the Act does not "arise under'' federal law but requires an *independent* source of federal jurisdiction, such as diversity or some other federal statute.

This line of cases raised still further questions: In cases that *do* involve foreign or interstate commerce, does the body of law fashioned by federal courts bind *state* courts as well? For example, would a Vermont court, in such a case, still be free to hold an arbitration agreement revocable, or is Vermont law to that effect preempted by the FAA?

Southland Corporation v. Keating

Supreme Court of the United States, 1984.
465 U.S. 1, 104 S.Ct. 852, 79 L.Ed.2d 1.

■ CHIEF JUSTICE BURGER delivered the opinion of the Court.

This case presents the questions (a) whether the California Franchise Investment Law, which invalidates certain arbitration agreements covered by the Federal Arbitration Act, violates the Supremacy Clause and (b) whether arbitration under the federal Act is impaired when a class-action structure is imposed on the process by the state courts.

Appellant Southland Corp. is the owner and franchisor of 7–Eleven convenience stores. Southland's standard franchise agreement provides each franchisee with a license to use certain registered trademarks, a lease or sublease of a convenience store owned or leased by Southland, inventory financing, and assistance in advertising and merchandising. The franchisees operate the stores, supply bookkeeping data, and pay Southland a fixed percentage of gross profits. The franchise agreement also contains the following provision requiring arbitration:

> ''Any controversy or claim arising out of or relating to this Agreement or the breach hereof shall be settled by arbitration in accordance with the Rules of the American Arbitration Association ... and judgment upon any award rendered by the arbitrator may be entered in any court having jurisdiction thereof.''

Appellees are 7–Eleven franchisees. Between September 1975 and January 1977, several appellees filed individual actions against Southland in California Superior Court alleging, among other things, fraud, oral misrepresentation, breach of contract, breach of fiduciary duty, and violation of the disclosure requirements of the California Franchise Investment Law, Cal.Corp.Code § 31000 et seq. Southland's answer, in all but one of the individual actions, included the affirmative defense of failure to arbitrate.

In May 1977, appellee Keating filed a class action against Southland on behalf of a class that assertedly includes approximately 800 California franchisees. Keating's principal claims were substantially the same as those asserted by the other franchisees. After the various actions were consolidated, Southland petitioned to compel arbitration of the claims in all cases, and appellees moved for class certification.

The Superior Court granted Southland's motion to compel arbitration of all claims except those claims based on the Franchise Investment Law. The court did not pass on appellees' request for class certification. Southland appealed from the order insofar as it excluded from arbitration the claims based on the California statute. Appellees filed a petition for a writ of mandamus or prohibition in the California Court of Appeal arguing that the arbitration should proceed as a class action.

The California Court of Appeal reversed the trial court's refusal to compel arbitration of appellees' claims under the Franchise Investment Law. That court interpreted the arbitration clause to require arbitration of all claims asserted under the Franchise Investment Law, and construed the Franchise Investment Law not to invalidate such agreements to arbitrate. Alternatively, the court concluded that if the Franchise Investment Law rendered arbitration agreements involving commerce unenforceable, it would conflict with § 2 of the Federal Arbitration Act and therefore be invalid under the Supremacy Clause. The Court of Appeal also determined that there was no "insurmountable obstacle" to conducting an arbitration on a classwide basis, and issued a writ of mandate directing the trial court to conduct class-certification proceedings.

The California Supreme Court, by a vote of 4–2, reversed the ruling that claims asserted under the Franchise Investment Law are arbitrable. The California Supreme Court interpreted the Franchise Investment Law to require judicial consideration of claims brought under that statute and concluded that the California statute did not contravene the federal Act.

* * *

The California Franchise Investment Law provides:

> "Any condition, stipulation or provision purporting to bind any person acquiring any franchise to waive compliance with any provision of this law or any rule or order hereunder is void." Cal.Corp.Code Ann. § 31512.

The California Supreme Court interpreted this statute to require judicial consideration of claims brought under the state statute and accordingly refused to enforce the parties' contract to arbitrate such claims. So interpreted the California Franchise Investment Law directly conflicts with § 2 of the Federal Arbitration Act and violates the Supremacy Clause.

In enacting § 2 of the federal Act, Congress declared a national policy favoring arbitration and withdrew the power of the states to require a judicial forum for the resolution of claims which the contracting parties agreed to resolve by arbitration. * * *

We discern only two limitations on the enforceability of arbitration provisions governed by the Federal Arbitration Act: they must be part of a written maritime contract or a contract "evidencing a transaction involving commerce" and such clauses may be revoked upon "grounds as exist at law or in equity for the revocation of any contract." We see nothing in the Act indicating that the broad principle of enforceability is subject to any additional limitations under state law.

The Federal Arbitration Act rests on the authority of Congress to enact substantive rules under the Commerce Clause. In Prima Paint Corp. v. Flood & Conklin Mfg. Co., 388 U.S. 395 (1967) [infra p. 94], the Court examined the legislative history of the Act and concluded that the statute "is based upon ... the incontestable federal foundations of 'control over interstate commerce and over admiralty.' " The contract in *Prima Paint,* as here, contained an arbitration clause. One party in that case alleged that the other had committed fraud in the inducement of the contract, although not of the arbitration clause in particular, and sought to have the claim of fraud adjudicated in federal court. The Court held that, notwithstanding a contrary state rule, consideration of a claim of fraud in the inducement of a contract "is for the arbitrators and not for the courts." The Court relied for this holding on Congress' broad power to fashion substantive rules under the Commerce Clause.

At least since 1824 Congress' authority under the Commerce Clause has been held plenary. Gibbons v. Ogden, 9 Wheat 1, 196 (1824). In the words of Chief Justice Marshall, the authority of Congress is "the power to regulate; that is, to prescribe the rule by which commerce is to be governed." The statements of the Court in *Prima Paint* that the Arbitration Act was an exercise of the Commerce Clause power clearly implied that the substantive rules of the Act were to apply in state as well as federal courts.

* * *

Although the legislative history is not without ambiguities, there are strong indications that Congress had in mind something more than making arbitration agreements enforceable only in the federal courts. The House Report plainly suggests the more comprehensive objectives:

> "The purpose of this bill is to make valid and enforceable agreements for arbitration contained *in contracts involving interstate commerce* or within the jurisdiction or admiralty, *or* which may be the subject of litigation in the Federal courts." HR Rep No. 96, 68th Cong, 1st Sess, 1 (1924). (emphasis added).

This broader purpose can also be inferred from the reality that Congress would be less likely to address a problem whose impact was confined to federal courts than a problem of large significance in the field of commerce. The Arbitration Act sought to "overcome the rule of equity, that equity will not specifically enforce an[y] arbitration agreement." The House Report accompanying the bill stated:

> The need for the law arises from.... the jealousy of the English courts for their own jurisdiction.... This jealousy survived for so lon[g] a period that the principle became firmly embedded in the English common law and was adopted with it by the American courts. The courts have felt that the precedent was too strongly fixed to be overturned without legislative enactment....

Surely this makes clear that the House Report contemplated a broad reach of the Act, unencumbered by state-law constraints.

* * *

Justice O'Connor argues that Congress viewed the Arbitration Act "as a procedural statute, applicable only in federal courts." If it is correct that Congress sought only to create a procedural remedy in the federal courts, there can be no explanation for the express limitation in the Arbitration Act to contracts "involving commerce." For example, when Congress has authorized this Court to prescribe the rules of procedure in the federal Courts of Appeals, District Courts, and bankruptcy courts, it has not limited the power of the Court to prescribe rules applicable only to causes of action involving commerce. We would expect that if Congress, in enacting the Arbitration Act, was creating what it thought to be a procedural rule applicable only in federal courts, it would not so limit the Act to transactions involving commerce. On the other hand, Congress would need to call on the Commerce Clause if it intended the Act to apply in state courts. Yet at the same time, its reach would be limited to transactions involving interstate commerce. We therefore view the "involving commerce" requirement in § 2, not as an inexplicable limitation on the power of the federal courts, but as a necessary qualification on a statute intended to apply in state and federal courts.

Under the interpretation of the Arbitration Act urged by Justice O'Connor, claims brought under the California Franchise Investment Law are not arbitrable when they are raised in state court. Yet it is clear beyond question that if this suit had been brought as a diversity action in a federal district court, the arbitration clause would have been enforceable. The interpretation given to the Arbitration Act by the California Supreme Court would therefore encourage and reward forum shopping. We are unwilling to attribute to Congress the intent, in drawing on the comprehensive powers of the Commerce Clause, to create a right to enforce an arbitration contract and yet make the right dependent for its enforcement on the particular forum in which it is asserted. And since the overwhelming proportion of all civil litigation in this country is in the state courts, we cannot believe Congress intended to limit the Arbitration Act to disputes subject only to *federal*-court jurisdiction.[9] Such an interpretation would frustrate congressional intent to place "[a]n arbitration agreement ... upon the same footing as other contracts, where it belongs." HR Rep No. 96, 68th Cong, 1st Sess, 1 (1924).

9. While the Federal Arbitration Act creates federal substantive law requiring the parties to honor arbitration agreements, it does not create any independent federal question jurisdiction under 28 USC § 1331 or otherwise. This seems implicit in the provisions in § 3 for a stay by a "court in which such suit is pending" and in § 4 that enforcement may be ordered by "any United States district court which, save for such agreement, would have jurisdiction under title 28, in a civil action or in admiralty of the subject matter of a suit arising out of the controversy between the parties."

In creating a substantive rule applicable in state as well as federal courts,[10] Congress intended to foreclose state legislative attempts to undercut the enforceability of arbitration agreements.[11] We hold that 31512 of the California Franchise Investment Law violates the Supremacy Clause.

The judgment of the California Supreme Court denying enforcement of the arbitration agreement is reversed; as to the question whether the Federal Arbitration Act precludes a class-action arbitration and any other issues not raised in the California courts, no decision by this Court would be appropriate at this time. As to the latter issues, the case is remanded for further proceedings not inconsistent with this opinion.

■ JUSTICE STEVENS, concurring in part and dissenting in part.

The Court holds that an arbitration clause that is enforceable in an action in a federal court is equally enforceable if the action is brought in a state court. I agree with that conclusion. Although Justice O'Connor's review of the legislative history of the Federal Arbitration Act demonstrates that the 1925 Congress that enacted the statute viewed the statute as essentially procedural in nature, I am persuaded that the intervening developments in the law compel the conclusion that the Court has reached. I am nevertheless troubled by one aspect of the case that seems to trouble none of my colleagues.

For me it is not "clear beyond question that if this suit had been brought as a diversity action in a federal district court, the arbitration clause would have been enforceable." The general rule prescribed by § 2 of the Federal Arbitration Act is that arbitration clauses in contracts involving interstate transactions are enforceable as a matter of federal law. That general rule, however, is subject to an exception based on "such grounds as exist at law or in equity for the revocation of any contract." I believe that

10. The contention is made that the Court's interpretation of § 2 of the Act renders §§ 3 and 4 "largely superfluous." This misreads our holding and the Act. In holding that the Arbitration Act preempts a state law that withdraws the power to enforce arbitration agreements, we do not hold that §§ 3 and 4 of the Arbitration Act apply to proceedings in state courts. Section 4, for example, provides that the Federal Rules of Civil Procedure apply in proceedings to compel arbitration. The Federal Rules do not apply in such state-court proceedings

11. * * * Justice Stevens dissents in part on the ground that § 2 of the Arbitration Act permits a party to nullify an agreement to arbitrate on "such grounds as exist at law or in equity for the revocation of any contract." We agree, of course, that a party may assert general contract defenses such as fraud to avoid enforcement of an arbitration agreement. We conclude, however, that the defense to arbitration found in the California Franchise Investment Law is not a ground that exists at law or in equity "for the revocation of *any* contract" but merely a ground that exists for the revocation of arbitration provisions in contracts subject to the California Franchise Investment Law. Moreover, under this dissenting view, "a state policy of providing special protection for franchisees ... can be recognized without impairing the basic purposes of the federal statute." If we accepted this analysis, states could wholly eviscerate Congressional intent to place arbitration agreements "upon the same footing as other contracts" simply by passing statutes such as the Franchise Investment Law. We have rejected this analysis because it is in conflict with the Arbitration Act and would permit states to override the declared policy requiring enforcement of arbitration agreements.

exception leaves room for the implementation of certain substantive state policies that would be undermined by enforcing certain categories of arbitration clauses.

The exercise of state authority in a field traditionally occupied by state law will not be deemed preempted by a federal statute unless that was the clear and manifest purpose of Congress. Moreover, even where a federal statute does displace state authority, it "rarely occupies a legal field completely, totally excluding all participation by the legal systems of the states. . . . Federal legislation, on the whole, has been conceived and drafted on an ad hoc basis to accomplish limited objectives. It builds upon legal relationships established by the states, altering or supplanting them only so far as necessary for the special purpose." P. Bator, P. Mishkin, D. Shapiro, & H. Wechsler, Hart and Wechsler's The Federal Courts and the Federal System 470–471 (2d ed. 1973).

The limited objective of the Federal Arbitration Act was to abrogate the general common-law rule against specific enforcement of arbitration agreements, and a state statute which merely codified the general common-law rule—either directly by employing the prior doctrine of revocability or indirectly by declaring all such agreements void—would be pre-empted by the Act. However, beyond this conclusion, which seems compelled by the language of § 2 and case law concerning the Act, it is by no means clear that Congress intended entirely to displace state authority in this field. Indeed, while it is an understatement to say that "the legislative history of the . . . Act . . . reveals little awareness on the part of Congress that state law might be affected," it must surely be true that given the lack of a "clear mandate from Congress as to the extent to which state statutes and decisions are to be superseded, we must be cautious in construing the act lest we excessively encroach on the powers which Congressional policy, if not the Constitution, would reserve to the states."

The textual basis in the Act for avoiding such encroachment is the clause of § 2 which provides that arbitration agreements are subject to revocation on such grounds as exist at law or in equity for the revocation of any contract. The Act, however, does not define what grounds for revocation may be permissible, and hence it would appear that the judiciary must fashion the limitations as a matter of federal common law. In doing so, we must first recognize that as the " 'saving clause' in § 2 indicates, the purpose of Congress in 1925 was to make arbitration agreements as enforceable as other contracts, but not more so." The existence of a federal statute enunciating a substantive federal policy does not necessarily require the inexorable application of a uniform federal rule of decision notwithstanding the differing conditions which may exist in the several States and regardless of the decisions of the States to exert police powers as they deem best for the welfare of their citizens. Indeed the lower courts generally look to state law regarding questions of formation of the arbitration agreement under § 2, which is entirely appropriate so long as the state rule does not conflict with the policy of § 2.

A contract which is deemed void is surely revocable at law or in equity, and the California Legislature has declared all conditions purporting to waive compliance with the protections of the Franchise Investment Laws, including but not limited to arbitration provisions, void as a matter of public policy. Given the importance to the State of franchise relationships, the relative disparity in the bargaining positions between the franchisor and the franchisee, and the remedial purposes of the California Act, I believe this declaration of state policy is entitled to respect.

* * *

[A] state policy of providing special protection for franchisees, such as that expressed in California's Franchise Investment Law, can be recognized without impairing the basic purposes of the federal statute. Like the majority of the California Supreme Court, I am not persuaded that Congress intended the pre-emptive effect of this statute to be "so unyielding as to require enforcement of an agreement to arbitrate a dispute over the application of a regulatory statute which a state legislature, in conformity with analogous federal policy, has decided should be left to judicial enforcement."

Thus * * * I respectfully dissent from [the Court's] conclusion concerning the enforceability of the arbitration agreement. On that issue, I would affirm the judgment of the California Supreme Court.

■ JUSTICE O'CONNOR, with whom JUSTICE REHNQUIST joins, dissenting.

The majority opinion decides three issues. First, it holds that § 2 creates federal substantive rights that must be enforced by the state courts. Second, though the issue is not raised in this case, the Court states that § 2 substantive rights may not be the basis for invoking federal-court jurisdiction under 28 U.S.C. § 1331. Third, the Court reads § 2 to require state courts to enforce § 2 rights using procedures that mimic those specified for federal courts by FAA §§ 3 and 4. The first of these conclusions is unquestionably wrong as a matter of statutory construction; the second appears to be an attempt to limit the damage done by the first; the third is unnecessary and unwise.

One rarely finds a legislative history as unambiguous as the FAA's. That history establishes conclusively that the 1925 Congress viewed the FAA as a procedural statute, applicable only in federal courts, derived, Congress believed, largely from the federal power to control the jurisdiction of the federal courts.

In 1925 Congress emphatically believed arbitration to be a matter of "procedure." At hearings on the Act congressional Subcommittees were told: "The theory on which you do this is that you have the right to tell the Federal courts how to proceed."

* * *

Since *Bernhardt*, a right to arbitration has been characterized as "substantive," and that holding is not challenged here. But Congress in 1925 did not characterize the FAA as this Court did in 1956. Congress believed that the FAA established nothing more than a rule of procedure, a rule therefore applicable only in the federal courts.

* * *

Yet another indication that Congress did not intend the FAA to govern state-court proceedings is found in the powers Congress relied on in passing the Act. The FAA might have been grounded on Congress' powers to regulate interstate and maritime affairs, since the Act extends only to contracts in those areas. There are, indeed, references in the legislative history to the corresponding federal powers. More numerous, however, are the references to Congress' pre-Erie power to prescribe "general law" applicable in all federal courts. At the congressional hearings, for example: "Congress rests solely upon its power to prescribe the jurisdiction and duties of the Federal courts." * * * Plainly, a power derived from Congress' Art III control over federal-court jurisdiction would not by any flight of fancy permit Congress to control proceedings in state courts.

* * *

Section 2, like the rest of the FAA, should have no application whatsoever in state courts. Assuming, to the contrary, that § 2 *does* create a federal right that the state courts must enforce, state courts should nonetheless be allowed, at least in the first instance, to fashion their own procedures for enforcing the right. Unfortunately, the Court seems to direct that the arbitration clause at issue here must be *specifically* enforced; apparently no other means of enforcement is permissible.[20]

It is settled that a state court must honor federally created rights and that it may not unreasonably undermine them by invoking contrary local procedure. " '[T]he assertion of federal rights, when plainly and reasonably made, is not to be defeated under the name of local practice.' " Brown v. Western Ry. Co. of Alabama, 338 U.S. 294, 299 (1949). But absent specific direction from Congress the state courts have always been permitted to apply their own reasonable procedures when enforcing federal rights. Before we undertake to read a set of complex and mandatory procedures into § 2's brief and general language, we should at a minimum allow state courts and legislatures a chance to develop their own methods for enforcing the new federal rights. Some might choose to award compensatory or punitive damages for the violation of an arbitration agreement; some might award litigation costs to the party who remained willing to arbitrate; some might affirm the "validity and enforceability" of arbitration agreements in other ways. Any of these approaches would vindicate § 2 rights in a

20. If my understanding of the Court's opinion is correct, the Court has made § 3 of the FAA binding on the state courts. But * * * § 3 by its own terms governs only *federal-court* proceedings. Moreover, if § 2, standing alone, creates a federal right to specific enforcement of arbitration agreements §§ 3 and 4 are, of course, largely superfluous. And if § 2 implicitly incorporates §§ 3 and 4 procedures for making arbitration agreements enforceable before arbitration begins, why not also § 9 procedures concerning venue, personal jurisdiction, and notice for enforcing an arbitrator's award after arbitration ends? One set of procedures is of little use without the other.

manner fully consonant with the language and background of that provision.

The unelaborated terms of § 2 certainly invite flexible enforcement. At common law many jurisdictions were hostile to arbitration agreements. That hostility was reflected in two different doctrines: "revocability," which allowed parties to repudiate arbitration agreements at any time before the arbitrator's award was made, and "invalidity" or "unenforceability," equivalent rules that flatly denied any remedy for the failure to honor an arbitration agreement. In contrast, common-law jurisdictions that enforced arbitration agreements did so in at least three different ways—through actions for damages, actions for specific enforcement, or by enforcing sanctions imposed by trade and commercial associations on members who violated arbitration agreements. In 1925 a forum allowing any one of these remedies would have been thought to recognize the "validity" and "enforceability" of arbitration clauses.

This Court has previously rejected the view that state courts can adequately protect federal rights only if "such courts in enforcing the Federal right are to be treated as Federal courts and subjected pro hac vice to [federal] limitations...." Minneapolis & St. Louis R. Co. v. Bombolis, 241 U.S. 211 (1916). As explained by Professor Hart:

> "The general rule, bottomed deeply in belief in the importance of state control of state judicial procedure, is that federal law takes the state courts as it finds them.... Some differences in remedy and procedure are inescapable if the different governments are to retain a measure of independence in deciding how justice should be administered. If the differences become so conspicuous as to affect advance calculations of outcome, and so to induce an undesirable shopping between forums, the remedy does not lie in the sacrifice of the independence of either government. It lies rather in provision by the federal government, confident of the justice of its own procedure, of a federal forum equally accessible to both litigants."

In summary, even were I to accept the majority's reading of § 2, I would disagree with the Court's disposition of this case. After articulating the nature and scope of the federal right it discerns in § 2, the Court should remand to the state court, which has acted, heretofore, under a misapprehension of federal law. The state court should determine, at least in the first instance, what procedures it will follow to vindicate the newly articulated federal rights.

The Court rejects the idea of requiring the FAA to be applied only in federal courts partly out of concern with the problem of forum shopping. The concern is unfounded. Because the FAA makes the federal courts equally accessible to both parties to a dispute, no forum shopping would be possible even if we gave the FAA a construction faithful to the congressional intent. In controversies involving incomplete diversity of citizenship there is simply no access to federal court and therefore no possibility of forum shopping. In controversies *with* complete diversity of citizenship the FAA grants federal-court access equally to both parties; no party can gain any advantage by forum shopping. Even when the party resisting arbitration initiates an action in state court, the opposing party can invoke FAA § 4 and promptly secure a federal court order to compel arbitration. See, e.g., Moses H. Cone Memorial Hospital v. Mercury Construction Corp., 460 U.S. 1 (1983).

Ironically, the FAA was passed specifically to rectify forum-shopping problems created by this Court's decision in Swift v. Tyson, 16 Pet. 1, 10 L.Ed. 865 (1842). By 1925 several major commercial States had passed state arbitration laws, but the federal courts refused to enforce those laws in diversity cases. The drafters of the FAA might have anticipated *Bernhardt* by legislation and required federal diversity courts to adopt the arbitration law of the State in which they sat. But they deliberately chose a different approach. As was pointed out at congressional hearings, an additional goal of the Act was to make arbitration agreements enforceable even in federal courts located in States that had no arbitration law. The drafters' plan for maintaining reasonable harmony between state and federal practices was not to bludgeon States into compliance, but rather to adopt a uniform federal law, patterned after New York's path-breaking state statute, and simultaneously to press for passage of coordinated state legislation. The key language of the Uniform Act for Commercial Arbitration was, accordingly, identical to that in § 2 of the FAA.

In summary, forum-shopping concerns in connection with the FAA are a distraction that do not withstand scrutiny. The Court ignores the drafters' carefully devised plan for dealing with those problems.

Today's decision adds yet another chapter to the FAA's already colorful history. In 1842 this Court's ruling in Swift v. Tyson set up a major obstacle to the enforcement of state arbitration laws in federal diversity courts. In 1925 Congress sought to rectify the problem by enacting the FAA; the intent was to create uniform law binding only in the federal courts. In Erie R. Co. v. Tompkins, 304 U.S. 64 (1938), and then in Bernhardt v. Polygraphic Co., 350 U.S. 198 (1956), this Court significantly curtailed federal power. In 1967 our decision in *Prima Paint* upheld the application of the FAA in a *federal-court* proceeding as a valid exercise of Congress' Commerce Clause and admiralty powers. Today the Court discovers a federal right in FAA § 2 that the state courts must enforce. Apparently confident that state courts are not competent to devise their own procedures for protecting the newly discovered federal right, the Court summarily prescribes a specific procedure, found nowhere in § 2 or its common-law origins, that the state courts are to follow.

Today's decision is unfaithful to congressional intent, unnecessary, and, in light of the FAA's antecedents and the intervening contraction of federal power, inexplicable. Although arbitration is a worthy alternative to litigation, today's exercise in judicial revisionism goes too far. I respectfully dissent.

NOTES AND QUESTIONS

1. The California Labor Code regulates in an elaborate way the payment of employee wages. (For example, § 201.5 requires that discharged employees in the motion picture business must be given their earned and unpaid wages within "24 hours after discharge excluding Saturdays, Sundays, and holidays."). Section 229 provides:

> Actions to enforce the provisions of this article for the collection of due and unpaid wages claimed by an individual may be maintained without regard to the existence of any private agreement to arbitrate.

In 1973 the Supreme Court sustained a challenge to this statute, commenting sympathetically that it "was due, apparently, to the legislature's desire to protect the worker from the exploitative employer who would demand that a prospective employee sign away in advance his right to resort to the judicial system for redress of an employment grievance. * * * It may be, too, that the legislature felt that arbitration was a less than adequate protection against awarding the wage earner something short of what was due compensation." Merrill Lynch, Pierce, Fenner & Smith, Inc. v. Ware, 414 U.S. 117, 131, 94 S.Ct. 383, 38 L.Ed.2d 348 (1973). More recently, however, the California statute has been struck down as in conflict with the FAA. Perry v. Thomas, 482 U.S. 483, 107 S.Ct. 2520, 96 L.Ed.2d 426 (1987).

2. Now that § 2 of the FAA makes arbitration agreements enforceable in state courts, does the enforcement mechanism provided by the *rest* of the Act accompany it? To what extent are state courts required to supply remedies equivalent to those in § 3 (stay of court proceedings) and § 4 (order to compel arbitration)? Compare footnote 10 of the majority opinion in *Southland* with footnote 20 of Justice O'Connor's dissent. What about Justice O'Connor's suggestion that specific performance of arbitration agreements is not necessary to vindicate the federal right because damages might be an acceptable alternative?

Section 4 provides for a jury determination of contested issues concerning the "making of the arbitration agreement." But a state might prefer that these issues be decided by a *court,* see Rosenthal v. Great Western Fin. Securities Corp., 14 Cal.4th 394, 58 Cal.Rptr.2d 875, 926 P.2d 1061 (1996).

> To have a court rather than a jury pass on the existence of an arbitration agreement hardly appears to undermine or frustrate the arbitration process; moreover, a bench trial of the issue should not be expected to "frequently and predictably" lead to different outcomes. State rules denying a jury trial are certainly consistent both with the summary nature of the proceeding, and with the traditional treatment of these specific performance actions as equitable—and they can only result in making arbitration a speedier and more efficient process. It is not particularly clear in any event what role the choice of a jury in § 4 was intended to play in the overall statutory scheme: For some reason it is only "the party alleged to be in default"—presumably the party who has "failed, neglected, or refused" to proceed with arbitration—who under § 4 is entitled to ask for a jury trial; the party "aggrieved" by such "failure, neglect, or refusal" has no equivalent right. After such an analysis it might be concluded that state law ought to govern

on such matters, even where the parties themselves have not expressly chosen to adopt such law.

Alan Rau, "Does State Arbitration Law Matter At All? Part II: A Continuing Role for State Law," in ADR & The Law 208, 211 (15th ed. 1999).

3. The same question can be raised in relation to other FAA provisions. Might § 12 (time limits for seeking to vacate or modify an award) apply to the states? See Jeereddi A. Prasad, M.D., Inc. v. Investors Associates, Inc., 82 F. Supp.2d 365 (D.N.J.2000)(state law permitted challenges to arbitration awards to be raised in opposition to a motion to confirm the award, even after 90 days; held, this contravenes federal policy favoring quick resolution of arbitrations and the enforcement of arbitration awards; "in the absence of contractual intent to the contrary, the FAA trumps the New York rule"). What about § 16 (appealability of trial-court orders dealing with arbitration)? See Bush v. Paragon Property, Inc., 165 Or.App. 700, 997 P.2d 882 (2000)("Congress is without power under Article I to require a state to modify its normal judicial procedures, at least when those procedures do not absolutely defeat the congressional purpose").

4. Virginia law requires automobile manufacturers to submit their standard franchise agreements to the Department of Motor Vehicles for approval. Saturn Corporation, a subsidiary of General Motors, includes binding arbitration clauses in all franchise agreements with its dealers. The Department refused to approve the Saturn agreement unless it contained "an opt out provision" for dealers; its position was that while arbitration clauses were permissible, they could not be made "nonnegotiable." Saturn's challenge to the Department's action was successful: State law that "singles out" arbitration clauses, or treats them "more harshly than other contracts," is preempted by the FAA; since Virginia "has no general contract law restricting nonnegotiable provisions in standardized contracts, Virginia may not bar automobile manufacturers from making arbitration provisions a nonnegotiable term of doing business. * * * If a dealer does not wish to agree to nonnegotiable arbitration provisions, the dealer need not do business with Saturn." Saturn Distribution Corp. v. Williams, 905 F.2d 719 (4th Cir.1990).

5. Under Florida law, every arbitration agreement between a securities dealer and a customer must give the customer "the option" of arbitrating before the AAA "or other independent nonindustry arbitration forum" as well as before an "industry forum" such as a stock exchange. On what grounds could it be argued that such state law conflicts with the FAA? See Securities Industry Ass'n v. Lewis, 751 F.Supp. 205 (S.D.Fla.1990).

6. Under the Michigan Franchise Investment Act, any "provision requiring *that arbitration or litigation* be conducted outside this state" is "void and unenforceable if contained in any document relating to a franchise." Is this part of the statute preempted by the FAA? See Flint Warm Air Supply Co., Inc. v. York Int'l Corp., 115 F. Supp.2d 820 (E.D.Mich.2000); see also OPE Int'l L.P. v. Chet Morrison Contractors, Inc., 258 F.3d 443 (5th Cir.2001).

7. Individual investors opened an account with a discount brokerage firm registered in Delaware; the account agreement contained an arbitration clause. The firm advised the investors to buy certain stock that declined dramatically in value. The investors complained to the Division of Securities of the Delaware Department of Justice, and the state later instituted proceedings against the firm, alleging "fraudulent and unethical practices" in violation of state law in connection with the sale of stock. The state sought to impose fines and to revoke the firm's registration, and it also sought rescission of the stock transactions between the firm and the individual investors. The brokerage firm then brought suit to enjoin the state from pursuing this rescission action on behalf of the investors, alleging that the state could not properly pursue rescission since the firm "had a contractual right to arbitrate [the investors'] claims." The rescission remedy "circumvents [the firm's] rights under the FAA and thus violates the Supremacy Clause." What result? See Olde Discount Corp. v. Tupman, 1 F.3d 202 (3d Cir.1993).

8. The FAA applies to any "maritime transaction" or "contract evidencing a transaction involving commerce." (§ 2). For many years it remained unclear just how broadly this language should be read as a Congressional exercise of control over "commerce." The FAA is the only federal statute that uses the word "involving" to describe a relation to interstate commerce, and different courts adopted different standards as to when transactions were considered to "involve" commerce for purposes of the Act. See, e.g., Metro Industrial Painting Corp. v. Terminal Construction Co., Inc., 287 F.2d 382, 388 (2d Cir.1961) (Lumbard, C.J., concurring) (FAA should apply only when the parties "contemplated substantial interstate activity," for only then would the Act advance their expectations at the time of contracting).

However, the Supreme Court has recently made it clear that § 2 is to be given the broadest possible scope. The phrase "involving" commerce is the "functional equivalent" of "affecting" commerce, the Court held, and both terms "signal an intent to exercise Congress's commerce power to the full." If a transaction "in fact" involves commerce, it is within the FAA even if the parties had never contemplated any connection to interstate commerce. The FAA therefore applied to a contract in which homeowners obtained a lifetime "Termite Protection Plan" from the local office of a Terminix franchisee. It followed that state courts were obligated to enforce the arbitration clause in such a contract—even though under a state statute invalidating pre-dispute arbitration agreements, the clause would be unenforceable. Allied–Bruce Terminix Cos., Inc. v. Dobson, 513 U.S. 265, 115 S.Ct. 834, 130 L.Ed.2d 753 (1995).

The Supreme Court of Alabama has since held that a contract between a religious order (which owned and operated a monastery in the state) and a local construction company for repairs to the monastery, did not come within the FAA. There was no evidence that tools, equipment, or workers had moved across state lines (although the contractor was in turn to pay a percentage of the project cost to a plaster specialist resident in Texas.) The

Alabama court found that the Supreme Court's decision in *Terminix* had been limited by the Court's opinion just three months later in United States v. Lopez, 514 U.S. 549, 115 S.Ct. 1624, 131 L.Ed.2d 626 (1995)—in which the Court upheld a challenge to the constitutionality of the Gun–Free School Zones Act of 1990 (which made it a federal offense for any individual to possess a firearm in a "school zone"). According to the Alabama court, after *Lopez* Congress' Commerce power could extend only to matters that "substantially affect interstate commerce." Sisters of the Visitation v. Cochran Plastering Co., Inc., 775 So.2d 759 (Ala.2000); see also Southern United Fire Ins. Co. v. Knight, 736 So.2d 582 (Ala.1999) (insurance policy issued in Alabama between Alabama resident and Alabama insurer to cover the former's pick-up truck for personal use does not come within FAA; the insurer "does not . . . allege that Knight has traveled outside the State or that he ever will").

Is *Sisters of the Visitation* a case of simple misunderstanding? Wasn't the real problem in *Lopez* that neither the statute, nor the underlying regulated behavior, had anything to do with "commerce" or any sort of economic enterprise *in the first place*—whether "interstate" or not? As emphasized by Justice Kennedy's concurring opinion, "here neither the actors nor their conduct have a commercial character, and neither the purpose nor the design of the statute have an evident commercial nexus." 514 U.S. at 580. See also United States v. Morrison, 529 U.S. 598, 120 S.Ct. 1740, 146 L.Ed.2d 658 (2000)(Congress has no authority to enact Violence Against Women Act providing a federal civil remedy for the victims of gender-motivated violence; "gender-motivated crimes of violence are not, in any sense of the phrase, economic activity"). By contrast, isn't it clear that Congress' power to regulate economic activity extends to activity "that might, through repetition elsewhere," or "when viewed in the aggregate," come to substantially affect commerce—even though the effect may be de minimis in an individual case? See Wickard v. Filburn, 317 U.S. 111, 63 S.Ct. 82, 87 L.Ed. 122 (1942)(upholding the application of the Agricultural Adjustment Act to the growing of wheat for home consumption).

Perhaps, however, there is more going on in the Supreme Court of Alabama than a simple misreading of constitutional precedent: The *Sisters of the Visitation* opinion stressed that an expansive application of the FAA "would tend to defeat the doctrine of federalism, making that doctrine a hollow shell," and would "stifle" the efforts of the states to develop "creative" solutions "other than those that catch the fancy of Congress." (The court noted that even though Alabama law makes pre-dispute arbitration clauses unenforceable, the state still does have a "robust alternative dispute resolution program"—apparently consisting of non-binding judicial mediation!) *Sisters of the Visitation,* 775 So.2d at 764. Cf. Stephen J. Ware, Money, Politics and Judicial Decisions: A Case Study of Arbitration in Alabama, 15 J. of Law and Politics 645 (1999), which concludes that there is a "strong correlation" in the state "between a justice's source of campaign funds and how that justice votes in arbitration cases": "Justices whose campaigns are funded by plaintiffs' lawyers are all Democrats and oppose arbitration, while justices whose campaigns are funded by business are nearly all Republicans and favor arbitration."

9. The question whether the FAA applies to individual employment agreements also remained unsettled for many years. See the proviso to § 1 of the Act. A consensus gradually emerged in the lower courts, under which the § 1 exclusion should be narrowly limited to workers—like seamen and railroad employees—who are actually engaged "in the transportation industries or in the actual movement of goods in interstate commerce." E.g., Hampton v. ITT Corp., 829 F.Supp. 202 (S.D.Tex.1993) ("plaintiffs' employment in the loan servicing industry does not place them within [this] narrow category"). On this interpretation, except for workers literally engaged in interstate transportation, the FAA would apply to employment contracts to the same extent as to any other contract. The Supreme Court, narrowly divided 5–4, finally ratified this general understanding in Circuit City Stores, Inc. v. Adams, 532 U.S. 105, 121 S.Ct. 1302, 149 L.Ed.2d 234 (2001). Justice Kennedy for the Court asserted that "the text of the FAA forecloses the construction" that all employment contracts are excluded from the scope of the Act: The "application of the maxim *ejusdem generis*" provides an "insurmountable textual obstacle" to that reading; in addition, "the plain meaning of the words 'engaged in commerce' [in § 1] is narrower than the more open-ended formulations 'affecting commerce' and 'involving commerce.' " And the Court should not, he added, "chip away at *Southland [v. Keating]* by indirection."

There has been little pressure to apply the Federal Arbitration Act to collective bargaining agreements, given the well-developed body of law enforcing arbitration clauses under § 301 of the Labor Management Relations Act—although, as the Supreme Court has noted, even in such cases "the federal courts have often looked to the [FAA] for guidance," United Paperworkers Int'l Union v. Misco, Inc., 484 U.S. 29, 40 n. 9, 108 S.Ct. 364, 98 L.Ed.2d 286 (1987). Cf. Coca–Cola Bottling Co. of New York v. Soft Drink & Brewery Workers, 242 F.3d 52 (2d Cir.2001)("Given the difference in eras [between the respective dates of the two statutes] and the intervening revolution in labor policy, adherence to the FAA in Section 301 cases may led to anomalous or even bizarre results").

10. An insured was injured in an automobile accident and made a claim under the uninsured motorist provision of his policy. The policy contained an arbitration clause, which provided that if the damages awarded by the arbitrators exceeded the statutory minimum coverage for uninsured motorists ($25,000), then either party might demand a trial de novo. The arbitrators awarded the insured $45,000. The court held that the insurer had no right to a new trial; the trial de novo provision was unenforceable since it "would result in complete frustration of the very essence of the public policy favoring arbitration" and would operate "to defeat goals designed to promote judicial economy and respect for the judicial system." Schmidt v. Midwest Family Mutual Ins. Co., 426 N.W.2d 870 (Minn.1988).

What precisely is the nature of the "public policy" argument here? Are you convinced?

b. PREEMPTION AND CHOICE OF LAW: THE PROBLEM OF MULTI-PARTY DISPUTES

Many disputes that may be amenable to settlement by arbitration are considerably more complex than the simple two-party disputes we have been considering throughout this chapter. In a number of common fact patterns, several related players have an interest in resolving a controversy that has arisen out of a single transaction. For example:

(i) The Owner of a new building will have entered into separate contracts with the General Contractor (who is responsible for construction) and with an Architect (who acts as the Owner's representative in designing and overseeing the project). Owner may make a claim against Contractor for alleged defects in construction; Contractor may answer that any defects are attributable to Architect's failings in specifying materials or in inspecting the work. Should Contractor's defense be upheld, Owner may wish to assert a claim against Architect for negligence. Another common scenario is a claim by Contractor against Owner: Contractor may claim that he was unable to comply with the plans and specifications for the project because they called for the use of materials that were unobtainable; this, he asserts, caused him delay and economic loss. Should Contractor's claim be upheld, Owner's position will be that he is entitled to indemnification from Architect for anything he owes to Contractor.[1]

(ii) An owner of a ship suitable for transporting cargo will typically concern himself only with building, financing, and maintaining the vessel, and will enter into a long-term lease of the ship to a Charterer. Charterer may himself be only a middleman speculating on increases in shipping rates; he may then "subcharter" the vessel to someone actually interested in carrying cargo for particular voyages. During the course of one such voyage, the ship may suffer structural damage. Shipowner will seek compensation from Charterer; Charterer in turn will claim that the Subcharterer is responsible for the damage and will seek indemnity from him.[2]

(iii) The Egyptian Government purchased wheat from four American suppliers; it then chartered a vessel from a Shipper to carry the cargo from Texas to Egypt. During loading, it was discovered that the wheat contained insects; Shipper had to delay loading to fumigate the cargo, and claimed damages for the delay from the Government. The Government naturally took the position that it could not be held liable: "The flour must have been contaminated either before loading, in which case the Suppliers would be liable, or after loading, in which case [the Shipper] would be liable."[3]

1. See, e.g., Consolidated Pacific Engineering, Inc. v. Greater Anchorage Area Borough, 563 P.2d 252 (Alaska 1977); Litton Bionetics, Inc. v. Glen Construction Co., Inc., 292 Md. 34, 437 A.2d 208 (1981).

2. See Miller, Consolidated Arbitrations in New York Maritime Disputes, 14 Int'l Bus.Lawyer 58 (1986).

3. In the Matter of the Arbitration Between the Egyptian Co. for Maritime Transport and Hamlet Shipping Co., Inc., 1982 A.M.C. 874 (S.D.N.Y.1981).

In these cases, the party "in the middle"—for example, the Owner in case (i)—has an obvious interest in a single proceeding to resolve the interrelated disputes. If the Owner must first assert a claim against Contractor, and only later seek to hold Architect responsible, he is faced with more than just the duplication of time and expense inherent in separate proceedings. There is in addition the real possibility of inconsistent results in the two forums. In a first proceeding, the Owner may be unable to overcome the Contractor's defense based on deficiencies in the project specifications. In a *later* proceeding, however, it may be found that the defect was caused by poor workmanship rather than by the Architect's negligence in preparing the plans—leaving the Owner "holding the bag" alone. In such a case the Owner would much prefer to be able to sit back and let the Contractor and Architect fight out between themselves the cause of the construction defects.

Suppose, now, that the agreement between Owner and Contractor contains a clause providing for the arbitration of all disputes; however, the agreement between Owner and Architect contains no arbitration clause. In such a case there will in all probability be no way to insure that all the claims are heard at the same time in a single proceeding. Certainly a party who has never agreed to arbitrate a dispute cannot be coerced into the process. By contrast, one powerful advantage of litigation is that a court with jurisdiction over all the interested parties can bring them all into the action. In a lawsuit against Contractor, Owner would be able to join a claim "in the alternative" against Architect (see Fed.R.Civ.P. 20(a)); if he is a defendant, Owner can "implead" Architect as a "third-party defendant." (See Fed.R.Civ.P. 14(a)). And if there are pending separate "actions involving a common question of law or fact," a court "may order a joint hearing or trial of any or all of the matters in issue in the actions" or may "order all the actions consolidated." (Fed.R.Civ.P. 42(a)).

What if *both* contracts (between Owner and Contractor, and between Owner and Architect) contain provisions for the arbitration of future disputes? In such a case the Owner might wish to have the various arbitration proceedings "consolidated"—that is, heard jointly before a common arbitration panel.

The long-standing policy of the AAA is that it will not consolidate separate arbitration proceedings unless all the parties consent or unless all the agreements explicitly provide for consolidation. The AAA has little incentive to force consolidation upon unwilling parties—and may, in fact, fear that doing so will impair the enforceability of the resulting award. So parties in the Owner's position will often attempt to seek a court order for the consolidation of the separate arbitrations. Once a court order has been issued, the AAA is off the hook and is then willing to administer the consolidated arbitrations.

The willingness of courts to order consolidated arbitration varies greatly. Some courts will do so even over the objections of one of the parties—at least when the arbitration agreement does not expressly forbid this. Such a power is asserted "as an incident of the jurisdiction statutorily conferred on a court generally to enforce arbitration agreements";[4] it will be stressed that "the same considerations of adjudicative economy that argue in favor of consolidating closely related court cases argue for consolidating closely related arbitrations."[5]

However, the general trend seems to be hostile to ordering consolidation of related arbitrations without the express consent of the parties to all the agreements. Many courts find the absence of "privity" between the Architect and the Contractor a barrier to ordering consolidated arbitration: To do so, it is suggested, would be to "rewrite" the contracts which these parties entered into. "A court is not permitted to interfere with private arbitration agreements in order to impose its own view of speed and economy."[6] And even if a court would generally be willing to order that the Owner–Contractor and the Owner–Architect arbitrations be heard together, further questions are still likely to arise. If it seems impossible to dovetail the provisions of two arbitration agreements that differ in important respects—for example, if one agreement calls for arbitration in Texas and the other in California, or if the agreements call for administration by different institutions—it may be expected that a court will refuse to consolidate the arbitrations.[7]

If the Owner—who may expect to be "in the middle" in most controversies—does not have the assurance that he will be able to settle all related disputes at the same time through consolidated arbitration, he might in some cases simply prefer to avoid arbitration completely. Some Owner–Contractor agreements in fact contain an "escape clause," freeing the Owner from any obligation to submit disputes with the Contractor to arbitration if the Owner, "in order to fully protect its interests, desires in good faith to bring in or make a party to any [dispute] * * * the Architect, or any other third party who has not agreed to participate in and be bound by the same arbitration proceeding."[8]

Assume, however, that the Owner has not been able to negotiate for the inclusion of such an "escape clause." The Owner is a party to an arbitration agreement with the Contractor, but not with the Architect. When the Contractor demands arbitration, the Owner may argue that for

4. Litton Bionetics, Inc., 437 A.2d at 217.

5. Connecticut General Life Ins. Co. v. Sun Life Assurance Co. of Canada, 210 F.3d 771 (7th Cir.2000)("practical considerations [are] relevant to disambiguating a contract, because parties to a contract generally aim at obtaining sensible results in a sensible way")(Posner, J.).

6. American Centennial Ins. Co. v. National Casualty Co., 951 F.2d 107 (6th Cir. 1991); see also Baesler v. Continental Grain Co., 900 F.2d 1193 (8th Cir.1990) (no power to consolidate "absent a provision in an arbitration agreement authorizing consolidation"); Government of the United Kingdom v. Boeing Co., 998 F.2d 68 (2d Cir.1993); Pueblo of Laguna v. Cillessen & Son, Inc., 101 N.M. 341, 682 P.2d 197 (1984).

7. See Hyundai America, Inc. v. Meissner & Wurst GmbH & Co., 26 F.Supp.2d 1217 (N.D.Cal.1998)(consolidation of related arbitrations—one to take place in San Francisco under California law, and the other to take place in Eugene, Oregon under Oregon law—"would run contrary to the principal goal of the FAA which is to enforce agreements into which the parties have entered.").

8. See Garden Grove Community Church v. Pittsburgh–Des Moines Steel Co., 140 Cal.App.3d 251, 191 Cal.Rptr. 15 (1983).

the sake of "efficiency," a court should refuse to compel arbitration so that the entire dispute can be resolved in one judicial proceeding.

This was the fact pattern presented to the Supreme Court in Moses H. Cone Memorial Hospital v. Mercury Construction Corp., 460 U.S. 1, 103 S.Ct. 927, 74 L.Ed.2d 765 (1983). Owner had filed a state court action against Contractor—seeking a declaratory judgment that their dispute was not arbitrable—and also against Architect, claiming indemnity for any liability to Contractor. Contractor then brought an action in *federal* court against Owner, under § 4 of the FAA, to compel arbitration. Owner, having taken the care in his own action to join a defendant who was not subject to an arbitration agreement, was then in a position to argue that Contractor's action should be stayed, so that the entire dispute could be disposed of in the parallel *state* action. Otherwise, he asserted, there would have to be "piecemeal litigation." The Supreme Court held that it was an abuse of discretion for the district court to grant a stay of the federal action, which at the time was "running well ahead of the state suit." To the Court, Owner's argument was misconceived: If the dispute between Owner and Contractor were in fact arbitrable, then "piecemeal litigation" was inevitable no matter *which* court, state or federal, decided the question of arbitrability. For "the relevant federal law *requires* piecemeal resolution when necessary to give effect to an arbitration agreement."

By contrast, however, some states have been more receptive to such arguments by the Owner. See, e.g., Prestressed Concrete, Inc. v. Adolfson & Peterson, Inc., 308 Minn. 20, 240 N.W.2d 551 (1976) ("Where arbitration would increase rather than decrease delay, complexity, and costs, it should not receive favored treatment"); Jefferson County v. Barton–Douglas Contractors, Inc., 282 N.W.2d 155 (Iowa 1979) ("prospect of multiple proceedings carrying a potential for inconsistent findings provides a basis for overriding the freedom to contract for arbitration"). In California, a statute expressly permits a court to order consolidation of separate arbitrations when "[t]he disputes arise from the same transactions or series of related transactions" and "[t]here is common issue or issues of law or fact creating the possibility of conflicting rulings by more than one arbitrator or panel of arbitrators." At the same time, however, the statute provides that a court may *stay arbitration,* or *refuse enforcement* of an arbitration agreement, if one of the parties is also a party to pending *litigation* with a third party "arising out of the same transaction," and if there is a "possibility of conflicting rulings on a common issue of law or fact." West's Ann.Cal.Code Civ.Proc. § 1281.2(c); § 1281.3. Following *Southland v. Keating,* would such a refusal or stay of arbitration pursuant to the California statute violate federal law?

Volt Information Sciences, Inc. v. Board of Trustees of the Leland Stanford Junior University

Supreme Court of the United States, 1989.
489 U.S. 468, 109 S.Ct. 1248, 103 L.Ed.2d 488.

■ CHIEF JUSTICE REHNQUIST delivered the opinion of the Court.

Unlike its federal counterpart, the California Arbitration Act, Cal.Civ. Proc.Code Ann. § 1280 et seq., contains a provision allowing a court to stay arbitration pending resolution of related litigation. We hold that application of the California statute is not pre-empted by the Federal Arbitration Act, in a case where the parties have agreed that their arbitration agreement will be governed by the law of California.

Appellant Volt Information Sciences, Inc. (Volt), and appellee Board of Trustees of Leland Stanford Junior University (Stanford) entered into a construction contract under which Volt was to install a system of electrical conduits on the Stanford campus. The contract contained an agreement to arbitrate all disputes between the parties "arising out of or relating to this contract or the breach thereof."[1] The contract also contained a choice-of-law clause providing that "[t]he Contract shall be governed by the law of the place where the Project is located." During the course of the project, a dispute developed regarding compensation for extra work, and Volt made a formal demand for arbitration. Stanford responded by filing an action against Volt in California Superior Court, alleging fraud and breach of contract; in the same action, Stanford also sought indemnity from two other companies involved in the construction project, with whom it did not have arbitration agreements. Volt petitioned the Superior Court to compel arbitration of the dispute.[2] Stanford in turn moved to stay arbitration pursuant to Cal.Civ.Proc.Code Ann. § 1281.2(c), which permits a court to stay arbitration pending resolution of related litigation between a party to the arbitration agreement and third parties not bound by it, where "there is a possibility of conflicting rulings on a common issue of law or fact."[3] The Superior Court denied Volt's motion to compel arbitration and stayed

1. The arbitration clause read in full as follows: "All claims, disputes and other matters in question between the parties to this contract, arising out of or relating to this contract or the breach thereof, shall be decided by arbitration in accordance with the Construction Industry Arbitration Rules of the American Arbitration Association then prevailing unless the parties mutually agreed [sic] otherwise.... This agreement to arbitrate ... shall be specifically enforceable under the prevailing arbitration law."

2. Volt's motion to compel was apparently brought pursuant to § 4 of the FAA, and the parallel provision of the California Arbitration Act, Cal.Civ.Proc.Code Ann. § 1281.2; the motion cited both Acts as authority, but did not specify the particular sections upon which reliance was placed. Volt also asked the court to stay the Superior Court litigation until the arbitration was completed, presumably pursuant to § 3 of the FAA, and the parallel provision of the California Arbitration Act, Cal.Civ.Proc.Code Ann. § 1281.2(c)(3).

3. Section 1281.2(c) provides, in pertinent part, that when a court determines that "[a] party to the arbitration agreement is also a party to a pending court action or special proceeding with a third party, arising out of the same transaction or series of related transactions and there is a possibility of conflicting rulings on a common issue of law or fact[,] ... the court (1) may refuse to enforce the arbitration agreement and may order intervention or joinder of all parties in a single action or special proceeding; (2) may order intervention or joinder as to all or only certain issues; (3) may order arbitration among the parties who have agreed to arbitration and stay the pending court action or special proceeding pending the outcome of the arbitration proceeding; or (4) may stay arbitration pending the outcome of the court action or special proceeding."

the arbitration proceedings pending the outcome of the litigation on the authority of § 1281.2(c).

The California Court of Appeal affirmed. The court acknowledged that the parties' contract involved interstate commerce, that the FAA governs contracts in interstate commerce, and that the FAA contains no provision permitting a court to stay arbitration pending resolution of related litigation involving third parties not bound by the arbitration agreement. However, the court held that by specifying that their contract would be governed by " 'the law of the place where the project is located,' "the parties had incorporated the California rules of arbitration, including § 1281.2(c), into their arbitration agreement. Finally, the court rejected Volt's contention that, even if the parties had agreed to arbitrate under the California rules, application of § 1281.2(c) here was nonetheless pre-empted by the FAA because the contract involved interstate commerce.

The court reasoned that the purpose of the FAA was " 'not [to] mandate the arbitration of all claims, but merely the enforcement ... of privately negotiated arbitration agreements.' "While the FAA therefore pre-empts application of state laws which render arbitration agreements unenforceable, "[i]t does not follow, however, that the federal law has preclusive effect in a case where the parties have chosen in their [arbitration] agreement to abide by state rules." To the contrary, because "[t]he thrust of the federal law is that arbitration is strictly a matter of contract," the parties to an arbitration agreement should be "at liberty to choose the terms under which they will arbitrate." Where, as here, the parties have chosen in their agreement to abide by the state rules of arbitration, application of the FAA to prevent enforcement of those rules would actually be "inimical to the policies underlying state and federal arbitration law," because it would "force the parties to arbitrate in a manner contrary to their agreement." The California Supreme Court denied Volt's petition for discretionary review. * * * We now hold that we have appellate jurisdiction and affirm.

Appellant devotes the bulk of its argument to convincing us that the Court of Appeal erred in interpreting the choice-of-law clause to mean that the parties had incorporated the California rules of arbitration into their arbitration agreement. Appellant acknowledges, as it must, that the interpretation of private contracts is ordinarily a question of state law, which this Court does not sit to review. But appellant nonetheless maintains that we should set aside the Court of Appeal's interpretation of this particular contractual provision for two principal reasons.

Appellant first suggests that the Court of Appeal's construction of the choice-of-law clause was in effect a finding that appellant had "waived" its "federally guaranteed right to compel arbitration of the parties' dispute," a waiver whose validity must be judged by reference to federal rather than state law. This argument fundamentally misconceives the nature of the rights created by the FAA. The Act was designed "to overrule the judiciary's longstanding refusal to enforce agreements to arbitrate," and place such agreements " 'upon the same footing as other contracts,' " Scherk v.

Alberto–Culver Co., 417 U.S. 506, 511, 94 S.Ct. 2449, 2453, 41 L.Ed.2d 270 (1974) (quoting H.R.Rep. No. 96, 68th Cong., 1st Sess., 1, 2 (1924)). Section 2 of the Act therefore declares that a written agreement to arbitrate in any contract involving interstate commerce or a maritime transaction "shall be valid, irrevocable, and enforceable, save upon such grounds as exist at law or in equity for the revocation of any contract," and § 4 allows a party to such an arbitration agreement to "petition any United States district court ... for an order directing that such arbitration proceed in the manner provided for in such agreement."

But § 4 of the FAA does not confer a right to compel arbitration of any dispute at any time; it confers only the right to obtain an order directing that "arbitration proceed *in the manner provided for in [the parties'] agreement.*" Here the Court of Appeal found that, by incorporating the California rules of arbitration into their agreement, the parties had agreed that arbitration would not proceed in situations which fell within the scope of Calif.Code Civ.Proc.Ann. § 1281.2(c). This was not a finding that appellant had "waived" an FAA-guaranteed right to compel arbitration of this dispute, but a finding that it had no such right in the first place, because the parties' agreement did not require arbitration to proceed in this situation. Accordingly, appellant's contention that the contract interpretation issue presented here involves the "waiver" of a federal right is without merit.

Second, appellant argues that we should set aside the Court of Appeal's construction of the choice-of-law clause because it violates the settled federal rule that questions of arbitrability in contracts subject to the FAA must be resolved with a healthy regard for the federal policy favoring arbitration. Brief for Appellant, citing Moses H. Cone Memorial Hospital v. Mercury Construction Corp., 460 U.S. 1, 24–25 (1983) (§ 2 of the FAA "create[s] a body of federal substantive law of arbitrability, applicable to any arbitration agreement within the coverage of the Act," which requires that "questions of arbitrability ... be addressed with a healthy regard for the federal policy favoring arbitration," and that "any doubts concerning the scope of arbitrable issues ... be resolved in favor of arbitration"); Mitsubishi Motors Corp. v. Soler Chrysler–Plymouth, Inc., 473 U.S. 614, 626 (1985) (in construing an arbitration agreement within the coverage of the FAA, "as with any other contract, the parties' intentions control, but those intentions are generously construed as to issues of arbitrability"). These cases of course establish that, in applying general state-law principles of contract interpretation to the interpretation of an arbitration agreement within the scope of the Act, due regard must be given to the federal policy favoring arbitration, and ambiguities as to the scope of the arbitration clause itself resolved in favor of arbitration.

But we do not think the Court of Appeal offended the *Moses H. Cone* principle by interpreting the choice-of-law provision to mean that the parties intended the California rules of arbitration, including the § 1281.2(c) stay provision, to apply to their arbitration agreement. There is no federal policy favoring arbitration under a certain set of procedural rules; the federal policy is simply to ensure the enforceability, according to their terms, of private agreements to arbitrate. Interpreting a choice-of-law clause to make applicable state rules governing the conduct of arbitration—rules which are manifestly designed to encourage resort to the arbitral process—simply does not offend the rule of liberal construction set forth in *Moses H. Cone,* nor does it offend any other policy embodied in the FAA.[5]

The question remains whether, assuming the choice-of-law clause meant what the Court of Appeal found it to mean, application of Cal.Civ. Proc.Code Ann. § 1281.2(c) is nonetheless pre-empted by the FAA to the extent it is used to stay arbitration under this contract involving interstate commerce. It is undisputed that this contract falls within the coverage of the FAA, since it involves interstate commerce, and that the FAA contains no provision authorizing a stay of arbitration in this situation. Appellee contends, however, that §§ 3 and 4 of the FAA, which are the specific sections claimed to conflict with the California statute at issue here, are not applicable in this state-court proceeding and thus cannot pre-empt application of the California statute. While the argument is not without some merit,[6] we need not resolve it to decide this case, for we conclude that even if §§ 3 and 4 of the FAA are fully applicable in state-court proceedings, they do not prevent application of Cal.Civ.Proc.Code Ann. § 1281.2(c) to stay arbitration where, as here, the parties have agreed to arbitrate in accordance with California law.

The FAA contains no express pre-emptive provision, nor does it reflect a congressional intent to occupy the entire field of arbitration. But even when Congress has not completely displaced state regulation in an area, state law may nonetheless be pre-empted to the extent that it actually conflicts with federal law—that is, to the extent that it "stands as an obstacle to the accomplishment and execution of the full purposes and objectives of Congress." The question before us, therefore, is whether application of Cal.Civ.Proc.Code Ann. § 1281.2(c) to stay arbitration under this contract in interstate commerce, in accordance with the terms of the arbitration agreement itself, would undermine the goals and policies of the FAA. We conclude that it would not.

5. Unlike the dissent, we think the California arbitration rules which the parties have incorporated into their contract generally foster the federal policy favoring arbitration. As indicated, the FAA itself contains no provision designed to deal with the special practical problems that arise in multiparty contractual disputes when some or all of the contracts at issue include agreements to arbitrate. California has taken the lead in fashioning a legislative response to this problem, by giving courts authority to consolidate or stay arbitration proceedings in these situations in order to minimize the potential for contradictory judgments. See Calif.Civ.Proc.Code Ann. § 1281.2(c).

6. While we have held that the FAA's "substantive" provisions—§§ 1 and 2—are applicable in state as well as federal court, see Southland Corp. v. Keating, we have never held that §§ 3 and 4, which by their terms appear to apply only to proceedings in federal court, are nonetheless applicable in state court. See Southland Corp. v. Keating, supra, n. 10 (expressly reserving the question whether "§§ 3 and 4 of the Arbitration Act apply to proceedings in state courts"); see also id. (O'Connor, J., dissenting) (§§ 3 and 4 of the FAA apply only in federal court).

The FAA was designed "to overrule the judiciary's long-standing refusal to enforce agreements to arbitrate," and to place such agreements " 'upon the same footing as other contracts.' " While Congress was no doubt aware that the Act would encourage the expeditious resolution of disputes, its passage "was motivated, first and foremost, by a congressional desire to enforce agreements into which parties had entered." Accordingly, we have recognized that the FAA does not require parties to arbitrate when they have not agreed to do so, nor does it prevent parties who do agree to arbitrate from excluding certain claims from the scope of their arbitration agreement. It simply requires courts to enforce privately negotiated agreements to arbitrate, like other contracts, in accordance with their terms.

In recognition of Congress' principal purpose of ensuring that private arbitration agreements are enforced according to their terms, we have held that the FAA pre-empts state laws which "require a judicial forum for the resolution of claims which the contracting parties agreed to resolve by arbitration." *Southland Corp. v. Keating; Perry v. Thomas.* But it does not follow that the FAA prevents the enforcement of agreements to arbitrate under different rules than those set forth in the Act itself. Indeed, such a result would be quite inimical to the FAA's primary purpose of ensuring that private agreements to arbitrate are enforced according to their terms. Arbitration under the Act is a matter of consent, not coercion, and parties are generally free to structure their arbitration agreements as they see fit. Just as they may limit by contract the issues which they will arbitrate, so too may they specify by contract the rules under which that arbitration will be conducted. Where, as here, the parties have agreed to abide by state rules of arbitration, enforcing those rules according to the terms of the agreement is fully consistent with the goals of the FAA, even if the result is that arbitration is stayed where the Act would otherwise permit it to go forward. By permitting the courts to "rigorously enforce" such agreements according to their terms, we give effect to the contractual rights and expectations of the parties, without doing violence to the policies behind by the FAA.

The judgment of the Court of Appeals is

Affirmed.

■ JUSTICE O'CONNOR took no part in the consideration or decision of this case.

■ JUSTICE BRENNAN, with whom JUSTICE MARSHALL joins, dissenting. * * *

The Federal Arbitration Act requires courts to enforce arbitration agreements in contracts involving interstate commerce. The California courts nonetheless rejected Volt's petition to compel arbitration in reliance on a provision of state law that, in the circumstances presented, permitted a court to stay arbitration pending the conclusion of related litigation. Volt, not surprisingly, suggested that the Supremacy Clause compelled a different result. The California Court of Appeal found, however, that the parties had agreed that their contract would be governed solely by the law of the State of California, to the exclusion of federal law. In reaching this conclusion the court relied on no extrinsic evidence of the parties' intent, but solely on the language of the form contract that the "law of the place where the project is located" would govern.

This Court now declines to review that holding, which denies effect to an important federal statute, apparently because it finds no question of federal law involved. I can accept neither the state court's unusual interpretation of the parties' contract, nor this Court's unwillingness to review it. * * *

Arbitration is, of course, "a matter of contract and a party cannot be required to submit to arbitration any dispute which he has not agreed so to submit." Steelworkers v. Warrior & Gulf Nav. Co., 363 U.S. 574, 582 (1960). I agree with the Court that "the FAA does not require parties to arbitrate when they have not agreed to do so." Since the FAA merely requires enforcement of what the parties have agreed to, moreover, they are free if they wish to write an agreement to arbitrate outside the coverage of the FAA. Such an agreement would permit a state rule, otherwise pre-empted by the FAA, to govern their arbitration. The substantive question in this case is whether or not they have done so. And that question, we have made clear in the past, is a matter of federal law.

Not only does the FAA require the enforcement of arbitration agreements, but we have held that it also establishes substantive federal law that must be consulted in determining whether (or to what extent) a given contract provides for arbitration. We have stated this most clearly in Moses H. Cone Memorial Hospital v. Mercury Construction Corp., 460 U.S. 1, 24–25:

> "Section 2 [of the FAA] is a congressional declaration of a liberal federal policy favoring arbitration agreements, notwithstanding any state substantive or procedural policies to the contrary. The effect of the section is to create a body of federal substantive law of arbitrability, applicable to any arbitration agreement within the coverage of the Act. * * * The Arbitration Act establishes that, as a matter of federal law, any doubts concerning the scope of arbitrable issues should be resolved in favor of arbitration, whether the problem at hand is the construction of the contract language itself or an allegation of waiver, delay, or a like defense to arbitrability." * * *

The Court recognizes the relevance of the *Moses H. Cone* principle but finds it unoffended by the Court of Appeal's decision, which, the Court suggests, merely determines what set of procedural rules will apply. I agree fully with the Court that "the federal policy is simply to ensure the enforceability, according to their terms, of private agreements to arbitrate," but I disagree emphatically with its conclusion that that policy is not frustrated here. Applying the California procedural rule, which stays arbitration while litigation of the same issue goes forward, means simply that the parties' dispute will be litigated rather than arbitrated. Thus, interpreting the parties' agreement to say that the California procedural rules apply rather than the FAA, where the parties arguably had no such intent, implicates the *Moses H. Cone* principle no less than would an interpretation of the parties' contract that erroneously denied the existence of an agreement to arbitrate.[8]

While appearing to recognize that the state court's interpretation of the contract does raise a question of federal law, the Court nonetheless refuses to determine whether the state court misconstrued that agreement. There is no warrant for failing to do so. The FAA requires that a court determining a question of arbitrability not stop with the application of state-law rules for construing the parties' intentions, but that it also take account of the command of federal law that "those intentions [be] generously construed as to issues of arbitrability." Thus, the decision below is based on both state and federal law, which are thoroughly intertwined. In such circumstances the state-court judgment cannot be said to rest on an "adequate and independent state ground" so as to bar review by this Court. With a proper application of federal law in this case, the state court's judgment might have been different, and our review is therefore not barred. * * *

Construed with deference to the opinion of the California Court of Appeal, yet "with a healthy regard for the federal policy favoring arbitration," it is clear that the choice-of-law clause cannot bear the interpretation the California court assigned to it.

Construction of a contractual provision is, of course, a matter of discerning the parties' intent. It is important to recall, in the first place, that in this case there is no extrinsic evidence of their intent. We must therefore rely on the contract itself. But the provision of the contract at issue here was not one that these parties drafted themselves. Rather, they incorporated portions of a standard form contract commonly used in the construction industry. That makes it most unlikely that their intent was in any way at variance with the purposes for which choice-of-law clauses are commonly written and the manner in which they are generally interpreted.

It seems to me beyond dispute that the normal purpose of such choice-of-law clauses is to determine that the law of one State rather than that of another State will be applicable; they simply do not speak to any interaction between state and federal law. A cursory glance at standard conflicts texts confirms this observation: they contain no reference at all to the relation between federal and state law in their discussions of contractual choice-of-law clauses. See, e.g., R. Weintraub, Commentary on the Conflict of Laws s 7.3C (2d ed. 1980); E. Scoles & P. Hay, Conflict of Laws 632–652 (1982); R. Leflar, L. McDougal, & R. Felix, American Conflicts Law § 147

8. Whether or not "the California arbitration rules ... generally foster the federal policy favoring arbitration" is not the relevant question. Section 2 of the FAA requires courts to enforce agreements to arbitrate, and in *Moses H. Cone* we held that doubts as to whether the parties had so agreed were to be resolved in favor of arbitration. Whether California's arbitration rules are more likely than federal law to foster arbitration, i.e., to induce parties to agree to arbitrate disputes, is another matter entirely. On that question it is up to Congress, not this Court, to "fashio[n] a legislative response," and in the meantime we are not free to substitute our notions of good policy for federal law as currently written.

(4th ed. 1986). The same is true of standard codifications. See Uniform Commercial Code § 1–105(1) (1978); Restatement (Second) of Conflict of Laws § 187 (1971). Indeed the Restatement of Conflicts notes expressly that it does not deal with "the ever-present problem of determining the respective spheres of authority of the law and courts of the nation and of the member States." Id., § 2, Comment c. * * * Choice-of-law clauses simply have never been used for the purpose of dealing with the relationship between state and federal law. There is no basis whatever for believing that the parties in this case intended their choice-of-law clause to do so.

Moreover, the literal language of the contract—"the law of the place"—gives no indication of any intention to apply only state law and exclude other law that would normally be applicable to something taking place at that location. By settled principles of federal supremacy, the law of any place in the United States includes federal law. * * * In the absence of any evidence to the contrary it must be assumed that this is what the parties meant by "the law of the place where the Project is located." * * *

Most commercial contracts written in this country contain choice-of-law clauses, similar to the one in the Stanford–Volt contract, specifying which State's law is to govern the interpretation of the contract. See Scoles & Hay, Conflict of Laws, at 632–633 ("Party autonomy means that the parties are free to select the law governing their contract, subject to certain limitations. They will usually do so by means of an express choice-of-law clause in their written contract"). Were every state court to construe such clauses as an expression of the parties' intent to exclude the application of federal law, as has the California Court of Appeal in this case, the result would be to render the Federal Arbitration Act a virtual nullity as to presently existing contracts. I cannot believe that the parties to contracts intend such consequences to flow from their insertion of a standard choice-of-law clause. Even less can I agree that we are powerless to review decisions of state courts that effectively nullify a vital piece of federal legislation. I respectfully dissent.

NOTES AND QUESTIONS

1. The *Volt* case raised many more questions than it answered. Even after *Volt,* the extent to which rules of state law that restrict arbitration can continue to be applicable in contracts otherwise falling within the FAA remained "murky." See Ian Macneil, Richard Speidel, & Thomas Stipanowich, Federal Arbitration Law § 10.9.2.2 (1994). This question will often recur throughout this chapter; see e.g., pp. 92–94 infra (state requirements of conspicuous notice for arbitration clauses); p. 100 infra (state law departing from rule of "separability"), pp. 228–236 infra (state law prohibiting arbitrators from awarding punitive damages).

2. In what sense is it accurate to say—as the Court does in *Volt*—that the California "rules" involved in that case "are manifestly designed to encourage resort to the arbitral process"?

3. Under Rule 81(a)(3) of the Federal Rules of Civil Procedure, the federal rules apply "in proceedings under" the FAA "to the extent that matters of procedure are not provided for" in that statute. When a federal court is asked to compel arbitration, does this Rule give it the same power to order consolidation of related arbitrations involving a "common question of law or fact" as it would have to consolidate "actions" under Rule 42(a)? Or does the Rule simply mean that a court can consolidate two *judicial* proceedings to compel *two separate* arbitrations, or to enforce two separate awards, where there are common issues going to arbitrability or enforcement? See Robinson v. Warner, 370 F.Supp. 828 (D.R.I.1974) (relying on Rule 81 to order consolidation of arbitration proceedings); cf. Government of the United Kingdom v. Boeing Co., 998 F.2d 68 (2d Cir.1993) (§ 4 of the FAA precludes use of the Federal Rules to consolidate arbitrations "absent the parties' consent.")

4. The result of the Supreme Court's decision in *Moses H. Cone* was that arbitrability would be decided in federal court, even though a state court proceeding raising the same question was pending. What might be the advantages to the plaintiff of a federal court determination of arbitrability? Note that under § 6 of the FAA, the plaintiff's request for an order compelling arbitration would be treated as a motion, the Act envisages "an expeditious and summary hearing, with only restricted inquiry into factual issues." The federal district court could therefore have resolved the matter "in very short order." 460 U.S. at 22 & n. 26. Are the summary procedures envisaged by the Act available in state as well as federal courts?

5. Even if an overall dispute must be settled in "piecemeal" fashion, in separate proceedings, it should at least be possible for any lawsuit (say, between the Owner and the Architect) to be stayed until the conclusion of the arbitration between the Owner and the Contractor. See Hikers Industries, Inc. v. William Stuart Industries (Far East) Ltd., 640 F.Supp. 175 (S.D.N.Y.1986). In *Hikers* the exclusive licensee of a trademark brought suit against both his licensor and a retailer to whom the licensor had sold goods allegedly in violation of the license. The licensee had an arbitration agreement only with the licensor; however, the court held that "sound judicial administration" dictated that the suit be stayed as to the *retailer* also. The court noted that since the licensee's claims against the retailer were "derivative" of his claims against the licensor, the arbitrator's decision would be "helpful" and would "provide the court with insight into the issues of law and fact." (Note that a stay would also prevent the licensee from taking advantage of federal discovery in order to aid it in arbitration with the licensor.) The stay was to be lifted, however, if the licensor-licensee arbitration was not completed within six months.

Does this procedure tend to avoid duplication of effort and inconsistent results? In the suit against the retailer, what would be the effect of an arbitrator's decision that the licensor's sales were not in violation of the license agreement?

Where two *arbitration* proceedings are pending which cannot for some reason be consolidated, may a court order that one proceeding be stayed until the other is concluded?

6. St. Margaret's Hospital entered into a number of written contracts concerning additions and renovations to the building—there was a contract with Triangle to perform electrical work, and a contract with McBro to act as construction manager. Each contract contained identical arbitration clauses. Triangle later brought suit in tort (for negligence and interference with contract) against McBro, alleging that McBro had harassed and hampered its work. McBro's motions for a stay pending arbitration, and for an order compelling arbitration, were granted: Although there was no written agreement between the parties, Triangle was "equitably estopped" from asserting this argument, since its claims were "intimately founded in and intertwined with the underlying contract obligations." "The close relationship of the three entities here involved," and "the close relationship of the alleged wrongs to McBro's contractual duties to perform as construction manager, give one pause." McBro Planning & Development Co. v. Triangle Electrical Construction Co., Inc., 741 F.2d 342 (11th Cir.1984). In the course of its opinion the court naturally had no occasion to discuss whether there should be consolidation of any related arbitration proceedings involving the three parties.

7."If the parties haven't expressly provided for consolidation in their agreements, then for a court to order consolidation would violate the principle that arbitration is consensual." True or false? See Dominique Hascher, Consolidation of Arbitration by American Courts: Fostering or Hampering International Commercial Arbitration, 1 J. Int'l Arb. 127, 134 (1984)(true; "if it had been the parties' intention to submit their disputes to a multiparty arbitration setting, they would have so provided in their contracts"); to the same effect is "A Critique of the Uniform Arbitration Act (2000)," World Arb. & Med. Rep., April 2001 at pp. 94, 100–101. But cf. Alan Rau & Edward Sherman, Tradition and Innovation in International Arbitration Procedure, 30 Tex. Int'l L.J. 89, 113–115 (1995)(false; "as in most cases of contractual silence we are left with the need for some sort of default rule"; the problem of multiparty disputes is best approached "as one more inquiry into the choice of an appropriate presumption").

8. The new Revised Uniform Arbitration Act follows California's statute in reversing the usual default rule and in creating a new background rule in favor of consolidation. Under § 10 of the Act, a court may order consolidation of separate arbitration proceedings where:

> (2) the claims subject to the agreements to arbitrate arise in substantial part from the same transaction or series of related transactions;
>
> (3) the existence of a common issue of law or fact creates the possibility of conflicting decisions in the separate arbitration proceedings; and
>
> (4) prejudice resulting from a failure to consolidate is not outweighed by the risk of undue delay or prejudice to the rights of or hardship to parties opposing consolidation.

Section 10 (c) also adds—through an unnecessary excess of caution—that a court may nevertheless not order consolidation "of the claims of a party to an agreement to arbitrate which prohibits consolidation."

3. THE AGREEMENT TO ARBITRATE

a. ARBITRATION CLAUSES AND CONTRACT FORMATION

Under the modern federal and state statutes we have just been introduced to, the first requisite, of course, is an *enforceable agreement* providing for arbitration between the parties to the dispute. Where an arbitration clause calls for arbitration of any *future* dispute that may arise out of a contractual relationship, the clause may well be a small, little-noticed part of a much more complex document. Parties are likely to plan primarily for their performance, and only desultorily for what may happen should trouble arise from non-performance. And where firms exchange forms printed in advance, without separately agreeing (or even paying particularly careful attention) to everything that these forms contain, the challenge to the legal system to make some sense out of the transaction is at its most intense. The stage is then set for what lawyers and law students are trained to call "the battle of the forms."

Whether an arbitration clause has become part of a valid and enforceable contract is at least in the first instance a question of ordinary contract law. You may recall in fact the rather tortured attempt of the Uniform Commercial Code to provide some solution to the "battle of the forms" problem. UCC § 2–207 provides that

> (1) A definite and seasonable expression of acceptance or a written confirmation which is sent within a reasonable time operates as an acceptance even though it states terms additional to or different from those offered or agreed upon, unless acceptance is expressly made conditional on assent to the additional or different terms.
>
> (2) The additional terms are to be construed as proposals for addition to the contract. Between merchants such terms become part of the contract unless:
>
> (a) the offer expressly limits acceptance to the terms of the offer;
>
> (b) they materially alter it; or
>
> (c) notification of objection to them has already been given or is given within a reasonable time after notice of them is received.

Assume that an exchange of forms creates a contract under UCC 2–207(1) but that only the *second* form contains a clause providing for the arbitration of future disputes. Does this clause become part of the contract?

The New York Court of Appeals considered this question in In the Matter of the Arbitration Between Marlene Industries Corp. v. Carnac Textiles, Inc., 45 N.Y.2d 327, 408 N.Y.S.2d 410, 380 N.E.2d 239 (1978). This case involved conflicting forms sent in confirmation of an *oral order* placed by the buyer; the seller's "acknowledgment" form, sent last, alone provided for arbitration but was not made "expressly conditional" on the buyer's assent to that or any other term. The Court of Appeals held that:

> the inclusion of an arbitration agreement materially alters a contract for the sale of goods, and thus, pursuant to section 2–207(2)(b) it will

not become a part of such a contract unless both parties explicitly agree to it.

It has long been the rule in this State that the parties to a commercial transaction "will not be held to have chosen arbitration as the forum for the resolution of their disputes in the absence of an express, unequivocal agreement to that effect; absent such an explicit commitment neither party may be compelled to arbitrate." The reason for this requirement, quite simply, is that by agreeing to arbitrate a party waives in large part many of his normal rights under the procedural and substantive law of the State, and it would be unfair to infer such a significant waiver on the basis of anything less than a clear indication of intent.

Since an arbitration agreement in the context of a commercial transaction "must be clear and direct, and must not depend upon implication, inveiglement or subtlety ... [its] existence ... should not depend solely upon the conflicting fine print of commercial forms which cross one another but never meet." Thus, at least under this so-called "New York Rule", it is clear that an arbitration clause is a material addition which can become part of a contract only if it is expressly assented to by both parties. Applying these principles to this case, we conclude that the contract between Marlene and Carnac does not contain an arbitration clause; hence, the motion to permanently stay arbitration should have been granted.

In New York, therefore, an arbitration clause has been said to be a "per se material alteration" of any agreement.[1] Cf. Jack Greenberg, Inc. v. Velleman Corp., 1985 U.S. Dist. Lexis 17132 *5 n. 1 (E.D.Pa.1985) (clause provided for arbitration under AAA rules "as supplemented or modified by the Meat Importers Council of America, Inc.'s Arbitration Rules"; held, "[e]ven assuming that it was not a per se material alteration, I would conclude that the clause here was material in that it would deprive Greenberg of its right to come into court to enforce the contract, without first bringing its claim before the Meat Importers Council of America").

NOTES AND QUESTIONS

1. The UCC does not define the term "materially alter." However Comment 4 to UCC § 2–207, in giving some examples, refers to clauses that would "result in surprise or hardship if incorporated without express awareness by the other party." The idea seems to be that a clause which is sufficiently important and unusual that a party would expect to have his attention specifically directed to it, should not come into the contract by way of a form that is by hypothesis commonly unread. Examples in Comment 5 of clauses which by contrast "involve no element of unreason-

1. Supak & Sons Mfg. Co., Inc. v. Pervel Industries, Inc., 593 F.2d 135, 136 (4th Cir.1979).

able surprise" are couched in terms of what is "within the range of trade practice" or "customary trade tolerances."

In many industries, of course, arbitration is a routinely-invoked, standard method of dispute resolution. Courts have even been willing to take "judicial notice" of the "common practice" of arbitration in the textile business. See Helen Whiting, Inc. v. Trojan Textile Corp., 307 N.Y. 360, 367, 121 N.E.2d 367, 370 (1954). Given the widespread acceptance of arbitration in these industries, could it be argued that an arbitration clause would not, in light of the policies behind UCC § 2–207, be a "material alteration"? See Schulze and Burch Biscuit Co. v. Tree Top, Inc., 831 F.2d 709 (7th Cir.1987) (given the prior course of dealing between the parties, the buyer "had ample notice" that the seller's confirmation might include an arbitration clause; the clause was therefore not a material alteration to the contract). Cf. Chelsea Square Textiles, Inc. v. Bombay Dyeing & Manufacturing Co., Ltd., 189 F.3d 289 (2d Cir.1999), which held that an importer was obligated to arbitrate with a textile manufacturer even though the arbitration clause was "nearly illegible" and was "printed on very thin, tissue-style paper, which resulted in some of the text being obscured by typing on the reverse side": "We believe that a textile buyer is generally on notice that an agreement to purchase textiles is not only likely, but almost certain, to contain a provision mandating arbitration in the event of disputes."

2. Might the practice of dispute resolution through arbitration be so widespread in a given trade, or so well-established in the prior dealings of the parties, that under ordinary contract principles arbitration might be an implied term of the bargain *from the very beginning* ? If so, then the arbitration term would not even be an "addition" to or an "alteration" of the contract *at all.* See UCC §§ 1–201(3), 1–205(3). In Schubtex, Inc. v. Allen Snyder, Inc., 49 N.Y.2d 1, 424 N.Y.S.2d 133, 399 N.E.2d 1154 (1979), a seller had confirmed a buyer's oral order by sending a form with an arbitration clause, and the buyer (as he had done several times in the past) retained the form without objection. The Court of Appeals conceded that "a determination that [the] oral agreement included a provision for arbitration could in a proper case be implied from a course of past conduct or the custom and practice in the industry," but concluded that such evidence was lacking in that case. Three judges, including the author of the *Marlene* opinion, concurred in the result but "strongly disagree[d]" with such a suggestion:

> It is true, of course, that evidence of a trade usage or of a prior course of dealings may normally be utilized to supplement the express terms of a contract for the sale of goods. General rules of contract law, however, are not always applicable to arbitration clauses because of overriding policy considerations. * * * "[T]he threshold for clarity of agreement to arbitrate is greater than with respect to other contractual terms." * * * Where there exists good reason to require an explicit agreement, * * * it would seem most imprudent to allow a presumption of intent to supplant the need for such an agreement.

3. Sometimes the writings exchanged by the parties will *not* create a contract under UCC § 2–207(1): A second form, for example, may simply provide that it is not an "Expression of Acceptance" at all, and that any acceptance is "expressly conditioned" on the other party's assent to its terms. E.g., Commerce & Industry Ins. Co. v. Bayer Corp., 433 Mass. 388, 742 N.E.2d 567 (2001)(only the first form contained an arbitration clause; held, arbitration agreement is not enforceable because "a contract never came into being"). Nevertheless, the parties may recognize the existence of a contract by their conduct—for example, by shipping, accepting, and paying for the goods before any dispute arises. In such a case, § 2–207(3) provides that the terms of the contract consist of "those terms on which the writings of the parties agree, together with any supplementary terms incorporated under any other provisions of this Act." May an agreement to arbitrate be brought into the contract in such circumstances as a "supplementary term" implied from custom and usage?

Recall that the FAA provides for the enforceability of "*a written provision*" in a contract to submit future disputes to arbitration. Section 6 of the Revised Uniform Arbitration Act makes enforceable "*an agreement contained in a record*" to arbitrate future disputes. (A "record" is defined as "information that is inscribed on a tangible medium or that is stored in an electronic or other medium and is retrievable in perceivable form."). Do either or both of these statutes require the arbitration clause to be an *express* part of a valid written agreement—preventing an arbitration provision from being incorporated into a contract solely on the basis of custom, trade usage, or past dealing? See C. Itoh & Co. (America) Inc. v. Jordan Intern. Co., 552 F.2d 1228 (7th Cir.1977).

4. The United Nations Convention on Contracts for the International Sale of Goods, ratified by the United States in 1986, applies to all contracts for the sale of goods between parties "whose places of business are in different [Contracting] states." With respect to the formation of contracts, the Convention provides that a second printed form (e.g., a seller's "acknowledgement") that contains any additions to or modifications or the original offer may be treated as an acceptance, unless the additions or modifications "materially alter" the offer. If they *do* "materially alter" it, then the second form is presumed to be a counter-offer rather than an acceptance—with the result that no contract is formed at all. And additional or different terms "relating to the settlement of disputes" are *always* deemed to be "material" alterations, thereby preventing the formation of any contract by correspondence. Art. 19(3).

5. A number of state statutes have traditionally imposed special requirements on the formation of arbitration agreements—presumably to guard against "surprise" and to insure that consent to arbitration has been knowing and informed. The Missouri arbitration statute, for example, requires a statement in ten point capital letters adjacent to or above the signature line, reading "THIS CONTRACT CONTAINS A BINDING ARBITRATION PROVISION WHICH MAY BE ENFORCED BY THE PARTIES." V.A.M.S. § 435.460. Another model singles out certain types of arbitration agreements and conditions their validity on the parties' having first received independent legal advice. The Texas statute requires that any agreement for arbitration in a contract where an individual acquires real or personal property, services, or money or credit, for an amount of $50,000 or less, must be signed by the attorneys of both parties. The same requirement applies to agreements to arbitrate any personal injury claim. Tex.Civ. Prac. & Rem.Code § 171.001.

All such statutes are now presumably dead letters in light of the Supreme Court's recent decision in Doctor's Associates, Inc. v. Casarotto, 517 U.S. 681, 116 S.Ct. 1652, 134 L.Ed.2d 902 (1996). In *Casarotto,* the Court was faced with a Montana statute requiring notice that a contract is subject to arbitration to be "typed in underlined capital letters on the first page of the contract": The Court struck down the state statute on the predictable ground that by enacting the FAA, "Congress precluded States from singling out arbitration provisions for suspect status, requiring instead that such provisions be placed upon the same footing as other contracts."

6. An arbitration agreement might also run afoul of disclosure requirements applied generally to wide classes of contracts. New York, for example, imposes precise legibility requirements (not less than "eight points in depth or five and one-half points in depth for upper case") for printed contracts in all "consumer transactions." An arbitration clause in a customer's agreement with a stockbroker was invalidated for failure to meet this requirement in Hacker v. Smith Barney, Harris Upham & Co., Inc., 131 Misc.2d 757, 501 N.Y.S.2d 977 (Special Term 1986), aff'd, 136 Misc.2d 169, 519 N.Y.S.2d 92 (Sup.Ct.1987).

The court in *Hacker v. Smith Barney* perfunctorily dismissed a preemption argument based on *Southland v. Keating*. But *Hacker* is rather easily distinguishable from *Southland* and *Casarotto,* isn't it?

7. What about the "New York Rule" on contract formation exemplified by the *Marlene* case, supra? Is it likely that the FAA has any preemptive effect on this rule? The Tenth Circuit, rejecting this argument, noted that UCC § 2–207 is "a general principle of state law controlling issues of contract formation." "Presumptions against including terms, such as the New York rule, are routinely applied to any term considered significant to the contracting parties," such as disclaimers of warranty; "§ 2–207 does nothing under its general, or its specific New York application, to restrict enforcement of agreements to arbitrate to which the parties have expressly assented." Avedon Engineering, Inc. v. Seatex, 126 F.3d 1279 (10th Cir. 1997). The Second Circuit, on the other hand, has pointed out that the *general* New York law of contracts (unlike the rule in *Marlene*) requires that "nonarbitration agreements be proven only by a mere preponderance of the evidence"; it therefore followed that *Marlene*'s "discriminatory treatment of arbitration agreements * * * is preempted." Progressive Casualty Ins. Co. v. C.A. Reaseguradora Nacional De Venezuela, 991 F.2d 42 (2d Cir.1993).

8. A Texas statute (now repealed) made all arbitration agreements unenforceable unless a notice of arbitration was "typed in underlined capital letters, or rubber-stamped prominently, on the first page of the contract." In one case, a contract provided that arbitration was to take place "pursuant to the laws of the State of Texas," but omitted the required statutory notice. The court held that on the authority of the *Volt* case, this choice-of-law provision allowed the notice requirement to escape federal preemption: "[T]he Texas Act prevails over the FAA and the arbitration agreement is unenforceable because it does not conform to the Texas Act." American Physicians Service Group, Inc. v. Port Lavaca Clinic Associates, 843 S.W.2d 675 (Tex.App.—Corpus Christi 1992); *accord,* Al's Formal Wear of Houston v. Sun, 869 S.W.2d 442, 443–44 n. 3 (Tex.App.—Houston 1993). Can this possibly be right? Does the "party autonomy" rationale of *Volt* have any relevance here?

9. The owner of containerized cargo equipment leased the equipment to two shipping companies, which in turn insured the equipment. The contract of insurance between the shipping companies and the insurer contained an arbitration clause. After the equipment was damaged, the owner brought suit against the insurer. (The two shipping companies had gone out of business.) Does the insurer have the right to stay the proceedings and compel arbitration? See Interpool Ltd. v. Through Transport Mutual Ins. Ass'n Ltd., 635 F.Supp. 1503 (S.D.Fla.1985).

An employee's agreement with his employer, a brokerage firm, provided that any future disputes arising out of his employment or termination of employment would be subject to arbitration. The employee later brought suit against the firm for wrongful termination; at the same time, his wife also filed suit alleging loss of consortium as a result of the firm's actions toward her husband. On the firm's motion to stay all the proceedings and compel arbitration, what result? See Prudential Ins. Co. of America v. Shammas, 865 F.Supp. 429 (W.D.Mich.1993) (motion granted); cf. Merrill Lynch, Pierce, Fenner & Smith, Inc. v. Longoria, 783 S.W.2d 229 (Tex. App.—Corpus Christi 1989) (motion properly denied as to wife).

b. THE "SEPARABILITY" OF THE ARBITRATION CLAUSE

Prima Paint Corp. v. Flood & Conklin Mfg. Co.

Supreme Court of the United States, 1967.
388 U.S. 395, 87 S.Ct. 1801, 18 L.Ed.2d 1270.

■ MR. JUSTICE FORTAS delivered the opinion of the Court.

This case presents the question whether the federal court or an arbitrator is to resolve a claim of "fraud in the inducement," under a contract governed by the United States Arbitration Act of 1925, where there is no evidence that the contracting parties intended to withhold that issue from arbitration.

The question arises from the following set of facts. On October 7, 1964, respondent, Flood & Conklin Manufacturing Company, a New Jersey corporation, entered into what was styled a "Consulting Agreement," with petitioner, Prima Paint Corporation, a Maryland corporation. This agreement followed by less than three weeks the execution of a contract pursuant to which Prima Paint purchased F & C's paint business. The consulting agreement provided that for a six-year period F & C was to furnish advice and consultation "in connection with the formulae, manufacturing operations, sales and servicing of Prima Trade Sales account." These services were to be performed personally by F & C's chairman, Jerome K. Jelin, "except in the event of his death or disability." F & C bound itself for the duration of the contractual period to make no "Trade Sales" of paint or paint products in its existing sales territory or to current customers. To the consulting agreement were appended lists of F & C customers, whose patronage was to be taken over by Prima Paint. In return for these lists, the covenant not to compete, and the services of Mr. Jelin, Prima Paint agreed to pay F & C certain percentages of its receipts from the listed customers and from all others, such payments not to exceed $25,000 over the life of the agreement. The agreement took into account the possibility that Prima Paint might encounter financial difficulties, including bankruptcy, but no corresponding reference was made to possible financial problems which might be encountered by F & C. The agreement states that it "embodies the entire understanding of the parties on the subject matter." Finally, the parties agreed to a broad arbitration clause, which read in part:

"Any controversy or claim arising out of or relating to this Agreement, or the breach thereof, shall be settled by arbitration in the City of New York, in accordance with the rules then obtaining of the American Arbitration Association...."

The first payment by Prima Paint to F & C under the consulting agreement was due on September 1, 1965. None was made on that date. Seventeen days later, Prima Paint did pay the appropriate amount, but into escrow. It notified attorneys for F & C that in various enumerated respects their client had broken both the consulting agreement and the earlier purchase agreement. Prima Paint's principal contention, so far as presently relevant, was that F & C had fraudulently represented that it was solvent and able to perform its contractual obligations, whereas it was in fact insolvent and intended to file a petition under Chapter XI of the Bankruptcy Act shortly after execution of the consulting agreement. Prima Paint noted that such a petition was filed by F & C on October 14, 1964, one week after the contract had been signed. F & C's response, on October 25, was to serve a "notice of intention to arbitrate." On November 12, three days before expiration of its time to answer this "notice," Prima Paint filed suit in the United States District Court for the Southern District of New York, seeking rescission of the consulting agreement on the basis of the alleged fraudulent inducement. The complaint asserted that the federal court had diversity jurisdiction.

Contemporaneously with the filing of its complaint, Prima Paint petitioned the District Court for an order enjoining F & C from proceeding with the arbitration. F & C cross-moved to stay the court action pending arbitration. F & C contended that the issue presented—whether there was fraud in the inducement of the consulting agreement—was a question for the arbitrators and not for the District Court. * * *

The District Court granted F & C's motion to stay the action pending arbitration, holding that a charge of fraud in the inducement of a contract containing an arbitration clause as broad as this one was a question for the arbitrators and not for the court. * * * The Court of Appeals for the Second Circuit dismissed Prima Paint's appeal.

* * *

[The Court first determined that "[t]here could not be a clearer case of a contract evidencing a transaction in interstate commerce."]

Having determined that the contract in question is within the coverage of the Arbitration Act, we turn to the central issue in this case: whether a claim of fraud in the inducement of the entire contract is to be resolved by the federal court, or whether the matter is to be referred to the arbitrators. The courts of appeals have differed in their approach to this question. The view of the Court of Appeals for the Second Circuit, as expressed in this case and in others, is that—except where the parties otherwise intend—arbitration clauses as a matter of federal law are "separable" from the contract in which they are embedded, and that where no claim is made that fraud was directed to the arbitration clause itself, a broad arbitration clause will be held to encompass arbitration of the claim that the contract itself was induced by fraud.[9] The Court of Appeals for the First Circuit, on the other hand, has taken the view that the question of "severability" is one of state law, and that where a State regards such a clause as inseparable a claim of fraud in inducement must be decided by the court.

With respect to cases brought in federal court involving maritime contracts or those evidencing transactions in "commerce," we think that Congress has provided an explicit answer. That answer is to be found in § 4 of the Act, which provides a remedy to a party seeking to compel compliance with an arbitration agreement. Under § 4, with respect to a matter within the jurisdiction of the federal courts save for the existence of an arbitration clause, the federal court is instructed to order arbitration to proceed once it is satisfied that "the making of the agreement for arbitration or the failure to comply [with the arbitration agreement] is not in issue." Accordingly, if the claim is fraud in the inducement of the arbitration clause itself—an issue which goes to the "making" of the agreement to arbitrate—the federal court may proceed to adjudicate it. But the statutory

9. The Court of Appeals has been careful to honor evidence that the parties intended to withhold such issues from the arbitrators and to reserve them for judicial resolution. We note that categories of contracts otherwise within the Arbitration Act but in which one of the parties characteristically has little bargaining power are expressly excluded from the reach of the Act. See § 1.

language does not permit the federal court to consider claims of fraud in the inducement of the contract generally. Section 4 does not expressly relate to situations like the present in which a stay is sought of a federal action in order that arbitration may proceed. But it is inconceivable that Congress intended the rule to differ depending upon which party to the arbitration agreement first invokes the assistance of a federal court. We hold, therefore, that in passing upon a § 3 application for a stay while the parties arbitrate, a federal court may consider only issues relating to the making and performance of the agreement to arbitrate. In so concluding, we not only honor the plain meaning of the statute but also the unmistakably clear congressional purpose that the arbitration procedure, when selected by the parties to a contract, be speedy and not subject to delay and obstruction in the courts.

* * *

In the present case no claim has been advanced by Prima Paint that F & C fraudulently induced it to enter into the agreement to arbitrate "[a]ny controversy or claim arising out of or relating to this Agreement, or the breach thereof." This contractual language is easily broad enough to encompass Prima Paint's claim that both execution and acceleration of the consulting agreement itself were procured by fraud. Indeed, no claim is made that Prima Paint ever intended that "legal" issues relating to the contract be excluded from arbitration, or that it was not entirely free so to contract. Federal courts are bound to apply rules enacted by Congress with respect to matters—here, a contract involving commerce—over which it has legislative power. The question which Prima Paint requested the District Court to adjudicate preliminarily to allowing arbitration to proceed is one not intended by Congress to delay the granting of a § 3 stay. Accordingly, the decision below dismissing Prima Paint's appeal is

Affirmed.

■ MR. JUSTICE BLACK, with whom MR. JUSTICE DOUGLAS and MR. JUSTICE STEWART join, dissenting.

The Court here holds that the United States Arbitration Act, as a matter of federal substantive law, compels a party to a contract containing a written arbitration provision to carry out his "arbitration agreement" even though a court might, after a fair trial, hold the entire contract—including the arbitration agreement—void because of fraud in the inducement. The Court holds, what is to me fantastic, that the legal issue of a contract's voidness because of fraud is to be decided by persons designated to arbitrate factual controversies arising out of a valid contract between the parties. And the arbitrators who the Court holds are to adjudicate the legal validity of the contract need not even be lawyers, and in all probability will be nonlawyers, wholly unqualified to decide legal issues, and even if qualified to apply the law, not bound to do so. I am by no means sure that thus forcing a person to forgo his opportunity to try his legal issues in the courts where, unlike the situation in arbitration, he may have a jury trial and right to appeal, is not a denial of due process of law. I am satisfied, however, that Congress did not impose any such procedures in the Arbitration Act. And I am fully satisfied that a reasonable and fair reading of that Act's language and history shows that both Congress and the framers of the Act were at great pains to emphasize that nonlawyers designated to adjust and arbitrate factual controversies arising out of valid contracts would not trespass upon the courts' prerogative to decide the legal question of whether any legal contract exists upon which to base an arbitration.

* * *

Let us look briefly at the language of the Arbitration Act itself as Congress passed it. Section 2, the key provision of the Act, provides that "[a] written provision in . . . a contract . . . involving commerce to settle by arbitration a controversy thereafter arising out of such contract . . . shall be valid, irrevocable, and enforceable, *save upon such grounds as exist at law or in equity for the revocation of any contract.*" (Emphasis added.) Section 3 provides that "[i]f any suit . . . be brought . . . *upon any issue referable to arbitration* under an agreement in writing for such arbitration, the court . . . *upon being satisfied that the issue involved in such suit . . . is referable to arbitration under such an agreement,* shall . . . stay the trial of the action until such arbitration has been had . . ." (Emphasis added.) The language of these sections could not, I think, raise doubts about their meaning except to someone anxious to find doubts. They simply mean this: an arbitration agreement is to be enforced by a federal court unless the court, not the arbitrator, finds grounds "at law or in equity for the revocation of any contract." Fraud, of course, is one of the most common grounds for revoking a contract. If the contract was procured by fraud, then, unless the defrauded party elects to affirm it, there is absolutely no contract, nothing to be arbitrated. Sections 2 and 3 of the Act assume the existence of a valid contract. They merely provide for enforcement where such a valid contract exists. These provisions were plainly designed to protect a person against whom arbitration is sought to be enforced from having to submit his legal issues as to validity of the contract to the arbitrator. * * *

Finally, it is clear to me from the bill's sponsors' understanding of the function of arbitration that they never intended that the issue of fraud in the inducement be resolved by arbitration. They recognized two special values of arbitration: (1) the expertise of an arbitrator to decide factual questions in regard to the day-to-day performance of contractual obligations,[13] and (2) the speed with which arbitration, as contrasted to litigation, could resolve disputes over performance of contracts and thus

13. "Not all questions arising out of contracts ought to be arbitrated. It is a remedy peculiarly suited to the disposition of the ordinary disputes between merchants as to questions of fact—quantity, quality, time of delivery, compliance with terms of payment, excuses for non-performance, and the like. It has a place also in the determination of the simpler questions of law—the questions of law which arise out of these daily relations between merchants as to the passage of title, the existence of warranties, or the questions of law which are complementary to the questions of fact which we have just mentioned." Cohen & Dayton, The New Federal Arbitration Law, 12 Va.L.Rev. 265, 281 (1926).

mitigate the damages and allow the parties to continue performance under the contracts. Arbitration serves neither of these functions where a contract is sought to be rescinded on the ground of fraud. On the one hand, courts have far more expertise in resolving legal issues which go to the validity of a contract than do arbitrators.[15] On the other hand, where a party seeks to rescind a contract and his allegation of fraud in the inducement is true, an arbitrator's speedy remedy of this wrong should never result in resumption of performance under the contract. And if the contract were not procured by fraud, the court, under the summary trial procedures provided by the Act, may determine with little delay that arbitration must proceed. The only advantage of submitting the issue of fraud to arbitration is for the arbitrators. Their compensation corresponds to the volume of arbitration they perform. If they determine that a contract is void because of fraud, there is nothing further for them to arbitrate. I think it raises serious questions of due process to submit to an arbitrator an issue which will determine his compensation.

* * *

The avowed purpose of the Act was to place arbitration agreements "upon the same footing as other contracts." The separability rule which the Court applies to an arbitration clause does not result in equality between it and other clauses in the contract. I had always thought that a person who attacks a contract on the ground of fraud and seeks to rescind it has to seek rescission of the whole, not tidbits, and is not given the option of denying the existence of some clauses and affirming the existence of others. Here F & C agreed both to perform consulting services for Prima and not to compete with Prima. Would any court hold that those two agreements were separable, even though Prima in agreeing to pay F & C not to compete did not directly rely on F & C's representations of being solvent? The simple fact is that Prima would not have agreed to the covenant not to compete or to the arbitration clause but for F & C's fraudulent promise that it would be financially able to perform consulting services.

* * *

Prima here challenged in the courts the validity of its alleged contract with F & C as a whole, not in fragments. If there has never been any valid contract, then there is not now and never has been anything to arbitrate. If Prima's allegations are true, the sum total of what the Court does here is to force Prima to arbitrate a contract which is void and unenforceable before arbitrators who are given the power to make final legal determinations of their own jurisdiction, not even subject to effective review by the highest court in the land. That is not what Congress said Prima must do. It seems

15. "It [arbitration] is not a proper remedy for ... questions with which the arbitrators have no particular experience and which are better left to the determination of skilled judges with a background of legal experience and established systems of law." Cohen & Dayton, supra, at 281.

to be what the Court thinks would promote the policy of arbitration. I am completely unable to agree to this new version of the Arbitration Act * * *.

NOTES AND QUESTIONS

1. There is a good review of authority in Ericksen, Arbuthnot, McCarthy, Kearney & Walsh, Inc. v. 100 Oak Street, 35 Cal.3d 312, 197 Cal.Rptr. 581, 673 P.2d 251 (1983). A law firm, complaining that the air conditioning in its offices was defective, brought suit against its landlord for breach of contract, of the covenant of quiet enjoyment, and of the warranty of habitability. The lease provided for arbitration "in the event of any dispute * * * with respect to the provisions of this Lease exclusive of those provisions relating to payment of rent." The lessor filed a motion to compel arbitration; the lessee responded that "[g]rounds exist for revocation of the agreement to arbitrate the alleged controversy in that [lessee] was falsely and fraudulently induced to enter into the lease agreement." The Supreme Court of California noted that "[t]he high courts of our sister states with cognate arbitration acts have followed the rule in *Prima Paint* with near unanimity" and held that the lessor's motion should have been granted:

> [T]he issue of fraud which is asserted here "seems inextricably enmeshed in the other factual issues of the case." Indeed, the claim of substantive breach—that the air conditioning did not perform properly—is totally embraced within the claim of fraud—that the lessor knew, at the time of the lease, that the air conditioning would not perform. Thus, if the trial court were to proceed to determine the fraud claim it would almost certainly have to decide the claim of substantive breach as well, and the original expectations of the parties—that such questions would be determined through arbitration—would be totally defeated. However the fraud claim were determined, there would be virtually nothing left for the arbitrator to decide.

Two dissenting judges found the majority's result "Incredible!" and commented that "[t]his is resupination: logic and procedure turned upside down."

2. The court in *Ericksen* apparently assumed that the contract between the parties did not fall within the FAA. When dealing with a contract that *is* within the scope of the Federal Act, would a state court be free in any event to ignore the rule of separability established by *Prima Paint?* Cf. Rhodes v. Consumers' Buyline, Inc., 868 F.Supp. 368 (D.Mass.1993) ("the parties intended" that New York arbitration law govern the arbitration clause, and "under New York law, the arbitration clause of a void and unenforceable contract is itself void and unenforceable").

3. The question of "separability" is posed also by challenges on a number of other contract-law grounds to the validity of the overall agreement. For example:

i. "Illegality"; see *Nuclear Electric Ins. Ltd. v. Central Power & Light Co.,* 926 F.Supp. 428 (S.D.N.Y.1996)(Texas Insurance Code rendered "unenforceable'' any contract of insurance entered into by an unauthorized insurer; held, since ''the claim of unenforceability does not specifically relate to the arbitration provision'' but to ''the entire policy,'' any claim that the policy is rendered unenforceable under Texas law ''must be submitted to the arbitrator''); Wolitarsky v. Blue Cross of California, 53 Cal.App.4th 338, 61 Cal.Rptr.2d 629 (1997)(policyholders argued that insurance dispute could not be arbitrated because the policy discriminated against women, in violation of the state Civil Rights Act, by imposing an additional deductible for maternity care; held, when ''the alleged illegality goes to only a portion of the contract (that does not include the arbitration agreement), the entire controversy, including the issue of illegality, remains arbitrable'').

ii. ''Unconscionability''; see Bondy's Ford, Inc. v. Sterling Truck Corp., 147 F.Supp.2d 1283 (M.D.Ala.2001)(''To the extent that Bondy's Ford claims that other provisions of the dealer's agreement, such as the waiver of punitive damages, render the contract void because they are unconscionable, the validity or invalidity of these provisions may be argued to the arbitral tribunal, and do not clearly implicate the arbitration clause itself'').

iii. Failure of a ''meeting of the minds,'' Bratt Enterprises, Inc. v. Noble International, Ltd., 99 F.Supp.2d 874 (S.D.Ohio 2000)(''Plaintiff does not claim that there was any 'mutual mistake' in the negotiation of the arbitration clause itself'').

iv. Duress and ''coercion through bribery,'' Republic of the Philippines v. Westinghouse Electric Corp., 714 F.Supp. 1362 (D.N.J.1989) (''if plaintiffs could demonstrate that the coercion or duress were directed specifically to the arbitration clause, this would satisfy *Prima Paint* and it would be appropriate to have a hearing on the issue'').

v. Frustration of purpose, Unionmutual Stock Life Ins. Co. of America v. Beneficial Life Ins. Co., 774 F.2d 524 (1st Cir.1985) (defendant ''never argued * * * that the arbitration clause itself was invalid because of either mutual mistake or frustration of purpose'').

vi. ''Agreement to Agree,'' Republic of Nicaragua v. Standard Fruit Co., 937 F.2d 469 (9th Cir.1991) (in determining whether ''Memorandum of Intent'' was a ''binding contract for the purchase and sale of bananas, or merely an 'agreement to agree' at some later date,'' the district court ''improperly looked to the validity of the contract as a whole'' and ''ignored strong evidence in the record that both parties intended to be bound by the arbitration clause''; court should instead have ''considered only the validity and scope of the arbitration clause itself'').

vii. Lack of ''Consideration,'' see Cline v. H.E. Butt Grocery Co., 79 F. Supp.2d 730 (S.D.Tex.1999)(employee claimed that the employer's unilateral right to amend or terminate its occupational injury plan made its promises ''illusory,'' but that ''is an attack on the [plan] as a whole, and not the arbitration provision itself,'' and is therefore ''properly referable to an arbitrator''); Matter of Exercycle Corp. v. Maratta, 9 N.Y.2d 329, 214 N.Y.S.2d 353, 174 N.E.2d 463 (N.Y. 1961)(although employment agreement contained an arbitration clause, the employer opposed arbitration, arguing that since the employee had the right to quit at any time, the employment contract was "lacking in mutuality" and therefore unenforceable; held, "the question whether the contract lacked mutuality of obligation" "is to be determined by the arbitrators, not the court").

4. Compare Stevens/Leinweber/Sullens, Inc. v. Holm Development & Management, Inc., 165 Ariz. 25, 795 P.2d 1308 (App.1990). In this case a General Contractor entered into a standard-form construction contract with the Owner, providing that future disputes would be submitted to arbitration in accordance with the Construction Industry Arbitration Rules of the AAA. The contract also contained a non-standard clause drafted by the Owner, giving the Owner "the unilateral option of selecting either arbitration or litigation as the means of dispute resolution"; the Owner in fact had the right to reconsider its choice of dispute resolution "at any time, prior to a final judgment in the ongoing proceeding." The court noted that Arizona's arbitration statute contained language very similar to § 4 of the FAA and that it therefore "embod[ied] the concept of separability endorsed by the United States Supreme Court in *Prima Paint.*" "Because under the separability doctrine the arbitration provision is an independent and separate agreement, [the Owner] cannot 'borrow' consideration from the principal contract to support the arbitration provision. As a result, we conclude that the arbitration provision, which clearly lacks mutuality, is void for lack of consideration. * * * [Owner's] contention that the arbitration provision should be considered in isolation from the principal contract only when it is necessary to preserve the parties' agreement to arbitrate is without merit."

Note that the *overall* construction contract in *Holm* was not challenged on the ground of lack of "mutuality" or "consideration." See 1 A. Corbin, Contracts §§ 125 ("One Consideration Exchanged for Several Promises"), 164 (1963). This is truly "separability" with a vengeance, isn't it?

5. In some cases, by contrast, courts rebel at carrying the notion of "separability" to its logical extreme. Are the following cases consistent with *Prima Paint* ?

i. Several local government authorities opened securities accounts with a brokerage firm, and later brought suit alleging that they had lost over $8 million as a result of the firm's unlawful conduct. The firm moved to stay the proceedings based on arbitration clauses in the customer agreements; the plaintiffs countered that the agreements were invalid because the individual purporting to sign on their behalf was not authorized to do so. The court held that this threshold issue whether the plaintiffs were bound by the customer agreements should be decided by the district court and not by the arbitrator: "A contrary rule would lead to untenable results. Party A could forge party B's name to a contract and compel party B to arbitrate the question of the genuineness of its signature." Three Valleys Municipal Water Dist. v. E.F. Hutton & Co., Inc., 925 F.2d 1136 (9th Cir.1991).

ii. A brokerage firm's customers (who could not read English) alleged that an employee of the firm had misrepresented to them that they were merely opening a money market account rather than a securities trading account. The court held that the customers were entitled to a trial on this issue, and that it was error to compel arbitration of the customers' claims before doing so: "Where misrepresentation of the character or essential terms of a proposed contract occurs, assent to the contract is impossible. In such a case there is no contract at all." Cancanon v. Smith Barney, Harris, Upham & Co., 805 F.2d 998 (11th Cir.1986). See also Strotz v. Dean Witter Reynolds, Inc., 223 Cal.App.3d 208, 272 Cal.Rptr. 680 (1990) (customer of brokerage firm alleged that she had not been told that the document entitled "Option Client Information" was actually a contract, the terms of which were set forth on the back of the form; "if a party is unaware he is signing any contract, obviously he also is unaware he is agreeing to arbitration").

6. The Supreme Court in Scherk v. Alberto–Culver Co., 417 U.S. 506, 94 S.Ct. 2449, 41 L.Ed.2d 270 (1974), characterized an agreement to arbitrate as "in effect, a specialized kind of forum-selection clause that posits not only the situs of suit but also the procedure to be used in resolving the dispute." Consider Marra v. Papandreou, 216 F.3d 1119 (D.C.Cir.2000). Here the plaintiff was an investor in a consortium that had won a license from the government of Greece to operate a casino near Athens. The license agreement contained no arbitration clause—it did, however, provide that any dispute concerning the license would be settled "by the Greek courts." After local political opposition to the casino developed, the Greek government revoked the license, citing legal defects. The plaintiff filed suit in the United States for breach of contract; it argued that—because the Greek government purported to have revoked the license "from the time it came into effect"—the government should be estopped from seeking refuge in the forum selection clause, which was a provision of a "nonexistent" license. The court nevertheless held that the forum selection clause was enforceable and that the plaintiff was required to file suit in Greece: The clause was properly understood as

> severable from the contract in which it is contained. Therefore while the Greek government's denial of its contractual obligations to Marra relieves her of her duty to perform her side of the contract's terms (for instance, she is no longer obligated to pay the annual license fee), that action does not work a repudiation of the forum-selection clause unless it is specifically directed at the clause itself. Were this not the case ... the value of a forum-selection clause would be significantly diminished, since it will often be the case that a plaintiff can plausibly allege that the defendant's nonperformance constitutes a "repudiation" of its contractual obligations precluding it from recourse to the clause.

c. CONTRACTS OF ADHESION AND UNCONSCIONABILITY

Broemmer v. Abortion Services of Phoenix, Ltd.

Supreme Court of Arizona, En Banc, 1992.
173 Ariz. 148, 840 P.2d 1013.

■ Moeller, Vice Chief Justice. * * *

In December 1986, plaintiff, an Iowa resident, was 21 years old, unmarried, and 16 or 17 weeks pregnant. She was a high school graduate earning less than $100.00 a week and had no medical benefits. The father-to-be insisted that plaintiff have an abortion, but her parents advised against it. Plaintiff's uncontested affidavit describes the time as one of considerable confusion and emotional and physical turmoil for her.

Plaintiff's mother contacted Abortion Services of Phoenix and made an appointment for her daughter for December 29, 1986. During their visit to the clinic that day, plaintiff and her mother expected, but did not receive, information and counselling on alternatives to abortion and the nature of the operation. When plaintiff and her mother arrived at the clinic, plaintiff was escorted into an adjoining room and asked to complete three forms, one of which is the agreement to arbitrate at issue in this case. The agreement to arbitrate included language that "any dispute aris[ing] between the Parties as a result of the fees and/or services" would be settled by binding arbitration and that "any arbitrators appointed by the AAA shall be licensed medical doctors who specialize in obstetrics/gynecology." The two other documents plaintiff completed at the same time were a 2–page consent-to-operate form and a questionnaire asking for a detailed medical history. Plaintiff completed all three forms in less than 5 minutes and returned them to the front desk. Clinic staff made no attempt to explain the agreement to plaintiff before or after she signed, and did not provide plaintiff with copies of the forms.

After plaintiff returned the forms to the front desk, she was taken into an examination room where pre-operation procedures were performed. She was then instructed to return at 7:00 a.m. the next morning for the termination procedure. Plaintiff returned the following day and Doctor Otto performed the abortion. As a result of the procedure, plaintiff suffered a punctured uterus that required medical treatment.

Plaintiff filed a malpractice complaint in June 1988, approximately 1 1/2 years after the medical procedure. By the time litigation commenced, plaintiff could recall completing and signing the medical history and consent-to-operate forms, but could not recall signing the agreement to arbitrate. Defendants moved to dismiss, contending that the trial court lacked subject matter jurisdiction because arbitration was required. In opposition, plaintiff submitted affidavits that remain uncontroverted. The trial court considered the affidavits, apparently treated the motion to dismiss as one for summary judgment, and granted summary judgment to the defendants. Plaintiff's motion to vacate, quash or set aside the order, or to stay the claim pending arbitration, was denied.

On appeal, the court of appeals held that although the contract was one of adhesion, it was nevertheless enforceable because it did not fall outside plaintiff's reasonable expectations and was not unconscionable. * * * We granted plaintiff's petition for review. * * *

Some of the parties and amici have urged us to announce a "bright-line" rule of broad applicability concerning the enforceability of arbitration agreements. Arbitration proceedings are statutorily authorized in Arizona,

A.R.S. §§ 12–1501 to–1518, and arbitration plays an important role in dispute resolution, as do other salutary methods of alternative dispute resolution. Important principles of contract law and of freedom of contract are intertwined with questions relating to agreements to utilize alternative methods of dispute resolution. We conclude it would be unwise to accept the invitation to attempt to establish some "bright-line" rule of broad applicability in this case. We will instead resolve the one issue which is dispositive: Under the undisputed facts in this case, is the agreement to arbitrate enforceable against plaintiff? We hold that it is not.

I. The Contract Is One of Adhesion

* * * [T]he enforceability of the agreement to arbitrate is determined by principles of general contract law. The court of appeals concluded, and we agree, that, under those principles, the contract in this case was one of adhesion.

An adhesion contract is typically a standardized form "offered to consumers of goods and services on essentially a 'take it or leave it' basis without affording the consumer a realistic opportunity to bargain and under such conditions that the consumer cannot obtain the desired product or services except by acquiescing in the form contract." Wheeler v. St. Joseph Hosp., 63 Cal.App.3d 345, 356, 133 Cal.Rptr. 775, 783 (1976). The *Wheeler* court further stated that "[t]he distinctive feature of a contract of adhesion is that the weaker party has no realistic choice as to its terms." Likewise, in Contractual Problems in the Enforcement of Agreements to Arbitrate Medical Malpractice, 58 Va.L.Rev. 947, 988 (1972), Professor Stanley Henderson recognized "the essence of an adhesion contract is that bargaining position and leverage enable one party 'to select and control risks assumed under the contract.' " (quoting Friedrich Kessler, Contracts of Adhesion—Some Thoughts About Freedom of Contract, 43 Colum.L.Rev. 629 (1943)).

The printed form agreement signed by plaintiff in this case possesses all the characteristics of a contract of adhesion. The form is a standardized contract offered to plaintiff on a "take it or leave it" basis. In addition to removing from the courts any potential dispute concerning fees or services, the drafter inserted additional terms potentially advantageous to itself requiring that any arbitrator appointed by the American Arbitration Association be a licensed medical doctor specializing in obstetrics/gynecology. The contract was not negotiated but was, instead, prepared by defendant and presented to plaintiff as a condition of treatment. Staff at the clinic neither explained its terms to plaintiff nor indicated that she was free to refuse to sign the form; they merely represented to plaintiff that she had to complete the three forms. The conditions under which the clinic offered plaintiff the services were on a "take it or leave it" basis, and the terms of service were not negotiable. Applying general contract law to the undisputed facts, the court of appeals correctly held that the contract was one of adhesion.

II. Reasonable Expectations

Our conclusion that the contract was one of adhesion is not, of itself, determinative of its enforceability. "[A] contract of adhesion is fully enforceable according to its terms unless certain other factors are present which, under established legal rules—legislative or judicial—operate to render it otherwise." Graham v. Scissor–Tail, Inc., 28 Cal.3d 807, 171 Cal.Rptr. 604, 611, 623 P.2d 165, 172 (1981) To determine whether this contract of adhesion is enforceable, we look to two factors: the reasonable expectations of the adhering party and whether the contract is unconscionable. As the court stated in *Graham:*

> Generally speaking, there are two judicially imposed limitations on the enforcement of adhesion contracts or provisions thereof. The first is that such a contract or provision which does not fall within the reasonable expectations of the weaker or "adhering" party will not be enforced against him. The second—a principle of equity applicable to all contracts generally—is that a contract or provision, even if consistent with the reasonable expectations of the parties, will be denied enforcement if, considered in its context, it is unduly oppressive or "unconscionable."

* * *

The comment to [Restatement (Second) of Contracts § 211] states in part: "Although customers typically adhere to standardized agreements and are bound by them without even appearing to know the standard terms in detail, they are not bound to unknown terms which are beyond the range of reasonable expectation." The Restatement focuses our attention on whether it was beyond plaintiff's reasonable expectations to expect to arbitrate her medical malpractice claims, which includes waiving her right to a jury trial, as part of the filling out of the three forms under the facts and circumstances of this case. Clearly, there was no conspicuous or explicit waiver of the fundamental right to a jury trial or any evidence that such rights were knowingly, voluntarily and intelligently waived. The only evidence presented compels a finding that waiver of such fundamental rights was beyond the reasonable expectations of plaintiff. Moreover, as Professor Henderson writes, "[i]n attempting to effectuate reasonable expectations consistent with a standardized medical contract, a court will find less reason to regard the bargaining process as suspect if there are no terms unreasonably favorable to the stronger party." In this case failure to explain to plaintiff that the agreement required all potential disputes, including malpractice disputes, to be heard only by an arbitrator who was a licensed obstetrician/gynecologist requires us to view the "bargaining" process with suspicion. It would be unreasonable to enforce such a critical term against plaintiff when it is not a negotiated term and defendant failed to explain it to her or call her attention to it.

Plaintiff was under a great deal of emotional stress, had only a high school education, was not experienced in commercial matters, and is still not sure "what arbitration is." Given the circumstances under which the agreement was signed and the nature of the terms included therein, [we are compelled] to conclude that the contract fell outside plaintiff's reasonable expectations and is, therefore, unenforceable. Because of this holding, it is unnecessary for us to determine whether the contract is also unconscionable.

III. A Comment on The Dissent

In view of the concern expressed by the dissent, we restate our firm conviction that arbitration and other methods of alternative dispute resolution play important and desirable roles in our system of dispute resolution. We encourage their use. When agreements to arbitrate are freely and fairly entered, they will be welcomed and enforced. They will not, however, be exempted from the usual rules of contract law * * *. * * *

The dissent is concerned that our decision today sends a "mixed message." It is, however, our intent to send a clear message. That message is: Contracts of adhesion will not be enforced unless they are conscionable and within the reasonable expectations of the parties. This is a well-established principle of contract law; today we merely apply it to the undisputed facts of the case before us.

Those portions of the opinion of the court of appeals inconsistent with this opinion are vacated. The judgment of the trial court is reversed and this case is remanded for further proceedings consistent with this opinion. * * *

■ MARTONE, JUSTICE, dissenting.

The court's conclusion that the agreement to arbitrate was outside the plaintiff's reasonable expectations is without basis in law or fact. I fear today's decision reflects a preference for litigation over alternative dispute resolution that I had thought was behind us. I would affirm the court of appeals.

We begin with the undisputed facts that the court ignores. At the top [of the agreement to arbitrate] it states in bold capital letters "PLEASE READ THIS CONTRACT CAREFULLY AS IT EFFECTS [sic] YOUR LEGAL RIGHTS." Directly under that in all capital letters are the words "AGREEMENT TO ARBITRATE." The recitals indicate that "the Parties deem it to be in their respective best interest to settle any such dispute as expeditiously and economically as possible." The parties agreed that disputes over services provided would be settled by arbitration in accordance with the rules of the American Arbitration Association. They further agreed that the arbitrators appointed by the American Arbitration Association would be licensed medical doctors who specialize in obstetrics/gynecology. Plaintiff, an adult, signed the document. * * *

The court seizes upon the doctrine of reasonable expectations to revoke this contract. But there is nothing in this record that would warrant a finding that an agreement to arbitrate a malpractice claim was not within the reasonable expectations of the parties. On this record, the exact opposite is likely to be true. For all we know, both sides in this case might wish to avoid litigation like the plague and seek the more harmonious waters of alternative dispute resolution. Nor is there anything in this record that would suggest that arbitration is bad. Where is the harm? In the end, today's decision reflects a preference in favor of litigation that is not shared by the courts of other states and the courts of the United States. * * *

NOTES AND QUESTIONS

1. Is it critical to the court's decision in *Broemmer* that under the contract the arbitrators were required to be "medical doctors who specialize in obstetrics/gynecology"?

Cf. Graham v. Scissor–Tail, Inc., 28 Cal.3d 807, 171 Cal.Rptr. 604, 623 P.2d 165 (1981), relied on by the court in *Broemmer. Graham* involved a contract for a series of concerts entered into between a promoter and Leon Russell, a recording artist and leader of a musical group. The contract was on a standard form prepared by Russell's union, the American Federation of Musicians, and provided that any disputes would be submitted to the International Executive Board of the Federation for final determination. After a dispute arose over the amount due to Russell out of the proceeds of the concerts, the Board issued an award in favor of Russell on the basis of a recommendation by a "referee"—a former executive officer of the union—named by the union president. The California Supreme Court refused to confirm this award. The court first found the agreement to be a "contract of adhesion"—"a standardized contract, which, imposed and drafted by the party of superior bargaining strength, relegates to the subscribing party only the opportunity to adhere to the contract or reject it." "All concert artists and groups of any significance or prominence" are members of the A.F. of M., and the promoter "was required by the realities of his business" to sign A.F. of M. form contracts with any concert artist with whom he wished to deal. Given that adhesion contracts are widely used and are "an inevitable fact of life for all citizens," that fact alone could not render the contract invalid. However, the court went on to find the agreement "unconscionable and unenforceable" because "it designates an arbitrator who, by reason of its status and identity, is presumptively biased in favor of one party":

> [W]hen as here the contract designating [the] arbitrator is the product of circumstances suggestive of adhesion, the possibility of overreaching by the dominant party looms large; contracts concluded in such circumstances, then, must be scrutinized with particular care to insure that the party of lesser bargaining power, in agreeing thereto, is not left in a position depriving him of any realistic and fair opportunity to prevail in a dispute under its terms. * * * [W]e * * * must insist—most especially in circumstances smacking of adhesion—that certain "minimum levels of integrity" be achieved if the arrangement in question is to pass judicial muster.

Further discussion of the selection of arbitrators and of arbitrator impartiality appears in Section D.1 infra.

2. Absent such elements of potential bias on the part of the arbitrators that the court found in *Graham,* under what circumstances is an arbitration clause in an adhesion contract likely to be found unenforceable?

Many state courts are inclined to strike down such clauses as "unconscionable" when they suspect that one party was not aware of the clause or that adequate efforts were not made to bring it to his attention. One such case is Wheeler v. St. Joseph Hospital, 63 Cal.App.3d 345, 133 Cal.Rptr. 775 (1976), also relied on in *Broemmer.* Wheeler was admitted to the hospital one evening "for an angiogram and catheterization studies in connection with a coronary insufficiency." On admission he signed a form entitled "CONDITIONS OF ADMISSION" which included a paragraph entitled "ARBITRATION OPTION." There was a blank space which the patient could initial to indicate his refusal of arbitration, but Wheeler did not do so. After the tests were performed, Wheeler suffered a brainstem infarction rendering him a total quadriplegic. The court held that he was not required to submit his malpractice claim to arbitration. According to his wife he had signed the admission form without reading it, and neither of them was aware that it contained an arbitration clause; "it was hurriedly signed under the stressful atmosphere of a hospital admitting room without any procedures calculated to alert the patient to the existence of the 'ARBITRATION OPTION.' Nor was the patient given a copy of the agreement to permit him to study its terms under less anxious circumstances":

> Although an express waiver of jury trial is not required, by agreeing to arbitration, the patient does forfeit a valuable right. The law ought not to decree a forfeiture of such a valuable right where the patient has not been made aware of the existence of an arbitration provision or its implications. Absent notification and at least some explanation, the patient cannot be said to have exercised a "real choice" in selecting arbitration over litigation. We conclude that in order to be binding, an arbitration clause incorporated in a hospital's "CONDITIONS OF ADMISSION" form should be called to the patient's attention and he should be given a reasonable explanation of its meaning and effect, including an explanation of any options available to the patient. These procedural requirements will not impose an unreasonable burden on the hospital. The hospital's admission clerk need only direct the patient's attention to the arbitration provision, request him to read it, and give him a simple explanation of its purpose and effect, including the available options. Compliance will not require the presence of the hospital's house counsel in the admission office.

4. A patient was admitted to the hospital for surgery. The hospital's "standard procedure" was to have the admitting clerk explain to patients that they were signing an arbitration agreement "to settle all grievances that they have against the hospital outside of court before an arbitration panel." The trial court found the arbitration agreement binding and dismissed the patient's malpractice action; *held,* reversed. The patient's waiver of his right to a jury trial was not "knowing," since there was insufficient evidence that he had read the agreement or was even aware that it contained an arbitration clause: "Surely, in a criminal proceeding, the prosecution could not withstand a *Miranda* challenge merely by presenting a police officer's testimony that it was his 'usual practice' to inform suspects of their rights before attempting to obtain confessions." Nor was the waiver "intelligent," since the agreement did not disclose the composition of the arbitration panel. Under Michigan law, one member of the panel was required to be a doctor or hospital administrator. The court found a "substantial likelihood that a health care provider's decisions will be swayed by *unconscious subliminal bias,* impossible to detect"; it therefore held that the patient must be fully informed in advance not only of the composition of the arbitration panel but also that doctors and hospital administrators on such panels may have "an incentive to minimize the number and size of malpractice awards, because their malpractice insurance rates are directly affected by those awards." Finally, the waiver was not "voluntary," in part because on signing the agreement upon admission to the hospital, the patient was in "considerable pain." Moore v. Fragatos, 116 Mich.App. 179, 321 N.W.2d 781 (1982).

5. If the patients in any of the preceding cases had had the opportunity to consult you in advance of treatment, would you have advised them that it was in their best interests to sign the arbitration agreement? Is it likely that the "disclosures" required in cases like *Wheeler and Moore* will have the same effect?

6. Investors entered into a margin account agreement with a stock brokerage firm. The firm later sold securities worth $3 million that were held in the account as collateral for the repayment of loans it had made to the investors. The investors brought suit claiming that this sale violated the agreement; the firm moved to compel arbitration in accordance with an arbitration clause. The investors asserted that they had been "fraudulently induced" to enter into the arbitration agreement by the firm's "failure to disclose the effect of the arbitration clause." The court held that the investors were not entitled to a jury trial of this issue:

> We know of no case holding that parties dealing at arm's length have a duty to explain to each other the terms of a written contract. We decline to impose such an obligation where the language of the contract clearly and explicitly provides for arbitration of disputes arising out of the contractual relationship. This is not a criminal case; the [plaintiffs'] argument that there was no "showing of intelligent and knowing waiver of the substantive rights at issue" is simply beside the point. * * * We see no unfairness in expecting parties to read contracts before they sign them.

Cohen v. Wedbush, Noble, Cooke, Inc., 841 F.2d 282 (9th Cir.1988). Is this consistent with the cases in the preceding notes? Cf. In re Rangel, 45 S.W.3d 783 (Tex.App.—Waco 2001), where the court enforced Orkin's "Limited Lifetime Subterranean Termite Agreement" containing an arbitration clause: The homeowner "was 75 years old, had never attended school, was functionally illiterate, and was hard of hearing." Nevertheless "at no time" did he "ask any questions regarding, or request any explanations of," the contract; the arbitration provision "was never hidden" from him, and he had "the opportunity to read and reject the terms of the contract within three business days."

7. In addition to one party's lack of awareness of the arbitration clause, what other defects might there be in an arbitration agreement which could give rise to an argument of unconscionability? See Henderson, Contractual Problems in the Enforcement of Agreements to Arbitrate Medical Malpractice, 58 Va.L.Rev. 947, 994 (1972):

> Assuming the conventional expectations test is applied widely to medical arbitration clauses, it is essential to underscore the point that the primary reason for application of such a test is that the disadvantaged bargaining party is harmed or unfairly overreached. The factor of harm or prejudice measures the range of reasonable expectation induced by a standardized contract. * * * So unless it can be said that a medical arbitration term operates in a coercive or oppressive manner, it is difficult to see that the courts will regard it as exceeding the expectations of the average patient who accepts it.

One possible illustration of an arbitration clause that "operates in a coercive or oppressive manner" might be Patterson v. ITT Consumer Financial Corp., 14 Cal.App.4th 1659, 18 Cal.Rptr.2d 563 (1993). Plaintiffs, "individuals of modest means, some self-employed or temporarily jobless," borrowed "relatively small amounts of money." The loan agreements provided that any disputes "shall be resolved by binding arbitration by the National Arbitration Forum, Minneapolis, Minnesota." The court found this arbitration provision "unconscionable and thus unenforceable." The NAF's rules were unclear as to just where the arbitration would be held, but "the provision on its face suggests that Minnesota would be the locus for the arbitration"—and "[w]hile arbitration per se may be within the reasonable expectation of most consumers, it is much more difficult to believe that arbitration in Minnesota would be within the reasonable expectation of California consumers." In addition, in order to obtain a participatory hearing the consumer was required to prepay a substantial hearing fee; a rule explaining the NAF's process for waiver of the fee was "incomprehensible."

8. The Bank of America's arbitration program for all its depositors and credit-card holders (see pp. 46–47 supra) was quickly challenged in court. The plaintiffs argued that "the Bank's unprecedented ADR provision does not fall within the reasonable expectations of the Bank's consumer account-holders," and that "the Bank's unilateral imposition of ADR deprives consumers without their consent of rights that are constitutionally guaranteed." (Plaintiffs' Trial Brief, pp. 23, 25). Outside of court, the plaintiffs' attorney put the matter somewhat more dramatically: "[A]rbitration, like sex, must be based on consent, not on coercion." 1 ABA Disp.Res.Mag., p. 5 (Summer 1994).

The plaintiffs were successful in having the Bank's arbitration clause held unenforceable in Badie v. Bank of America, 67 Cal.App.4th 779, 79 Cal.Rptr.2d 273 (1998). The credit-card agreements had provided that the Bank "may change any term, condition, service or feature of your Account at any time"—such change-of-terms provisions had in fact been standard industry practice since bank credit cards first became available in the 1960's. Nevertheless the court held that it was a violation of the covenant of good faith and fair dealing for the Bank to "attempt to 'recapture' a foregone opportunity by adding an entirely new term, which has no bearing on any subject * * * addressed in the original contract and which was not within the reasonable contemplation of the parties when the contract was entered into"; the absence of any such limitation "would open the door to a claim that the agreements are illusory." There was nothing that would have alerted a customer to the possibility that the Bank might one day in the future invoke this provision to add clauses that were not "integral to the Bank/creditor relationship". Nor was the customer's failure to close an account after receiving the "bill stuffers" sufficient to constitute a waiver of his right to a jury trial—because the Bank's notice was not "direct, clear and unambiguous" and was not "designed to achieve knowing consent" to arbitration. Federal policy favoring arbitration, added the court, "does not even come into play unless it is first determined that the Bank's customers agreed to use some form of ADR to resolve disputes regarding their deposit and credit card accounts"—a determination that in turn "requires analysis of the account agreements in light of ordinary state law principles" governing contracts.

9. The following year, Delaware enacted a statute that permitted a bank to amend any revolving credit plan "in any respect, whether or not the amendment * * * was originally contemplated or addressed by the parties or is integral to the relationship between the parties." Such amendment "may change terms by the addition of new terms" "of any kind whatsoever," expressly including "arbitration or other alternative dispute resolution mechanisms," and notice of any such amendment may be sent by the bank "in the same envelope with a periodic statement." 5 Del. Code § 952 (1999).

The Delaware statute was applied to bind credit card customers of First USA Bank to an arbitration clause in Marsh v. First USA Bank, N.A., 103 F.Supp.2d 909 (N.D.Tex.2000): It was enough for the Bank to show that notice of the arbitration clause was designed to be routinely included in monthly credit-card statements, and that there were in place "multi-level quality assurance controls" to "detect errors." To the same effect is Herrington v. Union Planters Bank, N.A., 113 F.Supp.2d 1026 (S.D.Miss.2000)("plaintiffs' apparent failure to read the revisions to their accounts is irrelevant to the issue of whether they agreed to arbitrate or are subject to those changes").

10. The use of arbitration clauses by Gateway in the direct sales of its computers (see p. 48 supra) has also been the subject of a flurry of recent litigation. The clause was enforced by the Seventh Circuit in Hill v.

Gateway 2000, Inc., 105 F.3d 1147 (7th Cir.1997). Under Gateway's standard terms, the "form in the box" would govern unless the customer returned the computer within 30 days. Therefore, the court held, the contract had not been formed when the telephone order was placed, nor when the goods were delivered—but only *after* the customer had retained the computer beyond that time limit. "By keeping the computer beyond 30 days, the Hills accepted Gateway's offer, including the arbitration clause." Judge Easterbrook pointed out that "cash now-terms later" transactions were quite common in our economy, for example, in air travel and insurance transactions; "cashiers cannot be expected to read legal documents to customers before ringing up sales." And of course, "a contract need not be read to be effective; people who accept take the risk that the unread terms may in retrospect prove unwelcome."

Hylton, Agreements to Waive or to Arbitrate Legal Claims: An Economic Analysis, 8 Sup. Ct. Econ. Rev. 209, 252 (2000), argues that "rational apathy" may justify enforcement of arbitration clauses in "shrink wrap" and other cases where consumers purchase goods before reading or understanding the contract terms. If consumers are likely to misperceive the probability that an injury will arise, one explanation is that "it is costly to discover information about the probability of loss, and the expected rewards for discovering such information are too low to justify the research costs. The expected rewards may be too low because either the probability or the severity of harm, even after the [possibility of filing a lawsuit] is removed, is extremely low." Rational apathy may exist because consumers "rationally discount the deterrence benefits connected to their right to sue. In other words, they do not expect a significant change in the firm's conduct if the parties agree to resolve their disputes in the arbitration regime."

At least one court has declined to follow *Hill*, and has insisted that the proper analysis should instead be under § 2–207 of the UCC. The court in Klocek v. Gateway, Inc., 104 F.Supp.2d 1332 (D.Kan.2000) denied Gateway's motion to dismiss a consumer's breach of warranty suit. For purposes of the motion, it assumed that an offer to purchase the computer had been made by the consumer, and that Gateway had accepted the offer, "either by completing the sales transaction in person or by agreeing to ship and/or shipping the computer to plaintiff." "Because the plaintiff was not a 'merchant,' " Gateway's "additional" arbitration term could become part of the agreement under § 2–207(2) only if the plaintiff had "expressly agreed" to it—and merely retaining the computer was insufficient to show such express agreement.

11. The terms of Gateway's standard arbitration clause were found to be "substantively unconscionable" in Brower v. Gateway 2000, Inc., 246 A.D.2d 246, 676 N.Y.S.2d 569 (1998). The clause, as originally drafted, provided for arbitration to take place in Chicago under ICC rules. The court held that the "possible inconvenience of the chosen site" did not "alone" rise to the level of unconscionability. However, "the excessive cost factor that is necessarily entailed in arbitrating before the ICC is unreasonable and surely serves to deter the individual consumer from invoking the process." (For the smallest of cases ICC rules required an advance payment of $4000—greater than the cost of most Gateway products—of which the $2000 registration fee was nonrefundable even if the consumer prevailed at the arbitration.). Nevertheless, the court did not strike down the arbitration clause in its entirety—instead, it remanded the case to the trial court "so that the parties have the opportunity to seek appropriate substitution of an arbitrator" pursuant to § 5 of the FAA. More recently, the standard Gateway arbitration clause has been amended so that it now requires an arbitration administered by the "National Arbitration Forum"; the arbitration is to be held "at any reasonable location near [the customer's] residence."

12. Are general state contract-law principles of unconscionability applicable to a contract within the coverage of the FAA? The Supreme Court suggested in *Perry v. Thomas* that under § 2 of the FAA "state law, whether of legislative or judicial origin, is applicable *if* that law arose to govern issues concerning the validity, revocability, and enforceability of contracts generally." However, a "state-law principle that takes its meaning precisely from the fact that a contract to arbitrate is at issue does not comport with this requirement of § 2. * * * Nor may a court rely on the uniqueness of an agreement to arbitrate as a basis for a state-law holding that enforcement would be unconscionable, for this would enable the court to effect what we hold today the state legislature cannot." 482 U.S. 483, 492–93 n. 9. Lower courts seem to have had considerable difficulty in applying this principle. See, e.g., Meyers v. Univest Home Loan, Inc., 1993 WL 307747 (N.D.Cal.1993) ("Notwithstanding *Perry,* the court reads the controlling precedent to require that the instant dispute be resolved under principles of federal law only").

13. "When introduced as a method to control soil erosion, kudzu was hailed as an asset to agriculture, but it has become a creeping monster. Arbitration was innocuous when limited to negotiated commercial contracts, but it developed sinister characteristics when it became ubiquitous." In re Knepp, 229 B.R. 821 (Bankr.N.D.Ala.1999).

The *Knepp* court held that an arbitration clause in a contract for the sale of a used car was "void under the doctrine of unconscionability": The buyer lacked "meaningful choice," since "in today's market it is virtually impossible" to purchase an automobile without the sales contract containing an arbitration clause. The court noted that since "automobiles are a necessity in our society, consumers can ill afford to forsake this necessity even at the price of their constitutional rights." Under such reasoning, what *other* clauses in a standard sales, employment, or insurance contract could one justify invalidating?

14. Contracts of adhesion drafted by franchisors, brokerage firms, or insurers often give rise to a large number of claims presenting common questions. The repercussions of the defendant's actions may be widespread, but the monetary harm to individual claimants may be so insignificant that the expense even of arbitration proceedings would not be warranted. And a victory in arbitration for one particularly determined claimant would not necessarily lead to any recovery for any others, or alter the defendant's behavior.

Presumably, a defendant's motion to compel arbitration may no longer be denied simply on the ground that a class action would be a more suitable means of resolving the problem. See Dunham, The Arbitration Clause as Class Action Shield, 16 Franchise L.J. 141 (1997)("strict enforcement of an arbitration clause should enable the franchisor to dramatically reduce its aggregate exposure"); Johnson v. West Suburban Bank, 225 F.3d 366 (3d Cir.2000)(consumer borrowers can be forced to arbitrate their claims under the Truth in Lending Act even if doing so prevents them from bringing class actions; while the statute "clearly contemplates" class actions, it does not "create a right to bring them"); cf. Caudle v. AAA, 230 F.3d 920 (7th Cir.2000)(Easterbrook, J.)("A procedural device aggregating multiple persons' claims in litigation does not entitle anyone to *be* in litigation; a contract promising to arbitrate the dispute removes the person from those eligible to represent a class of litigants").

But are class actions and arbitration agreements necessarily and inherently incompatible? Would it be feasible or desirable to expand the notion of "consolidation" to permit these similar cases to be heard together in a "class arbitration"? Cf. McCarthy v. Providential Corp., 1994 WL 387852 (N.D.Cal.)("Consolidation and class actions are both methods of adjudicating numerous individual actions involving common questions of law or fact"; the rationale of the consolidation cases "leads to the conclusion that the court cannot compel arbitration on a class basis where the agreement did not specifically provide for it"); cf. Blue Cross of California v. Superior Court of Los Angeles County, 67 Cal.App.4th 42, 78 Cal.Rptr.2d 779 (Cal.App.1998)(judicial consolidation of arbitrations is authorized by the California Code of Civil Procedure, see p. 78 supra, and "the interests of justice that would be served by ordering classwide arbitration are likely to be even more substantial in some cases than the interests that are thought to justify consolidation"). For a comprehensive discussion of this problem, see Sternlight, As Mandatory Binding Arbitration Meets the Class Action, Will the Class Action Survive?, 42 Wm. & Mary L. Rev. 1 (2000)(suggesting that the dispute over the permissibility of classwide arbitration may be simply a "decoy," which has "distracted observers from the companies' true goal: total evisceration of consumer and employment class actions").

15. Can an arbitration clause be enforceable if it purports to supersede class actions *that have already been filed*, where the consumer is a member of the putative class? The 2001 amendments to Fleet Bank (R.I.)'s credit card agreement so provide (arbitration "will not apply to Claims asserted in lawsuits filed by you against us ... before the Effective Date of this Arbitration Provision," but it will apply "to all other Claims, even if the facts and circumstances giving rise to the Claims existed before the [Effective Date] and even if some third party has initiated a class action against us, purporting to assert a Claim against us on your behalf prior to [the Effective Date]"; consequently the credit-card holder "may not participate in a class action or class-wide arbitration'' unless he is a member of a class ''which has already been certified on the effective date of this arbitration provision''). Cf. Jess Bravin, ''Banks Seek to Halt Suits By Cardholders,'' Wall St. J., May 2, 2001.

d. ''ARBITRABILITY''

Even if a valid agreement to arbitrate exists, that does not end the matter. The question may still arise whether the particular dispute falls within the ambit of the agreement—that is, whether the parties have agreed to submit *this* matter in controversy to decision by arbitration. In the United States this is often referred to as an inquiry into whether the dispute is ''arbitrable''—in effect, an inquiry into the ''subject matter jurisdiction'' of the arbitrator to hear the case.

AT & T Technologies, Inc. v. Communications Workers of America

Supreme Court of the United States, 1986.
475 U.S. 643, 106 S.Ct. 1415, 89 L.Ed.2d 648.

■ JUSTICE WHITE delivered the opinion of the Court.

The issue presented in this case is whether a court asked to order arbitration of a grievance filed under a collective-bargaining agreement must first determine that the parties intended to arbitrate the dispute, or whether that determination is properly left to the arbitrator.

I

AT & T Technologies, Inc. (AT & T or the Company) and the Communications Workers of America (the Union) are parties to a collective-bargaining agreement which covers telephone equipment installation workers. Article 8 of this agreement establishes that ''differences arising with respect to the interpretation of this contract or the performance of any obligation hereunder'' must be referred to a mutually agreeable arbitrator upon the written demand of either party. This Article expressly does not cover disputes ''excluded from arbitration by other provisions of this contract.''[1] Article 9 provides that, ''subject to the limitations contained in the provisions of this contract, but otherwise not subject to the provisions of the arbitration clause,'' AT & T is free to exercise certain management functions, including the hiring and placement of employees and the termi-

1. Article 8 provides, in pertinent part, as follows:

> If the National and the Company fail to settle by negotiation any differences arising with respect to the interpretation of this contract or the performance of any obligation hereunder, such differences shall (provided that such dispute is not excluded from arbitration by other provisions of this contract, and provided that the grievance procedures as to such dispute have been exhausted) be referred upon written demand of either party to an impartial arbitrator mutually agreeable to both parties.

nation of employment.[2] "When lack of work necessitates Layoff," Article 20 prescribes the order in which employees are to be laid off.[3]

On September 17, 1981, the Union filed a grievance challenging AT & T's decision to lay off 79 installers from its Chicago base location. The Union claimed that, because there was no lack of work at the Chicago location, the planned layoffs would violate Article 20 of the agreement. Eight days later, however, AT & T laid off all 79 workers, and soon thereafter, the Company transferred approximately the same number of installers from base locations in Indiana and Wisconsin to the Chicago base. AT & T refused to submit the grievance to arbitration on the ground that under Article 9, the Company's decision to lay off workers when it determines that a lack of work exists in a facility is not arbitrable.

The Union then sought to compel arbitration by filing suit in federal court pursuant to § 301(a) of the Labor Management Relations Act, 29 U.S.C. § 185(a). Ruling on cross-motions for summary judgment, the District Court reviewed the provisions of Articles 8, 9, and 20 and set forth the parties' arguments as follows:

> "Plaintiffs interpret Article 20 to require that there be an actual lack of work prior to employee layoffs and argue that there was no such lack of work in this case. Under plaintiffs' interpretation, Article 20 would allow the union to take to arbitration the threshold issue of whether the layoffs were justified by a lack of work. Defendant interprets Article 20 as merely providing a sequence for any layoffs which management, in its exclusive judgment, determines are necessary. Under defendant's interpretation, Article 20 would not allow for an arbitrator to decide whether the layoffs were warranted by a lack of work but only whether the company followed the proper order in laying off the employees."

Finding that "the union's interpretation of Article 20 was at least 'arguable,'" the court held that it was "for the arbitrator, not the court to decide whether the union's interpretation has merit," and accordingly, ordered the Company to arbitrate.

The Court of Appeals for the Seventh Circuit affirmed. The Court of Appeals understood the District Court to have ordered arbitration of the

2. Article 9 states:

> The Union recognizes the right of the Company (subject to the limitations contained in the provisions of this contract, but otherwise not subject to the provisions of the arbitration clause) to exercise the functions of managing the business which involve, among other things, the hiring and placement of Employees, the termination of employment, the assignment of work, the determination of methods and equipment to be used, and the control of the conduct of work.

3. Article 20 provides, in pertinent part, "[w]hen lack of work necessitates Layoff, Employees shall be Laid–Off in accordance with Term of Employment and by Layoff groups as set forth in the following [subparagraphs stating the order of layoff]." Article 1.11 defines the term "Layoff" to mean "a termination of employment arising out of a reduction in the force due to lack of work."

threshold issue of arbitrability. The court acknowledged the "general rule" that the issue of arbitrability is for the courts to decide unless the parties stipulate otherwise, but noted that this Court's decisions in *Steelworkers v. Warrior & Gulf Navigation Co.,* 363 U.S. 574 (1960), and *Steelworkers v. American Mfg. Co.,* 363 U.S. 564 (1960), caution courts to avoid becoming entangled in the merits of a labor dispute under the guise of deciding arbitrability. From this observation, the court announced an "exception" to the general rule, under which "a court should compel arbitration of the arbitrability issue where the collective bargaining agreement contains a standard arbitration clause, the parties have not clearly excluded the arbitrability issue from arbitration, and deciding the issue would entangle the court in interpretation of substantive provisions of the collective bargaining agreement and thereby involve consideration of the merits of the dispute."

All of these factors were present in this case. Article 8 was a "standard arbitration clause," and there was "no clear, unambiguous exclusion from arbitration of terminations predicated by a lack of work determination." Moreover, although there were "colorable arguments" on both sides of the exclusion issue, if the court were to decide this question it would have to interpret not only Article 8, but Articles 9 and 20 as well, both of which are "substantive provisions of the Agreement." The court thus "decline[d] the invitation to decide arbitrability," and ordered AT & T "to arbitrate the arbitrability issue."

* * *

We granted certiorari and now vacate the Seventh Circuit's decision and remand for a determination of whether the Company is required to arbitrate the Union's grievance.

II

The principles necessary to decide this case are not new. They were set out by this Court over 25 years ago in a series of cases known as the *Steelworkers Trilogy: Steelworkers v. American Mfg. Co.; Steelworkers v. Warrior & Gulf Navigation Co.*; and *Steelworkers v. Enterprise Wheel & Car Corp.,* 363 U.S. 593 (1960). These precepts have served the industrial relations community well, and have led to continued reliance on arbitration, rather than strikes or lockouts, as the preferred method of resolving disputes arising during the term of a collective-bargaining agreement. We see no reason either to question their continuing validity, or to eviscerate their meaning by creating an exception to their general applicability.

The first principle gleaned from the *Trilogy* is that "arbitration is a matter of contract and a party cannot be required to submit to arbitration any dispute which he has not agreed so to submit." This axiom recognizes the fact that arbitrators derive their authority to resolve disputes only because the parties have agreed in advance to submit such grievances to arbitration.

The second rule, which follows inexorably from the first, is that the question of arbitrability—whether a collective-bargaining agreement creates a duty for the parties to arbitrate the particular grievance—is undeniably an issue for judicial determination. Unless the parties clearly and unmistakably provide otherwise, the question of whether the parties agreed to arbitrate is to be decided by the court, not the arbitrator.

The Court expressly reaffirmed this principle in *John Wiley & Sons, Inc. v. Livingston,* 376 U.S. 543 (1964). The "threshold question" there was whether the court or an arbitrator should decide if arbitration provisions in a collective-bargaining contract survived a corporate merger so as to bind the surviving corporation. The Court answered that there was "no doubt" that this question was for the courts. " 'Under our decisions, whether or not the company was bound to arbitrate, as well as what issues it must arbitrate, is a matter to be determined by the Court on the basis of the contract entered into by the parties.' ... The duty to arbitrate being of contractual origin, a compulsory submission to arbitration cannot precede judicial determination that the collective bargaining agreement does in fact create such a duty."

The third principle derived from our prior cases is that, in deciding whether the parties have agreed to submit a particular grievance to arbitration, a court is not to rule on the potential merits of the underlying claims. Whether "arguable" or not, indeed even if it appears to the court to be frivolous, the union's claim that the employer has violated the collective-bargaining agreement is to be decided, not by the court asked to order arbitration, but as the parties have agreed, by the arbitrator. "The courts, therefore, have no business weighing the merits of the grievance, considering whether there is equity in a particular claim, or determining whether there is particular language in the written instrument which will support the claim. The agreement is to submit all grievances to arbitration, not merely those which the court will deem meritorious."

Finally, it has been established that where the contract contains an arbitration clause, there is a presumption of arbitrability in the sense that "[a]n order to arbitrate the particular grievance should not be denied unless it may be said with positive assurance that the arbitration clause is not susceptible of an interpretation that covers the asserted dispute. Doubts should be resolved in favor of coverage." *Warrior & Gulf,* 363 U.S. at 582–583. Such a presumption is particularly applicable where the clause is as broad as the one employed in this case, which provides for arbitration of "any differences arising with respect to the interpretation of this contract or the performance of any obligation hereunder.... " In such cases, "[i]n the absence of any express provision excluding a particular grievance from arbitration, we think only the most forceful evidence of a purpose to exclude the claim from arbitration can prevail." *Warrior & Gulf,* 363 U.S., at 584–585.

This presumption of arbitrability for labor disputes recognizes the greater institutional competence of arbitrators in interpreting collective bargaining agreements, "furthers the national labor policy of peaceful resolution of labor disputes and thus best accords with the parties' presumed objectives in pursuing collective bargaining." The willingness of parties to enter into agreements that provide for arbitration of specified disputes would be "drastically reduced," however, if a labor arbitrator had the "power to determine his own jurisdiction...." Cox, Reflections Upon Labor Arbitration, 72 Harv.L.Rev. 1482, 1509 (1959). Were this the applicable rule, an arbitrator would not be constrained to resolve only those disputes that the parties have agreed in advance to settle by arbitration, but instead, would be empowered "to impose obligations outside the contract limited only by his understanding and conscience." This result undercuts the longstanding federal policy of promoting industrial harmony through the use of collective-bargaining agreements, and is antithetical to the function of a collective-bargaining agreement as setting out the rights and duties of the parties.

With these principles in mind, it is evident that the Seventh Circuit erred in ordering the parties to arbitrate the arbitrability question. It is the court's duty to interpret the agreement and to determine whether the parties intended to arbitrate grievances concerning layoffs predicated on a "lack of work" determination by the Company. If the court determines that the agreement so provides, then it is for the arbitrator to determine the relative merits of the parties' substantive interpretations of the agreement. It was for the court, not the arbitrator, to decide in the first instance whether the dispute was to be resolved through arbitration.

The Union does not contest the application of these principles to the present case. Instead, it urges the Court to examine the specific provisions of the agreement for itself and to affirm the Court of Appeals on the ground that the parties had agreed to arbitrate the dispute over the layoffs at issue here. But it is usually not our function in the first instance to construe collective-bargaining contracts and arbitration clauses, or to consider any other evidence that might unmistakably demonstrate that a particular grievance was not to be subject to arbitration. The issue in the case is whether, because of express exclusion or other forceful evidence, the dispute over the interpretation of Article 20 of the contract, the layoff provision, is not subject to the arbitration clause. That issue should have been decided by the District Court and reviewed by the Court of Appeals; it should not have been referred to the arbitrator.

The judgment of the Court of Appeals is vacated, and the case is remanded for proceedings in conformity with this opinion.

■ JUSTICE BRENNAN, with whom THE CHIEF JUSTICE and JUSTICE MARSHALL join, concurring.

I join the Court's opinion and write separately only to supplement what has been said in order to avoid any misunderstanding on remand and in future cases.

The Seventh Circuit's erroneous conclusion that the arbitrator should decide whether this dispute is arbitrable resulted from that court's confusion respecting the "arbitrability" determination that we have held must be judicially made. Despite recognizing that Article 8 of the collective-bargaining agreement "is a standard arbitration clause, providing for arbitration of 'any differences arising with respect to the interpretation of this contract or the performance of any obligation hereunder,'" and that "there is no clear, unambiguous exclusion [of this dispute] from arbitration," the Court of Appeals thought that "there [were] colorable arguments both for and against exclusion." The "colorable arguments" referred to by the Court of Appeals were the parties' claims concerning the meaning of Articles 9 and 20 of the collective-bargaining agreement: the Court of Appeals thought that if the Union's interpretation of Article 20 was correct and management could not order lay-offs for reasons other than lack of work, the dispute was arbitrable; but if AT & T's interpretation of Article 20 was correct and management was free to order lay-offs for other reasons, the dispute was not arbitrable under Article 9. Because these were the very issues that would be presented to the arbitrator if the dispute was held to be arbitrable, the court reasoned that "determining arbitrability would enmesh a court in the merits of th[e] dispute," and concluded that the arbitrability issue should be submitted to the arbitrator.

The Court of Appeals was mistaken insofar as it thought that determining arbitrability required resolution of the parties' dispute with respect to the meaning of Articles 9 and 20 of the collective-bargaining agreement. This is clear from our opinion in *Steelworkers v. Warrior & Gulf Navigation Co.* In *Warrior & Gulf,* the Union challenged management's contracting out of labor that had previously been performed by Company employees. The parties failed to resolve the dispute through grievance procedures, and the Union requested arbitration; the Company refused, and the Union sued to compel arbitration under § 301 of the Labor Management Relations Act, 29 U.S.C. § 185. The collective-bargaining agreement contained a standard arbitration clause similar to Article 8 of the AT & T/CWA contract, i.e., providing for arbitration of all differences with respect to the meaning or application of the contract. We held that, in light of the congressional policy making arbitration the favored method of dispute resolution, such a provision requires arbitration "unless it may be said with positive assurance that the arbitration clause is not susceptible of an interpretation that covers the asserted dispute. Doubts should be resolved in favor of coverage."

The Company in *Warrior & Gulf* relied for its argument that the dispute was not arbitrable on a "Management Functions" clause which, like Article 9 of the AT & T/CWA agreement, excluded "matters which are strictly a function of management" from the arbitration provision. We recognized that such a clause "might be thought to refer to any practice of management in which, under particular circumstances prescribed by the agreement, it is permitted to indulge." However, we also recognized that to read the clause this way would make arbitrability in every case depend upon whether management could take the action challenged by the Union; the arbitrability of every dispute would turn upon a resolution of the merits, and "the arbitration clause would be swallowed up by the exception." Therefore, we held that, where a collective-bargaining agreement contains a standard arbitration clause and the "exception" found in the Management Functions clause is general, "judicial inquiry ... should be limited to the search for an explicit provision which brings the grievance under the cover of the [Management Functions] clause...." "In the absence of any express provision excluding a particular grievance from arbitration, ... only the most forceful evidence of a purpose to exclude the claim from arbitration can prevail...."

The Seventh Circuit misunderstood these rules of contract construction and did precisely what we disapproved of in *Warrior & Gulf*—it read Article 9, a general Management Functions clause, to make arbitrability depend upon the merits of the parties' dispute. As *Warrior & Gulf* makes clear, the judicial inquiry required to determine arbitrability is much simpler. The parties' dispute concerns whether Article 20 of the collective-bargaining agreement limits management's authority to order lay-offs for reasons other than lack of work. The question for the court is "strictly confined" to whether the parties agreed to submit disputes over the meaning of Article 20 to arbitration. Because the collective-bargaining agreement contains a standard arbitration clause, the answer must be affirmative unless the contract contains explicit language stating that disputes respecting Article 20 are not subject to arbitration, or unless the party opposing arbitration—here AT & T—adduces "the most forceful evidence" to this effect from the bargaining history. Under *Warrior & Gulf,* determining arbitrability does not require the court even to consider which party is correct with respect to the meaning of Article 20.

NOTES AND QUESTIONS

1. The presumption of arbitrability established by the *Steelworkers* "Trilogy" rested in large part on the unique value that arbitration was thought to have, as a "substitute for industrial strife," in the context of the administration of a collective bargaining agreement. See the excerpts from Justice Douglas' opinion in the *Warrior and Gulf* case, supra p. 38. Is there any reason to apply a similar presumption in other areas? See Schneider Moving & Storage Co. v. Robbins, 466 U.S. 364, 104 S.Ct. 1844, 80 L.Ed.2d 366 (1984) (*Steelworkers* presumption of arbitrability "is not a proper rule of construction" in a case brought against employers by the trustees of certain multi-employer trust funds).

In cases within the coverage of the FAA, the statute's "liberal federal policy favoring arbitration agreements" has led to a similar presumption that "any doubts concerning the scope of arbitrable issues should be resolved in favor of arbitration." Moses H. Cone Memorial Hospital v. Mercury Construction Corp., 460 U.S. 1, 24–25, 103 S.Ct. 927, 941, 74 L.Ed.2d 765 (1983); see also Mitsubishi Motors Corp. v. Soler Chrysler–Plymouth, infra p. 170. Courts applying the FAA will tend even in commercial arbitration cases to cite routinely and to rely indiscriminately on the labor precedents. See, e.g., In the Matter of the Arbitration Between the Singer Co. and Tappan Co., 403 F.Supp. 322, 330 (D.N.J.1975), aff'd, 544

F.2d 513 (3d Cir.1976) (if the policy of judicial noninterference in labor cases is grounded on the belief that "a labor arbitrator is better able to decide complex labor issues than a judge, then it can likewise be said here that the accounting complexities which led to disagreement between well known and highly regarded accounting firms should likewise be best left for arbitration").

2. The *Steelworkers* "Trilogy" is also thought to stand for the principle that questions of "arbitrability" are not affected by the fact that the claim asserted may clearly be without any substantive merit. "Issues do not lose their quality of arbitrability because they can be correctly decided only one way." New Bedford Defense Prods. Div. v. Local No. 1113, 258 F.2d 522, 526 (1st Cir.1958). Is the same proposition true, as a general matter, of the "subject matter jurisdiction" of a court?

In an influential article relied on by Justice Douglas in the "Trilogy," Professor Cox argued that a dispute can rarely be confidently labeled as "frivolous" until "its industrial context," "the parties' way of life and general industrial practice," have all been brought to light: "Since the true nature of a grievance often cannot be determined until there is a full hearing upon the facts, the reasonable course is to send all doubtful cases to arbitration * * *." Cox, Reflections Upon Labor Arbitration, 72 Harv. L.Rev. 1482, 1515, 1517 (1959). Recall also the frequently-made claim that in collective bargaining cases the airing even of claims that *are* clearly "frivolous" might have a "therapeutic" or "cathartic" value. Is this likely to be true of disputes outside of the collective bargaining area?

3. A collective bargaining agreement provided that any layoffs would be in order of seniority, provided that "aptitude and ability [were] equal." One year after the agreement had expired, the employer laid off a number of senior employees, and the Union brought a grievance. The Supreme Court (in a 5–4 decision) held that this dispute did not "arise under" the expired agreement and was therefore not arbitrable. The grievances "would be arbitrable only if they involve rights which accrued or vested under the Agreement, or rights which carried over after expiration of the Agreement * * * as continuing obligations under the contract," and this was not the case: Since aptitude and ability "do not remain constant, but change over time," they "cannot be said to vest or accrue." The Court rejected the Union's argument that this was an issue of contract interpretation that should be submitted in the first instance to the arbitrator: The presumption of arbitrability cannot be applied "wholesale in the context of an expired bargaining agreement, for to do so would make limitless the contractual obligation to arbitrate. * * * [W]e must determine whether the parties agreed to arbitrate this dispute, and we cannot avoid that duty because it requires us to interpret a provision of a bargaining agreement." A footnote in the opinion conceded that the Court's determination that the dispute was not arbitrable "does, of necessity, determine that * * * the employees lacked any vested contractual right to a particular order of layoff." Litton Financial Printing Div. v. NLRB, 501 U.S. 190, 111 S.Ct. 2215, 115 L.Ed.2d 177 (1991).

Is *Litton* consistent with *AT & T?* See also Independent Lift Truck Builders Union v. Hyster Co., 2 F.3d 233 (7th Cir.1993) (after *Litton,* "the rule that courts must decide arbitrators' jurisdiction takes precedence over the rule that courts are not to decide the merits of the underlying dispute").

4. Any "presumption" in favor of arbitration remains, at least in theory, only a rule of construction. The ultimate goal is to effectuate the parties' intent, and the presumption can be overcome by language or other evidence indicating an intent to *exclude* certain items or claims from the arbitrator's consideration. See, e.g., Instructional Television Corp. v. National Broadcasting Co., 45 A.D.2d 1004, 357 N.Y.S.2d 915 (1974) (clause provided that "[a]ny unresolved questions of fact, as distinguished from questions of law, shall at the behest of either party be submitted to arbitration").

Conversely, it is at least conceivable that the parties could go so far as to entrust to the arbitrator *alone* the authority to determine the scope of his own jurisdiction. After all, is not a dispute about "arbitrability" a dispute (in the language of the arbitration clause involved in *Warrior & Gulf*) "as to the meaning and application of [one of] the provisions of [the] Agreement"? However, is it likely that the parties will have wanted to do this? Are arbitrators likely to be entirely objective in deciding whether or not they have the authority to hear the merits of a case? "Once they have bitten into the enticing fruit of controversy, they are not apt to stay the satisfying of their appetite after one bite." Trafalgar Shipping Co. v. International Milling Co., 401 F.2d 568, 573–74 (2d Cir.1968) (Lumbard, C.J., dissenting). The Supreme Court has warned that lower courts "should not assume" that contracting parties have empowered the arbitrator to decide questions of arbitrability, in the absence of "clear and unmistakable evidence that they did so." First Options of Chicago v. Kaplan, 514 U.S. 938, 944, 115 S.Ct. 1920, 131 L.Ed.2d 985 (1995).

5. The AAA recommends the following standard arbitration clause for use in all commercial contracts:

> Any controversy or claim arising out of or relating to this contract, or the breach thereof, shall be settled by arbitration in accordance with the Commercial Arbitration Rules of the American Arbitration Association, and judgment upon the award rendered by the Arbitrator(s) may be entered in any Court having jurisdiction thereof.

One of the advantages of arbitration is that this grant of jurisdiction can be limited or tailored to meet the particular needs and circumstances of the parties. However, more detailed clauses are likely to invite litigation over arbitrability, and may invite courts to speculate as to just what the parties were aiming at. And the departure from hallowed formulas may leave the door open to idiosyncratic judicial rulings.

For example, in Beckham v. William Bayley Co., 655 F.Supp. 288 (N.D.Tex.1987) the parties had provided for arbitration of "any disagreement * * * as to the intent of this contract." The plaintiff, a general contractor, complained that the casements and doors delivered by the defendant were warped and otherwise defective. The court held that this complaint concerning the defendant's *performance* under the contract was not covered by the arbitration clause. The court did not suggest *why* the parties might have wanted to distinguish between disputes over "intent" and disputes over "performance." (Aren't issues of the quality of "performance" precisely the kind of factual questions for which arbitration may be most suited?) See also United Offshore Co. v. Southern Deepwater Pipeline Co., 899 F.2d 405 (5th Cir.1990) (clause provided for arbitration of "any controversy or claim * * * arising out of the interpretation of the provisions of the agreement"; held, arbitrator was "powerless to decide matters on which the agreement was silent; '[i]t is clear that the parties intended that only the contract be interpreted by the arbitrator and not general principles of justice or industry custom or course of dealing between the parties' ").

6. The "separability" principle of *Prima Paint* is also nominally a rule of construction. See fn. 9 of the Supreme Court's opinion, p. 96 supra. A court will frequently compel arbitration only after indulging in mock deference to the parties' presumed "intention" to entrust to the arbitrator the question whether the overall agreement had been induced by fraud. See, e.g., Weinrott v. Carp, 32 N.Y.2d 190, 344 N.Y.S.2d 848, 298 N.E.2d 42 (1973) (proceeding to confirm arbitration award; "technical argument about separability or nonseparability has often obscured the main goal of the court's inquiry which is to discern the parties' intent"). It need hardly be pointed out that this is usually little more than a fiction: It will be rare indeed that parties resisting arbitration will be able to present sufficient evidence to satisfy "their heavy burden of proving an intent not to arbitrate" the issue of fraudulent inducement. See Stateside Machinery Co., Ltd. v. Alperin, 591 F.2d 234 (3d Cir.1979).

Nevertheless, judicial reliance on rules of construction may occasionally entail some curious consequences in terms of party planning and drafting. In some circuits, for example, a clause that merely requires arbitration for "any disputes arising hereunder" will be considered a "narrow" clause—and thus, it may be held not to encompass an allegation of fraudulent inducement. Cf. RCM Technologies, Inc. v. Brignik Technology, Inc., 137 F.Supp.2d 550 (D.N.J.2001)("Because the arbitration clause at issue here is substantially narrower than the clause in *Prima Paint,* the court declines to compel arbitration of the fraudulent inducement claims on the basis of that case"). Nor may it encompass a tort claim for misappropriation of trade secrets—even though the defendant has allegedly used trade secrets and confidential information obtained during the term of a license agreement. The omission from the arbitration clause of the words "relating to," which appear in the AAA's standard clause, may be considered "significant." See Mediterranean Enterprises, Inc. v. Ssangyong Corp., 708 F.2d 1458 (9th Cir.1983) ("arising hereunder" is intended to cover "only those [disputes] relating to the interpretation and performance of the contract itself"); Tracer Research Corp. v. National Environmental Services Co., 42 F.3d 1292 (9th Cir.1994). At the same time, a court may seize on drafting distinctions—admittedly rather "subtle"—to order arbitration of fraudulent inducement questions where the agreement mandates arbitration of disputes "arising out of" the agreement, or disputes that "shall arise or occur under" the agreement, or "all claims and disputes of whatever nature arising under this contract"! Cf. Sweet Dreams Unlimited, Inc. v. Dial–A–Mattress Int'l, Ltd., 1 F.3d 639 (7th Cir.1993); S.A. Mineracao Da Trindade–Samitri v. Utah Int'l, Inc., 745 F.2d 190 (2d Cir.1984); Genesco, Inc. v. T. Kakiuchi & Co., 815 F.2d 840 (2d Cir.1987).

7. Should the attitude of a court be different if the case to be decided by an arbitrator falls towards the "interest" side of the dispute spectrum? In such cases should a court begin with a different presumption as to arbitrability?

Consider Bowmer v. Bowmer, 50 N.Y.2d 288, 428 N.Y.S.2d 902, 406 N.E.2d 760 (1980). Husband and wife entered into a 37–page separation agreement providing for payment of alimony and child support according to a complex formula. Certain matters such as adjustments to the formula in the event of changes in the tax laws or in the Government's cost of living index were expressly made arbitrable. The agreement also provided that:

> Any claim, dispute or misunderstanding arising out of or in connection with this Agreement, or any breach hereof, or any default in payment by the Husband, or any matter herein made the subject matter of arbitration, shall be arbitrated.

Five years later the husband gave notice that because of changed circumstances he would be reducing his support payments, and sought to compel arbitration of this issue. The court held that the husband's claim was not arbitrable since the arbitration clause "was not intended to encompass the dispute here":

> [What the husband] seeks, in essence, is to have the arbitrator rewrite the terms of the agreement because he now views them as onerous. This cannot be considered merely a claim arising from the contract. Instead, it requires the making of a new contract, not by the parties, but by the arbitrator. Obviously, the parties never agreed to such a procedure for it would mean that, once the agreement made provision for arbitration, the arbitrator would be completely unfettered by the terms of the contract in resolving disputes.

Compare Egol v. Egol, 118 A.D.2d 76, 503 N.Y.S.2d 726 (App.Div.), aff'd, 68 N.Y.2d 893, 508 N.Y.S.2d 935, 501 N.E.2d 584 (N.Y. 1986), where a husband and wife in a pre-divorce agreement expressly provided for arbitration of any claims for reduction in the husband's maintenance and support obligations should he "suffer a substantial, adverse and involuntary change in his financial circumstances, making his support obligations under this Agreement inequitable or a substantial hardship for him." The court granted a motion to compel arbitration: "This is not a case where the arbitrator is asked to reform the instrument. The arbitrator is called upon only to interpret it."

8. Agreements between brokerage firms and their employees commonly provide for arbitration of disputes "arising out of employment or the termination of employment." A former account executive brought suit against his employer for prima facie tort and slander, alleging that his superiors had (1) made defamatory statements to former customers and falsely informed others that his broker's license had been suspended, (2) attempted to "scrounge up" complaints from former customers concerning the handling of their investments, and (3) told fellow office workers that the plaintiff had stolen things from their desks at night. The court held that the first two claims were arbitrable, because they "involved significant aspects of the employment relationship," but that the third was not: "No customers or securities agencies are implicated, and no significant issue of [plaintiff's] job performance *qua* broker is implicated." Morgan v. Smith Barney, Harris Upham & Co., 729 F.2d 1163 (8th Cir.1984). See also Dean Witter Reynolds, Inc. v. Ness, 677 F.Supp. 866 (D.S.C.1988) (brokerage firm caused former employee to be arrested for trespass when he repeatedly visited the office; employee's suit for false arrest, imprisonment, and intentional infliction of emotional distress held not arbitrable).

9. Mr. and Mrs. Seifert contracted with U.S. Home for the construction of a house; the contract provided that "any controversy or claim arising out of or related to this Agreement" would be submitted to arbitration. After they moved into their home, their car was left running in the garage, and the air conditioning system located in the garage picked up the carbon monoxide emissions and distributed them into the house, killing Mr. Seifert. U.S. Home moved that Mrs. Seifert's claim for negligence be referred to arbitration. Mrs. Seifert "concedes that an action for breach of contract or any of the warranties or other rights and obligations arising out of the contract would be subject to arbitration": However, the court held, "because the wrongful death action here is predicated upon a tort theory of common law negligence unrelated to the rights and obligations of the contract," the action "was not contemplated by the parties when the contract was made and should not be subject to arbitration." According to the court, this result was also "supported" by "public policy"—since referral to arbitration would "deprive [the plaintiff] of her rights to a trial by jury, due process and access to the courts." A concurring judge concluded that "the authors of these arbitration provisions need to go back to the drafting board." Seifert v. U.S. Home Corp., 750 So.2d 633 (Fla.1999).

10. A defendant refuses to participate in arbitration, asserting that he never agreed to arbitrate the dispute. Should the plaintiff first seek an order under § 4 of the FAA to "compel" arbitration? Or should he simply proceed without the defendant? The AAA Commercial Arbitration Rules permit arbitrators to proceed despite the absence of one party, although the award may not be made solely by default and the party who is present must submit evidence supporting his claim. (Rule 31).

If the defendant fails to appear, and the arbitration does proceed without him, may the defendant later resist judicial enforcement of the resulting award? As in the case of default in litigation, the defendant has certainly lost the ability to defend the claim on the merits. May he also be found to have waived the right to assert any defense of lack of agreement?

Most commentators assume that a defendant who remains out of the proceeding may still at a later time challenge the existence of an agreement to arbitrate. See Martin Domke, Commercial Arbitration § 18:04 at 266 (rev. ed.); see also MCI Telecommunications Corp. v. Exalon Industries, Inc., 138 F.3d 426 (1st Cir.1998)(if there is no written agreement to arbitrate, "the actions of the arbitrator have no legal validity"; "in both the FAA and personal jurisdiction contexts, albeit for different reasons, the non-appearing party can subsequently challenge the authority of the decision-maker, but not the merits of the decision"); but cf. Ian Macneil, Richard Speidel, & Thomas Stipanowich, Federal Arbitration Law §§ 17.6, 40.1.3 (1994). This seems also to be the sense of the Revised Uniform Arbitration Act, which allows a court to vacate an arbitration award where "[t]here was no agreement to arbitrate, unless the person participated in the arbitration proceeding without raising the objection . . . not later than the commencement of the arbitration hearing." § 23(a)(5).

However, see Comprehensive Accounting Corp. v. Rudell, 760 F.2d 138 (7th Cir.1985). The defendants in this case refused to participate in an arbitration, and later opposed confirmation of the award on the ground that they did not actually know about the arbitration clause when they signed the agreement. The court commented that this was "irrelevant," even if the defendants could make out a claim of fraud in the inducement. "[A]fter an award has been entered, § 4 [of the FAA] is no longer in play." It was "too late" for the defendants to "sit back and allow the arbitration to go forward, and only after it was all done * * * say: oh by the way, we never agreed to the arbitration clause. That is a tactic that the law of arbitration, with its commitment to speed, will not tolerate." See also Ramonas v. Kerelis, 102 Ill.App.2d 262, 243 N.E.2d 711 (Ill.App.1968) ("in refusing to appear," defendant "acted at [his] own peril," and his "defense that he did not sign the contract nor was a party to the contract was lost due to a situation of his own creation").

On the other hand, if the defendant *does* appear before the arbitrators to raise and argue the contention that there was no agreement to arbitrate the dispute, he may also incur certain risks: Might his conduct be taken as a consent to allow *the arbitrators themselves* to determine the threshold question of their own jurisdiction? E.g., Yorkaire, Inc. v. Sheet Metal Workers Int'l Ass'n, 758 F.Supp. 248 (E.D.Pa.1990), aff'd mem., 931 F.2d 53 (3d Cir.1991) ("Although [the employer] vigorously argued from the start that the panel did not have jurisdiction to resolve the substance of the Union's grievances, it did not contest the arbitration panel's authority to determine whether the grievances fell within its jurisdiction"). And if the arbitrators go on to conclude that the dispute is in fact arbitrable, will that decision benefit from the same degree of deference that is enjoyed by arbitral awards generally?

See First Options of Chicago, Inc. v. Kaplan, 514 U.S. 938, 115 S.Ct. 1920, 131 L.Ed.2d 985 (1995). In this case the claimant brought an arbitration proceeding against the respondents and their wholly-owned investment company; the respondents—who had not personally signed any arbitration agreement—denied that the dispute was arbitrable and filed written objections to that effect with the arbitrators. The award in favor of the claimant was vacated by the Third Circuit and the Supreme Court affirmed:

> Did the parties agree to submit the arbitrability question itself to arbitration? If so, then the court's standard for reviewing the arbitrator's decision about *that* matter should not differ from the standard courts apply when they review any other matter that the parties have agreed to arbitrate. * * * But merely arguing the arbitrability issue to an arbitrator does not indicate a clear willingness to arbitrate that issue, *i.e.*, a willingness to be effectively bound by the arbitrator's decision on that point. To the contrary, insofar as the [respondents] were forcefully objecting to the arbitrators deciding their dispute with [the claimant], one naturally would think that they did *not* want the arbitrators to have binding authority over them. * * * [B]ecause the [respondents] did not clearly agree to submit the question of arbitrability to arbitration, the Court of Appeals was correct in finding that the arbitrability of the * * * dispute was subject to independent review by the courts.

What other steps are open to a defendant who does not believe that he is subject to a valid agreement to arbitrate?

Note: Loss of the Right to Arbitrate through Delay or "Waiver"

A particular dispute may be conceded to be within the scope of a valid arbitration clause. However, one of the parties may resist on the ground that the other has *lost* the right to arbitrate—perhaps through delay in asserting the right, or by engaging in some action supposedly "inconsistent" with arbitration. This defense may be phrased indiscriminately in terms of "waiver," or "laches," or may be based on the other party's failure to comply with time limits or procedures specified in the contract for seeking arbitration. Is this a matter for the court or the arbitrator to decide? And why does this matter?

The cases frequently distinguish between "substantive" and "procedural arbitrability" and hold that the latter is a question for the arbitrator: "Once it is determined * * * that the parties are obligated to submit the subject matter of a dispute to arbitration, 'procedural' questions which grow out of the dispute and bear on its final disposition should be left to the arbitrator." John Wiley & Sons, Inc. v. Livingston, 376 U.S. 543, 557, 84 S.Ct. 909, 11 L.Ed.2d 898 (1964). In *Wiley* the employer argued that the union had failed to follow the various grievance steps required in the collective bargaining agreement as prerequisites to arbitration; the Supreme Court held that this question was itself arbitrable. The Court noted that "procedural" questions will often be intertwined with the merits of the dispute, and that reserving "procedural" issues for the court "would thus not only create the difficult task of separating related issues, but would also produce frequent duplication of effort" and delay in a final decision. See also Trafalgar Shipping Co. v. International Milling Co., 401

F.2d 568 (2d Cir.1968) (laches) ("in the often esoteric field of commercial dealings," severity of prejudice suffered through delay should be submitted to "expertise of the arbitrators").

However, where the parties' agreement lays down precise time limits within which arbitration must be initiated, a court will often take this as an invitation to make the determination of arbitrability itself, rather than leave the matter to the arbitrator. See, e.g., Virginia Carolina Tools, Inc. v. International Tool Supply, Inc., 984 F.2d 113 (4th Cir.1993) (since "a broad, non-specific arbitration clause" was accompanied in the agreement by "an express termination date provision," an intention to arbitrate "the very continuation of contractual obligations * * * cannot properly be inferred"). Another example can be found in securities arbitration, where the rules of "self-regulatory organizations" like the NYSE and NASD commonly impose a limit of six years after which no customer claim "shall be eligible for submission to arbitration." Brokerage firms will usually prefer that the *courts* decide whether this time limit has passed, while on the other hand customers will argue that this should be an issue for the *arbitrators*. (Why?) *Compare* J.E. Liss & Co. v. Levin, 201 F.3d 848 (7th Cir.2000)("A majority of courts, including ours, applying the principle that courts decide issues of arbitrability unless the parties have clearly indicated that the arbitrators are to decide them, hold that whether the six-year limit has been exceeded is for the courts rather than the arbitrators to decide") *and* Smith Barney Shearson Inc. v. Sacharow, 91 N.Y.2d 39, 666 N.Y.S.2d 990, 992–93, 689 N.E.2d 884 (1997)(contractual proviso "limits the subject of, entitlement to, and range of arbitrable matters" and thus "creates a substantive feature that may affect the right and obligation to arbitrate"); *with* Prudential Securities Inc. v. Laurita, 1997 WL 109438 (S.D.N.Y.)(the "principle continues to be applied in this Circuit" that "any limitations defense—whether stemming from the arbitration agreement, arbitration association rule, or state statute—is an issue to be addressed by the arbitrators").

Another common scenario goes something like this: One party who now wishes to arbitrate will have earlier taken an active part in litigation concerning the very same dispute—for example, he may have earlier filed a counterclaim, or engaged in discovery. He may then be met with the assertion that he has "waived" his right to arbitration. In such cases, courts will often pass directly on the "waiver" issue, sometimes without expressly addressing the appropriateness of their doing so. It has in fact been suggested that a claim of waiver "predicated solely upon participation in the lawsuit by the party seeking arbitration" should be decided by a court, while the issue of waiver "by other conduct" should be for the arbitrator. See The Brothers Jurewicz, Inc. v. Atari, Inc., 296 N.W.2d 422 (Minn.1980). Why should this be true? See also Bridas Sociedad Anonima Petrolera Industrial Y Comercial v. International Standard Elec. Corp., 128 Misc.2d 669, 490 N.Y.S.2d 711 (Sup.Ct.1985) ("Logic would dictate" that where a claim of waiver turns on "the degree of a party's participation in a court action," then the issue of waiver should be determined by the court and not the arbitrator). Does the final proviso of § 3 of the FAA have any bearing at all on this question?

Some state courts seem to approach this question of waiver in a fairly rigid and mechanical way, asking whether the party now seeking arbitration had earlier acted in a way that is "inconsistent" with an assertion of the right to arbitrate or had made "an election" between a judicial and an arbitral forum. E.g., Sanford Construction Co., Inc. v. Rosenblatt, 25 Ohio Misc. 99, 266 N.E.2d 267 (Ohio Mun.Ct.1970) (defendant's statement, "If you want to collect, sue us!" constituted an "express waiver" of arbitration); Lapidus v. Arlen Beach Condominium Ass'n, Inc., 394 So.2d 1102 (Fla.App.1981) ("filing an answer without asserting the right for arbitration acts as waiver"). Such cases seem to counsel that a decision whether or not to pursue arbitration under an arbitration clause should be made at the earliest possible moment. See also Texas International Commercial Arbitration and Conciliation Act, V.T.C.A., Civ.Prac. & Rem.Code § 172.052 (court shall stay judicial proceedings in favor of arbitration if a party requests a stay "not later than the time the party submits the party's first statement on the substance of the dispute").

In contrast, many *federal* cases seem to be considerably slower in finding "waiver" where a party has vacillated and participated in litigation before moving to compel arbitration. Given the "strong federal policy favoring enforcement of arbitration agreements between knowledgeable business people," a finding of waiver is not favored in federal court; the party asserting waiver is said to bear a heavy burden of proof. Knorr Brake Corp. v. Harbil, Inc., 556 F.Supp. 489 (N.D.Ill.1983). But cf. Cabinetree of Wisconsin, Inc. v. Kraftmaid Cabinetry, Inc., 50 F.3d 388 (7th Cir.1995) (Posner, J.) ("[i]n determining whether a waiver has occurred, the court is not to place its thumbs on the scales").

The majority of federal courts therefore tend to ask whether one of the parties will have been "prejudiced" if his adversary is permitted to take part in litigation and then later demand arbitration. Without such a finding of "prejudice," the mere fact that a party has delayed in calling for arbitration will not be enough to cause a waiver of his right to arbitrate. (In many cases, of course, delay in demanding arbitration will simply reflect the fact that negotiations over a settlement of the dispute are being carried on.) Nor will the fact that he has filed pleadings in the lawsuit. So, for example, a party has been allowed to seek arbitration thirteen months after a suit was filed, even though he had answered the complaint, served several interrogatories and requests for the production of documents, and participated in a pretrial conference. Walker v. J.C. Bradford & Co., 938 F.2d 575 (5th Cir.1991). See also Stifel, Nicolaus & Co. Inc. v. Freeman, 924 F.2d 157 (8th Cir.1991) (brokerage firm sued customers for outstanding balances; customers filed a counterclaim and the parties engaged in written discovery; six months after filing suit, the brokerage firm moved to compel arbitration).

Whether a party has suffered enough "prejudice" to warrant a finding of waiver is obviously an inquiry heavily dependent on the facts of the particular case. Courts will often rely on the fact that the party resisting arbitration has incurred substantial costs in preparing for trial and in defending against the litigation moves of his opponent; see, e.g., Prudential–Bache Securities, Inc. v. Stevenson, 706 F.Supp. 533 (S.D.Tex.1989) (defendants "have incurred attorneys' fees and expenses in excess of $5,000 connected with the preparation of their answer"); Fraser v. Merrill Lynch Pierce, Fenner & Smith, Inc., 817 F.2d 250 (4th Cir.1987) (the parties "participated in four status conferences, five hearings on pending motions, and two pretrial conferences"; waiver was found in light of "the extent of the moving party's trial-oriented activity" and the "substantial time and effort" expended by the plaintiff). In addition, courts often find it important that the party now demanding arbitration has earlier benefited from using judicial discovery mechanisms that are not available as of right in arbitration. See, e.g., Zwitserse Maatschappij Van Levensverzekering En Lijfrente v. ABN Int'l Capital Markets Corp., 996 F.2d 1478 (2d Cir.1993) (defendant "suffered prejudice because the deposition-type discovery obtained [by plaintiff] in the Netherlands would not have been available" in securities arbitration in the United States). In other cases, however, the benefits of pre-trial discovery obtained by the party seeking arbitration seem to play a smaller role: A court may even note that the party resisting arbitration and claiming waiver will *itself* derive advantages from the discovery that has already taken place. See *Stifel, Nicolaus & Co.*, supra (defendants' claim of "waiver" rejected; "the limited discovery conducted will be usable in arbitration"). On the availability of discovery in arbitration, see generally Section D.2.d. infra.

NOTES AND QUESTIONS

1. Are the state cases and statutes referred to in the text consistent with federal policy? Is a separate state standard of waiver permissible in cases falling within the ambit of the FAA? See Alan Rau, The UNCITRAL Model Law in State and Federal Courts: The Problem of "Waiver," 6 Am.Rev.Int'l Arb. 223 (1995).

2. A finding of waiver is more readily made where it is the *plaintiff* in a lawsuit who later seeks to compel arbitration of the dispute. See, e.g., Christensen v. Dewor Developments, 33 Cal.3d 778, 191 Cal.Rptr. 8, 661 P.2d 1088 (1983) (plaintiff filed complaint in order to "have some feel for what the Defendants' position would be at arbitration"). See also Note, Contractual Agreements to Arbitrate Disputes: Waiver of the Right to Compel Arbitration, 52 So.Cal.L.Rev. 1513 (1979), which advocates that a plaintiff who files suit over an arbitrable issue should be "deemed" to have waived any right to arbitration. Are there any virtues in such a mechanical rule? What of the case where a plaintiff files a complaint and then, the same day, changes his mind and makes a formal demand for arbitration? See Cavac Compania Anonima Venezolana de Administracion y Comercio v. Board for Validation of German Bonds in the U.S., 189 F.Supp. 205 (S.D.N.Y.1960).

3. A plaintiff brings a lawsuit, and the defendant successfully moves for a stay on the ground that the parties had agreed to arbitrate. So the plaintiff acquiesces, and makes a demand for arbitration. Then the defendant tries to claim that the plaintiff—by originally instituting the suit—has waived his right to arbitration. Can the defendant thereby accomplish the "stunning tour de force" of denying the plaintiff any forum at all? See 795 Fifth Ave. Corp. v. Trusthouse Forte (Pierre) Management, Inc., 131 Misc.2d 291, 499 N.Y.S.2d 857 (1986) (no).

4. A finding that the right to arbitration has been "waived" is often a value-laden judgment, comprehensible only as a response to other, unarticulated policies. An extreme example of this point is Davis v. Blue Cross of Northern California, 25 Cal.3d 418, 158 Cal.Rptr. 828, 600 P.2d 1060 (1979). A number of insureds alleged in a class action that Blue Cross had refused to pay for hospital expenses to which they were entitled. Shortly after the filing of the complaint Blue Cross moved to submit the disputes to a "medical arbitration panel" as required by the policies. The trial court found that the arbitration clause had been "buried in an obscure provision" of the agreements and that Blue Cross, in rejecting claims, had failed to bring the arbitration procedure to its insureds' attention. The Supreme Court of California agreed with the trial court that Blue Cross had "breached its duty of good faith and fair dealing" to its insureds "by failing timely or adequately to apprise them of the availability" of arbitration and that "as a consequence, Blue Cross waived any right subsequently to compel its insureds to resort to arbitration."

Is this a case of "waiver"? How have the plaintiffs been prejudiced by Blue Cross's failure to inform them of the availability of arbitration? In the course of its opinion, the Supreme Court also noted that:

> Under hospitalization policies, in which disputes over benefits may frequently involve a simple disagreement between the insured's physician and the insurer's medical consultant as to the reasonableness of fees or the necessity for certain medical procedures, the existence of an arbitral process will often enable the insured to obtain an impartial review of the insurer's decision without the need to incur the significant expense of legal counsel; as a consequence, the reduced cost of the process may make it practicable for the insured to secure a binding resolution of disputes over smaller claims than would otherwise be financially feasible.

How does the court's finding of "waiver" respond to this rhetoric about the advantages of the arbitration process?

5. A defendant in an arbitration asserts that if the dispute had been litigated, the state's statute of limitations would have barred the underlying claim. The arbitrator finds that questions relating to the statute of limitations are within the scope of the arbitration clause, and rules in favor of the claimant. On a motion to vacate the award, what result? See NCR Corp. v. CBS Liquor Control, Inc., 874 F.Supp. 168 (S.D.Ohio 1993), aff'd, 43 F.3d 1076 (6th Cir.1995) ("the effect of a statute of limitations is to bar an action at law, not arbitration"); Hanes Corp. v. Millard, 531 F.2d 585

(D.C.Cir.1976) ("the arbitrator may be forced to decide at what point any breach might have occurred and when the [plaintiffs] did or should have acquired knowledge of the alleged breach. Such an inquiry will require considerable factual probing"). A New York statute permits a party, by application to the court, to assert the statute of limitations "as a bar to arbitration"; "the failure to assert such bar by such application shall not preclude its assertion before the arbitrators, who may, in their sole discretion, apply or not apply the bar." N.Y.C.P.L.R. § 7502(b).

4. Judicial Supervision and Review

For arbitration to function as an efficient process of private dispute resolution—to realize the benefits of expert decision-making with reduced cost and delay—litigation challenging the process, or aimed at upsetting the resulting award, must be minimized. One danger is exemplified by a tongue-in-cheek comment of a lawyer from Latin America, a region where arbitration is neither familiar nor generally accepted:

> "We lawyers like arbitration. It assures us three litigations: one before, one during and one after the arbitration."[1]

In addition, arbitrators faced with heightened judicial scrutiny might ultimately come to focus less on the merits of the particular dispute, or the relationship between the parties, and more on the task of producing opinions or building a record that would enable their awards to survive later challenge.

There is thus a need to prevent a "judicialization" of the arbitral process. But at the same time, some sort of "public" supervision and control may be necessary to protect wider social interests that may be ignored or jeopardized by "private" arbitrators. The inevitable tension between these two values is a theme that figures in much of these materials.

The occasion for judicial supervision and control of the arbitral process may arise at a number of different stages. Such supervision may be exercised at the time an award made by arbitrators comes before a court for review and enforcement. Or it may be exercised at a still earlier stage—when the question is posed whether a particular dispute is at all suitable for arbitration in the first place: This is the question whether "public policy" demands that the full panoply of judicial procedure remain available to an aggrieved party, despite his earlier agreement to submit to arbitration. Even at that threshold stage, however, an inquiry into whether "public policy" forbids arbitration of the dispute must take into account the fact that any ultimate award is likely to be treated with considerable deference by a reviewing court, even with respect to matters of "law." We begin, therefore, with an overview of the critical subject of the judicial review of arbitral awards.

1. Quoted in Nattier, International Commercial Arbitration in Latin America: Enforcement of Arbitral Agreements and Awards, 21 Tex.Int'l L.J. 397, 408 (1986).

a. JUDICIAL REVIEW OF ARBITRAL AWARDS

By far the greatest number of the many awards rendered by arbitrators are voluntarily complied with. This seems especially true in collective bargaining cases: Recent estimates suggest that less than 1% of labor arbitration awards in the private sector are ever challenged in court.[2] However, where one party is recalcitrant, official sanctions to enforce the award may be needed. Modern arbitration statutes make available the assistance of courts in enforcing arbitration awards: See, for example, §§ 9 and 13 of the FAA. How closely will a court scrutinize an arbitration award? Under what circumstances will it decline to give the award legal effect?

The conventional wisdom is that successful challenges to arbitration awards are rare. Thirty years ago one commentator could write that in "the overwhelming majority of that miniscule portion which are appealed, only an infinitesimal few have ever been vacated."[3] In more recent years, the amount of "litigious wrangling" over the enforcement of awards—and thus the number of successful challenges—has unquestionably increased, so as to make that something of an overstatement.[4] Nonetheless the essential point about judicial deference to arbitral awards still appears to be valid.[5]

Modern arbitration statutes provide only limited grounds on the basis of which a court may refuse to enforce an award. See §§ 10 and 11 of the FAA. What does it mean to say (as in § 10(d)) that an award can be overturned if the arbitrators have "exceeded their powers"? Among other things, this can often be a peg on which to hang a challenge—even after an award is rendered—to the "arbitrability" of the dispute, at least if the point has been preserved by a proper objection before the arbitrator. The question then becomes whether the arbitrator has in fact determined an issue which the parties in their agreement have empowered him to decide. See also § 11(b).

Does § 10 of the FAA have a bearing on *other* challenges to arbitration awards besides assertions that under the agreement the underlying dispute was not "arbitrable"? And are the grounds specified in the federal statute *exclusive*? Or are there other grounds on which a court can rely in refusing

2. Feuille & LeRoy, Grievance Arbitration Appeals in the Federal Courts: Facts and Figures, 45 Arb.J. 35 (Mar. 1990).

3. Jones, Evidentiary Concepts in Labor Arbitration: Some Modern Variations on Ancient Legal Themes, 13 U.C.L.A.L.Rev. 1241, 1296 (1966).

4. See Gould, Judicial Review of Labor Arbitration Awards—Thirty Years of the *Steelworkers Trilogy*: The Aftermath of *AT & T* and *Misco,* 64 Notre Dame L.Rev. 464, 467, 474 (1989). Gould attributes this phenomenon at least in part to the decline in the number of employees represented by unions, which has "simultaneously encouraged and emboldened employers to challenge arbitration awards and unions as well."

5. While "the odds of a successful appeal have improved somewhat" in recent years, federal courts are still enforcing labor arbitration awards approximately 70% of the time. See LeRoy & Feuille, The *Steelworkers Trilogy* and Grievance Arbitration Appeals: How the Federal Courts Respond, 13 Ind.Rel. L.J. 78, 103, 117 (1991); Calvin Sharpe, Judicial Review of Labor Arbitration Awards: A View from the Bench, Proceedings, 52nd Annual Meeting, National Academy of Arbitrators 126, 142 (2000).

to enforce an award? In the materials that follow you will come across a number of variant formulations, sometimes in terms borrowed from labor arbitration cases. Do these constitute alternative grounds to vacate an award? Or do they instead amount to nothing more than dressing up the same idea in different semantic garb?

United Paperworkers International Union v. Misco, Inc.

Supreme Court of the United States, 1987.
484 U.S. 29, 108 S.Ct. 364, 98 L.Ed.2d 286.

■ JUSTICE WHITE delivered the opinion of the Court.

The issue for decision involves several aspects of when a federal court may refuse to enforce an arbitration award rendered under a collective-bargaining agreement.

I

Misco, Inc. operates a paper converting plant in Monroe, Louisiana. The Company is a party to a collective-bargaining agreement with the United Paperworkers International Union, AFL–CIO, and its union local; the agreement covers the production and maintenance employees at the plant. Under the agreement, the Company or the Union may submit to arbitration any grievance that arises from the interpretation or application of its terms, and the arbitrator's decision is final and binding upon the parties. The arbitrator's authority is limited to interpretation and application of the terms contained in the agreement itself. The agreement reserves to management the right to establish, amend, and enforce "rules and regulations regulating the discipline or discharge of employees" and the procedures for imposing discipline. Such rules were to be posted and were to be in effect "until ruled on by grievance and arbitration procedures as to fairness and necessity." For about a decade, the Company's rules had listed as causes for discharge the bringing of intoxicants, narcotics, or controlled substances on to plant property or consuming any of them there, as well as reporting for work under the influence of such substances.[2] At the time of the events involved in this case, the Company was very concerned about the use of drugs at the plant, especially among employees on the night shift.

Isiah Cooper, who worked on the night shift for Misco, was one of the employees covered by the collective-bargaining agreement. He operated a slitter-rewinder machine, which uses sharp blades to cut rolling coils of paper. The arbitrator found that this machine is hazardous and had caused numerous injuries in recent years. Cooper had been reprimanded twice in a few months for deficient performance. On January 21, 1983, one day after

2. Rule II.1 lists the following as causes for discharge:

"Bringing intoxicants, narcotics, or controlled substances into, or consuming intoxicants, narcotics or controlled substances in the plant, or on plant premises. Reporting for duty under the influence of intoxicants, narcotics, or controlled substances."

the second reprimand, the police searched Cooper's house pursuant to a warrant, and a substantial amount of marijuana was found. Contemporaneously, a police officer was detailed to keep Cooper's car under observation at the Company's parking lot. At about 6:30 p.m., Cooper was seen walking in the parking lot during work hours with two other men. The three men entered Cooper's car momentarily, then walked to another car, a white Cutlass, and entered it. After the other two men later returned to the plant, Cooper was apprehended by police in the backseat of this car with marijuana smoke in the air and a lighted marijuana cigarette in the front-seat ashtray. The police also searched Cooper's car and found a plastic scales case and marijuana gleanings. Cooper was arrested and charged with marijuana possession.[3]

On January 24, Cooper told the Company that he had been arrested for possession of marijuana at his home; the Company did not learn of the marijuana cigarette in the white Cutlass until January 27. It then investigated and on February 7 discharged Cooper, asserting that in the circumstances, his presence in the Cutlass violated the rule against having drugs on the plant premises.[4] Cooper filed a grievance protesting his discharge the same day, and the matter proceeded to arbitration. The Company was not aware until September 21, five days before the hearing before the arbitrator was scheduled, that marijuana had been found in Cooper's car. That fact did not become known to the Union until the hearing began. At the hearing it was stipulated that the issue was whether the Company had "just cause to discharge the Grievant under Rule II.1" and, "[i]f not, what if any should be the remedy."

The arbitrator upheld the grievance and ordered the Company to reinstate Cooper with backpay and full seniority. The arbitrator based his finding that there was not just cause for the discharge on his consideration of seven criteria.[5] In particular, the arbitrator found that the Company failed to prove that the employee had possessed or used marijuana on company property: finding Cooper in the backseat of a car and a burning cigarette in the front-seat ashtray was insufficient proof that Cooper was using or possessed marijuana on company property. The arbitrator refused to accept into evidence the fact that marijuana had been found in Cooper's car on company premises because the Company did not know of this fact when Cooper was discharged and therefore did not rely on it as a basis for the discharge.[6]

3. Cooper later pleaded guilty to that charge, which was not related to his being in a car with a lighted marijuana cigarette in it. The authorities chose not to prosecute for the latter incident.

4. The Company asserted that being in a car with a lit marijuana cigarette was a direct violation of the company rule against having an illegal substance on company property.

5. These considerations were the reasonableness of the employer's position, the notice given to the employee, the timing of the investigation undertaken, the fairness of the investigation, the evidence against the employee, the possibility of discrimination, and the relation of the degree of discipline to the nature of the offense and the employee's past record.

6. The arbitrator stated: "One of the rules in arbitration is that the Company

The Company filed suit in District Court, seeking to vacate the arbitration award on several grounds, one of which was that ordering reinstatement of Cooper, who had allegedly possessed marijuana on the plant premises, was contrary to public policy. The District Court agreed that the award must be set aside as contrary to public policy because it ran counter to general safety concerns that arise from the operation of dangerous machinery while under the influence of drugs, as well as to state criminal laws against drug possession. The Court of Appeals affirmed, with one judge dissenting. The court ruled that reinstatement would violate the public policy "against the operation of dangerous machinery by persons under the influence of drugs or alcohol." The arbitrator had found that Cooper was apprehended on company premises in an atmosphere of marijuana smoke in another's car and that marijuana was found in his own car on the company lot. These facts established that Cooper had violated the Company's rules and gave the company just cause to discharge him. The arbitrator did not reach this conclusion because of a "narrow focus on Cooper's procedural rights" that led him to ignore what he "knew was in fact true: that Cooper *did* bring marijuana onto his employer's premises." [The Court of Appeals also suggested that the arbitrator's "baffling view of evidence that would with ease have sustained a civil verdict and probably a criminal conviction" might in part be explained by his formal training "as an engineer and not as a lawyer." 768 F.2d 739, 741 n. 2.] * * *

Because the Courts of Appeals are divided on the question of when courts may set aside arbitration awards as contravening public policy, we granted the Union's petition for a writ of certiorari, and now reverse the judgment of the Court of Appeals.

II

The Union asserts that an arbitral award may not be set aside on public policy grounds unless the award orders conduct that violates the positive law, which is not the case here. But in the alternative, it submits that even if it is wrong in this regard, the Court of Appeals otherwise exceeded the limited authority that it had to review an arbitrator's award entered pursuant to a collective-bargaining agreement. Respondent, on the other hand, defends the public policy decision of the Court of Appeals but alternatively argues that the judgment below should be affirmed because of erroneous findings by the arbitrator. We deal first with the opposing alternative arguments.

A

Collective-bargaining agreements commonly provide grievance procedures to settle disputes between union and employer with respect to the interpretation and application of the agreement and require binding arbitration for unsettled grievances. In such cases, and this is such a case, the

must have its proof in hand before it takes disciplinary action against an employee. The Company does not take the disciplinary action and then spend eight months digging up supporting evidence to justify its actions. * * * "

Court made clear almost 30 years ago that the courts play only a limited role when asked to review the decision of an arbitrator. The courts are not authorized to reconsider the merits of an award even though the parties may allege that the award rests on errors of fact or on misinterpretation of the contract. "The refusal of courts to review the merits of an arbitration award is the proper approach to arbitration under collective bargaining agreements. The federal policy of settling labor disputes by arbitration would be undermined if courts had the final say on the merits of the awards." *Steelworkers v. Enterprise Wheel & Car Corp.*, 363 U.S. 593, 596 (1960). As long as the arbitrator's award "draws its essence from the collective bargaining agreement," and is not merely "his own brand of industrial justice," the award is legitimate.

> "The function of the court is very limited when the parties have agreed to submit all questions of contract interpretation to the arbitrator. It is confined to ascertaining whether the party seeking arbitration is making a claim which on its face is governed by the contract. Whether the moving party is right or wrong is a question of contract interpretation for the arbitrator. In these circumstances the moving party should not be deprived of the arbitrator's judgment, when it was his judgment and all that it connotes that was bargained for." * * * *Steelworkers v. American Mfg. Co.*, 363 U.S. 564, 567–568 (1960).

The reasons for insulating arbitral decisions from judicial review are grounded in the federal statutes regulating labor-management relations. These statutes reflect a decided preference for private settlement of labor disputes without the intervention of government. * * * Because the parties have contracted to have disputes settled by an arbitrator chosen by them rather than by a judge, it is the arbitrator's view of the facts and of the meaning of the contract that they have agreed to accept. Courts thus do not sit to hear claims of factual or legal error by an arbitrator as an appellate court does in reviewing decisions of lower courts. To resolve disputes about the application of a collective-bargaining agreement, an arbitrator must find facts and a court may not reject those findings simply because it disagrees with them. The same is true of the arbitrator's interpretation of the contract. The arbitrator may not ignore the plain language of the contract; but the parties having authorized the arbitrator to give meaning to the language of the agreement, a court should not reject an award on the ground that the arbitrator misread the contract. So, too, where it is contemplated that the arbitrator will determine remedies for contract violations that he finds, courts have no authority to disagree with his honest judgment in that respect. If the courts were free to intervene on these grounds, the speedy resolution of grievances by private mechanisms would be greatly undermined. Furthermore, it must be remembered that grievance and arbitration procedures are part and parcel of the ongoing process of collective bargaining. It is through these processes that the supplementary rules of the plant are established. * * * [A]s long as the arbitrator is even arguably construing or applying the contract and acting within the scope of his authority, that a court is convinced he committed serious error does not suffice to overturn his decision. Of course, decisions procured by the parties through fraud or through the arbitrator's dishonesty need not be enforced. But there is nothing of that sort involved in this case.

B

The Company's position, simply put, is that the arbitrator committed grievous error in finding that the evidence was insufficient to prove that Cooper had possessed or used marijuana on company property. But the Court of Appeals, although it took a distinctly jaundiced view of the arbitrator's decision in this regard, was not free to refuse enforcement because it considered Cooper's presence in the white Cutlass, in the circumstances, to be ample proof that Rule II.1 was violated. No dishonesty is alleged; only improvident, even silly, factfinding is claimed. This is hardly sufficient basis for disregarding what the agent appointed by the parties determined to be the historical facts.

Nor was it open to the Court of Appeals to refuse to enforce the award because the arbitrator, in deciding whether there was just cause to discharge, refused to consider evidence unknown to the Company at the time Cooper was fired. The parties bargained for arbitration to settle disputes and were free to set the procedural rules for arbitrators to follow if they chose. Section VI of the agreement, entitled "Arbitration Procedure," did set some ground rules for the arbitration process. It forbade the arbitrator to consider hearsay evidence, for example, but evidentiary matters were otherwise left to the arbitrator. Here the arbitrator ruled that in determining whether Cooper had violated Rule II.1, he should not consider evidence not relied on by the employer in ordering the discharge, particularly in a case like this where there was no notice to the employee or the Union prior to the hearing that the Company would attempt to rely on after-discovered evidence. This, in effect, was a construction of what the contract required when deciding discharge cases: an arbitrator was to look only at the evidence before the employer at the time of discharge. As the arbitrator noted, this approach was consistent with the practice followed by other arbitrators.[8] And it was consistent with our observation in *John Wiley & Sons, Inc. v. Livingston*, 376 U.S. 543, 557 (1964), that when the subject matter of a dispute is arbitrable, "procedural" questions which grow out of the dispute and bear on its final disposition are to be left to the arbitrator.

Under the Arbitration Act, the federal courts are empowered to set aside arbitration awards on such grounds only when "the arbitrators were guilty of misconduct . . . in refusing to hear evidence pertinent and material to the controversy." If we apply that same standard here and assume that the arbitrator erred in refusing to consider the disputed evidence, his error was not in bad faith or so gross as to amount to affirmative

8. Labor arbitrators have stated that the correctness of a discharge "must stand or fall upon the reason given at the time of discharge," see, e.g., West Va. Pulp & Paper Co., 10 Lab.Arb. 117, 118 (1947), and arbitrators often, but not always, confine their considerations to the facts known to the employer at the time of the discharge.

misconduct.[10] Finally, it is worth noting that putting aside the evidence about the marijuana found in Cooper's car during this arbitration did not forever foreclose the Company from using that evidence as the basis for a discharge.

Even if it were open to the Court of Appeals to have found a violation of Rule II.1 because of the marijuana found in Cooper's car, the question remains whether the court could properly set aside the award because in its view discharge was the correct remedy. Normally, an arbitrator is authorized to disagree with the sanction imposed for employee misconduct. In *Enterprise Wheel,* for example, the arbitrator reduced the discipline from discharge to a 10–day suspension. The Court of Appeals refused to enforce the award, but we reversed, explaining that though the arbitrator's decision must draw its essence from the agreement, he "is to bring his informed judgment to bear in order to reach a fair solution of a problem. *This is especially true when it comes to formulating remedies.*" The parties, of course, may limit the discretion of the arbitrator in this respect; and it may be, as the Company argues, that under the contract involved here, it was within the unreviewable discretion of management to discharge an employee once a violation of Rule II.1 was found. But the parties stipulated that the issue before the arbitrator was whether there was "just" cause for the discharge, and the arbitrator, in the course of his opinion, cryptically observed that Rule II.1 merely listed causes for discharge and did not expressly provide for immediate discharge. Before disposing of the case on the ground that Rule II.1 had been violated and discharge was therefore proper, the proper course would have been remand to the arbitrator for a definitive construction of the contract in this respect.

C

The Court of Appeals did not purport to take this course in any event. Rather, it held that the evidence of marijuana in Cooper's car required that the award be set aside because to reinstate a person who had brought drugs onto the property was contrary to the public policy "against the operation of dangerous machinery by persons under the influence of drugs or alcohol." We cannot affirm that judgment.

A court's refusal to enforce an arbitrator's award under a collective-bargaining agreement because it is contrary to public policy is a specific application of the more general doctrine, rooted in the common law, that a court may refuse to enforce contracts that violate law or public policy. *W.R. Grace & Co. v. Rubber Workers,* 461 U.S. 757, 766 (1983). That doctrine

10. Even in the very rare instances when an arbitrator's procedural aberrations rise to the level of affirmative misconduct, as a rule the court must not foreclose further proceedings by settling the merits according to its own judgment of the appropriate result, since this step would improperly substitute a judicial determination for the arbitrator's decision that the parties bargained for in the collective-bargaining agreement. Instead, the court should simply vacate the award, thus leaving open the possibility of further proceedings if they are permitted under the terms of the agreement. The court also has the authority to remand for further proceedings when this step seems appropriate. See [FAA] § 10(e).

derives from the basic notion that no court will lend its aid to one who founds a cause of action upon an immoral or illegal act, and is further justified by the observation that the public's interests in confining the scope of private agreements to which it is not a party will go unrepresented unless the judiciary takes account of those interests when it considers whether to enforce such agreements. In the common law of contracts, this doctrine has served as the foundation for occasional exercises of judicial power to abrogate private agreements.

In *W.R. Grace,* we recognized that "a court may not enforce a collective-bargaining agreement that is contrary to public policy," and stated that "the question of public policy is ultimately one for resolution by the courts." We cautioned, however, that a court's refusal to enforce an arbitrator's interpretation of such contracts is limited to situations where the contract as interpreted would violate "some explicit public policy" that is "well defined and dominant, and is to be ascertained 'by reference to the laws and legal precedents and not from general considerations of supposed public interests.' " In *W.R. Grace,* we identified two important public policies that were potentially jeopardized by the arbitrator's interpretation of the contract: obedience to judicial orders and voluntary compliance with Title VII. We went on to hold that enforcement of the arbitration award in that case did not compromise either of the two public policies allegedly threatened by the award. Two points follow from our decision in *W.R. Grace.* First, a court may refuse to enforce a collective-bargaining agreement when the specific terms contained in that agreement violate public policy. Second, it is apparent that our decision in that case does not otherwise sanction a broad judicial power to set aside arbitration awards as against public policy. Although we discussed the effect of that award on two broad areas of public policy, our decision turned on our examination of whether the award created any explicit conflict with other "laws and legal precedents" rather than an assessment of "general considerations of supposed public interests." At the very least, an alleged public policy must be properly framed under the approach set out in *W.R. Grace,* and the violation of such a policy must be clearly shown if an award is not to be enforced.

As we see it, the formulation of public policy set out by the Court of Appeals did not comply with the statement that such a policy must be "ascertained 'by reference to the laws and legal precedents and not from general considerations of supposed public interests.' " The Court of Appeals made no attempt to review existing laws and legal precedents in order to demonstrate that they establish a "well defined and dominant" policy against the operation of dangerous machinery while under the influence of drugs. Although certainly such a judgment is firmly rooted in common sense, we explicitly held in *W.R. Grace* that a formulation of public policy based only on "general considerations of supposed public interests" is not the sort that permits a court to set aside an arbitration award that was entered in accordance with a valid collective-bargaining agreement.

Even if the Court of Appeals' formulation of public policy is to be accepted, no violation of that policy was clearly shown in this case. In pursuing its public policy inquiry, the Court of Appeals quite properly considered the established fact that traces of marijuana had been found in Cooper's car. Yet the assumed connection between the marijuana gleanings found in Cooper's car and Cooper's actual use of drugs in the workplace is tenuous at best and provides an insufficient basis for holding that his reinstatement would actually violate the public policy identified by the Court of Appeals "against the operation of dangerous machinery by persons under the influence of drugs or alcohol." A refusal to enforce an award must rest on more than speculation or assumption.

In any event, it was inappropriate for the Court of Appeals itself to draw the necessary inference. To conclude from the fact that marijuana had been found in Cooper's car that Cooper had ever been or would be under the influence of marijuana while he was on the job and operating dangerous machinery is an exercise in factfinding about Cooper's use of drugs and his amenability to discipline, a task that exceeds the authority of a court asked to overturn an arbitration award. The parties did not bargain for the facts to be found by a court, but by an arbitrator chosen by them who had more opportunity to observe Cooper and to be familiar with the plant and its problems. Nor does the fact that it is inquiring into a possible violation of public policy excuse a court for doing the arbitrator's task. If additional facts were to be found, the arbitrator should find them in the course of any further effort the Company might have made to discharge Cooper for having had marijuana in his car on company premises. Had the arbitrator found that Cooper had possessed drugs on the property, yet imposed discipline short of discharge because he found as a factual matter that Cooper could be trusted not to use them on the job, the Court of Appeals could not upset the award because of its own view that public policy about plant safety was threatened. In this connection it should also be noted that the award ordered Cooper to be reinstated in his old job or in an equivalent one for which he was qualified. It is by no means clear from the record that Cooper would pose a serious threat to the asserted public policy in every job for which he was qualified.[12]

The judgment of the Court of Appeals is reversed.

So ordered.

■ JUSTICE BLACKMUN, with whom JUSTICE BRENNAN joins, concurring.

I join the Court's opinion, but write separately to underscore the narrow grounds on which its decision rests and to emphasize what it is *not* holding today. In particular, the Court does not reach the issue upon which certiorari was granted: whether a court may refuse to enforce an arbitration award rendered under a collective-bargaining agreement on public

12. We need not address the Union's position that a court may refuse to enforce an award on public policy grounds only when the award itself violates a statute, regulation, or other manifestation of positive law, or compels conduct by the employer that would violate such a law.

policy grounds only when the award itself violates positive law or requires unlawful conduct by the employer. The opinion takes no position on this issue. See n. 12. Nor do I understand the Court to decide, more generally, in what way, if any, a court's authority to set aside an arbitration award on public policy grounds differs from its authority, outside the collective-bargaining context, to refuse to enforce a contract on public policy grounds. Those issues are left for another day.

I agree with the Court that the judgment of the Court of Appeals must be reversed and I summarize what I understand to be the three alternative rationales for the Court's decision:

1. The Court of Appeals exceeded its authority in concluding that the company's discharge of Cooper was proper under the collective-bargaining agreement. The Court of Appeals erred in considering evidence that the arbitrator legitimately had excluded from the grievance process, in second-guessing the arbitrator's factual finding that Cooper had not violated Rule II.1, and in assessing the appropriate sanction under the agreement. Absent its overreaching, the Court of Appeals lacked any basis for disagreeing with the arbitrator's conclusion that there was not "just cause" for discharging Cooper.

2. Even if the Court of Appeals properly considered evidence of marijuana found in Cooper's car and legitimately found a Rule II.1 violation, the public policy advanced by the Court of Appeals does not support its decision to set aside the award. The reinstatement of Cooper would not contravene the alleged public policy "against the operation of dangerous machinery by persons under the influence of drugs or alcohol." The fact that an employee's car contains marijuana gleanings does not indicate that the employee uses marijuana on the job or that he operates his machine while under the influence of drugs, let alone that he will report to work in an impaired state in the future. Moreover, nothing in the record suggests that the arbitrator's award, which gives the company the option of placing Cooper in a job equivalent to his old one, would require Cooper to operate hazardous machinery.

3. The public policy formulated by the Court of Appeals may not properly support a court's refusal to enforce an otherwise valid arbitration award. In *W.R. Grace & Co. v. Rubber Workers,* 461 U.S. 757 (1983), we stated that the public policy must be founded on "laws and legal precedents." The Court of Appeals identified no law or legal precedent that demonstrated an "explicit public policy" against the operation of dangerous machinery by persons under the influence of drugs. Far from being "well defined and dominant," as *W.R. Grace* prescribed, the Court of Appeals' public policy was ascertained merely "from general considerations of supposed public interests." I do not understand the Court, by criticizing the company's public policy formulation, to suggest that proper framing of an alleged public policy under the approach set out in *W.R. Grace* would be sufficient to justify a court's refusal to enforce an arbitration award on public policy grounds. Rather, I understand the Court to hold that such compliance is merely a necessary step if an award is not to be enforced.

It is on this understanding that I join the opinion of the Court.

NOTES AND QUESTIONS

1. In Hill v. Norfolk and Western Ry. Co., 814 F.2d 1192, 1194–95 (7th Cir.1987), Judge Posner wrote that

> As we have said too many times to want to repeat again, the question for decision by a federal court asked to set aside an arbitration award—whether the award is made under the Railway Labor Act, the Taft–Hartley Act, or the United States Arbitration Act—is not whether the arbitrator or arbitrators erred in interpreting the contract; it is not whether they clearly erred in interpreting the contract; it is not whether they grossly erred in interpreting the contract; it is whether they interpreted the contract. * * * A party can complain if the arbitrators don't interpret the contract—that is, if they disregard the contract and implement their own notions of what is reasonable and fair. * * * But a party will not be heard to complain merely because the arbitrators' interpretation is a misinterpretation. Granted, the grosser the apparent misinterpretation, the likelier it is that the arbitrators weren't interpreting the contract at all. But once the court is satisfied that they were interpreting the contract, judicial review is at an end, provided there is no fraud or corruption and the arbitrators haven't ordered anyone to do an illegal act.

In *Hill,* the district court had refused to disturb an award against a discharged employee. Finding that the employee's appeal was "based largely on frivolous grounds," the Seventh Circuit on its own initiative imposed sanctions on his attorney. Judge Posner remarked that "[t]his court has been plagued by groundless lawsuits seeking to overturn arbitration awards * * *. [W]e have said repeatedly that we would punish such tactics, and we mean it." Cf. Miller Brewing Co. v. Brewery Workers Local Union No. 9, 739 F.2d 1159 (7th Cir.1984) ("because there are so few grounds for attacking arbitration awards, it is easy to pronounce most such attacks utterly groundless").

2. Different arbitrators may on different occasions come to hear cases arising under the same collective bargaining agreement, and they may, on identical facts, give opposite or conflicting interpretations of the same contractual provision. In such circumstances a court may well conclude that *neither* award should be vacated, since *each* "draws its essence" from the agreement. E.g., Graphic Arts Int'l Union Local 97–B v. Haddon Craftsmen, Inc., 489 F.Supp. 1088 (M.D.Pa.1979); Consolidation Coal Co. v. United Mine Workers of America, 213 F.3d 404 (7th Cir.2000). Cf. Connecticut Light & Power Co. v. Local 420, Int'l Brotherhood of Elec. Workers, 718 F.2d 14 (2d Cir.1983) (first arbitrator had issued cease and desist order for the future; where both awards could not be implemented, the court must "select that interpretation which most nearly conforms to the intent of the parties").

3. Assume that after the Supreme Court's decision in *Misco,* the employer wishes to discharge Cooper on the ground that it *now* knows marijuana was found in his car on company premises on January 21: Would this be consistent with the arbitral award ordering that the employee be reinstated? See part "II.B." of the Supreme Court's opinion. In a similar case, an employee was discharged for sexual harassment, and the arbitrator ordered reinstatement. The employer acquiesced in the confirmed award and reinstated the employee, but then discharged him *the same day* on the basis of earlier incidents which had come to light after the original termination, but which the arbitrator had refused to consider. The union requested that the employer be held in contempt for attempting to evade the court's order enforcing the award but the district court denied the motion "because it concluded that [the employer] had complied with its order by reinstating [the employee]". The court of appeals affirmed in Chrysler Motors Corp. v. International Union, Allied Industrial Workers of America, 2 F.3d 760 (7th Cir.1993).

Compare United States Postal Service v. National Ass'n of Letter Carriers, 64 F.Supp.2d 633 (S.D.Tex.1999), in which an employee was discharged for committing workers' compensation fraud; the arbitrator, finding a "procedural defect" in the process by which the worker was terminated, ordered reinstatement. The employer then sent a second notice of termination predicated on the same misconduct and began a disciplinary process in an attempt to "cure the procedural defect." The arbitrator determined that the collective bargaining agreement precluded a "collateral attack" on the original award through a second discipline, and the court confirmed this award: The remedy sought by the employer "is analogous to a police department's illegally executing a search warrant, seizing evidence, and on seeing it suppressed, returning the evidence to the apartment, correctly executing the warrant, and attempting to reintroduce it at trial." The worker should not become "a pinata that the government strikes until it gets a 'good' result." Is this case distinguishable from *Chrysler Motors*?

Note: Arbitral Decision–Making and Legal "Rules"

Some years ago a survey of commercial arbitrators found that 80 per cent of the studied arbitrators "thought that they ought to reach their decisions within the context of the principles of substantive rules of law, but almost 90 per cent believed that they were free to ignore these rules whenever they thought that more just decisions would be reached by so doing."[1] The readiness of arbitrators to depart from legal "rules" varies, of course. It will depend in part on the presumed willingness of the parties to allow them to do so, as well as on the presence or absence of attorneys and the arbitrator's own profession and degree of expertness. For example, in the highly informal "Autoline" program administered by the Better Business Bureau, volunteer arbitrators are expressly enjoined not to try to interpret state law or even the language of the automobile manufacturer's warranty. Rather than basing a decision on the fact that a car may be "out

1. Mentschikoff, Commercial Arbitration, 61 Col.L.Rev. 846, 861 (1961).

of warranty," for example, they are told instead to be more "flexible" and to decide only on the basis of the "facts."

At the other end of the spectrum, international commercial contracts regularly contain provisions that stipulate which substantive law the arbitrator is to apply. In international transactions the choice of law is likely to affect any number of questions, from warranty obligations to prejudgment interest, as to which the various national legal systems involved may give radically different answers. Where the parties are of different nationalities they may think it fairer to insure that the transaction is governed by the law of a *third* country, unrelated to either. Another possibility is exemplified by a contract between a German and an English company, where the arbitrators were instructed to apply German law if the English company was the claimant, and English law if the German company was the claimant![2] However, there does exist a familiar alternative in international arbitration. The parties may sometimes expressly provide that the arbitrators shall decide "according to natural justice and equity" or "ex aequo et bono." (The comparable French phrase, rooted in civil law tradition, is that the arbitrators shall act as "*amiables compositeurs.*") The rules of international arbitral institutions such as the ICC make this device available to parties who choose to give the arbitrator such authority, as do the Arbitration Rules promulgated by the United Nations Commission on International Trade Law ("UNCITRAL") for non-administered arbitrations. In what sorts of cases might the parties prefer that their arbitrators proceed on the basis of general "equitable" standards of fairness? In what sorts of cases might they prefer instead that their arbitrators apply a particular body of national law?

The extent to which arbitrators are expected to follow external legal "rules" has given rise to considerable controversy in labor relations cases. The classic statement of the dilemma usually goes like this: Assume that an industrial plant begins Sunday operations; when work crews cannot be filled with volunteers, the employer selects workers for Sunday work on a rotating basis. An employee refuses to work on Sunday for religious reasons; he is discharged and a grievance is filed which proceeds to arbitration. The collective bargaining agreement forbids discharge without "just cause." Title VII of the 1964 Civil Rights Act makes it unlawful for an employer to discriminate on the basis of religion unless he can demonstrate "that he is unable to reasonably accommodate" the employee's religious practices "without undue hardship" on the conduct of his business. How should the arbitrator proceed?

The "orthodox" position among labor arbitrators has been that the arbitrators should adhere to the agreement and "ignore the law." The arbitrator, on this view, is merely:

> the parties' officially designated "reader" of the contract. He (or she) is their joint *alter ego* for the purpose of striking whatever supplementary bargain is necessary to handle the anticipated unanticipated omissions

2. See Kerr, International Arbitration v. Litigation, [1980] J.Bus.Law 164, 172.

of the initial agreement. * * * [T]he arbitrator's mandate is plain: tell the parties (and the courts) what the contract means and let them worry about the legal consequences.[3]

Finding "the law" and interpreting statutes and cases are tasks likely to be beyond the special competence of most arbitrators, whether legally trained or not—beyond, that is, the reasons for which they were chosen by the parties, and beyond the reasons supporting the presumption of arbitrability and the practice of deference to arbitral awards.[4] So the conventional view is that whether an agreement is in accord with the external "law" is "irrelevant";[5] it is a question best "postponed" for later determination by the courts.[6] The fear is frequently expressed that by presuming to decide such questions themselves, arbitrators might actually be inviting closer judicial scrutiny and thus more active judicial intervention in the arbitral process—for professional arbitrators, one of the most menacing of nightmares.

There exist in the literature all sorts of nuanced variations on this "orthodox" view. An exception is usually made for situations where the parties themselves seem to "invite" the arbitrator to decide according to the law: It is, for example, increasingly common to find cases where the parties have expressly tracked the language of a statute in their agreement, or have stipulated that the award must be "consistent with applicable laws" and in such cases it is likely that they will be found to have "necessarily bargained for the arbitrator's interpretation of the law."[7] It may be, though, that this entire subject is of more academic than practical

3. St. Antoine, Judicial Review of Labor Arbitration Awards: A Second Look at *Enterprise Wheel* and its Progeny, 75 Mich.L.Rev. 1137, 1140, 1142 (1977).

4. In a 1975 survey of the members of the National Academy of Arbitrators concerning the arbitration of discrimination cases, only 52% of the respondents indicated that they regularly read labor advance sheets to keep abreast of current developments under Title VII; only 14% indicated that they felt confident they could accurately define basic employment-discrimination terms like "bona fide occupational qualification." (another 30% thought they could make a good "educated guess."). Only 54% of the respondents were attorneys; of the total number of employment discrimination cases heard by the respondents, both parties were represented by counsel in only 53%. Harry Edwards, Arbitration of Employment Discrimination Cases: An Empirical Study, Proceedings, 28th Annual Meeting, Nat'l Academy of Arbitrators 59 (1976).

5. Feller, Arbitration and the External Law Revisited, 37 St. Louis U.L.J. 973, 975 (1993).

6. Meltzer, Ruminations about Ideology, Law and Labor Arbitration, Proceedings, 20th Annual Meeting, Nat'l Academy of Arbitrators 1, 17 n. 40 (1967).

7. American Postal Workers Union v. United States Postal Serv., 789 F.2d 1, 6 (D.C.Cir.1986) (Edwards, J.).

See, e.g., In re GTE North Inc., 113 Lab. Arb. 665, 672 (1999)(contract contained both a non-discrimination clause and a "Conflict with Law" provision; "[f]urthermore, compliance with the ADA can be viewed * * * as a component of 'just cause,' a necessary element for discharge"; "[f]or all these reasons, this Arbitrator is going to address the Union's ADA argument"); In re Los Angeles Community College District, 112 Lab. Arb. 733, 738 (1999)(employer agreed "to comply with all federal * * * laws regarding nondiscrimination"; "[I]t becomes, then, the Arbitrator's unenviable task to decide the matter, even if it presents a novel issue under the ADA not previously settled by the courts").

interest. The paradigm case—where both law and agreement are clear and irreconcilably in conflict—will not often arise. There is usually plenty of room to reinterpret the agreement in light of the arbitrator's understanding of the requirements of the external law, and most arbitrators can be expected to deploy adequate resourcefulness to avoid any contradiction.[8]

After an arbitral award has been handed down, the *Misco* case clearly teaches that the arbitrator should not be treated as a sort of "lower court": A court will not decline enforcement of an award merely because the arbitrator has decided the case differently from the way a trial judge would. For over a century the cases have been full of reminders to this effect:

> If an arbitrator makes a mistake either as to law or fact, it is the misfortune of the party, and there is no help for it. There is no right of appeal, and the court has no power to revise the decisions of "judges who are of the parties' own choosing."[9]

Of course, in thinking about judicial review on matters of "law" we should distinguish between mere rules of construction, which come into play in the absence of a contrary agreement, and mandatory rules. After all, most "rules" of contract or commercial law are nothing more than "gap-fillers." They supply a term where the parties have not expressly supplied one themselves; modern commercial law looks in particular to industry custom and course of dealing to furnish the "framework of common understanding controlling any general rules of law which hold only when there is no such understanding."[10] But where the parties have bargained for dispute resolution through arbitration, the method *they* have chosen to fill any gaps in the agreement is the arbitrator's interpretation. His interpretation *is* their bargain. In contrast, legal "rules" in other areas may reflect stronger and overriding governmental or societal interests. In such cases, obviously, some greater degree of arbitral deference should be expected.

In addition, the whole subject of assuring compliance with legal "rules" can often take on an air of unreality. This is particularly true in the commercial area. The obvious lesson of innumerable commercial arbitration cases is that lack of a reasoned opinion will help to insulate an award from judicial scrutiny. Consider, for example, Stroh Container Co. v. Delphi Industries, Inc., 783 F.2d 743 (8th Cir.1986). In confirming an award in this contract dispute, the court first considered whether §§ 10 and 11 of the FAA were the exclusive grounds on the basis of which an award could be vacated or modified:

8. For a recent review of the controversy—and a demonstration that "the debate is narrower than it first appears"—see Laura Cooper, Dennis Nolan, & Richard Bales, ADR in the Workplace 153–180 (2000).

9. Patton v. Garrett, 116 N.C. 847, 21 S.E. 679, 682–83 (1895).

10. UCC § 1–205 comment 4; see also §§ 1–102(3), (4).

Some courts * * * have suggested that an award may be set aside if it is in "manifest disregard of the law," is completely irrational in that it fails to draw its "essence" from the agreement, or contravenes a deeply rooted public policy. * * *

We need not decide, however, whether to adopt any of these exceptions since, under any one of them, the award must nevertheless be affirmed. * * * [N]either the award itself nor the record before us suggests that the arbitrators in any way manifestly disregarded the law in reaching their decision. In Wilko v. Swan, 346 U.S. 427, 436 (1953), the Court carefully distinguished an arbitrator's interpretation of the law, which is insulated from review, from an arbitrator's disregard of the law, which may open the door for judicial scrutiny. Further, such disregard must "be made clearly to appear," and may be found "when arbitrators understand and correctly state the law, but proceed to disregard the same." In the case before us, the arbitrators' decision does not clearly delineate the law applied, nor expound the reasoning and analysis used. Rather, the award presents, as the district court stated, "only a cursory discussion of what the arbitrators considered to be the key points underlying the award." It therefore cannot be said that it clearly appears that the arbitrators identified applicable law and proceeded to reach a contrary position in spite of it. Nor does the absence of express reasoning by the arbitrators support the conclusion that they disregarded the law. Arbitrators are not required to elaborate their reasoning supporting an award, and to allow a court to conclude that it may substitute its own judgment for the arbitrator's whenever the arbitrator chooses not to explain the award would improperly subvert the proper functioning of the arbitral process.

See also Perini Corp. v. Greate Bay Hotel & Casino, Inc., 129 N.J. 479, 610 A.2d 364 (1992). In this case one of the judges noted that "after four years and sixty-four days, the arbitrators simply awarded $14 million to [the plaintiff] without any explanation whatsoever other than a finding that [the defendant] had 'failed to properly perform its obligations as construction manager pursuant to the contract * * *.' There are no reasons, no findings of fact, no conclusions of law, nothing other than the foregoing. For all we know, the arbitrators concluded that the sun rises in the west, the earth is flat, and damages have nothing to do with the intentions of the parties or the foreseeability of the consequences of a breach." 129 N.J. at 534–35, 610 A.2d at 392 (Wilentz, C.J., concurring). The award was confirmed.

Alan Rau, Contracting Out of the Arbitration Act, 8 American Review of International Arbitration 225 (1997)

The parties to an international joint venture agreed to arbitration to be held under ICC Rules in San Francisco. Under the terms of their arbitration clause, the arbitration panel was instructed to issue a written award that was to include "detailed findings of fact and conclusions of law"; the federal district court for the Northern District of California could then:

> vacate, modify or correct any award (i) based upon any of the grounds referred to in the Federal Arbitration Act, (ii) where the arbitrators' findings of fact are not supported by substantial evidence, or (iii) where the arbitrators' conclusions of law are erroneous.

An award was ultimately rendered, but the district court resolutely refused to look into the arbitrators' findings of fact or conclusions of law: It found that its "options" were "limited" by the provisions of the FAA "and may not be extended by agreement of the parties." "The role of the federal courts cannot be subverted to serve private interests at the whim of contracting parties." So the court restricted its inquiry to the "permissible statutory grounds" found in § 10 of the Act, and summarily confirmed the award. The arbitrators had not "exceeded their powers." While they had indeed—as instructed—applied at least some version of California law, they were hardly required to apply California law "without error."

* * *

This [is] the celebrated case of *Lapine Technology Corp. v. Kyocera Corp.* And to no-one's particular surprise, I think, the court of appeals soon reversed, remanding "for review of the decision by use of the agreed-to standard."[4] The Ninth Circuit thereby [committed itself] to the proposition that precisely how "binding" an award is to be is a matter for the parties themselves to determine.

I must say that I have been astonished at the extent to which this issue seems to have excited the attention of the arbitration community. It might, then, not be out of place for me to say just why I think the Ninth Circuit is so clearly right. Had it not been for the strong differences of opinion that *Kyocera* has evoked, I would have thought that the case deserved to be relegated to some routine and workmanlike set of continuing legal education materials, mentioned in passing as one more minor but interesting corollary to everything that we have known for a long time.

* * *

II. WHAT IS THE POINT OF § 10?

It seems symptomatic of a particularly rigid cast of mind to assume that where the arbitration statute allocates certain powers to a court, then—by that very fact—any *contractual re-allocation* by the parties themselves must necessarily be forbidden. Section 3 of the FAA, for example, tells us that before staying litigation, the court must be "satisfied that the issue involved in such suit or proceeding is referable to arbitration." Are we really and truly required to conclude from this that the courts have "exclusive jurisdiction" to determine whether an arbitration clause covers

4. 130 F.3d 884, 891 (9th Cir.1997).

a particular dispute—even *though the parties themselves* may have agreed to entrust this question of "arbitrability" to the arbitrator? The Supreme Court has sensibly indicated that the answer to this question is "no"[25]—that is, that the statute's default allocation of authority *between courts and arbitrators* need not implicate in any way the power of the *parties themselves* to structure the arbitration mechanism so as to advance their own interests.

Similarly, §§ 9 and 10 of the Act direct courts to confirm awards unless certain specified grounds for *vacatur* are present; the "merits"—that is, arbitral determinations of fact and interpretations of law—are not reviewable, being presumably left to the arbitrators. Are we really and truly required to conclude from this that *the parties themselves* may not entrust to courts—rather than to the arbitrators—the final authority to decide legal and factual questions? Must we conclude [as some commentators have argued] that giving effect to such an agreement would constitute a "patent violation" of the Act? Presented with such an assertion—and with no attempt at a functional or purposive reading of the statute—the diagnosis seems justified that we are in the presence of that most common of legal ailments, "hardening of the categories."

By contrast, I have always thought that the principal purpose of § 10 of the FAA—and for that matter, of equivalent provisions found in all modern arbitration laws—is rather to insulate from parochial or intrusive judicial review awards *that the parties intended in the usual sense to be binding*. That is, § 10 serves to assure the parties to an arbitral proceeding that they need not fear an officious or meddlesome inquiry into the merits which would impair the efficacy of the arbitral process for them. But such a purpose has nothing at all, as far as I can see, to do with the situation where the parties are eager to depart from the protective rule of § 10. It is one thing to say that their awards must have legal currency in accordance with the parties' presumed wishes; it is something totally different to say that their awards *will* have this currency, by God, over the parties' expressed wishes to the contrary. I should think that such interference with private autonomy would have to be justified—and on other than paternalistic grounds.

It is in this sense then that I see the provisions of § 10, not as an imperative command of public policy, but as no more than a set of "default rules" intended to reflect the traditional historical understanding concerning the binding effect of arbitral awards. Like any default rules, these supply a ready-made stock of implied terms, allocating the burden of being explicit and chosen at least in part to mirror the "hypothetical bargain" that the parties are assumed to have intended. And so whatever we can

25. *See* First Options of Chicago, Inc. v. Kaplan, 514 U.S. 938, 943, 115 S.Ct. 1920, 131 L.Ed.2d 985 (1995)(the question "who has the primary power to decide arbitrability" "turns upon what the parties agreed about that matter"; if the parties agreed to submit the arbitrability question to arbitration, "then the court's standard for reviewing the arbitrator's decision about that matter should not differ from the standard courts apply when they review any other matter that parties have agreed to arbitrate").

characterize as a "default rule" may naturally be varied by an express agreement of the parties, who may stray in the direction of expanding the statutory grounds of review—or even, perhaps, in the direction of restricting them still further.

Since a default rule is no more than a rebuttable presumption—the mere beginning of the inquiry—it by definition grants the ultimate power of decisionmaking to the parties rather than to the State. * * * Now it is of course entirely a separate question whether § 10 represents the *most desirable background* rule to govern arbitral determinations of "legal" issues. The arbitration law of England, for example, adopts more or less the opposite presumption: Judicial review for errors of law is possible, at least with leave of the court, unless the parties expressly exclude it.[33] But the English legislation at least demonstrates that it is plausible to treat this issue as I am suggesting it should be treated—as the search for the appropriate presumption—and for the moment, the default rule of § 10 is the only default rule we have.

III. ARBITRABILITY AND COMPARATIVE ADVANTAGE

It is at least plausible to say—it is, after all, a proposition of some antiquity—that arbitration has its greatest utility in providing expert determinations of contested matters of fact (such as the "determination of the quality of a commodity or the amount of money due under a contract").[34] By contrast, the legitimacy of the arbitration process—and any comparative advantage that it may possess over litigation—may be weakest when arbitrators attempt to follow national courts in laying down disputed legal norms. In fact such a judgment once reflected our dominant view of arbitration, and presumably explains the traditional reluctance of courts in

33. *See* Arbitration Act 1996 (1996 c.23) § 69.

In the *absence* of an exclusion agreement, the right to appeal on questions of law is generally discretionary with the court. But note that under the English Arbitration Act no leave of court is necessary if all the parties agree to such an appeal. And such an "agreement" for appeal may be contained in a predispute arbitration clause, or even in "rules incorporated into that clause;" *see* David St. John Sutton et al., Russell on Arbitration 428 & n.14 (21st ed. 1997). In that respect at least the English regime is not too different from what was approved by the Ninth Circuit in *Kyocera*.

34. Wilko v. Swan, 346 U.S. 427, 435, 74 S.Ct. 182, 98 L.Ed. 168 (1953). *See* also Philip G. Phillips, *Rules of Law or Laissez–Faire in Commercial Arbitration,* 47 Harv. L. Rev. 590, 599–600, 626 (1934)("the attention of business has been on arbitration as an escape from the jury method of fact determination and not as an escape from substantive law"); Paul L. Sayre, *Development of Commercial Arbitration Law,* 37 Yale L. J. 595, 615 (1928)(the "full usefulness of arbitration lies" in making it serve as a substitute for the preliminary stages of a court trial; "arbitration works much more cheaply and quickly when the arbitrators confine themselves to their specialty, that of passing on technical questions of fact in modem business"); Julius Henry Cohen & Kenneth Dayton, *The New Federal Arbitration Law,* 12 Va. L. Rev. 265, 281 (1926)("[n]ot all questions arising out of contracts ought to be arbitrated;" arbitration "is a remedy peculiarly suited to the disposition of the ordinary disputes between merchants as to questions of fact—quantity, quality, time of delivery, compliance with terms of payment, excuses for non-performance, and the like") * * *.

decisions like *Wilko v. Swan,*[35] or *Alexander v. Gardner–Denver,*[36] to defer to arbitrators—or even to find arbitration permissible—in cases where the decisionmaker was called upon to interpret and apply regulatory legislation.

Now of course, the law has progressed far beyond the stage where the competence of arbitrators to decide difficult "legal" questions was systematically doubted—and cases like *Wilko*, as restrictions on the arbitral process in the name of "public policy," are long dead. But might not *the parties themselves*—who are, after all, the ultimate consumers of the process—still reasonably adopt the same attitude in individual cases?

I am at a loss to understand why parties to commercial transactions should ever be compelled to adopt one unitary model of arbitration—making judicial oversight of awards, for example, into a Procrustean bed to which the parties must adapt themselves even at the cost of amputated limbs. But that is precisely what it means to assert that once parties choose arbitration, they must necessarily accept arbitral determinations on all "legal issues." * * *

I had always assumed it to be a commonplace that parties to a contract are able—and indeed, should be encouraged—to tailor the scope of "arbitrable issues" to fit their own particular needs, circumstances, or desires. The ability to do this is in fact one of the principal selling points of the arbitration process: As the prophets of private ordering suggested long ago, arbitration is in this respect "the parties' dream."[39] The parties are free, as the Supreme Court wrote in *Volt,* "to structure their arbitration agreements as they see fit. Just as they may limit by contract the issues which they will arbitrate, so too may they specify by contract the rules under which that arbitration will be conducted." So, for example, they are free, if they think it advisable, to:

- draw a distinction between disputes over fees "due and owing" under a distributorship agreement, and disputes over alleged copyright and trademark infringement—and choose to arbitrate only the former;[41] * * *

35. Wilko v. Swan, 346 U.S. 427, 437, 74 S.Ct. 182, 98 L.Ed. 168 (1953)("the protective provisions of the Securities Act require the exercise of judicial direction to fairly assure their effectiveness").

36. Alexander v. Gardner–Denver Co., 415 U.S. 36, 56–57, 94 S.Ct. 1011, 39 L.Ed.2d 147 (1974)(employee's statutory right to trial under Title VII of the Civil Rights Act of 1964 is not foreclosed by prior submission of his claim to arbitration under arbitration clause in collective bargaining agreement; "[a]rbitral procedures, while well suited to the resolution of contractual disputes, make arbitration a comparatively inappropriate forum for the final resolution of rights created by Title VII";"the specialized competence of arbitrators pertains primarily to the law of the shop, not the law of the land"). [See pp. 192–193 infra].

39. Henry M. Hart, Jr. & Albert M. Sacks, The Legal Process: Basic Problems in the Making and Application of Law 310 (1994 ed.). [See also pp. 238–239 infra].

41. Zenger–Miller, Inc. v. Training Team, GmbH, 757 F.Supp. 1062 (N.D.Cal. 1991); *see also* Coady v. Ashcraft & Gerel, 996 F.Supp. 95, 98, 109 (D.Mass.1998)(employment agreement provided for arbitration of "any ambiguities or questions of interpretation of this contract"; held, claim of breach of fiduciary duty is not subject to arbitration

- draw a distinction between disputes over past breaches of contract, and disputes relating to future adjustments of the contract—and choose to arbitrate only the former.

Certain well-established "rules" of arbitration law are also in essence little more than background presumptions, which the parties may vary by redefining in their contract the scope of arbitrable issues. So, for example, the parties may:

- draw a distinction between disputes over breach of contract and disputes alleging fraudulent inducement of the contract—and choose to arbitrate only the former, thereby reversing the default rule of *Prima Paint*[44] * * *.
- Now, given this familiar background, is it not understandable that the parties—relying here on hoary considerations of comparative advantage—might choose to draw a distinction between "any unresolved questions of fact" and "questions of law"? If they do so, they may prefer to draft an arbitration clause by which they agree to submit only the former to arbitration—thereby entrusting factual determinations to arbitrators chosen specifically for that purpose, while *withholding* from their arbitrators the power to make ultimate determinations of "legal" issues.

Would this not, in fact, be just one more example of the unremarkable, everyday practice by which parties "agree to submit to arbitration only some of the disputes that may arise between them"? The contract in *Kyocera* might then be understood simply as an attempt to limit the scope of authority of the arbitrators and to carve out a particular class of disputes as "arbitrable": And from this point of view, the Ninth Circuit's decision becomes nothing more than a natural corollary of a half-dozen or more cases in which the Supreme Court's "presumption of arbitrability" left abundant room for an inquiry into whether the parties had agreed on anything to the contrary.

* * *

since "fiduciary duties arise out of agency law and do not depend on any interpretation of the Employment Agreement"); Tracer Research Corp. v. National Environmental Services Co., 42 F.3d 1292, 1295 (9th Cir.1994)(arbitration clause covering "any controversy or claim arising out of this Agreement" refers only to disputes "relating to the interpretation and performance of the contract itself"; tort claim for misappropriation of trade secrets is not arbitrable).

Or they may draw a distinction between disputes over the terms of a charter agreement, and tort disputes arising out of a collision between the vessel and a dock; *see* Texaco, Inc. v. American Trading Transport. Co., Inc., 644 F.2d 1152 (5th Cir.1981).

44. *See* Carro v. Parade of Toys, Inc., 950 F.Supp. 449, 452 (D.P.R.1996) (agreement to arbitrate any dispute arising under this "Purchase Order" reflected "an intent to arbitrate only a limited range of disputes," those "relating to the interpretation and performance of a contract," and did not cover allegations of fraud in the inducement of the entire contract, nor claims for negligent misrepresentation or conversion). * * *

IV. CONTRACTING FOR NON-BINDING ARBITRATION

We can arrive at precisely the same result reached by the Ninth Circuit in *Kyocera* by taking a somewhat different route. While it would be unusual to do so, the parties to an agreement might wish to alter in some respects the binding effect of an arbitral award. * * * [There are cases, for example,] where commercial parties dealing at arm's length have stipulated that their arbitral award shall be completely non-binding. These are the cases where the parties may see the virtues of what is in effect an "advisory opinion" as an aid to evaluating a case for settlement purposes—although they may be unwilling to give up all notion of recourse to litigation. In particular the parties may think that a "trial run" of the case, ending in a prediction by a neutral expert, may cause the more recalcitrant among them to reassess their own partisan estimates of the likely outcome of adjudication. Another object may be for attorneys or management representatives to be able to use the opinion of a third party to "sell" a compromise settlement to reluctant clients or constituents, allowing them to withdraw without loss of face from hardened positions. In this respect "non-binding arbitration" has much in common with other formal "reality testing" devices such as "court-annexed arbitration," the "summary jury trial," the "mini-trial," and fact finding in public-sector employment disputes. The utility of such non-binding evaluative processes has long been recognized, to the point that they have become commonplace and unremarkable remedies in the ADR armamentarium.

Such agreements for non-binding arbitration have been held to be within the Federal Arbitration Act for the purposes of stays or orders to compel under §§ 3 and 4. (The leading case probably remains *AMF Inc. v. Brunswick*,[71] but there are a number of more recent holdings to the same effect.)[72] However, the applicability of the FAA seems to be a question of largely theoretical interest—given the undoubted power of a court to enforce such agreements as a matter of ordinary contract law.[73] A federal court with the requisite jurisdiction over the case would be expected routinely to apply this general corpus of state law—under which compliance with the prescribed arbitration process becomes merely a precondition

71. AMF Inc. v. Brunswick Corp., 621 F.Supp. 456, 458 (E.D.N.Y.1985)(settlement agreement between competitors provided that any future dispute involving an advertised claim of "data based comparative superiority" would be submitted to the National Advertising Division of the Council of Better Business Bureaus "for the rendition of an advisory opinion"). * * *

72. *See* Wolsey, Ltd. v. Foodmaker, Inc., 144 F.3d 1205 (9th Cir.1998)(agreement between franchiser of Jack in the Box restaurants and Hong Kong corporation established a three-step dispute resolution process, in which non-binding arbitration under AAA rules could be followed by litigation in federal court); Kelley v. Benchmark Homes, Inc., 250 Neb. 367, 550 N.W.2d 640, 642–43 (1996)(warranty contract entered into by home buyers provided for arbitration which "shall not be legally binding, but shall be a condition precedent to the commencement of any litigation"). * * *

73. Whether an agreement for non-binding arbitration falls within the FAA can of course have practical, as well as mere "theoretical," significance should a party seek to invoke one of the other procedural provisions of the Act designed to support the arbitration process—e.g., § 5 (court appointment of arbitrator), § 6 (any application to the court to be heard as a motion). * * *

to litigation in accordance with the intention *of* the parties.[74] Should the process fail in its goal of inducing settlement, the court would then of course proceed to hear the case in the usual manner.

From this point of view, then, aren't *Kyocera* and similar cases—which honor the parties' wishes that arbitral determinations of "legal" issues not be binding—merely natural corollaries *of AMF Inc. v. Brunswick?* The thesis that the parries may preserve the right to reject an arbitrator's "conclusions of law" should be fairly unobjectionable, should it not, once one concedes an even broader proposition—that they may preserve the right to a trial *de novo* on *all issues* in the case?

In stark contrast to this analysis, [some distinguished commentators have argued that]:

> Obtaining a resolution of a dispute ... in a speedy and efficient manner provides a compelling reason for limiting the scope of judicial review to the bare essentials needed to afford due process and to protect the state's own interests.... [I]f arbitral awards could be reviewed for errors of law or fact, arbitration would easily degenerate into a device for adding still another instance to the usual three instances of litigation in the ordinary courts.... [P]ermitting contractual modification of the scope of judicial review would undermine the public policy of encouraging arbitration. For it would inexorably cause arbitral awards to be final dispositions to a far lesser extent and thus lessen the social desirability of arbitration.[76]

But I find the argument that parties should not be permitted to alter the binding character of their awards, "because it would impair the efficacy of arbitration," to be extremely troubling. More than anything, it reminds

74. * * * Similar results are reached without difficulty in other cases that do not even consider it necessary to use the word "arbitration." *See, e.g.,* Haertl Wolff Parker, Inc. v. Howard S. Wright Construction Co., 1989 WL 151765 (D.Or.)(parties agreed to submit future disputes to a neutral third party "for a recommendation;" held, claim dismissed "with leave to refile without prejudice if the disputes are not resolved after referral" to the neutral; "the court cannot say that it would be futile to refer the deadlocked issues to him"); DeValk Lincoln Mercury, Inc. v. Ford Motor Co., 811 F.2d 326, 334–38 (7th Cir.1987)(agreement between automobile dealership and manufacturer provided that any claim by the dealer arising out of termination or nonrenewal "shall be appealed" to the company's Dealer Policy Board as "a condition precedent to the Dealer's right to pursue any other remedy;" the company, but not the dealer, "shall be bound by the decision of the Policy Board;" held, because "the mediation (sic) clause demands strict compliance with its requirement of appeal," summary judgment ordered for manufacturer).

76. Hans Smit, *Contractual Modification of the Scope of Judicial Review of Arbitral Awards,* 8 Am. Rev. Int'l Arb. 147, 149, 150 (1997). *See also* Andreas Lowenfeld, *Can Arbitration Coexist with Judicial Review? A Critique of* LaPine v. Kyocera, ADR Currents, Sept. 1998 at pp. 1, 15 ("judicial review of the merits would inevitably prolong the process, negating the expeditiousness that is one of the important advantages of arbitration") * * *.

This has long been a familiar point. Cf. Fudickar v. Guardian Mut. Life Ins. Co., 62 N.Y. 392, 400 (1875)("If courts should assume to judge the decision of arbitrators upon the merits, the value of this method of settling controversies would be destroyed, and an award instead of being a final determination of a controversy would become but one of the steps in its progress").

me of the stereotypical librarian resentful of the whole practice of borrowing books—because the annoying tendency of patrons to do so disrupts the symmetry and orderly appearance of the shelves, and the comforting assurance that everything can always be found in its rightful place.

However, the arbitration process—just like the public library—exists and is designed above all to serve the interests of its users, not those of the guardians of the temple. The Supreme Court has reminded us often enough that "efficiency" is not an ultimate value in arbitration: The overriding goal of the FAA, in the eyes of the Court, is not "to promote the expeditious resolution of claims" but rather to "rigorously enforce agreements to arbitrate"—even though this admittedly "thwarts" our interest in "speedy and efficient decisionmaking." But in any event there is a more fundamental point: It is to the practice of contracting parties—and to that exclusively—that we must look to determine what under the circumstances is efficient *for them*. The quoted argument strikes me as excellent drafting advice—a sage warning to transactional attorneys that inserting into their arbitration agreements a clause of the sort involved in *Kyocera* may be folly.[78] But would it not be just a tad dogmatic to assert that there exist no cases where the parties might ever rationally choose to make a different choice?

So in high-stakes cases I can imagine that a desire to ensure predictability in the application of legal standards, a desire to guard against a "rogue tribunal," or against the distortions of judgment that can often result from the dynamics of tripartite arbitration—may all weigh heavily in the decision to limit by contract the binding effect of an arbitral award. Parties who, through risk aversion or inadequate confidence, have ex *ante* the perspective of a "potential loser" may particularly be impelled in this direction. * * * Similarly, I find it quite plausible to assert that review of awards for "errors of law"—with all the formality and need for reasoned opinions that are likely to come in its wake—is quite likely to impair the ability of arbitrators to "fashion creative solutions"; arbitrators might shun reasonable solutions if they had to worry that courts might not be willing or able to endorse the legal bases on which they rest. Indeed I have argued elsewhere that it is precisely an arbitrator's "freedom from overbroad rules or time-honored categories" that makes possible arbitration's "flexibility in decisionmaking and a maximum attention to context." But in the absence of externalities, here too surely the proper tradeoff is for the parties

78. It is interesting to note, though, that among all the reasons why parties prefer to submit their disputes to arbitration rather than litigation, savings in time and in cost appear—at least in international cases—to be factors of "slight" or even "non-existent" importance, *see* Christian Bühring-Uhle, Arbitration and Mediation in International Business 137–39 (1996). This survey of practitioner attitudes also suggests that the "absence of appeals" is a somewhat "ambivalent" attribute of the arbitration process: For a large number of respondents, this was "crucial for the aim of obtaining a final decision within a reasonable time span"—although "according to some of the practitioners interviewed [the absence of appeals was] seen as a disadvantage since the possibility to correct even grave errors of the arbitral tribunal is very restricted." Id. at 137.

themselves—who may be less enamored of clever and creative solutions than those of us who do not have to live with the practical consequences.

* * *

During oral argument before the Ninth Circuit in *Kyocera,* Judge Kozinski asked pointedly what could account for the sudden popularity of clauses in which the binding effect of awards was restricted: What, he wondered, "was happening in the middle of the 1980's that caused the parties to start drafting arbitration agreements that departed from the standard clause.... [T]here's no case law there, there's no legislation. Suddenly it starts popping up." He didn't receive much of an answer, but the question was certainly a good one.

Reasons for drafting clauses of the sort involved in *Kyocera* have always existed, of course, but in light of a number of developments the moment does indeed seem "right" for lawyers increasingly to resort to them. The blanket assumption of arbitral competence that has in recent years swept whole areas of statutory and regulatory law into arbitration has certainly contributed to a countervailing impulse—the desire to ensure that awards in such cases are not too discordant with "public" jurisprudence. The growing use of custom-tailored arbitration clauses—whether intended to diminish the finality of awards or to increase formality in arbitral procedure—is surely but one manifestation of what is often described and decried as the "judicialization" or "legalization" of arbitration; it is in a sense the natural consequence of the capture of the ADR movement by lawyers intent on remaking all dispute resolution in the image of the courtroom. In international cases, this process has been attributed to an increased involvement on the part of American litigators in transnational arbitration;[142] the habits—and perceived duties—of such litigators, may, it is said, lead them "to push to enlarge the limited means of appeal and therefore expand the control of the courts over private justice."

The increasingly altered appearance of arbitration may also suggest that one of the principal messages of the ADR movement—that parties can experiment with dispute resolution, shaping and adapting different processes to meet their own particular needs—is at last beginning to percolate through the profession. On a more mundane level, the diffusion of information about particular innovations in dispute resolution will inevitably encourage, if not coerce, imitation. * * *

One can expect that it is attorneys least familiar and comfortable with the peculiar nature of arbitration who will be most tempted to tinker with the default rules that govern arbitral finality. Long-term, repeat users will

142. *See* Yves Dezalay & Bryant G. Garth, Dealing in Virtue: International Commercial Arbitration and the Construction of a Transnational Legal Order 33–58 (1996)("Arbitration as Litigation"; electing arbitration, says an American practitioner, "doesn't mean that I necessarily want to give up all the trappings of full-scale litigation and what might come with it"; "[o]ne understands the irritation of the founding fathers confronted by these newcomers who permit themselves to transform the nature of arbitration by multiplying the incidents of procedure and technical appeals").

by contrast have the greatest stake in the proper functioning of the system—and will be most likely to understand that combining private justice with judicial oversight of the merits represents some considerable conceptual confusion, certain over time to lessen the potential utility of arbitration to contracting parties. In this sense I am tempted to join Professor Lowenfeld in the hope that what he calls "arbitration plus" "does not catch on" generally.[148] But clearly there will be occasions when limits on the binding effect of an award may be critical to acceptance of the process: For some litigators, I imagine, arbitration will only be tolerated at all with what appears to be the added safeguard of a controlled outcome firmly grounded in "the law." In such cases, the persistent feeling that people will unfailingly make the wrong decisions if allowed to choose for themselves is a poor basis for lawmaking.

NOTES AND QUESTIONS

1. The standard of judicial review of arbitration awards "has taken on various hues and colorations in its formulations," some courts suggesting that awards may be set aside if they are "arbitrary and capricious" or "completely irrational." "Although the differences in phraseology have caused a modicum of confusion, we deem them insignificant. We regard the standard of review undergirding these various formulations as identical, no matter how pleochroic their shadings and what terms of art have been employed to ensure that the arbitrator's decision relies on his interpretation of the contract as contrasted with his own beliefs of fairness and justice. However nattily wrapped, the packages are fungible." Advest, Inc. v. McCarthy, 914 F.2d 6, 9 (1st Cir.1990).

2. One California judge has advised commercial arbitrators that in the event "they feel impelled by some uncontrollable urge, literary fluency, good conscience, or mere garrulousness to express themselves about a case they have tried, the opinion should be a separate document and not part of the award itself." Loew's, Inc. v. Krug (Cal.Super.1953); *quoted in* Sherman, Analysis of Pennsylvania's Arbitration Act of 1980, 43 U.Pitts.L.Rev. 363, 397 n. 94 (1982). Or, as the AAA's Guide for Commercial Arbitrators (1985) puts it, "The obligations to the parties are better fulfilled when the award leaves no room for attack."

3. Section 20(d) of the Revised Uniform Arbitration Act permits a reviewing court to resubmit a case to the arbitrators "to clarify the award," and courts proceeding under the FAA have asserted a similar power to demand "clarification." Such power is occasionally used to determine the effect or scope of an award—to determine just what it was that the arbitrator had in fact decided. See, e.g., Diapulse Corp. of America v. Carba, Ltd., 626 F.2d 1108 (2d Cir.1980) (arbitrator's injunction against sale of competing "similar devices" was not adequately specific as to definition of devices nor as to geographical scope or duration of injunction). But such power is rarely if ever used to compel the arbitrator to explain his reasoning process.

148. Lowenfeld, supra n.76 at 17.

See Sargent v. Paine Webber Jackson & Curtis, Inc., 882 F.2d 529 (D.C.Cir.1989). In this case the arbitrators, without any explanation, had awarded the plaintiffs a fraction of the amount they were claiming. The district court vacated the award and remanded to the arbitrators "for a full explanation of the manner in which damages were computed," reasoning that in order for the court to be able to engage in "meaningful judicial review" the "basis for the calculations underlying the award must be made known." However, the court of appeals reversed. It noted that "the absence of a duty to explain is presumably one of the reasons why arbitration should be faster and cheaper than an ordinary lawsuit"; the interest "in assuring that judgment be swift and economical * * * must generally prevail" over any interest "in rooting out possible error." See also Robbins v. Day, 954 F.2d 679 (11th Cir.1992) ("an arbitration award that only contains a lump sum award is presumed to be correct"; the burden is on the party seeking to overturn the award to refute "every rational basis upon which the arbitrator could have relied"); Container Technology Corp. v. J. Gadsden Pty., Ltd., 781 P.2d 119 (Colo.App.1989) (taking deposition of arbitrators is not permitted if the purpose is to inquire into their "thought processes").

4. Except in the most complex or technical cases, it is not common practice to make a record or transcript of the proceedings in commercial arbitration. See Martin Domke, Commercial Arbitration § 24:07 (rev. ed.). This of course reinforces the absence of a reasoned opinion in making the work of a reviewing court that much more problematical. See House Grain Co. v. Obst, 659 S.W.2d 903 (Tex.App.1983) (in absence of transcript, there was insufficient evidence to support trial court's finding that arbitration award was the result of "such gross mistake as would imply bad faith and failure to exercise honest judgment").

5. A common rationale for deference to arbitration is that the parties have bargained for the judgment of an arbitrator rather than a court to resolve their disputes and that this bargain, once made, should be respected. Might it follow that the scope of judicial review should be broader in arbitrations arising out of "adhesion" contracts? Consider, for example, the arbitration of uninsured motorist claims under standard automobile insurance policies. Is judicial deference due to an arbitrator's award of $500 (one-sixth of funeral expenses) to the widow of a 23–year old man with two children? Such an award was confirmed in In the Matter of the Arbitration of Torano and Motor Vehicle Accident Indemnification Corp., 15 N.Y.2d 882, 258 N.Y.S.2d 418, 206 N.E.2d 353 (1965). A dissenting judge noted that "[i]t is to incongruities of this sort that the critics of arbitration point when they argue that in the long run it is better to leave disposition of litigation with professional judges and not with occasional amateurs."

6. Is even greater judicial deference due to an award in an "interest" arbitration? Why should this be true? See Local 58, Int'l Brotherhood of Elec. Workers v. Southeastern Mich. Chapter, Nat'l Elec. Contractors Ass'n, Inc., 43 F.3d 1026 (6th Cir.1995) (because the arbitrator is "acting as a legislator, fashioning new contractual obligations" rather than "as a judicial officer, construing the terms of an existing agreement and applying them to a particular set of facts").

7. A number of states have enacted statutes that purport to govern international commercial arbitrations (that is, arbitrations arising out of contracts between parties of different nationalities or that envisage performance abroad). Such statutes are patterned after the "Model Law" adopted by UNCITRAL in 1985, and provide—in accordance with the general understanding in international arbitration—that the arbitral tribunal may "decide ex aequo and bono * * * if the parties have expressly authorized it to do so." See, e.g., Cal.Code Civ.Pro. § 1297.284; Tex. Int'l Commercial Arbitration and Conciliation Act, Tex.Civ.Prac. & Rem.Code § 172.251(d). What is the effect of such provisions? Are these statutes not in fact more restrictive than the general practice in American commercial arbitration? After all, isn't it true that when American arbitrators decide *ex aequo et bono,* they "do not think of themselves as doing anything special"? See W. Laurence Craig, William Park, & Jan Paulsson, International Chamber of Commerce Arbitration 110 (3rd ed. 2000); see also Rene David, Arbitration in International Trade 119, 332 (1985).

8. Imagine that you have agreed to act as arbitrator in one of the cases discussed in note 3. Will the process by which you reach a decision be different depending on whether you are obligated to write an opinion which explains and justifies the reasons for your result? In what ways? Consider the following excerpt.

Alan Rau, On Integrity in Private Judging, 14 Arbitration International 115, 146–150 (1998)

It is a familiar enough proposition that an arbitrator's freedom from the need to explain or justify his award is closely linked to his lack of accountability in terms of judicial review: The naked award that is the norm in domestic commercial arbitrations can be explained as much by a desire to insulate decisions from judicial scrutiny as to any desire to avoid the delay or added expense that written opinions would entail. And this tactic of ensuring the finality of arbitration by harnessing Delphic decisions to a hard-to-rebut presumption of validity has been extremely effective. Conversely, one can expect that any attempt to impose reasoned awards on arbitrators will be motivated at least in part by the desire to expand judicial supervision of the process.

For arbitrators as for jurors, our present lack of accountability can be both liberating and intoxicating. And for arbitrators and jurors equally, decisionmaking that is so safe and easy can just as readily lead to lazy and uninformed judgment—where minds have not been concentrated nor strenuous efforts made to question initial impulses.[149] From this point of view,

149. See Christine Cooper, 'Where Are We Going with Gilmer?—Some Ruminations on the Arbitration of Discrimination Claims, 11 St Louis U. Pub. Law. Rev. 203, 219

reasoned opinions can be seen as one means of imposing transparency on the decisionmaking process and in particular, of imposing a certain self-discipline on the decisionmakers themselves. This is the phenomenon in which the judge or arbitrator supposedly finds—at the point where it becomes necessary to turn inclination into reasoned judgment—that it simply "will not write":[150] Forced to think through the implications of his decision, he may in the course of explanation be surprised to find that it is not internally consistent, that it does not take account of all relevant interests, that it overlooks authority or ignores factual complexities. "[W]hen institutional designers have grounds for believing that decisions will systematically be the product of bias, self-interest, insufficient reflection, or simply excess haste, requiring decisionmakers to give reasons may counteract some of these tendencies."[151]

However, one need not be inordinately cynical to suspect that in arbitration, a requirement of reasoned awards would be somewhat less likely to affect outcomes in this way than it would be to serve merely as a challenge to an arbitrator's craftsmanship. It is hard to take issue with the proposition that a mandate to give reasons will "drive out illegitimate reasons when they are the only plausible explanation for particular outcomes"[152]—but surely in most cases we can expect the qualifying phrase to swallow up whatever possible interest inheres in the original claim. Surely an arbitrator obligated to make a reasoned award may be expected to deploy his rhetorical ability, ingenuity, creativity and imagination in articulating the narrowest, the most plausible, or the most conventional rationale for his decision—all in the interest of commanding the acquiescence of the

(1992)(an arbitrator "who is not a professional arbitrator and who knows the scope of judicial review cannot be expected to view the case as seriously as a federal judge who is developing public law"); Margaret Jacobs, "Men's Club: Riding Crop and Slurs: How Wall Street Dealt With a Sex-Bias Case," Wall St J, June 9, 1994, at A 1, A8 (arbitrator in employment discrimination case explained that "[u]sually you see and hear things and you get a feeling, and the decision is based on that").

I think it would be a serious error, though, to underestimate the sobering and disciplining effects on decisionmaking that one sees simply as a result of deliberation on a panel of three arbitrators—especially when the members of the panel are experienced attorneys and businesspeople, willing to invest some care in taking apart the elements of a dispute, and anxious to demonstrate to their colleagues that they have done so.

150. See * * * Frederick Schauer, Giving Reasons, 47 Stan. L. Rev. 633, 652 (1995); see also Rt. Hon. Lord Justice Bingham, Reasons and Reasons for Reasons: Differences Between a Court Judgment and an Arbitration Award, 4 Arb. Int'l 141, 143 (1988) ("I cannot, I hope, be the only person who has sat down to write a judgment, having formed the view that A must win, only to find in the course of composition that there are no sustainable grounds for that conclusion and that on any rational analysis B must succeed").

151. Schauer, supra n. 150 at 657. The CPR's "Non-Administered Arbitration Rules" provide that awards "shall state the reasoning on which the award rests unless the parties agree otherwise," Rule 13.2. In its Commentary, the drafting Committee suggested that it would be "good discipline for arbitrators to require them to spell out their reasoning. Sometimes this process gives rise to second thoughts as to the soundness of the result."

152. Schauer, supra n.150 at 657–58.

disputing parties or a reviewing court.[153] The claim here is not that reasoned opinions must always and necessarily be products of a conscious "Houdini-like manipulation"—when they are not indeed the result of self-deception or rationalization[154]—although this will very often be the case. The point is just that even under the very best of circumstances, the process of crafting reasoned awards will not be congruent with the decision-making process; the award must be an imperfect "reconstruction" after the fact of actual decision, the product of a struggle to marshal arguments in support of the result in such a way that it will "pass without objection in the trade."

European academics and arbitrators, accustomed to reasoned awards as a matter of course, often find it paradoxical that it is only in this country—where a common law, case-based jurisprudence has become so highly developed—that we are so willing to dispense with such opinions from arbitrators. But as with most paradoxes, this observation makes possible a further leap of insight. I should think that it is precisely our common law background that enables us to do this: More particularly, it is precisely because our legal education has so carefully honed the skills of deconstructing judicial opinions, and so laboriously trained us to debunk their explanatory power, that we can no longer believe in the presence of such opinions as an indispensable element of a just decision.

* * *

While reasoned opinions often do not constrain choice as much as we would like to believe, there is also a counter-proposition that may seem somewhat paradoxical—that at the same time they often constrain more than we would think desirable. The case for "naked" awards thus has an important positive as well as a defensive aspect. Here the continual dialectic between "rule-based decisionmaking" on the one hand, and "particularistic decisionmaking" or "case by case optimization" on the other—which lies at the heart of the judicial enterprise—has a particular resonance. When we talk about the arbitrator's freedom from reasoned awards, it will frequently be the case that we are really talking about his freedom from over-broad rules or time-honored categories that might otherwise appear to dictate a result he would prefer to avoid. This is, then, a freedom that makes possible an arbitrator's flexibility in decisionmaking and a maximum attention to context.

Some concrete examples may illustrate the point. Where a buyer has refused to perform under an installment sales contract, an arbitrator's

153. This of course has been a commonplace of Realist insight for some time. See, e.g., Letter from O.W. Holmes, Jr. to Harold Laski, 19 Februarv 1920, in 1 Holmes–Laski Letters 243 (1953) ("I always say in conference that no case can be settled by general propositions, that I will admit any general proposition you like and decide the case either way") * * *.

154. See Scott Altman, Beyond Candor, 89 Mich. L. Rev. 296, 311 (1990) ("Houdini is willing to manipulate. By manipulation, I mean intentionally ignoring what one believes to be the most convincing argument and instead offering legal arguments that one believes to be less strong, while failing to disclose one's reasons for doing so").

decision may award damages to the seller for breach but at the same time relieve the buyer of any further performance. As a teacher of Contracts, I would find it rather difficult to rationalize this result in doctrinal terms—but it may nevertheless make some rough sense in terms of the business situation and the equities of the parties. Or again, a strong claim may be made based on fraud for the rescission of a joint venture agreement; the arbitrators may be sympathetic to the claim but feel that the plaintiff is at least in part responsible for its own dilemma and at least in part to blame for its reliance—and so they may resort to the analogy of "comparative negligence" to reduce its recovery. Here too, lawyer-arbitrators obligated to justify this result in the form of a reasoned opinion might well feel the need to do so in terms of existing contract doctrine: Should they find that they are not in fact up to the task, they would inexorably be led to apply "that most ubiquitous of principles, winner-take-all, which is more typical of a judicial forum."

It has been suggested that a major source of the common law's commitment to an "all-or-nothing bias" has been the "combative aspects of the search for reality in our courts": It is a "reflection of the egocentric dialectic of the adversary system," and of our "fighting instinct." But the prevalence of hard-fought arbitrations suggests that this may give us at best an incomplete account. Perhaps a more satisfactory explanation might be found in the mandate to our courts to rationalize results in written opinions. It is striking that by contrast to the judicial forum, arbitration shares with other processes of private settlement two major characteristics: both a tendency to look for intermediate solutions—responsive to the uniqueness of each dispute—and the absence of any need to justify the outcome.

So a naked award in the cases I mentioned above might appear at first glance to be nothing more than further examples of unprincipled arbitral "compromise". Yet such awards do not readily fit our usual understanding of "compromise" as a response to factual or legal indeterminacy, or as the reflection of an arbitrator's insecurity of tenure, or of his inadequate energy or care. Still less do they strike us as a kind of "formless and unpredictable qadi justice." Lack of a reasoned opinion here may make possible an arbitral decisionmaking which, while departing from the judicial model, is nevertheless infused with attention to such things as commercial understanding, good business practice and notions of honorable behavior, and with practical reasoning from familiar legal norms.[164] And we should remember that private dispute settlement—which lacks any adjudicative dimension whatever—may often work in the same way. In a sense, then, we are returning here to where we began—with the premise that the

164. Cf. Lisa Bernstein, Opting Out of the Legal System: Extralegal Contractual Relations in the Diamond Industry, 21 J. Leg. Stud. 115, 127 (1992)(arbitrators in the diamond industry's arbitration mechanism "explain that they decide complex cases on the basis of trade custom and usage, a little common sense, some Jewish law, and, last, common-law legal principles").

process of arbitration can only be understood in terms of bargain and contract, as part of a private exercise in the planning of transactions.

Note: Judicial Review of Awards and "Public Policy"

At the end of his shift a worker suffered a nervous breakdown; he "flew into a rage," attacked other employees, and damaged company property. He was discharged and later spent 30 days in a hospital psychiatric ward. The arbitrator found that the likelihood of a recurrence was "remote" and that he was "not at fault for his outburst"; the company was ordered to reinstate him. The district court vacated the award, noting "public policy concerns regarding the safety of the workplace." The Court of Appeals reversed, E.I. DuPont de Nemours & Co. v. Grasselli Employees Ind. Ass. of East Chicago, Inc., 790 F.2d 611 (7th Cir.1986). In his concurring opinion, Judge Easterbrook wrote:

> Suppose DuPont's contract expressly excused a single psychotic tantrum, provided the problem was unlikely to recur, or suppose a contract excused a single episode of larceny from the employer. If the firm, honestly implementing its contract with the employees, reinstated the berserker or the thief (or never discharged him), no public policy would stand in the way. If the person's immediate supervisor fired him, and someone higher in the line of command reversed that decision as a result of a grievance, there would be no greater reason for review. A contract of arbitration transfers the power of this manager to the arbitrator. If the arbitrator carries out the contract, the decision should be treated the same as the management's own. Firms may place decisionmaking authority where they please, and the Arbitration Act restricts the court to ascertaining that the arbitrator was a faithful agent of the contracting parties. * * *
>
> [I]f because of potential liability to its workers for having an unsafe working environment no firm would adopt a clause giving a psychotic worker a second chance, an arbitrator who provides a second chance is expressing sympathy, administering home-brewed justice rather than the contract. Public policy may be a useful guide to the sorts of provisions that will not appear in contracts, and when no one will write the provisions expressly arbitrators may not infer them. If a court concludes, however, that the implication of a rule by the arbitrator is not a frolic, that a rational firm could have such a rule and apply it prospectively, then the only further role for public policy is to determine whether the rule violates positive law.

The Supreme Court seems to have adopted Judge Easterbrook's position in Eastern Associated Coal Corp. v. United Mine Workers of America, 531 U.S. 57, 121 S.Ct. 462 (2000). Here a truck driver twice tested positive for marijuana, was twice discharged, and was twice reinstated by arbitrators who found that there was no "just cause" for termination. (The second arbitrator made reinstatement conditional on suspension without pay, participation in a substance abuse program, and continued random drug testing). The employer claimed that "considerations of public policy" made the second award unenforceable, but both the lower courts and the Supreme Court disagreed. Six Justices joined Justice Breyer's opinion:

> In considering this claim, we must assume that the collective-bargaining agreement itself calls for [the employee's] reinstatement. That is because both employer and union have granted to the arbitrator the authority to interpret the meaning of their contract's language, including such words as "just cause." They have "bargained for" the "arbitrator's construction" of their agreement. * * * Hence we must treat the arbitrator's award as if it represented an agreement between [the employer] and the union as to the proper meaning of the contract's words "just cause." For present purposes, the award is not distinguishable form the contractual agreement. * * * To put the question more specifically, does a contractual agreement to reinstate [the employee] with specified conditions run contrary to an explicit, well-defined, and dominant public policy, as ascertained by reference to positive law and not from general considerations of supposed public interests?

In this case, "neither Congress [in the Omnibus Transportation Employee Testing Act of 1991, 49 U.S.C. § 31306(b)(1)(A)] nor the Secretary [of Transportation] has seen fit to mandate the discharge of a worker who twice tests positive for drugs."

NOTES AND QUESTIONS

1. During an overnight layover the "Pilot in Command" of a Delta flight consumed large quantities of alcohol, and when he arrived at the airport the next morning shortly before departure, "[h]is face was very red; his eyes were glassed over; and he appeared to be very disoriented." He nevertheless flew the aircraft between Bangor, Maine and Boston. A later blood test indicated that at the time of the flight his blood alcohol level was .13. The pilot's license was suspended by the FAA, and Delta discharged him. An arbitrator, however, found that the discharge was "without just cause," since Delta had not enforced its alcohol policy "uniformly or fairly" and the pilot, after being discharged, "had pursued a rehabilitation program with effective results." Delta was ordered to reinstate him and to cooperate with him and with the FAA so that he could be relicensed. The court set aside the award: "We emphasize that we have found no state that approves of operation of an aircraft while drunk." Delta Air Lines, Inc. v. Air Line Pilots Ass'n Int'l, 861 F.2d 665 (11th Cir.1988).

An arbitrator concluded that a registered nurse had engaged in "serious substandard nursing practices"—failure to monitor the condition of a four-month old infant admitted to hospital with second-degree burns—and that her conduct had contributed to the baby's death. The arbitrator nevertheless ordered reinstatement, finding that the nurse had not "callously disregarded" the welfare of the patient, and that discharge was "too harsh" a sanction given the nurse's unblemished ten-year record. The court vacated the award: "If the recognized policy favoring optimal health care is to have practical meaning, an otherwise preventable death occasioned by negligence simply must warrant the most severe employment penalty—discharge." "This Court has found no case where reinstatement has been ordered against a public policy argument after a preventable death." Boston Medical Center v. Service Employees Int'l Union, 113 F.Supp.2d 169 (D.Mass.2000).

Is it likely that in these cases the process of labor arbitration—so oriented towards "industrial due process" and the maintenance of good working relations between employer and union—will adequately protect the interests of society generally? How would Judge Easterbrook or Justice Breyer have voted to decide these cases?

2. Stroehmann Bakeries discharged one of its drivers for "immoral conduct while on duty" after a store clerk complained that he had sexually assaulted her when he was making a delivery. The arbitrator found that the driver had been dismissed without just cause, and the employer was ordered to reinstate him with full back pay and benefits. "Considerations referred to by the arbitrator in conjecturing on the matter" included the observation that the victim lacked a social life, had a female roommate, was "unattractive and frustrated," and that she might have fabricated the entire incident in order to "titillate herself and attract her mother's caring attention." The court vacated the award and remanded the matter for a *de novo* hearing before another arbitrator: The arbitrator's "reasoning process, language, tone, considerations, and award violate public policy." "The manner in which the award was reached could easily deter other victims," and the award also "sends a message" to the company's other employees and to the public "that complaints of sexual assault are not treated seriously [or] sensitively." Stroehmann Bakeries, Inc. v. Local 776 Int'l Brotherhood of Teamsters, 762 F.Supp. 1187 (M.D.Pa.1991), aff'd, 969 F.2d 1436 (3d Cir.1992). Cf. Note, Arbitral Decision–Making and Legal "Rules," supra.

3. In an effort to promote the sale of its fighter aircraft to Saudi Arabia, Northrop entered into a "marketing agreement" with Triad. In exchange for commissions on sales, Triad was to act as Northrop's exclusive agent in soliciting contracts for aircraft for the Saudi Air Force. Some of the sales were to be made through the United States Government as a result of contracts between Northrop and the Defense Department. The agreement was to be governed by California law and contained an arbitration clause.

Several years later the Saudi Arabian government issued a decree prohibiting the payment of commissions in connection with armaments contracts, and requiring that existing obligations for the payment of commissions be suspended. Northrop ceased paying commissions and the dispute was submitted to arbitrators, who awarded Triad over $31 million. The district court held that the arbitrator's award was "contrary to law and public policy." California's Civil Code provides that "performance of an obligation" is "excused" when it is "prevented * * * by the operation of law." The court interpreted the Saudi decree as applying to and indeed "formulated specifically with the Northrop–Triad agency relationship in mind." In addition, it noted that the Defense Department "wished to conform its policy precisely to that announced by Saudi Arabia" and was now requiring that arms suppliers under contract to the Department certify that their price included no costs for agent's commissions not approved by the purchasing country.

On appeal, what result? See Northrop Corp. v. Triad Int'l Marketing S.A., 811 F.2d 1265 (9th Cir.1987).

4. Party Yards borrowed $160,000 from Templeton in order to meet production costs and expenses in connection with an important contract. In addition to interest at 18% (the maximum interest rate allowed under state usury laws), Templeton was to receive a "commission" on the gross revenue of all of Party Yard products for a period ending twenty years after Templeton's death. The contract contained an arbitration clause and the lower court ordered arbitration; the court of appeals, however, found "that the trial court's reliance on *Prima Paint* was misplaced because that case is inapplicable": "A party who alleges and offers colorable evidence that a contract is illegal cannot be compelled to arbitrate the threshold issue of the existence of the agreement to arbitrate; only a court can make that determination." "A court's failure to first determine whether the contract violates Florida's usury laws could breathe life into a contract that not only violates state law, but also is criminal in nature, by use of an arbitration provision." Party Yards, Inc. v. Templeton, 751 So.2d 121 (Fla.App.2000).

Do you agree that "the separability doctrine (à la *Prima Paint*) should have insulated the arbitral clause from automatic ricochet invalidity"? World Arb. & Med. Rep., April 2000, at p. 103. See pp. 100–101 (illegality), supra. Cf. Harbour Assurance Co. (UK) Ltd. v. Kansa General Int'l Assurance Co. Ltd., [1993] Q.B. 701, 704 (C.A. 1993)(Hoffmann, L.J.):

> [I]t is particularly necessary to have regard to the purpose and policy of the rule which invalidates the contract and to ask * * * whether the rule strikes down the arbitration clause as well. There may be cases in which the policy of the rule is such that it would be liable to be defeated by allowing the issue to be determined by a tribunal chosen by the parties. This may be especially true of *contrats d'adhésion* in which the arbitrator is in practice the choice of the dominant party. Thus, saying that arbitration clauses, because separable, are never affected by the illegality of the principal contract is as much a case of false logic as saying that they must be.

5. A "weighmaster" at a town landfill was terminated after pleading nolo contendere to the charge of larceny by embezzlement for pocketing daily landfill fees. He purportedly made the decision to enter the plea because he could not afford the legal fees he would incur by contesting the charges at trial. Because the city relied exclusively on the plea, and did not seek to independently prove the charge, an arbitrator found that the city lacked "just cause" for the termination and ordered reinstatement. The court vacated the award on the ground that it "violated the clear public policy against embezzlement," which "encompasses the policy that an employer should not be compelled to reinstate an employee who has been convicted of embezzling the employer's funds, irrespective of whether the conviction followed a trial, a guilty plea or a nolo contendere plea." The employer "is entitled to expect that he be able to trust an employee who is in a position of financial responsibility." Town of Groton v. United Steelworkers of America, 254 Conn. 35, 757 A.2d 501 (2000).

What exactly is the "public policy" implicated here? Is the term being used in the same sense as in the foregoing cases?

6. The United Nations Convention on the Recognition and Enforcement of Foreign Arbitral Awards (the "New York Convention") has been ratified by most important commercial nations, including the United States. See Appendix B. This Convention requires participating states to enforce commercial arbitration awards, rendered in another state, with the same effect as if they were domestic awards (Art. III). There are a number of exceptions to the mandate of Art. III.

See, for example, Art. V(2)(b). American cases have narrowly confined the defense of Art. V(2)(b) to the exceptional situation "where enforcement would violate the forum country's most basic notions of morality and justice." Parsons & Whittemore Overseas Co., Inc. v. Société Générale De l'Industrie Du Papier (RAKTA), 508 F.2d 969, 974 (2d Cir.1974). See also Brandeis Intsel Ltd. v. Calabrian Chemicals Corp., 656 F.Supp. 160 (S.D.N.Y.1987) (defense of "manifest disregard of the law" does not rise to the level of a "public policy" violation within the meaning of Art. V).

b. "PUBLIC POLICY" AND ARBITRABILITY

Mitsubishi Motors Corp. v. Soler Chrysler–Plymouth, Inc.

Supreme Court of the United States, 1985.
473 U.S. 614, 105 S.Ct. 3346, 87 L.Ed.2d 444.

■ JUSTICE BLACKMUN delivered the opinion of the Court.

The principal question presented by these cases is the arbitrability, pursuant to the federal Arbitration Act and the Convention on the Recognition and Enforcement of Foreign Arbitral Awards (Convention), of claims arising under the Sherman Act, 15 U.S.C. § 1 et seq., and encompassed within a valid arbitration clause in an agreement embodying an international commercial transaction.

I

Petitioner-cross-respondent Mitsubishi Motors Corporation (Mitsubishi) is a Japanese corporation which manufactures automobiles and has its principal place of business in Tokyo, Japan. Mitsubishi is the product of a joint venture between, on the one hand, Chrysler International, S.A. ("CISA"), a Swiss corporation registered in Geneva and wholly owned by Chrysler Corporation, and, on the other, Mitsubishi Heavy Industries, Inc., a Japanese corporation. The aim of the joint venture was the distribution through Chrysler dealers outside the continental United States of vehicles manufactured by Mitsubishi and bearing Chrysler and Mitsubishi trademarks. Respondent-cross-respondent Soler Chrysler–Plymouth, Inc. (Soler), is a Puerto Rico corporation with its principal place of business in Pueblo Viejo, Guaynabo, Puerto Rico.

On October 31, 1979, Soler entered into a Distributor Agreement with CISA which provided for the sale by Soler of Mitsubishi-manufactured vehicles within a designated area, including metropolitan San Juan. On the same date, CISA, Soler, and Mitsubishi entered into a Sales Procedure Agreement (Sales Agreement) which, referring to the Distributor Agreement, provided for the direct sale of Mitsubishi products to Soler and governed the terms and conditions of such sales. Paragraph VI of the Sales Agreement, labeled "Arbitration of Certain Matters," provides:

> "All disputes, controversies or differences which may arise between [Mitsubishi] and [Soler] out of or in relation to Articles I–B through V of this Agreement or for the breach thereof, shall be finally settled by arbitration in Japan in accordance with the rules and regulations of the Japan Commercial Arbitration Association."

Initially, Soler did a brisk business in Mitsubishi-manufactured vehicles. As a result of its strong performance, its minimum sales volume, specified by Mitsubishi and CISA, and agreed to by Soler, for the 1981 model year was substantially increased. In early 1981, however, the new-car market slackened. Soler ran into serious difficulties in meeting the expected sales volume, and by the spring of 1981 it felt itself compelled to request that Mitsubishi delay or cancel shipment of several orders. About the same time, Soler attempted to arrange for the transshipment of a quantity of its vehicles for sale in the continental United States and Latin America. Mitsubishi and CISA, however, refused permission for any such diversion, citing a variety of reasons, and no vehicles were transshipped. Attempts to work out these difficulties failed. Mitsubishi eventually withheld shipment of 966 vehicles, apparently representing orders placed for May, June, and July 1981 production, responsibility for which Soler disclaimed in February 1982.

The following month, Mitsubishi brought an action against Soler in the United States District Court for the District of Puerto Rico under the federal Arbitration Act and the Convention.[2] Mitsubishi sought an order to compel arbitration in accord with ¶ VI of the Sales Agreement. Shortly after filing the complaint, Mitsubishi filed a request for arbitration before the Japan Commercial Arbitration Association.

2. The complaint alleged that Soler had failed to pay for 966 ordered vehicles; that it had failed to pay contractual "distress unit penalties," intended to reimburse Mitsubishi for storage costs and interest charges incurred because of Soler's failure to take shipment of ordered vehicles; that Soler's failure to fulfill warranty obligations threatened Mitsubishi's reputation and good will; * * * and that the Distributor and Sales Agreements had expired by their terms or, alternatively, that Soler had surrendered its rights under the Sales Agreement.

Soler denied the allegations and counterclaimed against both Mitsubishi and CISA. It alleged numerous breaches by Mitsubishi of the Sales Agreement, raised a pair of defamation claims, and asserted causes of action under the Sherman Act; the federal Automobile Dealers' Day in Court Act; the Puerto Rico competition statute; and the Puerto Rico Dealers' Contracts Act. In the counterclaim premised on the Sherman Act, Soler alleged that Mitsubishi and CISA had conspired to divide markets in restraint of trade. To effectuate the plan, according to Soler, Mitsubishi had refused to permit Soler to resell to buyers in North, Central, or South America vehicles it had obligated itself to purchase from Mitsubishi; had refused to ship ordered vehicles or the parts, such as heaters and defoggers, that would be necessary to permit Soler to make its vehicles suitable for resale outside Puerto Rico; and had coercively attempted to replace Soler and its other Puerto Rico distributors with a wholly owned subsidiary which would serve as the exclusive Mitsubishi distributor in Puerto Rico.

After a hearing, the District Court ordered Mitsubishi and Soler to arbitrate each of the issues raised in the complaint and in all the counterclaims save two and a portion of a third. [The Court of Appeals agreed that the arbitration clause "encompass[ed] virtually all the claims arising under the various statutes, including all those arising under the Sherman Act."[9] It held, however, that arbitration of Soler's antitrust claims could not be compelled.]

* * *

II

At the outset, we address the contention raised in Soler's cross-petition that the arbitration clause at issue may not be read to encompass the statutory counterclaims stated in its answer to the complaint. In making this argument, Soler does not question the Court of Appeals' application of ¶ VI of the Sales Agreement to the disputes involved here as a matter of standard contract interpretation. Instead, it argues that as a matter of law a court may not construe an arbitration agreement to encompass claims arising out of statutes designed to protect a class to which the party

9. As the Court of Appeals saw it, "[t]he question ... is not whether the arbitration clause mentions antitrust or any other particular cause of action, but whether the factual allegations underlying Soler's counterclaims—and Mitsubishi's bona fide defenses to those counterclaims—are within the scope of the arbitration clause, whatever the legal labels attached to those allegations." * * *

The court read the Sherman Act counterclaim to raise issues of wrongful termination of Soler's distributorship, wrongful failure to ship ordered parts and vehicles, and wrongful refusal to permit transshipment of stock to the United States and Latin America. Because the existence of just cause for termination turned on Mitsubishi's allegations that Soler had breached the Sales Agreement by, for example, failing to pay for ordered vehicles, the wrongful termination claim implicated [several] provisions within the arbitration clause [including]: Article I-D(1), which rendered a dealer's orders "firm" * * * and Article I-F, specifying payment obligations and procedures. The court therefore held the arbitration clause to cover this dispute.

* * *

resisting arbitration belongs "unless [that party] has expressly agreed" to arbitrate those claims, by which Soler presumably means that the arbitration clause must specifically mention the statute giving rise to the claims that a party to the clause seeks to arbitrate. Soler reasons that, because it falls within the class for whose benefit the federal and local antitrust laws and dealers' acts were passed, but the arbitration clause at issue does not mention these statutes or statutes in general, the clause cannot be read to contemplate arbitration of these statutory claims.

We do not agree, for we find no warrant in the Arbitration Act for implying in every contract within its ken a presumption against arbitration of statutory claims. * * *

[T]he first task of a court asked to compel arbitration of a dispute is to determine whether the parties agreed to arbitrate that dispute. The court is to make this determination by applying the "federal substantive law of arbitrability, applicable to any arbitration agreement within the coverage of the Act." And that body of law counsels "that * * * any doubts concerning the scope of arbitrable issues should be resolved in favor of arbitration * * *." Thus, as with any other contract, the parties' intentions control, but those intentions are generously construed as to issues of arbitrability.

There is no reason to depart from these guidelines where a party bound by an arbitration agreement raises claims founded on statutory rights. * * * Of course, courts should remain attuned to well-supported claims that the agreement to arbitrate resulted from the sort of fraud or overwhelming economic power that would provide grounds "for the revocation of any contract." [FAA, § 2]. But, absent such compelling considerations, the Act itself provides no basis for disfavoring agreements to arbitrate statutory claims by skewing the otherwise hospitable inquiry into arbitrability.

That is not to say that all controversies implicating statutory rights are suitable for arbitration. There is no reason to distort the process of contract interpretation, however, in order to ferret out the inappropriate. Just as it is the congressional policy manifested in the federal Arbitration Act that requires courts liberally to construe the scope of arbitration agreements covered by that Act, it is the congressional intention expressed in some other statute on which the courts must rely to identify any category of claims as to which agreements to arbitrate will be held unenforceable. For that reason, Soler's concern for statutorily protected classes provides no reason to color the lens through which the arbitration clause is read. By agreeing to arbitrate a statutory claim, a party does not forego the substantive rights afforded by the statute; it only submits to their resolution in an arbitral, rather than a judicial, forum. It trades the procedures and opportunity for review of the courtroom for the simplicity, informality, and expedition of arbitration. We must assume that if Congress intended the substantive protection afforded by a given statute to include protection against waiver of the right to a judicial forum, that intention will be deducible from text or legislative history. Having made the bargain to arbitrate, the party should be held to it unless Congress itself has evinced an intention to preclude a waiver of judicial remedies for the statutory rights at issue. Nothing, in the meantime, prevents a party from excluding statutory claims from the scope of an agreement to arbitrate.

In sum, the Court of Appeals correctly conducted a two-step inquiry, first determining whether the parties' agreement to arbitrate reached the statutory issues, and then, upon finding it did, considering whether legal constraints external to the parties' agreement foreclosed the arbitration of those claims. We endorse its rejection of Soler's proposed rule of arbitration-clause construction.

III

We now turn to consider whether Soler's antitrust claims are nonarbitrable even though it has agreed to arbitrate them. In holding that they are not, the Court of Appeals followed the decision of the Second Circuit in *American Safety Equipment Corp. v. J.P. Maguire & Co.,* 391 F.2d 821 (1968). Notwithstanding the absence of any explicit support for such an exception in either the Sherman Act or the federal Arbitration Act, the Second Circuit there reasoned that "the pervasive public interest in enforcement of the antitrust laws, and the nature of the claims that arise in such cases, combine to make ... antitrust claims ... inappropriate for arbitration." We find it unnecessary to assess the legitimacy of the *American Safety* doctrine as applied to agreements to arbitrate arising from domestic transactions. As in *Scherk v. Alberto–Culver Co.,* 417 U.S. 506 (1974), we conclude that concerns of international comity, respect for the capacities of foreign and transnational tribunals, and sensitivity to the need of the international commercial system for predictability in the resolution of disputes require that we enforce the parties' agreement, even assuming that a contrary result would be forthcoming in a domestic context.

* * *

[The Court in *Scherk*] Court emphasized:

> "A contractual provision specifying in advance the forum in which disputes shall be litigated and the law to be applied is ... an almost indispensable precondition to achievement of the orderliness and predictability essential to any international business transaction....
>
> "A parochial refusal by the courts of one country to enforce an international arbitration agreement would not only frustrate these purposes, but would invite unseemly and mutually destructive jockeying by the parties to secure tactical litigation advantages.... [It would] damage the fabric of international commerce and trade, and imperil the willingness and ability of businessmen to enter into international commercial agreements."

* * *

Thus, we must weigh the concerns of *American Safety* against a strong belief in the efficacy of arbitral procedures for the resolution of international commercial disputes and an equal commitment to the enforcement of freely negotiated choice-of-forum clauses.

At the outset, we confess to some skepticism of certain aspects of the *American Safety* doctrine. As distilled by the First Circuit, the doctrine comprises four ingredients. First, private parties play a pivotal role in aiding governmental enforcement of the antitrust laws by means of the private action for treble damages. Second, "the strong possibility that contracts which generate antitrust disputes may be contracts of adhesion militates against automatic forum determination by contract." Third, antitrust issues, prone to complication, require sophisticated legal and economic analysis, and thus are "ill-adapted to strengths of the arbitral process, i.e., expedition, minimal requirements of written rationale, simplicity, resort to basic concepts of common sense and simple equity." Finally, just as "issues of war and peace are too important to be vested in the generals, . . . decisions as to antitrust regulation of business are too important to be lodged in arbitrators chosen from the business community—particularly those from a foreign community that has had no experience with or exposure to our law and values."

Initially, we find the second concern unjustified. The mere appearance of an antitrust dispute does not alone warrant invalidation of the selected forum on the undemonstrated assumption that the arbitration clause is tainted. A party resisting arbitration of course may attack directly the validity of the agreement to arbitrate. See *Prima Paint Corp.* Moreover, the party may attempt to make a showing that would warrant setting aside the forum-selection clause—that the agreement was "[a]ffected by fraud, undue influence, or overweening bargaining power"; that "enforcement would be unreasonable and unjust"; or that proceedings "in the contractual forum will be so gravely difficult and inconvenient that [the resisting party] will for all practical purposes be deprived of his day in court." But absent such a showing—and none was attempted here—there is no basis for assuming the forum inadequate or its selection unfair.

Next, potential complexity should not suffice to ward off arbitration. We might well have some doubt that even the courts following *American Safety* subscribe fully to the view that antitrust matters are inherently insusceptible to resolution by arbitration, as these same courts have agreed that an undertaking to arbitrate antitrust claims entered into after the dispute arises is acceptable. And the vertical restraints which most frequently give birth to antitrust claims covered by an arbitration agreement will not often occasion the monstrous proceedings that have given antitrust litigation an image of intractability. In any event, adaptability and access to expertise are hallmarks of arbitration. The anticipated subject matter of the dispute may be taken into account when the arbitrators are appointed, and arbitral rules typically provide for the participation of experts either employed by the parties or appointed by the tribunal. Moreover, it is often a judgment that streamlined proceedings and expeditious results will best serve their needs that cause parties to agree to arbitrate their disputes; it is typically a desire to keep the effort and expense required to resolve a dispute within manageable bounds that prompts them mutually to forgo access to judicial remedies. In sum, the factor of potential complexity alone does not persuade us that an arbitral tribunal could not properly handle an antitrust matter.

For similar reasons, we also reject the proposition that an arbitration panel will pose too great a danger of innate hostility to the constraints on business conduct that antitrust law imposes. International arbitrators frequently are drawn from the legal as well as the business community; where the dispute has an important legal component, the parties and the arbitral body with whose assistance they have agreed to settle their dispute can be expected to select arbitrators accordingly.[18] We decline to indulge the presumption that the parties and arbitral body conducting a proceeding will be unable or unwilling to retain competent, conscientious, and impartial arbitrators.

We are left, then, with the core of the *American Safety* doctrine—the fundamental importance to American democratic capitalism of the regime of the antitrust laws. Without doubt, the private cause of action plays a central role in enforcing this regime. As the Court of Appeals pointed out:

> "A claim under the antitrust laws is not merely a private matter. The Sherman Act is designed to promote the national interest in a competitive economy; thus, the plaintiff asserting his rights under the Act has been likened to a private attorney-general who protects the public's interest."

The treble-damages provision wielded by the private litigant is a chief tool in the antitrust enforcement scheme, posing a crucial deterrent to potential violators.

The importance of the private damages remedy, however, does not compel the conclusion that it may not be sought outside an American court. Notwithstanding its important incidental policing function, the treble-damages cause of action conferred on private parties by § 4 of the Clayton Act, and pursued by Soler here by way of its third counterclaim, seeks primarily to enable an injured competitor to gain compensation for that injury.

> "Section 4 ... is in essence a remedial provision. It provides treble damages to '[a]ny person who shall be injured in his business or property by reason of anything forbidden in the antitrust laws....' Of course, treble damages also play an important role in penalizing

18. * * * [T]he arbitration panel selected to hear the parties' claims here is composed of three Japanese lawyers, one a former law school dean, another a former judge, and the third a practicing attorney with American legal training who has written on Japanese antitrust law.

The Court of Appeals was concerned that international arbitrators would lack "experience with or exposure to our law and values." The obstacles confronted by the arbitration panel in this case, however, should be no greater than those confronted by any judicial or arbitral tribunal required to determine foreign law. See, e.g., Fed.Rule Civ.Proc. 44.1. Moreover, while our attachment to the antitrust laws may be stronger than most, many other countries, including Japan, have similar bodies of competition law.

wrongdoers and deterring wrongdoing, as we also have frequently observed.... It nevertheless is true that the treble-damages provision, which makes awards available only to injured parties, and measures the awards by a multiple of the injury actually proved, is designed primarily as a remedy." *Brunswick Corp. v. Pueblo Bowl-O-Mat, Inc.*, 429 U.S. 477, 485–486 (1977).

* * *

There is no reason to assume at the outset of the dispute that international arbitration will not provide an adequate mechanism. To be sure, the international arbitral tribunal owes no prior allegiance to the legal norms of particular states; hence, it has no direct obligation to vindicate their statutory dictates. The tribunal, however, is bound to effectuate the intentions of the parties. Where the parties have agreed that the arbitral body is to decide a defined set of claims which includes, as in these cases, those arising from the application of American antitrust law, the tribunal therefore should be bound to decide that dispute in accord with the national law giving rise to the claim.[19] And so long as the prospective litigant effectively may vindicate its statutory cause of action in the arbitral forum, the statute will continue to serve both its remedial and deterrent function.

Having permitted the arbitration to go forward, the national courts of the United States will have the opportunity at the award enforcement stage to ensure that the legitimate interest in the enforcement of the antitrust laws has been addressed. The Convention reserves to each signatory country the right to refuse enforcement of an award where the "recognition or enforcement of the award would be contrary to the public policy of that

19. In addition to the clause providing for arbitration before the Japan Commercial Arbitration Association, the Sales Agreement includes a choice-of-law clause which reads: "This Agreement is made in, and will be governed by and construed in all respects according to the laws of the Swiss Confederation as if entirely performed therein." The United States raises the possibility that the arbitral panel will read this provision not simply to govern interpretation of the contract terms, but wholly to displace American law even where it otherwise would apply. Brief for United States as *Amicus Curiae* 20. The International Chamber of Commerce opines that it is "[c]onceivabl[e], although we believe it unlikely, [that] the arbitrators could consider Soler's affirmative claim of anti-competitive conduct by CISA and Mitsubishi to fall within the purview of this choice-of-law provision, with the result that it would be decided under Swiss law rather than U.S. Sherman Act." Brief for International Chamber of Commerce as *Amicus Curiae* 25. At oral argument, however, counsel for Mitsubishi conceded that American law applied to the antitrust claims and represented that the claims had been submitted to the arbitration panel in Japan on that basis. The record confirms that before the decision of the Court of Appeals the arbitral panel had taken these claims under submission.

We therefore have no occasion to speculate on this matter at this stage in the proceedings, when Mitsubishi seeks to enforce the agreement to arbitrate, not to enforce an award. Nor need we consider now the effect of an arbitral tribunal's failure to take cognizance of the statutory cause of action on the claimant's capacity to reinitiate suit in federal court. We merely note that in the event the choice-of-forum and choice-of-law clauses operated in tandem as a prospective waiver of a party's right to pursue statutory remedies for antitrust violations, we would have little hesitation in condemning the agreement as against public policy.

country." Art. V(2)(b). While the efficacy of the arbitral process requires that substantive review at the award-enforcement stage remains minimal, it would not require intrusive inquiry to ascertain that the tribunal took cognizance of the antitrust claims and actually decided them.[20]

As international trade has expanded in recent decades, so too has the use of international arbitration to resolve disputes arising in the course of that trade. The controversies that international arbitral institutions are called upon to resolve have increased in diversity as well as in complexity. Yet the potential of these tribunals for efficient disposition of legal disagreements arising from commercial relations has not yet been tested. If they are to take a central place in the international legal order, national courts will need to "shake off the old judicial hostility to arbitration," and also their customary and understandable unwillingness to cede jurisdiction of a claim arising under domestic law to a foreign or transnational tribunal. To this extent, at least, it will be necessary for national courts to subordinate domestic notions of arbitrability to the international policy favoring commercial arbitration.

Accordingly, we "require this representative of the American business community to honor its bargain," by holding this agreement to arbitrate "enforce[able] . . . in accord with the explicit provisions of the Arbitration Act."

The judgment of the Court of Appeals is affirmed in part and reversed in part, and the cases are remanded for further proceedings consistent with this opinion.

■ JUSTICE STEVENS, with whom JUSTICE BRENNAN joins, and with whom JUSTICE MARSHALL joins except as to Part II, dissenting.

One element of this rather complex litigation is a claim asserted by an American dealer in Plymouth automobiles that two major automobile companies are parties to an international cartel that has restrained competition in the American market. Pursuant to an agreement that is alleged to have violated § 1 of the Sherman Act, those companies allegedly prevented the dealer from transshipping some 966 surplus vehicles from Puerto Rico to other dealers in the American market.

The petitioner denies the truth of the dealer's allegations and takes the position that the validity of the antitrust claim must be resolved by an arbitration tribunal in Tokyo, Japan. Largely because the auto manufacturers' defense to the antitrust allegation is based on provisions in the dealer's franchise agreement, the Court of Appeals concluded that the arbitration clause in that agreement encompassed the antitrust claim. * * *

* * * Because I am convinced that the Court of Appeals' construction of the arbitration clause is erroneous, and because I strongly disagree with

20. See n. 19, supra. We note, for example, that the rules of the Japan Commercial Arbitration Association provide for the taking of a "summary record" of each hearing, for the stenographic recording of the proceedings where the tribunal so orders or a party requests one, and for a statement of reasons for the award unless the parties agree otherwise. * * *

this Court's interpretation of the relevant federal statutes, I respectfully dissent. In my opinion, (1) a fair construction of the language in the arbitration clause in the parties' contract does not encompass a claim that auto manufacturers entered into a conspiracy in violation of the antitrust laws; (2) an arbitration clause should not normally be construed to cover a statutory remedy that it does not expressly identify; (3) Congress did not intend § 2 of the Federal Arbitration Act to apply to antitrust claims; and (4) Congress did not intend the Convention on the Recognition and Enforcement of Foreign Arbitral Awards to apply to disputes that are not covered by the Federal Arbitration Act.

* * *

Until today all of our cases enforcing agreements to arbitrate under the Arbitration Act have involved contract claims. * * * [T]his is the first time the Court has considered the question whether a standard arbitration clause referring to claims arising out of or relating to a contract should be construed to cover statutory claims that have only an indirect relationship to the contract. In my opinion, neither the Congress that enacted the Arbitration Act in 1925, nor the many parties who have agreed to such standard clauses, could have anticipated the Court's answer to that question.

* * *

In view of the Court's repeated recognition of the distinction between federal statutory rights and contractual rights, together with the undisputed historical fact that arbitration has functioned almost entirely in either the area of labor disputes or in "ordinary disputes between merchants as to questions of fact," it is reasonable to assume that most lawyers and executives would not expect the language in the standard arbitration clause to cover federal statutory claims. Thus, in my opinion, both a fair respect for the importance of the interests that Congress has identified as worthy of federal statutory protection, and a fair appraisal of the most likely understanding of the parties who sign agreements containing standard arbitration clauses, support a presumption that such clauses do not apply to federal statutory claims.

* * *

It was Chief Justice Hughes who characterized the Sherman Anti–Trust Act as "a charter of freedom" that may fairly be compared to a constitutional provision. * * * More recently, the Court described the weighty public interests underlying the basic philosophy of the statute:

> "Antitrust laws in general, and the Sherman Act in particular, are the Magna Carta of free enterprise. They are important to the preservation of economic freedom and our free-enterprise system as the Bill of Rights is to the protection of our fundamental personal freedoms. And the freedoms guaranteed each and every business, no matter how small, is the freedom to compete—to assert with vigor, imagination,

devotion, and ingenuity whatever economic muscle it can muster." * * * *United States v. Topco Associates, Inc.*, 405 U.S. 596, 610 (1972).

The Sherman and Clayton Acts reflect Congress' appraisal of the value of economic freedom; they guarantee the vitality of the entrepreneurial spirit. Questions arising under these Acts are among the most important in public law.

The unique public interest in the enforcement of the antitrust laws is repeatedly reflected in the special remedial scheme enacted by Congress. Since its enactment in 1890, the Sherman Act has provided for public enforcement through criminal as well as civil sanctions.

* * *

The provision for mandatory treble damages—unique in federal law when the statute was enacted—provides a special incentive to the private enforcement of the statute, as well as an especially powerful deterrent to violators. What we have described as "the public interest in vigilant enforcement of antitrust laws through the instrumentality of the private treble damage action" is buttressed by the statutory mandate that the injured party also recover costs, "including a reasonable attorney's fee." The interest in wide and effective enforcement has thus, for almost a century, been vindicated by enlisting the assistance of "private Attorneys General"; we have always attached special importance to their role because "[e]very violation of the antitrust laws is a blow to the free-enterprise system envisaged by Congress."

There are, in addition, several unusual features of the antitrust enforcement scheme that unequivocally require rejection of any thought that Congress would tolerate private arbitration of antitrust claims in lieu of the statutory remedies that it fashioned. * * * [A]n antitrust treble damage case "can only be brought in a District Court of the United States." The determination that these cases are "too important to be decided otherwise than by competent tribunals" surely cannot allow private arbitrators to assume a jurisdiction that is denied to courts of the sovereign States.

* * *

Arbitration awards are only reviewable for manifest disregard of the law, and the rudimentary procedures which make arbitration so desirable in the context of a private dispute often mean that the record is so inadequate that the arbitrator's decision is virtually unreviewable.[31] Despotic decision making of this kind is fine for parties who are willing to agree in advance to settle for a best approximation of the correct result in order to resolve quickly and inexpensively any contractual dispute that may

31. The arbitration procedure in this case does not provide any right to evidentiary discovery or a written decision, and requires that all proceedings be closed to the public. Moreover, Japanese arbitrators do not have the power of compulsory process to secure witnesses and documents, nor do witnesses who are available testify under oath. Cf. 9 U.S.C. § 7 (arbitrators may summon witnesses to attend proceedings and seek enforcement in a district court).

arise in an ongoing commercial relationship. Such informality, however, is simply unacceptable when every error may have devastating consequences for important businesses in our national economy and may undermine their ability to compete in world markets.[32] Instead of "muffling a grievance in the cloakroom of arbitration," the public interest in free competitive markets would be better served by having the issues resolved "in the light of impartial public court adjudication."

* * *

In my opinion, the elected representatives of the American people would not have us dispatch an American citizen to a foreign land in search of an uncertain remedy for the violation of a public right that is protected by the Sherman Act. This is especially so when there has been no genuine bargaining over the terms of the submission, and the arbitration remedy provided has not even the most elementary guarantees of fair process. Consideration of a fully developed record by a jury, instructed in the law by a federal judge, and subject to appellate review, is a surer guide to the competitive character of a commercial practice than the practically unreviewable judgment of a private arbitrator.

Unlike the Congress that enacted the Sherman Act in 1890, the Court today does not seem to appreciate the value of economic freedom. I respectfully dissent.

NOTES AND QUESTIONS

1. Consider carefully footnote 19 to the Court's opinion in *Mitsubishi*. The ICC's concession that it was "unlikely" the arbitrators would apply Swiss law in deciding Soler's antitrust claims "came as a bad surprise to many long time users of ICC arbitration," according to one commentator: One of "the very basics" of arbitration is that it functions within the limits fixed by the agreement of the parties, and "what is indeed very unlikely, to say the least, is that arbitrators would accept to apply U.S. antitrust law to claims to be ruled, according to [the] parties' clear will, by Swiss law!" Werner, A Swiss Comment on *Mitsubishi,* 3 J. of Int'l Arb. 81, 83 (1986). Cf. Lowenfeld, The *Mitsubishi* Case: Another View, 2 Arb.Int'l 178, 186 (1986) ("antitrust law is 'mandatory law,' on the same level as export controls, criminal law, or tax law, i.e., law that cannot ordinarily be avoided by party choice of law in the same way that, for instance, otherwise applicable statutes of limitations, or law governing the extent of implied warranties, or the measure of damages for breach of contract, can be avoided by the parties through a choice of law clause."). The opposing views are canvassed thoroughly in Mayer, Mandatory Rules of Law in International Arbitration, 2 Arb.Int'l 274 (1986).

32. The greatest risk, of course, is that the arbitrator will condemn business practices under the antitrust laws that are efficient in a free competitive market. In the absence of a reviewable record, a reviewing district court would not be able to undo the damage wrought. Even a Government suit or an action by a private party might not be available to set aside the award.

2. In PPG Industries, Inc. v. Pilkington Plc, 825 F.Supp. 1465 (D.Ariz. 1993), the contract between the parties contained a clause by which "the Agreement shall be governed by the laws of England." The court compelled arbitration but warned that:

> the Court may, and certainly will, withdraw the reference to arbitration if U.S. antitrust law does not govern the substantive resolution of [the plaintiff's] claims. In addition, the Court directs that any damages determination, or arbitral award, made by the arbitrators shall be determined according to U.S. antitrust law irrespective of any conflict that may exist between those laws and the laws of England.

Similar questions have arisen in a number of recent securities fraud cases brought against Lloyd's of London, in which underwriters have suffered massive losses arising out of liability for asbestos and toxic-waste damage. Standardized contracts in such cases did not mandate arbitration, but they commonly joined an English choice-of-law clause with a choice-of-forum clause giving jurisdiction to English courts. See, e.g., Haynsworth v. The Corporation, 121 F.3d 956 (5th Cir.1997)("The view that every foreign forum's remedies must duplicate those available under American law would render all forum selection clauses worthless and would severely hinder Americans' ability to participate in international commerce"; "[t]he plaintiffs' remedies in England are adequate to protect their interests and the policies behind the statutes at issue"); Lipcon v. Underwriters at Lloyd's, London, 148 F.3d 1285 (11th Cir.1998)("the Court in *Mitsubishi* recognized and affirmed *Scherk's* policy of treating international commercial agreements as *sui generis*"; "[w]e will not invalidate choice clauses ... simply because the remedies available in the contractually chosen forum are less favorable than those available in the courts of the United States"); Richards v. Lloyd's of London, 135 F.3d 1289 (9th Cir.1998)("Without question this case would be easier to decide if [footnote 19] in *Mitsubishi* had not been inserted").

3. How convincing is the Supreme Court's assurance that the arbitral award, once rendered, can be effectively reviewed at the enforcement stage to "ensure that the legitimate interest in the enforcement of the antitrust laws has been addressed"? In light of the highly restricted scope of judicial review of the merits of awards, is this a realistic prospect? Will it be enough if a reviewing court is satisfied that the Japanese arbitrators merely "took cognizance of the antitrust claims and actually decided them"? Or will *Mitsubishi* encourage courts to engage in a more extensive review of the substantive issues?

4. Professor Eric Posner notes that the *Mitsubishi* case has been much criticized on the ground that "the holding of the majority and the dicta in footnote 19 contradict each other": "If the Court meant to hold that all arbitration clauses must be enforced, then international arbitration will flourish but arbitrators will not respect mandatory rules in the hope of attracting clients." If, on the other hand, the Court included footnote 19 "in order to signal that courts will review arbitration clauses in de novo trials, then courts can ensure that mandatory rules are enforced but international arbitration will lose its value." Posner argues, however, that these polar solutions are not the only ones possible: The "optimal strategy" of courts may instead be to engage in *random* de novo review of awards—a strategy that would result "in arbitrators frequently respecting mandatory rules" (since they would "fear the possibility of de novo review"), and courts refraining from *always* reviewing arbitration awards ("creating savings in congestion"). And he goes on to argue that the Court in *Mitsubishi* implemented precisely this strategy ("though perhaps not intentionally")—by creating conditions of "ambiguous threat": If parties are "not sure whether American courts will review arbitration awards or not—and if American courts occasionally do review arbitration awards—that would be a good thing." Eric A. Posner, Arbitration and the Harmonization of International Commercial Law: A Defense of *Mitsubishi,* 39 Va. J. Int'l L. 647, 651–52, 667–68 (1999).

5. Justice Blackmun's opinion claims that the Court found it "unnecessary to assess the legitimacy of the *American Safety* doctrine as applied to agreements to arbitrate arising from domestic transactions." Is this disingenuous? Can the rationale of *Mitsubishi* possibly be limited to international arbitration? Or is an antitrust claim now arbitrable even if it arises out of a purely domestic transaction? See Nghiem v. NEC Electronic, Inc., 25 F.3d 1437 (9th Cir.1994) (referring to *Mitsubshi*'s "meticulous step-by-step disembowelment of the *American Safety* doctrine"); Kotam Electronics, Inc. v. JBL Consumer Products, Inc., 93 F.3d 724 (11th Cir.1996)(holding that arbitration agreements concerning domestic antitrust claims are enforceable "in light of *Mitsubishi* and its progeny, as well as the persuasive authority from our sister circuits").

6. ILC Peripherals Leasing Corp. v. International Business Machines Corp., 458 F.Supp. 423 (1978) was a suit against IBM for monopolizing or attempting to monopolize various markets in the computer industry. The trial lasted for five months and consumed 96 trial days; the parties called 87 witnesses whose testimony filled more than 19,000 pages of transcript. After deliberating for 19 days, the jury reported itself hopeless deadlocked, and the court declared a mistrial. "Throughout the trial, the court felt that the jury was having trouble grasping the concepts that were being discussed by the expert witnesses." Only one of the jurors had even "limited technical education." "While the court was appreciative of the effort they put into deciding the case, it is understandable that people with such backgrounds would have trouble applying concepts like cross-elasticity of supply and demand, market share and market power, reverse engineering, product interface manipulation, discriminatory pricing, barriers to entry, exclusionary leasing, entrepreneurial subsidiaries, subordinated debentures, stock options, modeling, and etc." Cf. John R. Allison, Arbitration Agreements and Antitrust Claims: The Need for Enhanced Accommodation of Conflicting Public Policies, 64 N. Car. L. Rev. 219., 246 (1986)("One is led to wonder whether the rule prohibiting arbitration of antitrust claims actually contributes to the interest that a party with a weak claim has in generating confusion.").

7. Separation agreements usually contain detailed provisions relating to the children of the marriage. Where children are involved, the unraveling of the family can never be complete, and so there will be a need to lay down ground rules for all sorts of matters: custody and visitation rights, child support, and various other continuing incidents of the family relationship (such as the choice of a school or summer camp, religious training, medical treatment, or trips and vacations). With increasing frequency, agreements provide that the inevitable disputes over such matters will be settled by arbitration. Some courts deny on grounds of "public policy" that such disputes are arbitrable. See, e.g., Glauber v. Glauber, 192 A.D.2d 94, 600 N.Y.S.2d 740 (App.Div.1993) ("when circumstances require determining which living arrangements are in the best interests of children, the courts alone must undertake the task"). Other courts enforce arbitration agreements, but with the caveat that "a special review" of the resulting award is necessary: "The courts should conduct a de novo review unless it is clear on the face of the award that the award could not adversely affect the substantial best interests of the child." Faherty v. Faherty, 97 N.J. 99, 477 A.2d 1257 (1984); see also Miller v. Miller, 423 Pa.Super. 162, 620 A.2d 1161 (1993) ("an award rendered by an arbitration panel would be subject to the supervisory power of the court in its parens patriae capacity in a proceeding to determine the best interests of the child"; if the court finds that the award is in the child's best interests, "the court may adopt the decision as its own").

What is the justification for compelling arbitration of a domestic dispute—but at the same time treating the process as something of a rehearsal for a separate judicial inquiry, with an inevitable duplication of time and expense? Are there aspects of arbitration that make it particularly attractive as a device for resolving domestic disputes over child support and custody? Cf. Agur v. Agur, 32 A.D.2d 16, 298 N.Y.S.2d 772 (App.Div.1969) (separation agreement provided that custody disputes would be decided by three arbitrators, including an Orthodox rabbi, versed in "Jewish religious law"; court refused to order arbitration). One court has observed that "the process of arbitration, useful when the mundane matter of the amount of support is in issue, is less so when the delicate balancing of the factors comprising the best interests of a child is the issue. The judicial process is more broadly gauged and better suited in protecting these interests." Nestel v. Nestel, 38 A.D.2d 942, 331 N.Y.S.2d 241 (App.Div.1972). What precisely do you think this means? Do you agree?

8. A law firm's partnership agreement provided for post-retirement benefits, but also called for the forfeiture of all such benefits if a partner engaged in a competing practice of law within three years after retirement. An arbitrator found that a former partner had forfeited his entitlement to post-employment benefits under this provision. On the partner's motion to vacate, the trial court declined to review the award de novo, giving "great deference" to the arbitrator's finding of fact and legal conclusions. The Supreme Court of Connecticut, however, concluded that the arbitrator's decision "implicated a legitimate public policy—facilitating clients' access to an attorney of their choice"—a policy that was embodied in Rule 5.6 of the Rules of Professional Conduct. In such circumstances, the court held, the trial court should have conducted a de novo review: Given that "courts have greater expertise and knowledge" in the identification and application of state public policy, "it comports with logic for the court to review the arbitrator's interpretation of an ethics rule de novo rather than to leave it to the arbitrators themselves to attempt to apply pertinent public policy." "So too is a reviewing court better suited to evaluate whether certain facts, as found by the arbitrator, comport with the specific public policy that is at issue." Nevertheless, "adher[ing] to the long-standing principle that findings of fact are ordinarily left undisturbed upon judicial review," the court noted that it would "defer to the arbitrator's interpretation of the agreements regarding the scope of the forfeiture upon competition provision." Schoonmaker v. Cummings & Lockwood, 252 Conn. 416, 747 A.2d 1017 (2000).

9. An important tenet of American patent law is that the validity of patents must be freely challengeable, so as not to impede free competition in the exploitation of the "public domain." Invalid patents are "vicious Zombis." Aero Spark Plug Co. v. B.G. Corp., 130 F.2d 290, 299 (2d Cir.1942) (Frank, J., concurring). Patent licensees, therefore, are free to attack the patents of their licensors. Lear, Inc. v. Adkins, 395 U.S. 653, 89 S.Ct. 1902, 23 L.Ed.2d 610 (1969). And once a patent has been successfully challenged in court, its invalidity is established not only between the litigants but as to the world generally; the owner of the patent will be estopped from claiming infringement in a later suit against a third party. Blonder–Tongue Labs., Inc. v. University of Illinois Found., 402 U.S. 313, 91 S.Ct. 1434, 28 L.Ed.2d 788 (1971).

Given this public interest in challenging invalid patents, it was traditionally assumed that patent disputes were not arbitrable. See, e.g., Diematic Mfg. Corp. v. Packaging Industries, Inc., 381 F.Supp. 1057 (S.D.N.Y. 1974), appeal dismissed, 516 F.2d 975 (2d Cir.1975) ("Questions of patent law are not mere private matters"). In 1982, however, Congress expressly authorized the arbitration of "any dispute relating to patent validity or infringement." 35 U.S.C.A. § 294. The statute provides that the arbitration award is to be "final and binding between the parties to the arbitration," but that it "shall have no force or effect on any other person." What does this language mean? See Goldstein, Arbitration of Disputes Relating to Patent Validity or Infringement, 72 Ill.Bar.J. 350, 351 (1984) ("phrase is intended to remove the defense of collateral estoppel and permit the patentee to enforce a patent against others").

It appears that as yet the potential for arbitration in patent cases has not been widely exploited. One recent survey of practice in patent disputes suggests that corporations "overwhelmingly favor arbitration for disputes involving smaller stakes," but "only a very small percentage prefer arbitration where the risks exceed six figures." Wesley & Peterson, "Patent Arbitration," BNA ADR Rep., vol. 4 no. 2 (1990), at 30. Similar results were found in Field & Rose, Prospects for ADR in Patent Disputes: An

Empirical Assessment of Attorneys' Attitudes, 32 Idea 309, 317–18 (1992). Why might this be true?

10. The Magnuson–Moss Act, 15 U.S.C. § 2301, was enacted in 1974 "to make warranties on consumer products more readily understood and enforceable": It requires sellers or manufacturers who give written warranties on consumer products to "fully and conspicuously disclose in simple and readily understood language the terms and conditions" of their warranties, and lays down federal minimum standards that must be met before a warrantor can designate a warranty as a "full" (as opposed to a "limited") warranty. Consumers may bring claims "under a written warranty [or] implied warranty" in federal court, and prevailing plaintiffs may recover reasonable attorneys' fees in addition to damages. Warrantors are also encouraged to establish "informal dispute settlement procedures" under FTC guidelines: If the "written warranty" so provides, a consumer must "initially" resort to such procedure before bringing any suit under the Act; the decision in the "procedure" is, however, admissible in any later civil action.

May a seller or a manufacturer of a mobile home rely on a pre-dispute arbitration clause to force a warranty claim into an arbitration process intended to be binding on the consumer? A number of courts have recently held that the Magnuson–Moss Act makes such arbitration clauses unenforceable when a claim is made under a written warranty: "Congress's intent [was] that any non-judicial dispute resolution procedures would be non-binding, and [that] consumers would always retain the right of final access to court"; the "informal dispute resolution procedures" may therefore be a "prerequisite, but not a bar, to relief in court." See Wilson v. Waverlee Homes, Inc., 954 F.Supp. 1530 (M.D.Ala.1997)(warranty claim against manufacturer, not a signatory to arbitration agreement; held, defendant may not, by relying on the agreement between the consumer and the dealer, "do by surrogate or vicarious means what it is forbidden to do on its own behalf"); Federal Trade Commission, Final Action Concerning Review of Interpretations of Magnuson–Moss Warranty Act, 64 Fed. Reg. 19700, 19708–09 (April 22, 1999)(FTC rules "will continue to prohibit warrantors from including [clauses in their contracts] that would require consumers to submit warranty disputes to binding arbitration," although "warrantors are not precluded from offering a binding arbitration option to consumers after a warranty dispute has arisen.") *Contra*, In re American Homestar of Lancaster, Inc., 50 S.W.3d 480 (Tex.2001)("we find no clear congressional intent in the Magnuson–Moss Act to override the FAA policy favoring arbitration"). Cf. Boyd v. Homes of Legend, Inc., 981 F.Supp. 1423 (M.D.Ala.1997)(warranty claim against dealer; "it is only with respect to *written* warranties that Congress sought in the Magnuson–Moss Act to protect consumers from exploitation by more powerful manufacturers and suppliers who desired to impose the requirement that disputes be resolved by binding arbitration"; the court could discern "no contrary congressional intent regarding binding arbitration of *non-written or implied warranty* claims").

11. Plaintiff, a minor, brought suit against Cigna Healthplans for medical malpractice, and also for violation of the California Consumer Legal Remedies Act [CLRA]—claiming that Cigna had deceptively advertised the quality of medical services which would be provided under its health care plan. Alleging that the plaintiff's mother had received "substandard prenatal medical services" that caused the plaintiff to suffer severe injuries at birth, the suit asked for actual and punitive damages and for "an order enjoining [Cigna's] deceptive practices." The trial court granted the motion to compel arbitration of the medical malpractice action, but denied the motion as to the CLRA claim, and Cigna appealed. The Supreme Court of California held that the plaintiff's damage claim under CLRA was indeed "fully arbitrable," but that his claim for an injunction was not. Distinguishing *Mitsubishi,* the court held that there was an "inherent conflict" between arbitration and the injunctive relief provisions of the CLRA: The "evident purpose" of the latter was not to "resolve a private dispute" or to "compensate for an individual wrong," but instead to "prohibit and enjoin conduct injurious to the general public"; in seeking an injunction, the plaintiff was in effect here "playing the role of a private attorney general." Furthermore, arbitration would not be a "suitable forum" because of "evident institutional shortcomings": A court, unlike an arbitrator, could "retain its jurisdiction over a public injunction until it is dissolved," providing "a necessary continuity and consistency for which a series of arbitrators is an inadequate substitute"; also unlike arbitrators, courts are "publicly accountable" and thus "the most appropriate overseers of injunctive remedies explicitly designed for public protection." Broughton v. Cigna Healthplans of California, 21 Cal.4th 1066, 90 Cal.Rptr.2d 334, 988 P.2d 67 (1999).

Note: Investor/Broker Disputes Under the Securities Acts

The Securities Act of 1933 imposes liability for making misleading statements in the sale of a security "by means of a prospectus or oral communication."[1] The SEC's Rule 10b–5, promulgated under the Securities Exchange Act of 1934, prohibits the making of false statements or the failure to disclose material facts in connection with the sale of securities, and also makes it unlawful to engage "in any act, practice, or course of business which operates or would operate as a fraud or deceit upon any person, in connection with the purchase or sale of any security."[2] Provisions of this Rule have been used to attack a wide variety of securities practices such as "insider trading" and the "churning" of customer accounts by brokers (making numerous trades in order to increase commissions); a private cause of action for those injured by violations of the Rule has long been implied.

For many years, disputes arising under both of these statutes were thought to be not arbitrable as a matter of "public policy." The Supreme Court held in Wilko v. Swan, 346 U.S. 427, 74 S.Ct. 182, 98 L.Ed. 168

1. 15 U.S.C.A. §§ 77a, 77l.

2. 15 U.S.C.A. §§ 78a, 78j; 17 C.F.R. § 240.10b–5.

(1953), that an investor could litigate a misrepresentation claim against a brokerage firm under the Securities Act of 1933, despite the fact that the investor's agreement with the firm contained an arbitration clause. The Court noted that arbitrators must make determinations "without judicial instruction on the law" and that an award "may be made without explanation of their reasons and without a complete record of their proceedings"; it concluded that "the protective provisions of the Securities Act require the exercise of judicial direction to fairly assure their effectiveness." The statute should therefore be read as preventing a "waiver of judicial trial and review," and any agreement to arbitrate future disputes was invalid.

However, the Supreme Court—in line with its increasing tendency to presume arbitral competence even as to statutory or "public policy" matters—has recently reversed course. In Shearson/American Express, Inc. v. McMahon, 482 U.S. 220, 107 S.Ct. 2332, 96 L.Ed.2d 185 (1987), the Court held that arbitration of claims against a broker under the Securities Exchange Act and Rule 10b–5 could be compelled where the customer had earlier signed an arbitration agreement. The Court reached this conclusion by relying heavily on *Mitsubishi,* noting that "the mistrust of arbitration that formed the basis for the *Wilko* opinion in 1953 is difficult to square with the assessment of arbitration that has prevailed since that time." The Court pointed to the fact that the SEC had specifically approved the arbitration procedures of the various stock exchanges, and has exercised its "oversight authority" to ensure that the procedures of the exchanges "adequately protect statutory rights." Nor were arbitration agreements made unenforceable by § 29(a) of the Securities Exchange Act, which prohibits any agreement by which a party undertakes "to waive compliance with any provision of [the Act]"[3]. The Court—in what has now become a familiar rhetorical move—concluded that by "agreeing to arbitrate a statutory claim, a party does not forego the substantive rights afforded by the statute; it only submits to their resolution in an arbitral, rather than a judicial, forum."

At the same time the Supreme Court held in *McMahon* that claims under the Racketeer Influenced and Corrupt Organizations Act ("RICO") were also subject to arbitration under a pre-dispute arbitration clause. "RICO" makes it unlawful to use any money derived "from a pattern of racketeering activity" in the operation of an interstate enterprise.[4] As Justice O'Connor noted in *McMahon,* the scope of RICO has in recent years been dramatically extended far beyond the activities of "the archetypal, intimidating mobster," to reach ordinary business disputes involving "respected and legitimate" enterprises.[5] The RICO statute follows the model of the antitrust laws in giving a private cause of action, including the right to attorney's fees and treble damages, to persons injured by such conduct.

3. 15 U.S.C.A. § 78cc(a).

4. 18 U.S.C.A. § 1961.

5. "Racketeering activity" under the statute is defined as the violation of certain predicate statutes—for example, those dealing with bribery and narcotics sales, but also including "mail fraud" and "fraud in the sale of securities"; a "pattern" of such activity is found when at least two such violations occur within a period of ten years.

"Although the holding in *Mitsubishi* was limited to the international context, much of its reasoning is equally applicable here." 482 U.S. at 239.

While the *McMahon* case did not expressly overrule *Wilko v. Swan,* it did not take long for the Supreme Court to give *Wilko* a formal burial: In Rodriguez de Quijas v. Shearson/American Express, Inc., 490 U.S. 477, 109 S.Ct. 1917, 104 L.Ed.2d 526 (1989), the Court held that claims under the Securities Act of 1933 were also arbitrable where the parties had entered into a pre-dispute arbitration agreement.

At the present time, virtually all brokerage firms require customers to sign a pre-dispute arbitration agreement as a condition for opening an account, particularly in the case of margin or option accounts. Broker-customer contracts commonly provide for arbitration under the auspices of an industry organization such as the New York Stock Exchange (NYSE) or the National Association of Securities Dealers (NASD). Of the more than 6600 arbitration cases filed with these organizations in 1997, approximately 90% were filed with the NASD and about 8% with the NYSE. Under current NASD rules, cases involving more than $50,000 are presumptively to be heard by a panel of three arbitrators, a majority of whom must be "public" arbitrators, "not from the securities industry."

These exchange-administered arbitrations have been the subject of frequent and vocal criticism for many years. See, e.g., "When Investors Bring Claims Against Brokers," New York Times, March 29, 1987, Sec. 3, pp. 1, 8 (lawyer who represents investors says, "I would rather defend a capitalist before the comrades' court than a client before an arbitration panel of the New York Stock Exchange"). Following the Supreme Court's decision in *McMahon,* the industry's arbitration rules were amended in an attempt to address some of these concerns. The definition of just who can serve as a "public" arbitrator has been clarified and tightened: Not only individuals associated with brokers and dealers, but also attorneys or accountants who have devoted 20% of their work to securities industry clients, persons who are retired from the industry, and the spouses and immediate family members of all such persons, are excluded.[6] In addition, it is now required that arbitral awards contain a "summary of the issues" and "a statement of [the] issues resolved"; the awards, along with the names of the parties—and those of the arbitrators—are to be made publicly available.[7]

One frequently-expressed concern has been that in disputes between customers and "repeat players" like brokers, the decisions of arbitrators who hope to decide a large number of cases may be affected by the desire to obtain future assignments—and an appearance of partiality toward the industry may be exacerbated by a tendency of some exchanges to call frequently on particular arbitrators.[8] Under the NYSE rules the exchange

6. NASD Code of Arbitration Procedure, R. 10308(a)(4),(5).

7. NASD Code of Arbitration Procedure, R. 10330.

8. See U.S. General Accounting Office, Securities Arbitration: How Investors Fare 57–58 (1992) (at the Chicago Board Options Exchange, one arbitrator had decided 47% of

itself—rather than the parties—names the members of the arbitration panel. This was formerly the NASD's practice as well, but in 1998 the NASD moved to a system of arbitration selection similar to that of the AAA—in which the parties are provided lists of potential arbitrators, strike the names of those found to be unacceptable, and rank the remaining names in order of preference.[9] A software program will now generate names for forwarding to the parties "on a rotating basis," listing first those potential arbitrators who have participated least often in the process.[10]

A 1992 study conducted by the United States General Accounting Office could find "no indication of pro-industry bias in arbitration decisions at industry-sponsored forums." Investors were successful in about 59% of the cases in which they initiated claims against broker-dealers, and those receiving awards got an overall average of 61% of the amount they claimed.[11] More recent figures show a similar pattern.[12] Since investors with small monetary claims against broker-dealers often have difficulty obtaining legal representation in arbitration, around 40% of investors represent themselves in securities arbitration—and as might be expected, investors represented by counsel achieve a significantly higher recovery rate than pro se claimants.[13]

the cases the GAO reviewed—and he decided 71% of these in favor of the broker-dealer). See also Robbins, Securities Arbitration from the Arbitrators' Perspective, 23 Rev.Sec. & Commodities Reg. 171, 175 (1990) ("One too often sees the same faces week after week at certain arbitration forums. With all due respect, arbitration should not be a supplement to social security. * * * [W]hen they sit on cases day after day, arbitrators build up an immunity to outrageous conduct"). Arbitrators in securities cases are compensated for their services (although not handsomely—at the NASD, they receive $200 for an eight-hour day).

9. NASD Code of Arbitration Procedure, R. 10308(b),(c); NYSE Arbitration Rules R. 607(b), R. 608, R. 609 (each party has right to one peremptory challenge, and unlimited challenges for cause). See generally p. 241, infra.

10. See generally Cheryl Nichols, Arbitrator Selection at the NASD: Investor Perception of a Pro–Securities Industry Bias, 15 Ohio St. J. Disp. Res. 63, 107–112 (1999).

11. U.S. G.A.O., Securities Arbitration, supra n.8 at 35.

12. See *http://www.nasdadr.com* (customers were awarded damages in 61% of cases decided by the NASD in 1999). A GAO study published in June 2000 found that the percentage of cases favoring investors averaged around 51% in the years 1992–1996, then rose to 57% in 1998. The amount of awards made to investors as a percentage of what they had claimed declined to about 51% during those years, although an increase in the percentage of cases settled—generally 50–60% of the total cases concluded—"may have changed the mix of cases going to a final arbitration award." U.S. General Accounting Office, Securities Arbitration: Actions Needed to Address Problem of Unpaid Awards (2000). Investors claimed punitive damages in about 20% of the cases decided in 1998, and were awarded punitives in about 34% of decided cases in which such damages were requested—a significant increase from the 12% reported in 1992. The 2000 GAO report also found, however, that 49% of the awards rendered in 1998 were not paid at all, and an additional 12% were only partially paid—although when investors complained, suspensions or the threat of suspensions by the NASD against noncomplying broker-dealers resulted in many of these awards being satisfied. Most of the unpaid awards had been rendered against broker-dealers who were no longer in business.

13. See U.S. Securities and Exchange Commission, Office of Inspector General, "Oversight of Self–Regulatory Organization Arbitration" (1999).

In any event the suspicion has persisted (in the words of Justice Blackmun's dissent in *McMahon*) that "[t]he uniform opposition of investors to compelled arbitration and the overwhelming support of the securities industry for the process suggest that there must be *some* truth to the investors' belief that the securities industry has an advantage in a forum under its own control."[14] Arbitration of disputes between members of a trade and "outsiders" often brings to the surface a tension between two widely-accepted values underlying the arbitration process. On the one hand, there are the often-cited advantages of expert knowledge and experience on the part of decision-makers familiar with industry practice. The task, for example, of educating a jury or even the average judge in the conventions of securities or commodities trading may be a daunting one. On the other hand, there is a need to preserve the fairness of the process by avoiding onesidedness. Even decision-makers who think of themselves as scrupulously neutral are often hard put to avoid the predispositions and preconceptions that seem to accompany technical "expertise." This is particularly true where one of the parties claims to have observed "trade standards," and the dispute seems likely to call into question long-standing practices and patterns of behavior widespread throughout an entire industry. "Expertise provides a powerful basis to determine what behavior is reasonable, economically efficient, or even economically necessary." And "[p]ressures to decide cases quickly without an intrusive investigation into motives and the like * * * may enforce the failure to challenge" long-standing practices.[15] The arbitration of broker-customer disputes illustrates the inevitable tension; how to draw the balance between these values is a persistent theme in discussions of arbitration. Cf. Section D.1.b. infra ("Arbitral Impartiality").

Note: Employment Disputes and the Statutory Rights of Employees

A large number of federal statutes have been enacted in recent years that extend protection to employees against various forms of discrimination in the workplace. Perhaps the most important of these is Title VII of the Civil Rights Act of 1964, which makes it an "unlawful employment practice" to "fail or refuse to hire or to discharge any individual, or otherwise to discriminate against any individual with respect to his compensation, terms, conditions, or privileges of employment, because of such individual's race, color, religion, sex, or national origin." 42 U.S.C. § 2000e–2(a)(1). When—if at all—may claims brought under such statutes be subject to mandatory and binding arbitration? This is a question that has been the focus of much litigation—and the cause of considerable and continuing confusion.

14. See also Nichols, supra n.10 at 129 (amended NASD rules illustrate "the difficulty, maybe the impossibility, of eliminating the perception of pro-securities industry bias in the NASD arbitrator pool when an economically dependent relationship exists between one of the parties (securities industry respondents) and the arbitrators deciding the dispute").

15. Garth, Privatization and the New Market for Disputes: A Framework for Analysis and a Preliminary Assessment, 12 Studies in Law, Politics and Society 367, 382 (1992).

In Alexander v. Gardner–Denver Co., 415 U.S. 36, 94 S.Ct. 1011, 39 L.Ed.2d 147 (1974), the Supreme Court was presented with a collective bargaining agreement protecting employees from discharge without "just cause," and also prohibiting "discrimination against any employee on account of race." After being fired, an employee claimed at an arbitration hearing that his discharge was the result of racial discrimination. The arbitrator made no explicit reference to the racial discrimination claim but found that the employee had been fired for "just cause," and denied the grievance. The employee then sued the employer, alleging that his discharge was in violation of Title VII. The district court granted the employer's motion for summary judgment, finding "that the claim of racial discrimination had been submitted to the arbitrator and resolved adversely" to the employee: Having "voluntarily elected to pursue his grievance to final arbitration under the nondiscrimination clause of the collective bargaining agreement," the employee "was bound by the arbitral decision and thereby precluded from suing his employer under Title VII." Before the Supreme Court, the employer argued that federal courts should defer to arbitral decisions on discrimination claims, at least "where (i) the claim was before the arbitrator; (ii) the collective-bargaining agreement prohibited the form of discrimination charged in the suit under Title VII; and (iii) the arbitrator has authority to rule on the claim and to fashion a remedy."

The Supreme Court, however, rejected this argument and reversed:

> The purpose and procedures of Title VII indicate that Congress intended federal courts to exercise final responsibility for enforcement of Title VII; deferral to arbitral decisions would be inconsistent with that goal. * * * [The employer's] deferral rule is necessarily premised on the assumption that arbitral processes are commensurate with judicial processes and that Congress impliedly intended federal courts to defer to arbitral decisions on Title VII issues. We deem this supposition unlikely.

Gardner–Denver was followed by two other important cases, also dealing with the effects of an arbitral award under a collective bargaining agreement on the statutory rights of employees. In Barrentine v. Arkansas–Best Freight System, Inc., 450 U.S. 728, 101 S.Ct. 1437, 67 L.Ed.2d 641 (1981), an employee had unsuccessfully submitted wage claims to arbitration; the Court held that this did not preclude a later suit, based on the same underlying facts, alleging a violation of the minimum wage provisions of the Fair Labor Standards Act.

In McDonald v. City of West Branch, 466 U.S. 284, 104 S.Ct. 1799, 80 L.Ed.2d 302 (1984), a police officer was discharged by a city and filed a grievance pursuant to the collective bargaining agreement. Here too the arbitrator ruled against him, finding that there was "just cause" for the discharge. McDonald did not challenge the award, but later filed an action against the city under 42 U.S.C. § 1983 (imposing liability on any person who "under color of" state law deprives another "of any rights, privileges, or immunities secured by the Constitution and laws" of the United States; McDonald alleged that he had been discharged for exercising his First

Amendment rights.) The court of appeals concluded that McDonald's First Amendment claims were barred by res judicata and collateral estoppel, but the Supreme Court, relying heavily on *Gardner–Denver,* reversed: While "arbitration is well suited to resolving contractual disputes," it said, it cannot in a § 1983 action "provide an adequate substitute for a judicial trial. Consequently, according preclusive effect to arbitration awards in § 1983 actions would severely undermine the protection of federal rights that the statute is designed to provide."

The Court buttressed this conclusion by pointing to a number of characteristics of arbitration. Noting first that "many arbitrators are not lawyers," the Court suggested that:

> [A]n arbitrator's expertise "pertains primarily to the law of the shop, not the law of the land." An arbitrator may not, therefore, have the expertise required to resolve the complex legal questions that arise in § 1983 actions.
>
> Second, because an arbitrator's authority derives solely from the contract, an arbitrator may not have the authority to enforce § 1983. As we explained in *Gardner–Denver:* "The arbitrator ... has no general authority to invoke public laws that conflict with the bargain between the parties.... If an arbitral decision is based 'solely upon the arbitrator's view of the requirements of enacted legislation,' rather than on an interpretation of the collective-bargaining agreement, the arbitrator has 'exceeded the scope of the submission,' and the award will not be enforced." * * *
>
> Third, when, as is usually the case, the union has exclusive control over the "manner and extent to which an individual grievance is presented," there is an additional reason why arbitration is an inadequate substitute for judicial proceedings. The union's interests and those of the individual employee are not always identical or even compatible. As a result, the union may present the employee's grievance less vigorously, or make different strategic choices, than would the employee. Thus, were an arbitration award accorded preclusive effect, an employee's opportunity to be compensated for a constitutional deprivation might be lost merely because it was not in the union's interest to press his claim vigorously.
>
> Finally, arbitral factfinding is generally not equivalent to judicial factfinding. * * * The record of the arbitration proceedings is not as complete; the usual rules of evidence do not apply; and rights and procedures common to civil trials, such as discovery, compulsory process, cross-examination, and testimony under oath, are often severely limited or unavailable.

In all three cases, however, the Court suggested that—even though an arbitral award would not preclude a later action by the employee—the award might still be admitted as evidence in the lawsuit. The weight to be given the award "must be determined in the court's discretion with regard to the facts and circumstances of each case":

> Relevant factors include the existence of provisions in the collective-bargaining agreement that conform substantially with [the statute or Constitution], the degree of procedural fairness in the arbitral forum, adequacy of the record with respect to the issue [in the judicial proceeding], and the special competence of particular arbitrators. Where an arbitral determination gives full consideration to an employee's [statutory or constitutional] rights, a court may properly accord it great weight. This is especially true where the issue is solely one of fact, specifically addressed by the parties and decided by the arbitrator on the basis of an adequate record.

See, e.g., Wilmington v. J.I. Case Co., 793 F.2d 909 (8th Cir.1986) ("the arbitrator's decision [that the employee was fired for "just cause"] was simply another piece of evidence presented to the jury, and it was for the jury to decide what weight to give it"; however, the trial court properly refused to admit into evidence the text of the award, since the arbitrator's comments and findings "would either usurp the jury's role in assessing credibility [of witnesses who also testified at trial] or would be unfairly prejudicial").

Some years later, however, the relentless federal policy favoring arbitration caused the pendulum to swing in the opposite direction. Gilmer v. Interstate/Johnson Lane Corporation, 500 U.S. 20, 111 S.Ct. 1647, 114 L.Ed.2d 26 (1991), involved an individual employee who was hired as a "Manager of Financial Services" by a brokerage house, and required to register as a securities representative with the New York Stock Exchange; NYSE rules at the time required the arbitration of any dispute "arising out of the employment or termination of employment" of registered representatives. Gilmer later brought suit against his employer alleging that he had been discharged in violation of the Age Discrimination in Employment Act of 1967 (ADEA), 290 U.S.C. § 621. The Supreme Court—relying again on *Mitsubishi,* supra p. 1701, as well as on *Shearson/American Express, Inc. v. McMahon* and *Rodriguez de Quijas v. Shearson/American Express*, supra pp. 188–189, held that arbitration of the claim should be compelled. Again the Court repeated that "[b]y agreeing to arbitrate a statutory claim, a party does not forgo the substantive rights afforded by the statute; it only submits to their resolution in an arbitral, rather than a judicial, forum." Again the Court stressed that "generalized attacks" on arbitration—to the effect that the arbitration process may not adequately permit vindication of the claimant's statutory rights—rested on an unwarranted "suspicion of arbitration," and were "far out of step with our current strong endorsement of the federal statutes favoring this method of resolving disputes."

For example, while it is true that discovery permitted in arbitration is more limited than in the federal courts, the Court found it "unlikely"

> that age discrimination claims require more extensive discovery than other claims that we have found to be arbitrable, such as RICO and antitrust claims. Moreover, there has been no showing in this case that the NYSE discovery provisions, which allow for document production, information requests, depositions, and subpoenas, will prove insuffi-

cient to allow ADEA claimants such as Gilmer a fair opportunity to present their claims. Although those procedures might not be as extensive as in the federal courts, by agreeing to arbitrate, a party "trades the procedures and opportunity for review of the courtroom for the simplicity, informality, and expedition of arbitration." Indeed, an important counterweight to the reduced discovery in NYSE arbitration is that arbitrators are not bound by the rules of evidence.

Nor was the Court persuaded by the contention that "there often will be unequal bargaining power between employers and employees.":

> Mere inequality in bargaining power * * * is not a sufficient reason to hold that arbitration agreements are never enforceable in the employment context. Relationships between securities dealers and investors, for example, may involve unequal bargaining power, but we nevertheless held in *Rodriguez de Quijas* and *McMahon* that agreements to arbitrate in that context are enforceable. * * * There is no indication in this case * * * that Gilmer, an experienced businessman, was coerced or defrauded into agreeing to the arbitration clause in his registration application. As with the claimed procedural inadequacies discussed above, this claim of unequal bargaining power is best left for resolution in specific cases.

How could *Gilmer* be distinguished from earlier cases like *Alexander v. Gardner–Denver* and its progeny? Most notably, the Court pointed out, "because the arbitration in those cases occurred in the context of a collective-bargaining agreement, the claimants there were represented by their unions in the arbitration proceedings. An important concern therefore was the tension between collective representation and individual statutory rights, a concern not applicable to the present case." Other purported distinctions seem considerably less persuasive—and more like mere makeweights. The Court also pointed out, for example, that the *Gardner–Denver* line of cases, unlike *Gilmer,* were not decided under the FAA—which "reflects a liberal federal policy favoring arbitration agreements." And it also stressed that those cases

> did not involve the issue of the enforceability of an agreement to arbitrate statutory claims. Rather, they involved the quite different issue whether arbitration of contract-based claims precluded subsequent judicial resolution of statutory claims. Since the employees there had not agreed to arbitrate their statutory claims, and the labor arbitrators were not authorized to resolve such claims, the arbitration in those cases understandably was held not to preclude subsequent statutory actions.

The relationship between *Gilmer* and *Gardner-Denver* was revisited—although inconclusively—by the Supreme Court in Wright v. Universal Maritime Service Corp., 525 U.S. 70, 119 S.Ct. 391, 142 L.Ed.2d 361 (1998). Here, an employee subject to a collective bargaining agreement filed suit alleging an employer's violation of the Americans with Disability Act of 1990, 42 U.S.C. § 12101. The Supreme Court acknowledged that there was "obviously some tension between these two lines of cases." The employee's contention—that "federal forum rights" could not be waived at all in union-negotiated collective bargaining agreements, even if they could be waived in individually executed contracts—"assuredly finds support in the text of *Gilmer.*" The employer, on the other hand, argued that *Gilmer* "has sufficiently undermined *Gardner-Denver*" that henceforth a union too should be able to surrender an employee's right to litigate a statutory claim. The Court found it "unnecessary to resolve" this question: For "*Gardner-Denver* at least stands for the proposition that the right to a federal judicial forum is of sufficient importance to be protected against less-than-explicit union waiver in a [collective bargaining agreement]." Matters which "go beyond the interpretation and application of contract terms"—like the meaning of a federal statute—will not be presumed to be arbitrable, but any such requirement in a collective bargaining agreement must instead be "particularly clear." And since the agreement in *Wright* could not meet such a standard, the employer's attempt to compel arbitration was denied. In *Gilmer*, by contrast—since it involved "an individual's waiver of his own rights, rather than a union's waiver of the rights of represented employees"—such a "clear and unmistakable" standard did not apply.

NOTES AND QUESTIONS

1. In 1990, Congress enacted the Older Workers Benefit Protection Act, 29 U.S.C. § 626(f), which amended the ADEA to prohibit waiver of "any right or claim" under the Act that is not "knowing and voluntary." Any such waiver must be "written in a manner calculated to be understood" by the employee; the employee must be "advised in writing to consult with an attorney" prior to signing it, and in any event there could be no waiver of "rights or claims that may arise after the date the waiver is executed." Should this amendment affect the validity of agreements providing for the arbitration of ADEA claims? *Compare* Thiele v. Merrill Lynch, Pierce, Fenner & Smith, 59 F.Supp.2d 1060 (S.D.Cal.1999)(arbitration clause "did not contain a knowing and voluntary waiver of Thiele's right to a jury trial, as required by the OWBPA, and it is therefore unenforceable with respect to his ADEA claim"), *with* Rosenberg v. Merrill Lynch, Pierce, Fenner & Smith, Inc., 170 F.3d 1 (1st Cir.1999)(to interpret the OWBPA to include "the right to a judicial forum" "would be to ignore the Supreme Court's repeated statements that arbitral and judicial fora are both able to give effect to the policies that underlie legislation").

2. The holding in *Gilmer* has been routinely applied by lower courts to other federal legislation extending rights to individual employees against job discrimination. See, e.g., Alford v. Dean Witter Reynolds, Inc., 939 F.2d 229 (5th Cir.1991) (Title VII); Koveleskie v. SBC Capital Markets, Inc., 167 F.3d 361 (7th Cir.1999)(Title VII); Bercovitch v. Baldwin School, Inc., 133 F.3d 141 (1st Cir.1998)(Americans with Disabilities Act).

See also McNulty v. Prudential–Bache Securities, Inc., 871 F.Supp. 567 (E.D.N.Y.1994) (claim under Jurors' Act, making it unlawful to discharge an employee "by reason of such employee's jury service"); Saari v. Smith Barney, Harris Upham & Co., Inc., 968 F.2d 877 (9th Cir.1992) (claim under Employee Polygraph Protection Act); Jones v. Fujitsu Network Communications, Inc., 81 F.Supp.2d 688 (N.D.Tex.1999)(claim under Family Medical Leave Act). In Williams v. Katten, Muchin & Zavis, 837 F.Supp. 1430 (N.D.Ill.1993), a claim under the Civil Rights Act of 1870 [42 U.S.C.A. § 1981, equal rights "to make and enforce contracts"] was held arbitrable; the court rejected arguments that racial discrimination is a more serious offense "morally distinguishable" from gender and age claims, and that § 1981 is more "constitutional in nature" than statutes enacted pursuant to the commerce clause such as Title VII. *But see* Nguyen v. City of Cleveland, 121 F.Supp.2d 643 (N.D.Ohio 2000)(claim under whistleblower protection provision of the False Claims Act, [31 U.S.C. § 3730(h)], is not arbitrable; "an employee who brings a claim against his employers on behalf of the federal government should not be forced by unequal bargaining power to accept a forum demanded as a condition of employment by the very party on which he informed").

3. The district court in *Alexander v. Gardner–Denver* had granted summary judgment to the employer; it feared that "[t]o hold that an employee has a right to an arbitration of a grievance which is binding on an employer but is not binding on the employee—a trial balloon for the employee, but a moon shot for the employer—would sound the death knell for arbitration clauses in labor contracts." 346 F.Supp. 1012, 1019 (D.Colo.1971). This prediction has not of course been borne out. Many collective bargaining agreements now include non-discrimination clauses and often incorporate Title VII or similar state statutes; labor arbitrators regularly decide such cases and engage in interpreting this language. See the discussion at pp. 146–149 supra ("Arbitral Decision–Making and Legal 'Rules' "). But given the holdings in *Gardner–Denver* and *McDonald,* what incentive is there for employers to agree to submit such disputes to arbitration if employees are able to get "a second bite of the apple"?

4. Strictly speaking, *Gardner–Denver* and *McDonald* were only concerned with the preclusive effect of *a prior arbitration award* on a *later* judicial claim. However, it seems clear that an employee subject to a collective bargaining agreement may always proceed *directly* to pursue litigation under Title VII or other civil rights statutes, without first exhausting his rights under the agreement. See 2 Larson, Employment Discrimination §§ 49.14, 49.15 (1990) (since courts in Title VII actions are not bound by the results of grievance and arbitration procedures in collective bargaining agreements, requiring exhaustion would "needlessly prolong the deprivation of rights"). This option of course no longer remains open to an employee in the position of Robert Gilmer. Is it not something of a paradox that statutory rights against discrimination are apparently subject to binding arbitration only in individual employment agreements—which are so often contracts of adhesion—and not in the hard-fought and actually "dickered" collective bargaining agreements between employers and unions?

5. In the securities industry, employees like Gilmer were for many years required by NASD and NYSE rules to submit employment disputes to arbitration before industry fora, under the same procedures as customers. A 1994 study found that arbitrators in such fora were not selected on the basis of any particular "expertise" in employment or discrimination law, and that most of them were "white men, averaging 60 years of age." U.S. General Accounting Office, Employment Discrimination: How Registered Representatives Fare in Discrimination Disputes 2, 8, 12 (1994)(of the 726 arbitrators in NYSE's New York arbitrator pool, 89% were men; of the 349 arbitrators whose race could be identified, 97% were white).

Commentators predictably seized on this fact to conclude that the awards of such arbitrators must tend to disfavor minority or female complainants—indeed, the presence of at least "unconscious bias" is usually taken to be self-evident without the need for any further discussion. How, though, would you characterize the typical federal judge? See Alan Rau, On Integrity in Private Judging, 14 Arb. Int'l 115, 135–40 (1998).

A number of recent accounts of the security industry's arbitration procedures in employment discrimination cases have been highly critical and widely-publicized. One NYSE panel apparently decided against the claimant in a sexual harassment case because her supervisor's behavior "was common within the industry"; the arbitrators were unfamiliar with the current state of antidiscrimination law and, in the words of one law professor, were "10 years behind where the courts are." One article concluded that "So grim are the prospects for most women who go through the securities-industry arbitration process that lawyers say they now advise their clients not to bother with arbitration at all. Instead, they urge women to take modest settlements and walk away." See Jacobs, "Men's Club: Riding Crop and Slurs: How Wall Street Dealt With a Sex–Bias Case," Wall St.J., June 9, 1994 at p. A1.

Studies and articles like these have naturally prompted calls for legislation to restrict the use of arbitration in resolving employment discrimination claims. See, e.g., 11 World Arb. & Mediation Rep. 153 (June 2000)(proposed "Civil Rights Procedures Protection Act," supported by the Department of Justice, would amend the FAA to exclude from arbitration claims of unlawful discrimination in employment on the basis of race, religion, gender, age or disability). Recent amendments to the rules of both the NASD and the NYSE have eliminated any industry-wide requirement of mandatory arbitration with respect to statutory discrimination claims. (However, industry employees are still required under these rules to arbitrate any common-law claims, such as wrongful termination or infliction of emotional distress. In addition, under the new NASD rules individual brokerage firms remain free to insert pre-dispute arbitration clauses in their employment agreements should they wish to do so, thereby making mandatory the arbitration of even discrimination claims). See SEC, Release No. 34–40109, 1998 WL 339422 (F.R.); SEC, Release No. 34–40858, 1999 WL 3315 (F.R.). As part of the settlement of a class action gender-discrimination suit, Merrill Lynch has agreed to waive any contractual right to insist on arbitration with respect to all future discrimination claims brought by employees. See 66 U.S.L.W. 2697 (May 19, 1998).

6. Outside the (now much diminished) sphere of cases like *Gardner–Denver* and *McDonald,* arbitration awards can be expected to have res judicata and collateral estoppel effects on later proceedings. The Restatement of Judgments, for example, generally provides that "a valid and final award by arbitration" will have the same preclusive effects as a judgment of a court. "If the arbitration award were not treated as the equivalent of a judicial adjudication for purposes of claim preclusion, the obligation to arbitrate would be practically illusory." Restatement (Second) of Judgments, § 84 and comment b. In addition, the arbitrators' determination of a particular *issue* will prevent later relitigation of the same issue (i.e., will have "collateral estoppel" effect), at least where the proceedings possess "the elements of adjudicatory procedure"—including notice to the parties, the right to present and rebut evidence and legal argument, and "such other procedural elements as may be necessary to constitute the proceeding a sufficient means of conclusively determining the matter in question." Id. at §§ 84(3), 83(2). Under modern arbitration statutes, once an award is confirmed by a court it is given "the same force and effect" as a judgment rendered in a suit, FAA § 13. But judicial confirmation is not necessary in order for an award to have a preclusive effect barring later relitigation. See generally 4 Ian Macneil, Richard Speidel, & Thomas Stipanowich, Federal Arbitration Law § 39.6 (1994).

In some cases, however, the collateral estoppel effects of an arbitration award may be limited by the "informality" of the arbitration proceeding. For example, where there is no transcript and where the arbitrators do not write a reasoned opinion, it may often be difficult to tell just what it is that they have actually decided. See, e.g., Tamari v. Bache & Co. (Lebanon) S.A.L., 637 F.Supp. 1333 (N.D.Ill.1986). In this case a customer initiated arbitration proceedings against a brokerage firm, seeking to hold it accountable for the acts of its subsidiary, and the arbitrators denied the claim without an opinion. This was held not to preclude a later suit against the subsidiary itself, since "it is impossible to tell" the basis for the arbitrators' award. After all, the court reasoned, the arbitrators could have found *either* that the subsidiary had done nothing wrongful, *or* that the subsidiary had simply not been acting as an agent of the parent. See also Clark v. Bear Stearns & Co., Inc., 966 F.2d 1318 (9th Cir.1992) (dismissal by arbitrators of state-law claims against broker did not preclude a later suit on federal-law claims; the award did not mention the applicable law selected by the arbitrators and if they chose California law "the defendants' alleged negligence need not have been addressed by the arbitrators at all," since the common-law claim would be barred by the state's statute of limitations); Shell, Res Judicata and Collateral Estoppel Effects of Commercial Arbitration, 35 U.C.L.A. L.Rev. 623 (1988).

In addition, even a confirmed arbitration award may not be given a *nonmutual* collateral estoppel effect in the absence of some express agreement between the parties. This is the situation in which A & B arbitrate a particular dispute, and A loses. In later litigation between A & C involving some of the same issues, C argues that A should be bound by adverse findings made by the arbitrator in the earlier proceeding. The Supreme Court of California rejected that argument in Vandenberg v. Superior Court, 21 Cal.4th 815, 88 Cal.Rptr.2d 366, 982 P.2d 229 (1999). The earlier arbitration had been between a landowner and its lessee for contamination of soil and groundwater; the court held that findings adverse to the lessee did not prevent him, in a later indemnification action against his insurers, from arguing that the discharge was "sudden and accidental" and thus not excluded from pollution coverage under the policy. The court noted that while in arbitration the parties have voluntarily traded "the safeguards and formalities of court litigation for an expeditious, sometimes roughshod means of resolving their dispute," "these same features can be serious, unexpected disadvantages if issues decided by the arbitrators are given leveraged effect in favor of strangers to the arbitration." But cf. Witkowski v. Welch, 173 F.3d 192 (3d Cir.1999)(the arbitrator had dismissed plaintiff's claim against an investment advisor alleging that his conveyance of real property acquired with the plaintiff's retirement funds had been fraudulent and should be set aside; held, summary judgment should be granted to the transferee of the disputed property in a later action brought against him by the plaintiff; "the fraud and fraudulent conveyance issues brought against [the investment advisor and the transferee] are so inextricably intertwined with one another that the disposal of the claims against the one is necessarily fatal to the alleged claim against the other").

7. After an employee was discharged in 1989, her union filed a grievance alleging unjust termination under the collective bargaining agreement; she also filed discrimination charges with the state Commission on Human Rights and with the EEOC. Two years later, the employer and the employee agreed to be bound by an arbitration decision. A "Stipulated Arbitration Award" was later confirmed by a state court: Under it, the employee was to be reinstated and compensated for lost wages, and she was to withdraw the discrimination charges filed with state and federal agencies. The employee later filed a lawsuit alleging a series of unlawful acts—up to and including her 1989 termination—which allegedly constituted discrimination and retaliation under Title VII and a deprivation of her civil rights under 42 U.S.C. § 1983. The employer moved to dismiss. The court noted that "if the prior resolution was an arbitration award, the plaintiff may proceed with the case, even if the only act of discrimination she can prove is the 1989 termination"—for, as in *Gardner-Denver,* "the arbitration was limited to determining the plaintiff's rights under a collective bargaining agreement." On the other hand, "if the prior resolution was a settlement," the plaintiff can only recover if she can prove "discriminatory acts which occurred *after* the settlement"—for an employee "who freely settles her demand with the employer may not sue on the same cause of action later merely because she grows dissatisfied with the payment for which she settled." For purposes of the motion to dismiss, the court accepted the plaintiff's characterization of the earlier resolution as "an arbitration award," and denied the motion. Tang v. State of Rhode Island Department of Elderly Affairs, 904 F.Supp. 69 (D.R.I.1995).

Armendariz v. Foundation Health Psychcare Services, Inc.

Supreme Court of California, 2000.
24 Cal.4th 83, 99 Cal.Rptr.2d 745, 6 P.3d 669.

MOSK, J.

* * *

I. STATEMENT OF FACTS AND PROCEDURAL ISSUES

Marybeth Armendariz and Dolores Olague–Rodgers (hereafter the employees) filed a complaint for wrongful termination against their former employer, Foundation Health Psychcare Services, Inc. (hereafter the employer). The complaint and certain documents filed in support of the employer's petition to compel arbitration provide us with the basic factual background of this case. In July and August of 1995, the employer hired the employees in the "Provider Relations Group" and they were later given supervisory positions with annual salaries of $38,000. On June 20, 1996, they were informed that their positions were "being eliminated" and that they were "being terminated." During their year of employment, they claim that their supervisors and coworkers engaged in sexually based harassment and discrimination. The employees alleged that they were "terminated ... because of their perceived and/or actual sexual orientation (heterosexual)."

Both employees had filled out and signed employment application forms, which included an arbitration clause pertaining to any future claim of wrongful termination. Later, they executed a separate employment arbitration agreement, containing the same arbitration clause. The clause states in full: "I agree as a condition of my employment, that in the event my employment is terminated, and I contend that such termination was wrongful or otherwise in violation of the conditions of employment or was in violation of any express or implied condition, term or covenant of employment, whether founded in fact or in law, including but not limited to the covenant of good faith and fair dealing, or otherwise in violation of any of my rights, I and Employer agree to submit any such matter to binding arbitration * * * . I and Employer further expressly agree that in any such arbitration, my exclusive remedies for violation of the terms, conditions or covenants of employment shall be limited to a sum equal to the wages I would have earned from the date of any discharge until the date of the arbitration award. I understand that I shall not be entitled to any other remedy, at law or in equity, including but not limited to reinstatement and/or injunctive relief."

The employees' complaint against the employer alleges a cause of action for violation of the [California Fair Employment and Housing Act,

Gov. Code § 12900 (FEHA)] and three additional causes of action for wrongful termination based on tort and contract theories of recovery. The complaint sought general damages, punitive damages, injunctive relief, and the recovery of attorney fees and costs of suit.

The employer countered by filing a motion for an order to compel arbitration * * *. [T]he trial court denied the motion on the ground that the arbitration provision in question was an unconscionable contract, * * * [finding] that several of the provisions of the contract are "so one-sided as to shock the conscience." * * *

After the employer filed a timely appeal, the Court of Appeal reversed. * * * We granted review.

II. DISCUSSION

A. Arbitrability of FEHA Claims

The employees urge us to adopt the conclusion of the United States Court of Appeals for the Ninth Circuit in Duffield v. Robertson Stephens & Co., 144 F.3d 1182 (9th Cir.1998) (*Duffield*), which held that the Civil Rights Act of 1991 prohibits the enforcement of mandatory employment agreements to arbitrate claims under Title VII of the Civil Rights Act of 1964, or equivalent state antidiscrimination statutes, such as the FEHA. *Duffield* involved a securities broker who sought to litigate Title VII and FEHA claims against her employer after alleged sexual discrimination and harassment, and who was subject to a mandatory arbitration agreement. The starting point for the *Duffield* court is the fact that the 1991 Act "was primarily designed to 'overrule' hostile Supreme Court decisions in order to make discrimination claims easier both to bring and to prove in federal courts...." It is against this background that the court examined section 118 of the 1991 Act, which provides: "Where appropriate and to the extent authorized by law, the use of alternative means of dispute resolution, including ... arbitration, is encouraged to resolve disputes arising under the Acts or provisions of Federal law amended by this title." The *Duffield* court found the language "where appropriate and to the extent authorized by law" to be indicative of a congressional intent to outlaw compulsory arbitration of employee civil rights claims, despite the apparently pro-arbitration thrust of section 118. The court reasoned as follows: The term "where appropriate," must be considered in the context of the statute as a whole, which provided "for a vast strengthening of employees' rights"; " 'Where appropriate,' as used in the Act, would appear to mean where arbitration furthers the purpose and objective of the Act—by affording victims of discrimination an opportunity to present their claims in an alternative forum, a forum that they find desirable—not by forcing an unwanted forum upon them."

Likewise, the *Duffield* court explained the phrase "to the extent authorized by law" in context: "As the Supreme Court has stated, we should examine initially the statute with an eye toward determining Congress' perception of the law that it was shaping or reshaping. The overwhelming weight of the law at the time Congress drafted section 118, and it was reported out of the House Education and Labor Committee, was to the effect that compulsory agreements to arbitrate Title VII claims were unenforceable. In other words, such agreements were not 'authorized by law.' To the contrary, the law at that time prohibited employers from compelling employees to arbitrate Title VII claims pursuant to collective bargaining agreements, 'in large part' because of the Court's recognition of the critical role that Congress envisioned for the independent federal judiciary in advancing Title VII's societal goal. [citing *Alexander v. Gardner–Denver* and *McDonald v. West Branch,* supra pp. 192–193]. This reading of the statute is especially supported by the legislative history, particularly the report of the House Committee on Education and Labor (the House report), which stated of the bill that was to become the 1991 Act: 'The Committee emphasizes ... that the use of alternative dispute mechanisms is ... intended to supplement, not supplant, the remedies provided by Title VII. Thus, for example, the committee believes that any agreement to submit disputed issues to arbitration, whether in the context of collective bargaining or in an employment contract, does not preclude the affected person from seeking relief under the enforcement provisions of Title VII. This view is consistent with the Supreme Court's interpretation of Title VII in Alexander v. Gardner–Denver Co.... The Committee does not intend this section to be used to preclude rights and remedies that would otherwise be available.' H.R.Rep. No. 40(I) at 97."*

Finally, the *Duffield* court reasoned that if the 1991 Act precluded the enforcement of mandatory employment arbitration agreements with respect to Title VII claims, the employee's FEHA claims must also be exempted from mandatory arbitration. Because "parallel state anti-discrimination laws are explicitly made part of Title VII's enforcement scheme, FEHA claims are arbitrable to the same extent as Title VII claims."

As the employer points out, the Ninth Circuit stands alone in its interpretation of the 1991 Act. Aside from the fact that *Duffield* is a minority of one, we find its reasoning unpersuasive. First and foremost, it is difficult to believe that Congress would have chosen to ban mandatory employment arbitration by means of a clause that encourages the use of arbitration and has no explicit prohibitory language, when it could have simply and straightforwardly proscribed mandatory employment arbitration of Title VII claims. Second, the *Duffield* court's analysis of the phrase "to the extent authorized by law" would perhaps be credible but for the fact that, as the court acknowledged, the United States Supreme Court decided *Gilmer* shortly before the passage of the 1991 Act. *Gilmer* modified the *Gardner-Denver* decision referred to in the congressional legislative history quoted above. * * *

The *Gilmer* court did not decide whether employment contracts are generally subject to the FAA, nor definitively rule on whether Title VII

* [This House report on the 1991 Act, from which the court quotes, was dated just 19 days before the Supreme Court handed down its decision in *Gilmer*. As the Supreme Court of California goes on to point out, however, *Gilmer* had been decided by the time Congress actually passed the Act.—Eds.]

claims were arbitrable. But at the very least, it was not at all clear at the time the 1991 Act was enacted that mandatory arbitration of Title VII claims (outside of the collective bargaining context) was prohibited according to judicial interpretation of Title VII, and in fact the contrary appeared to be more likely the case. The fact that the authors of the House report may have believed that section 118 of the 1991 Act was intended to incorporate a broad reading of the *Gardner-Denver* line of cases to preclude mandatory employment arbitration agreements of all types does not negate the fact that at the time Congress passed the 1991 Act, *Gilmer* was the law. Congress must be presumed to have been aware of *Gilmer* when it used the phrase "to the extent authorized by law."

Nor can the phrase "where appropriate" bear the weight given to it by the *Duffield* court. There is no reason to suppose that Congress believed mandatory arbitration agreements of civil rights claims to be inappropriate, provided that arbitration gives claimants the full opportunity to pursue such claims. Although the *Gilmer* court acknowledged that federal statutes may provide exceptions to the rule of arbitrability found in the FAA, it held that "questions of arbitrability must be addressed with healthy regard for the federal policy favoring arbitration." We cannot discern in the general phrase "where appropriate and to the extent authorized by law" a specific congressional intent to ban mandatory employment arbitration agreements.

We therefore conclude that nothing in the 1991 Act prohibits mandatory employment arbitration agreements that encompass state and federal antidiscrimination claims.

* * *

C. Arbitration of FEHA Claims

The United States Supreme Court's dictum that a party in agreeing to arbitrate a statutory claim, "does not forgo the substantive rights afforded by the statute but only submits to their resolution in an arbitral ... forum" (*Mitsubishi Motors Corp.*, 473 U.S. at p. 628) is as much prescriptive as it is descriptive. That is, it sets a standard by which arbitration agreements and practices are to be measured, and disallows forms of arbitration that in fact compel claimants to forfeit certain substantive statutory rights.

Of course, certain statutory rights can be waived. But arbitration agreements that encompass unwaivable statutory rights must be subject to particular scrutiny. This unwaivability derives from two statutes that are themselves derived from public policy. First, Civil Code section 1668 states: "All contracts which have for their object, directly or indirectly, to exempt anyone from responsibility for his own fraud, or willful injury to the person or property of another, or violation of law, whether willful or negligent, are against the policy of the law." "Agreements whose object, directly or indirectly, is to exempt [their] parties from violation of the law are against public policy and may not be enforced." Second, Civil Code section 3513 states, "Anyone may waive the advantage of a law intended solely for his benefit. But a law established for a public reason cannot be contravened by a private agreement."

There is no question that the statutory rights established by the FEHA are "for a public reason." * * * As we stated in [Rojo v. Kliger, 276 Cal. Rptr. 130, (1990)]: "The public policy against sex discrimination and sexual harassment in employment, moreover, is plainly one that inures to the benefit of the public at large rather than to a particular employer or employee. No extensive discussion is needed to establish the fundamental public interest in a workplace free from the pernicious influence of sexism. So long as it exists, we are all demeaned." It is indisputable that an employment contract that required employees to waive their rights under the FEHA to redress sexual harassment or discrimination would be contrary to public policy and unlawful.

In light of these principles, it is evident that an arbitration agreement cannot be made to serve as a vehicle for the waiver of statutory rights created by the FEHA. * * *

The employees argue that arbitration contains a number of shortcomings that will prevent the vindication of their rights under the FEHA. In determining whether arbitration is considered an adequate forum for securing an employee's rights under FEHA, we begin with the extensive discussion of this question in Cole v. Burns Intern. Security Services, 105 F.3d 1465 (*Cole*), in the context of Title VII claims. In that case, the employee, a security guard, filed Title VII claims against his former employer alleging racial discrimination and harassment. He had signed an arbitration form committing himself to arbitrate such claims.

The court began its analysis by acknowledging the difficulties inherent in arbitrating employees' statutory rights, difficulties not present in arbitrating disputes arising from employee rights under collective bargaining agreements. "The reasons for this hesitation to extend arbitral jurisprudence from the collective bargaining context are well-founded. The fundamental distinction between contractual rights, which are created, defined, and subject to modification by the same private parties participating in arbitration, and statutory rights, which are created, defined, and subject to modification only by Congress and the courts, suggests the need for a public, rather than private, mechanism of enforcement for statutory rights." Although *Gilmer* had held that statutory employment rights outside of the collective bargaining context are arbitrable, the *Cole* court recognized that *Gilmer*, both explicitly and implicitly, placed limits on the arbitration of such rights. "Obviously, *Gilmer* cannot be read as holding that an arbitration agreement is enforceable no matter what rights it waives or what burdens it imposes. Such a holding would be fundamentally at odds with our understanding of the rights accorded to persons protected by public statutes like the ADEA and Title VII. The beneficiaries of public statutes are entitled to the rights and protections provided by the law."

* * *

Based on *Gilmer*, and on the basic principle of nonwaivability of statutory civil rights in the workplace, the *Cole* court formulated five minimum requirements for the lawful arbitration of such rights pursuant to a mandatory employment arbitration agreement. Such an arbitration agreement is lawful if it "(1) provides for neutral arbitrators, (2) provides for more than minimal discovery, (3) requires a written award, (4) provides for all of the types of relief that would otherwise be available in court, and (5) does not require employees to pay either unreasonable costs or any arbitrators' fees or expenses as a condition of access to the arbitration forum. Thus, an employee who is made to use arbitration as a condition of employment effectively may vindicate [his or her] statutory cause of action in the arbitral forum."

Except for the neutral-arbitrator requirement, which we have held is essential to ensuring the integrity of the arbitration process and is not at issue in this case, the employees claim that the present arbitration agreement fails to measure up to the Cole requirements enumerated above. We consider below the validity of those requirements and whether they are met by the employer's arbitration agreement.[8]

1. Limitation of Remedies

The principle that an arbitration agreement may not limit statutorily imposed remedies such as punitive damages and attorney fees appears to be undisputed.

* * *

The employer does not contest that the damages limitation would be unlawful if applied to statutory claims, but instead contends that the limitation applies only to contract claims, pointing to the language in the penultimate sentence that refers to "my exclusive remedy for violation of the terms, conditions or covenants of employment. . . ." Both the trial court and the Court of Appeal correctly rejected this interpretation. While the above quoted language is susceptible to the employer's interpretation, the final sentence—"I understand that I shall not be entitled to any other remedy. . . ."—makes clear that the damages limitation was all-encompassing. We conclude this damages limitation is contrary to public policy and unlawful.

2. Adequate Discovery

The employees argue that employers typically have in their possession many of the documents relevant for bringing an employment discrimina-

8. We emphasize at the outset that our general endorsement of the *Cole* requirements occurs in the particular context of mandatory employment arbitration agreements, in order to ensure that such agreements are not used as a means of effectively curtailing an employee's FEHA rights. These requirements would generally not apply in situations in which an employer and an employee knowingly and voluntarily enter into an arbitration agreement after a dispute has arisen. In those cases, employees are free to determine what trade-offs between arbitral efficiency and formal procedural protections best safeguard their statutory rights. Absent such freely negotiated agreements, it is for the courts to ensure that the arbitration forum imposed on an employee is sufficient to vindicate his or her rights under the FEHA.

tion case, as well as having in their employ many of the relevant witnesses. The denial of adequate discovery in arbitration proceedings leads to the de facto frustration of the employee's statutory rights. They cite a report by the Department of Labor's Commission on the Future of Worker–Management Relations, chaired by former Secretary of Labor John Dunlop and including employee and employer representatives, which concludes that "if private arbitration is to serve as a legitimate form of private enforcement of public employment law," it must among other things provide "a fair and simple method by which the employee can secure the necessary information to present his or her claim." (Com. on the Future of Worker–Management Relations, Reported Recommendations (1994) p. 31 (hereafter Dunlop Commission Report).)

We agree that adequate discovery is indispensable for the vindication of FEHA claims. The employer does not dispute the point, but contends that the arbitration agreement at issue in this case does provide for adequate discovery by incorporating by reference all the rules set forth in the CAA. Adequate provisions for discovery are set forth in the CAA at Code of Civil Procedure section 1283.05, subdivision (a).[10]

The employees point out that the provisions of Code of Civil Procedure section 1283.05 are only "conclusively deemed to be incorporated into" an agreement to arbitrate under section 1283.1 if the dispute arises "out of ... any injury to, or death of, a person caused by the wrongful act or neglect of another", and argue that this language does not apply to FEHA claims. They further argue that because adequate discovery is not guaranteed under the arbitration agreement, FEHA claims should not be deemed arbitrable.

We note that one Court of Appeal case has held that a FEHA sexual harassment claim is considered an "injury to ... a person" within the meaning of Code of Civil Procedure section 1283.1, subdivision (a). * * * The scope of this provision is not before us. But even assuming that the claim in this case is not the sort of injury encompassed by section 1283.1, subdivision (a), subdivision (b) of that section permits parties to agree to incorporate section 1283.05. We infer from subdivision (b), and from the fundamentally contractual nature of arbitration itself, that parties incorporating the CAA into their arbitration agreement are also permitted to agree to something less than the full panoply of discovery provided in section

10. Code of Civil Procedure section 1283.05, subdivision (a), states: "To the extent provided in Section 1283.1 depositions may be taken and discovery obtained in arbitration proceedings as follows:

(a) After the appointment of the arbitrator or arbitrators, the parties to the arbitration shall have the right to take depositions and to obtain discovery regarding the subject matter of the arbitration, and, to that end, to use and exercise all of the same rights, remedies, and procedures, and be subject to all of the same duties, liabilities, and obligations in the arbitration with respect to the subject matter thereof, * * * as if the subject matter of the arbitration were pending before a superior court of this state in a civil action other than a limited civil case, subject to the limitations as to depositions set forth in subdivision (e) of this section." Subdivision (e) states that depositions may only be taken with the approval of the arbitrator.

1283.05. We further infer that when parties agree to arbitrate statutory claims, they also implicitly agree, absent express language to the contrary, to such procedures as are necessary to vindicate that claim. As discussed above, it is undisputed that some discovery is often necessary for vindicating a FEHA claim. Accordingly, whether or not the employees in this case are entitled to the full range of discovery provided in Code of Civil Procedure section 1283.05, they are at least entitled to discovery sufficient to adequately arbitrate their statutory claim, including access to essential documents and witnesses, as determined by the arbitrator(s) * * *.[11]

Therefore, although the employees are correct that they are entitled to sufficient discovery as a means of vindicating their sexual discrimination claims, we hold that the employer, by agreeing to arbitrate the FEHA claim, has already impliedly consented to such discovery. Therefore, lack of discovery is not grounds for holding a FEHA claim inarbitrable.

3. Written Arbitration Award and Judicial Review

The employees argue that lack of judicial review of arbitration awards makes the vindication of FEHA rights in arbitration illusory. * * * Arbitration, they argue, cannot be an adequate means of resolving a FEHA claim if the arbitrator is essentially free to disregard the law.

* * *

We are not faced in this case with a petition to confirm an arbitration award, and therefore have no occasion to articulate precisely what standard of judicial review is "sufficient to ensure that arbitrators comply with the requirements of [a] statute." (*McMahon*, 482 U.S. at p. 232.) All we hold today is that in order for such judicial review to be successfully accomplished, an arbitrator in a FEHA case must issue a written arbitration decision that will reveal, however briefly, the essential findings and conclusions on which the award is based. While such written findings and conclusions are not required under the CAA, nothing in the present arbitration agreement precludes such written findings, and to the extent it applies to FEHA claims the agreement must be interpreted to provide for such findings. In all other respects, the employees' claim that they are unable to vindicate their FEHA rights because of inadequate judicial review of an arbitration award is premature.

4. Employee Not to Pay Unreasonable Costs and Arbitration Fees

The employees point to the fact that the agreement is governed by Code of Civil Procedure section 1284.2, which provides that "each party to the arbitration shall pay his pro rata share of the expenses and fees of the neutral arbitrator, together with other expenses of the arbitration incurred

11. We recognize, of course, that a limitation on discovery is one important component of the "simplicity, informality and expedition of arbitration." (*Gilmer*, 500 U.S. at p. 31.) The arbitrator and reviewing court must balance this desirable simplicity with the requirements of the FEHA in determining the appropriate discovery, absent more specific statutory or contractual provisions.

or imposed by the neutral arbitrator." They argue that requiring them to share the often substantial costs of arbitrators and arbitration effectively prevents them from vindicating their FEHA rights.

In considering the employees' claim, we start with the extensive discussion of this issue in *Cole*. The *Cole* court held that it was unlawful to require an employee who is the subject of a mandatory employment arbitration agreement to have to pay the costs of arbitration. The issue in that case was an arbitration agreement that was to be governed by the rules of the American Arbitration Association (AAA). Under these rules, the court noted that the employee may well be obliged to pay arbitrators' fees ranging from $500 to $1,000 per day or more, a $500 filing fee, and administrative fees of $150 per day, in addition to room rental and court reporter fees. The court's reasons for requiring employer-financed arbitration are worth quoting at length:

> In *Gilmer* the Supreme Court endorsed a system of arbitration in which employees are not required to pay for the arbitrator assigned to hear their statutory claims. There is no reason to think that the Court would have approved arbitration in the absence of this arrangement. Indeed, we are unaware of any situation in American jurisprudence in which a beneficiary of a federal statute has been required to pay for the services of the judge assigned to hear her or his case. Under *Gilmer*, arbitration is supposed to be a reasonable substitute for a judicial forum. Therefore, it would undermine Congress's intent to prevent employees who are seeking to vindicate statutory rights from gaining access to a judicial forum and then require them to pay for the services of an arbitrator when they would never be required to pay for a judge in court.
>
> There is no doubt that parties appearing in federal court may be required to assume the cost of filing fees and other administrative expenses, so any reasonable costs of this sort that accompany arbitration are not problematic. However, if an employee like Cole is required to pay arbitrators' fees ranging from $500 to $1,000 per day or more, . . . in addition to administrative and attorney's fees, is it likely that he will be able to pursue his statutory claims? We think not. * * * [I]t is unacceptable to require Cole to pay arbitrators' fees, because such fees are unlike anything that he would have to pay to pursue his statutory claims in court.
>
> Arbitration will occur in this case only because it has been mandated by the employer as a condition of employment. Absent this requirement, the employee would be free to pursue his claims in court without having to pay for the services of a judge. In such a circumstance—where arbitration has been imposed by the employer and occurs only at the option of the employer—arbitrators' fees should be borne solely by the employer.

The Tenth and Eleventh Circuit Courts of Appeal have adopted a position on arbitration fees for statutory employment claims essentially in accord with *Cole*. In Shankle [v. B–G Maintenance Management of Colorado, Inc., 163 F.3d 1230, (10th Cir.1999)], the court estimated that the employee would have to pay between $1,875 and $5,000 in forum costs to resolve his claim. As the court stated: "Mr. Shankle could not afford such a fee, and it is unlikely other similarly situated employees could either. The Agreement thus placed Mr. Shankle between the proverbial rock and a hard place—it prohibited use of the judicial forum, where a litigant is not required to pay for a judge's services, and the prohibitive cost substantially limited use of the arbitral forum. Essentially, B–G Maintenance required Mr. Shankle to agree to mandatory arbitration as a term of continued employment, yet failed to provide an accessible forum in which he could resolve his statutory rights. Such a result clearly undermines the remedial and deterrent functions of the federal anti-discrimination laws."

* * *

[I]f it is possible that the employee will be charged substantial forum costs, it is an insufficient judicial response to hold that he or she may be able to cancel these costs at the end of the process through judicial review. Such a system still poses a significant risk that employees will have to bear large costs to vindicate their statutory right against workplace discrimination, and therefore chills the exercise of that right. Because we conclude the imposition of substantial forum fees is contrary to public policy, and is therefore grounds for invalidating or "revoking" an arbitration agreement and denying a petition to compel arbitration, * * * we hold that the cost issues should be resolved not at the judicial review stage but when a court is petitioned to compel arbitration.

Accordingly, consistent with the majority of jurisdictions to consider this issue, we conclude that when an employer imposes mandatory arbitration as a condition of employment, the arbitration agreement or arbitration process cannot generally require the employee to bear any type of expense that the employee would not be required to bear if he or she were free to bring the action in court. This rule will ensure that employees bringing FEHA claims will not be deterred by costs greater than the usual costs incurred during litigation, costs that are essentially imposed on an employee by the employer.

Three principal objections have been raised to imposing the forum costs of arbitration on the employer. The first is that such a system will compromise the neutrality of the arbitrator. As the *Cole* court recognized, however, it is not the fact that the employer may pay an arbitrator that is most likely to induce bias, but rather the fact that the employer is a "repeat player" in the arbitration system who is more likely to be a source of business for the arbitrator. Furthermore, as the *Cole* court recognized, there are sufficient institutional safeguards, such as scrutiny by the plaintiff's bar and appointing agencies like the AAA, to protect against corrupt arbitrators.

The second objection is that although employees may have large forum costs, the cost of arbitration is generally smaller than litigation, so that the employee will realize a net benefit from arbitration. Although it is true that the costs of arbitration is on average smaller than that of litigation, it is also true that amount awarded is on average smaller as well. The payment of large, fixed, forum costs, especially in the face of expected meager awards, serves as a significant deterrent to the pursuit of FEHA claims.

To be sure, it would be ideal to devise a method by which the employee is put in exactly the same position in arbitration, costwise, as he or she would be in litigation. But the factors going into that calculus refuse to admit ready quantification. Turning a motion to compel arbitration into a mini-trial on the comparative costs and benefits of arbitration and litigation for a particular employee would not only be burdensome on the trial court and the parties, but would likely yield speculative answers. Nor would there be an advantage to apportioning arbitration costs at the conclusion of the arbitration rather than at the outset. Without clearly articulated guidelines, such a post-arbitration apportionment would create a sense of risk and uncertainty among employees that could discourage the arbitration of meritorious claims.

Moreover, the above rule is fair, inasmuch as it places the cost of arbitration on the party that imposes it. Unlike the employee, the employer is in a position to perform a cost/benefit calculus and decide whether arbitration is, overall, the most economical forum. Nor would this rule necessarily present an employer with a choice between paying all the forum costs of arbitration or forgoing arbitration altogether and defending itself in court. There is a third alternative. Because this proposed rule would only apply to mandatory, predispute employment arbitration agreements, and because in many instances arbitration will be considered an efficient means of resolving a dispute both for the employer and the employee, the employer seeking to avoid both payment of all forum costs and litigation can attempt to negotiate postdispute arbitration agreements with its aggrieved employees.

The third objection to requiring the employer to shoulder most of the costs of arbitration is that it appears contrary to statute. As noted, Code of Civil Procedure section 1284.2 provides that unless the arbitration agreement provides otherwise, each party to the arbitration must pay his or her pro rata share of arbitration costs. But section 1284.2 is a default provision, and the agreement to arbitrate a statutory claim is implicitly an agreement to abide by the substantive remedial provisions of the statute. As noted, FEHA rights are unwaivable. * * * We do not believe the FEHA contemplates that employees may be compelled to resolve their antidiscrimination claims in a forum in which they must pay for what is the equivalent of the judge's time and the rental of the courtroom.

* * *

We therefore hold that a mandatory employment arbitration agreement that contains within its scope the arbitration of FEHA claims impliedly obliges the employer to pay all types of costs that are unique to arbitration. Accordingly, we interpret the arbitration agreement in the present case as providing, consistent with the above, that the employer must bear the arbitration forum costs. The absence of specific provisions on arbitration costs would therefore not be grounds for denying the enforcement of an arbitration agreement.

D. Unconscionability of the Arbitration Agreement

1. General Principles of Unconscionability

In the previous section of this opinion, we focused on the minimum requirements for the arbitration of unwaivable statutory claims. In this section, we will consider objections to arbitration that apply more generally to any type of arbitration imposed on the employee by the employer as a condition of employment, regardless of the type of claim being arbitrated. These objections fall under the rubric of "unconscionability."

We explained the judicially created doctrine of unconscionability in [*Graham v. Scissor–Tail,* see p. 108 supra]. Unconscionability analysis begins with an inquiry into whether the contract is one of adhesion. "The term [contract of adhesion] signifies a standardized contract, which, imposed and drafted by the party of superior bargaining strength, relegates to the subscribing party only the opportunity to adhere to the contract or reject it." If the contract is adhesive, the court must then determine whether "other factors are present which, under established legal rules—legislative or judicial—operate to render it [unenforceable]." "Generally speaking, there are two judicially imposed limitations on the enforcement of adhesion contracts or provisions thereof. The first is that such a contract or provision which does not fall within the reasonable expectations of the weaker or 'adhering' party will not be enforced against him. The second—a principle of equity applicable to all contracts generally—is that a contract or provision, even if consistent with the reasonable expectations of the parties, will be denied enforcement if, considered in its context, it is unduly oppressive or 'unconscionable.' " * * *

Because unconscionability is a reason for refusing to enforce contracts generally, it is also a valid reason for refusing to enforce an arbitration agreement under Code of Civil Procedure section 1281, which, as noted, provides that arbitration agreements are "valid, irrevocable, and enforceable, save upon such grounds as exist at law or in equity for the revocation of any contract." The United States Supreme Court, in interpreting the same language found in section 2 of the FAA, recognized that "generally applicable contract defenses, such as fraud, duress, or unconscionability, may be applied to invalidate arbitration agreements. . . . "

"[U]nconscionability has both a 'procedural' and a 'substantive' element," the former focusing on "oppression" or "surprise" due to unequal bargaining power, the latter on "overly harsh" or "one-sided" results. "The prevailing view is that [procedural and substantive unconscionability] must both be present in order for a court to exercise its discretion to refuse to enforce a contract or clause under the doctrine of unconscionability." But they need not be present in the same degree. "Essentially a sliding scale is invoked which disregards the regularity of the procedural process of the contract formation, that creates the terms, in proportion to the greater harshness or unreasonableness of the substantive terms themselves." In other words, the more substantively oppressive the contract term, the less evidence of procedural unconscionability is required to come to the conclusion that the term is unenforceable, and vice versa.

2. Unconscionability and Mandatory Employment Arbitration

Applying the above principles to this case, we first determine whether the arbitration agreement is adhesive. There is little dispute that it is. It was imposed on employees as a condition of employment and there was no opportunity to negotiate.

* * *

Aside from FEHA issues discussed in the previous part of this opinion, the employees contend that the agreement is substantively unconscionable because it requires only employees to arbitrate their wrongful termination claims against the employer, but does not require the employer to arbitrate claims it may have against the employees. In asserting that this lack of mutuality is unconscionable, they rely primarily on the opinion of the Court of Appeal Stirlen v. Supercuts, Inc., 60 Cal. Rptr.2d 138 (Cal.App. 1997). The employee in that case was hired as a vice president and chief financial officer; his employment contract provided for arbitration "in the event there is any dispute arising out of [the employee's] employment with the Company," including "the termination of that employment." The agreement specifically excluded certain types of disputes from the scope of arbitration, including those relating to the protection of the employer's intellectual and other property and the enforcement of a post-employment covenant not to compete, which were to be litigated in state or federal court. The employee was to waive the right to challenge the jurisdiction of such a court. The arbitration agreement further provided that the damages available would be limited to "the amount of actual damages for breach of contract, less any proper offset for mitigation of such damages." When an arbitration claim was filed, payments of any salary or benefits were to cease "without penalty to the Company," pending the outcome of the arbitration.

The *Stirlen* court concluded that the agreement was one of adhesion, even though the employee in question was a high-level executive, because of the lack of opportunity to negotiate. The court then concluded that the arbitration agreement was substantively unconscionable. * * * The employee pursuing claims against the employer had to bear not only with the inherent shortcomings of arbitration—limited discovery, limited judicial review, limited procedural protections—but also significant damage limitations imposed by the arbitration agreement. The employer, on the other hand, in pursuing its claims, was not subject to these disadvantageous limitations and had written into the agreement special advantages, such as a waiver of jurisdictional objections by the employee if sued by the employer.

The *Stirlen* court did not hold that all lack of mutuality in a contract of adhesion was invalid. "We agree a contract can provide a 'margin of safety' that provides the party with superior bargaining strength a type of extra protection for which it has a legitimate commercial need without being unconscionable. However, unless the 'business realities' that create the special need for such an advantage are explained in the contract itself, which is not the case here, it must be factually established." The *Stirlen* court found no "business reality" to justify the lack of mutuality, concluding that the terms of the arbitration clause were " 'so extreme as to appear unconscionable according to the mores and business practices of the time and place.' "

* * *

We conclude that *Stirlen* [is] correct in requiring this "modicum of bilaterality" in an arbitration agreement. Given the disadvantages that may exist for plaintiffs arbitrating disputes, it is unfairly one-sided for an employer with superior bargaining power to impose arbitration on the employee as plaintiff but not to accept such limitations when it seeks to prosecute a claim against the employee, without at least some reasonable justification for such one-sidedness based on "business realities." As has been recognized unconscionability turns not only on a "one-sided" result, but also on an absence of "justification" for it. If the arbitration system established by the employer is indeed fair, then the employer as well as the employee should be willing to submit claims to arbitration. Without reasonable justification for this lack of mutuality, arbitration appears less as a forum for neutral dispute resolution and more as a means of maximizing employer advantage. Arbitration was not intended for this purpose

The employer cites a number of cases that have held that a lack of mutuality in an arbitration agreement does not render the contract illusory as long as the employer agrees to be bound by the arbitration of employment disputes. We agree that such lack of mutuality does not render the contract illusory, i.e., lacking in mutual consideration. We conclude, rather, that in the context of an arbitration agreement imposed by the employer on the employee, such a one-sided term is unconscionable. Although parties are free to contract for asymmetrical remedies and arbitration clauses of varying scope, *Stirlen* [is] correct that the doctrine of unconscionability limits the extent to which a stronger party may, through a contract of adhesion, impose the arbitration forum on the weaker party without accepting that forum for itself.

* * *

Applying these principles to the present case, we note the arbitration agreement was limited in scope to employee claims regarding wrongful termination. Although it did not expressly authorize litigation of the employer's claims against the employee, as was the case in *Stirlen*, such was the clear implication of the agreement. Obviously, the lack of mutuality can be manifested as much by what the agreement does not provide as by what it does.

This is not to say that an arbitration clause must mandate the arbitration of all claims between employer and employee in order to avoid invalidation on grounds of unconscionability. Indeed, as the employer points out, the present arbitration agreement does not require arbitration of all conceivable claims that an employee might have against an employer, only wrongful termination claims. But an arbitration agreement imposed in an adhesive context lacks basic fairness and mutuality if it requires one contracting party, but not the other, to arbitrate all claims arising out of the same transaction or occurrence or series of transactions or occurrences. The arbitration agreement in this case lacks mutuality in this sense because it requires the arbitration of employee—but not employer—claims arising out of a wrongful termination. An employee terminated for stealing trade secrets, for example, must arbitrate his or her wrongful termination claim under the agreement while the employer has no corresponding obligation to arbitrate its trade secrets claim against the employee.

The unconscionable one-sidedness of the arbitration agreement is compounded in this case by the fact that it does not permit the full recovery of damages for employees, while placing no such restriction on the employer. Even if the limitation on FEHA damages is severed as contrary to public policy, the arbitration clause in the present case still does not permit full recovery of ordinary contract damages. The arbitration agreement specifies that damages are to be limited to the amount of back pay lost up until the time of arbitration. This provision excludes damages for prospective future earnings, so-called "front pay," a common and often substantial component of contractual damages in a wrongful termination case. The employer, on the other hand, is bound by no comparable limitation should it pursue a claim against its employees.

The employer in this case, as well as the Court of Appeal, claim the lack of mutuality was based on the realities of the employees' place in the organizational hierarchy. As the Court of Appeal stated: "We ... observe that the wording of the agreement most likely resulted from the employees' position within the organization and may reflect the fact that the parties did not foresee the possibility of any dispute arising from employment that was not initiated by the employee. Plaintiffs were lower-level supervisory employees, without the sort of access to proprietary information or control over corporate finances that might lead to an employer suit against them."

The fact that it is unlikely an employer will bring claims against a particular type of employee is not, ultimately, a justification for a unilateral arbitration agreement. It provides no reason for categorically exempting employer claims, however rare, from mandatory arbitration. Although an employer may be able, in a future case, to justify a unilateral arbitration agreement, the employer in the present case has not done so.

E. Severability of Unconscionable Provisions

The employees contend that the presence of various unconscionable provisions or provisions contrary to public policy leads to the conclusion that the arbitration agreement as a whole cannot be enforced. The employer contends that, insofar as there are unconscionable provisions, they should be severed and the rest of the agreement enforced.

Civil Code section 1670.5, subdivision (a) provides that "if the court as a matter of law finds the contract or any clause of the contract to have been unconscionable at the time it was made the court may refuse to enforce the contract, or it may enforce the remainder of the contract without the unconscionable clause, or it may so limit the application of any unconscionable clause as to avoid any unconscionable result." Comment 2 of the Legislative Committee Comment on section 1670.5, incorporating the comments from the Uniform Commercial Code, states: "Under this section the court, in its discretion, may refuse to enforce the contract as a whole if it is permeated by the unconscionability, or it may strike any single clause or group of clauses which are so tainted or which are contrary to the essential purpose of the agreement, or it may simply limit unconscionable clauses so as to avoid unconscionable results."

Thus, the statute appears to give a trial court some discretion as to whether to sever or restrict the unconscionable provision or whether to refuse to enforce the entire agreement. But it also appears to contemplate the latter course only when an agreement is "permeated" by unconscionability.

* * *

Two reasons for severing or restricting illegal terms rather than voiding the entire contract appear implicit in case law. The first is to prevent parties from gaining undeserved benefit or suffering undeserved detriment as a result of voiding the entire agreement—particularly when there has been full or partial performance of the contract. Second, more generally, the doctrine of severance attempts to conserve a contractual relationship if to do so would not be condoning an illegal scheme. The overarching inquiry is whether "the interests of justice ... would be furthered" by severance. Moreover, courts must have the capacity to cure the unlawful contract through severance or restriction of the offending clause, which, as discussed below, is not invariably the case.

* * *

In this case, two factors weigh against severance of the unlawful provisions. First, the arbitration agreement contains more than one unlawful provision; it has both an unlawful damages provision and an unconscionably unilateral arbitration clause. Such multiple defects indicate a systematic effort to impose arbitration on an employee not simply as an alternative to litigation, but as an inferior forum that works to the employer's advantage. In other words, given the multiple unlawful provisions, the trial court did not abuse its discretion in concluding that the arbitration agreement is permeated by an unlawful purpose.[13]

13. We need not decide whether the unlawful damages provision in this arbitration agreement, by itself, would be sufficient to warrant a court's refusal to enforce that agreement. We note, however, that in the analogous case of overly broad covenants not to compete, courts have tended to invalidate rather than restrict such covenants when it appears they were drafted in bad faith, i.e., with a knowledge of their illegality. The rea-

Second, in the case of the agreement's lack of mutuality, such permeation is indicated by the fact that there is no single provision a court can strike or restrict in order to remove the unconscionable taint from the agreement. Rather, the court would have to, in effect, reform the contract, not through severance or restriction, but by augmenting it with additional terms. * * * Code of Civil Procedure section 1281.2 authorizes the court to refuse arbitration if grounds for revocation exist, not to reform the agreement to make it lawful. Nor do courts have any such power under their inherent, limited authority to reform contracts. (See Kolani v. Gluska, 64 Cal. App. 4th 402, 407–408 (1998)) [power to reform limited to instances in which parties make mistakes, not to correct illegal provisions]. Because a court is unable to cure this unconscionability through severance or restriction, and is not permitted to cure it through reformation and augmentation, it must void the entire agreement.

* * *

The approach described above is consistent with our holding in *Scissor–Tail.* In that case, we found an arbitration agreement to be unconscionable because the agreement provided for an arbitrator likely to be biased in favor of the party imposing the agreement. We nonetheless recognized that "the parties have indeed agreed to arbitrate" and that there is a "strong public policy of this state in favor of resolving disputes by arbitration." The court found a way out of this dilemma through the [California Arbitration Act,] specifically Code of Civil Procedure section 1281.6, which provides in part: "In the absence of an agreed method [for appointing an arbitrator], or if the agreed method fails or for any reason cannot be followed, or when an arbitrator appointed fails to act and his or her successor has not been appointed, the court, on petition of a party to the arbitration agreement, shall appoint the arbitrator." Citing this provision, the court stated: "We therefore conclude that upon remand the trial court should afford the parties a reasonable opportunity to agree on a suitable arbitrator and, failing such agreement, the court should on petition of either party appoint the arbitrator." Other cases, both before and after *Scissor-Tail,* have also held that the part of an arbitration clause providing

son for this rule is that if such bad faith restrictive covenants are enforced, then "employers are encouraged to overreach; if the covenant is overbroad then the court will redraft it for them." This reasoning applies with equal force to arbitration agreements that limit damages to be obtained from challenging the violation of unwaivable statutory rights. An employer will not be deterred from routinely inserting such a deliberately illegal clause into the arbitration agreements it mandates for its employees if it knows that the worst penalty for such illegality is the severance of the clause after the employee has litigated the matter. In that sense, the enforcement of a form arbitration agreement containing such a clause drafted in bad faith would be condoning, or at least not discouraging, an illegal scheme, and severance would be disfavored unless it were for some other reason in the interests of justice. The refusal to enforce such a clause is also consistent with the rule that a party may waive its right to arbitration through bad faith or willful misconduct. Because we resolve this case on other grounds, we need not decide whether the state of the law with respect to damages limitations was sufficiently clear at the time the arbitration agreement was signed to lead to the conclusion that this damages clause was drafted in bad faith.

for a less-than-neutral arbitration forum is severable from the rest of the clause.

Thus, in *Scissor-Tail* and the other cases cited above, the arbitration statute itself gave the court the power to reform an arbitration agreement with respect to the method of selecting arbitrators. There is no comparable provision in the arbitration statute that permits courts to reform an unconscionably one-sided agreement.

* * *

The employer also points to two cases in which unconscionably one-sided provisions in arbitration agreements were severed and the agreement enforced. [Saika v. Gold, 56 Cal. Rptr.2d 922 (Cal.App.1996)] involved an arbitration agreement with a provision that would make the arbitration nonbinding if the arbitration award were $25,000 or greater. In Beynon v. Garden Grove Medical Group [161 Cal. Rptr. 146 (Cal.App.1980)], a provision of the arbitration agreement gave one party, but not the other, the option of rejecting the arbitrator's decision. The courts in both instances concluded, in *Saika* implicitly, in *Beynon* explicitly, that the offending clause was severable from the rest of the arbitration agreement.

The provisions in these two cases are different from the one-sided arbitration provision at issue in this case in at least two important respects. First, the one-sidedness in the above two cases were confined to single provisions regarding the rights of the parties after an arbitration award was made, not a provision affecting the scope of the arbitration. As such, the unconscionability could be cured by severing the unlawful provisions. Second, in both cases, the arguments against severance were made by the party that had imposed the unconscionable provision in order to prevent enforcement of an arbitration award against them, and the failure to sever would have had the effect of accomplishing the precise unlawful purpose of that provision the invalidation of the arbitration award. As discussed, courts will generally sever illegal provisions and enforce a contract when nonenforcement will lead to an undeserved benefit or detriment to one of the parties that would not further the interests of justice. In *Beynon* and *Saika*, the interests of justice would obviously not have been furthered by nonenforcement. The same considerations are not found in the present case.

The judgment of the Court of Appeal upholding the employer's petition to compel arbitration is reversed, and the cause is remanded to the Court of Appeal with directions to affirm the judgment of the trial court.

■ BROWN, J., CONCURRING. Although I agree with most of the majority's reasoning, I write separately on the issue of apportioning arbitral costs. The majority takes the simple approach: where the employer imposes mandatory arbitration and the employee asserts a statutory claim, the employer must bear all costs "unique to arbitration." Simplicity, however, is not a proxy for correctness. * * *

In adopting the bright-line approach advocated by *Cole,* supra, the majority argues that the mere risk that an employee may have to bear certain arbitral costs necessarily "chills the exercise" of her statutory rights. Thus, arbitration is not a reasonable substitute for a court if arbitral costs, such as the arbitrator's fees, may be imposed on the employee. The majority, however, assumes too much. "Arbitration is often far more affordable to plaintiffs and defendants alike than is pursuing a claim in court." Because employees may incur fewer costs and attorney fees in arbitration than in court, the potential imposition of arbitration forum costs does not automatically render the arbitral forum more expensive than—and therefore inferior to—the judicial forum.

The majority's approach also ignores the unique circumstances of each case. Not all arbitrations are costly, and not all employees are unable to afford the unique costs of arbitration. Thus, the imposition of some arbitral costs does not deter or discourage employees from pursuing their statutory claims in every case. (See, e.g., Williams v. Cigna Financial Advisors Inc.,197 F.3d 752, 764–765 (5th Cir.1999) [compelling arbitration because the employee did not show that he was unable to pay the arbitral costs or that these costs would deter him from pursuing his claims]; McCaskill v. SCI Management Corp., 2000 WL 875396 (N.D.Ill.) [compelling arbitration because there was no evidence that the costs of arbitration would be prohibitively expensive for the employee]; Cline v. H.E. Butt Grocery Co.,79 F. Supp. 2d 730, 733 (S.D.Tex.1999) [compelling arbitration because there was no evidence that the employee would have to pay any costs or that the employee could not afford to do so]. Indeed, the uniqueness of each case makes it impossible for any court to "conclude that the payment of fees will constitute a barrier to the vindication of ... statutory rights" without knowing the exact amount the employee must pay.

Accordingly, I would reject the majority's approach and follow the approach suggested by courts in several other jurisdictions. As long as the mandatory arbitration agreement does not require the employee to front the arbitration forum costs or to pay a certain share of these costs, apportionment should be left to the arbitrator. When apportioning costs, the arbitrator should consider the magnitude of the costs unique to arbitration, the ability of the employee to pay a share of these costs, and the overall expense of the arbitration as compared to a court proceeding. Ultimately, any apportionment should ensure that the costs imposed on the employee, if known at the onset of litigation, would not have deterred her from enforcing her statutory rights or stopped her from effectively vindicating these rights.

If the employee feels that the arbitrator's apportionment of costs is unreasonable, then she can raise the issue during judicial review of the arbitration award. I believe such an approach is preferable because it accounts for the particular circumstances of each case without sacrificing the employee's statutory rights.

NOTES AND QUESTIONS

1. As the *Armendariz* case indicates, arbitration agreements are increasingly common in nonunion employment agreements outside of the securities industry. Companies like Rockwell International, Brown and Root, Borg–Warner, and Hughes Electronics are now requiring such clauses, which usually call for arbitration under the auspices of an organization like the AAA. The General Accounting office estimated in 1995 that about 10% of companies with more than 100 employees were using binding arbitration to resolve employment discrimination claims (although arbitration was not made mandatory in all cases); another 8.4% were considering instituting such a policy. Most of these arbitration policies had been implemented in the previous five years, and the number would certainly be considerably larger today. GAO, Employment Discrimination: Most Private–Sector Employers Use Alternative Dispute Resolution 6–8, 28 (July 1995).

2. Does Justice Brown have the better of the argument when he urges that the issue of costs should be postponed, until such time as a court is asked to confirm or vacate the award? This was in fact the approach of the United States Supreme Court in a recent non-employment case, Green Tree Financial Corp.-Alabama v. Randolph, 531 U.S. 79, 121 S.Ct. 513, 148 L.Ed.2d 373 (2000). Here a buyer of a mobile home had financed the purchase, and later brought suit against the lender alleging violations of the Truth in Lending Act, 15 U.S.C. § 1601. The Eleventh Circuit held that the arbitration clause in the agreement was unenforceable: Since the agreement was silent with respect to the payment of filing fees and arbitrator compensation, there was a risk that the plaintiff's ability to assert her statutory rights under the TILA would be undone by "steep" arbitration costs. The Supreme Court reversed.

The Court acknowledged the possibility that "the existence of large arbitration costs could preclude a litigant such as [the plaintiff] from effectively vindicating her federal statutory rights in the arbitral forum." However, if a party seeks to invalidate an arbitration agreement on the ground that arbitration "would be prohibitively expensive," she must "bear the burden of showing the likelihood of incurring such costs." Here, the "risk" that the plaintiff "will be saddled with prohibitive costs is too speculative to justify the invalidation of an arbitration agreement," and the agreement's silence on the subject of costs "alone is plainly insufficient to render it unenforceable." Four dissenting justices would have preferred to remand for "clarification" and "further consideration of the accessibility of the arbitral forum" to the plaintiff, rather than "leaving the issue unsettled until the end of the line," that is, until after the arbitration. They noted that under the AAA's Consumer Arbitration Rules, consumers in small-claims arbitration incur no filing fee and are required to pay only $125 of the total fees charged by the arbitrator—but stressed that "there is no reliable indication in this record that [the plaintiff's] claim will be arbitrated under any consumer-protective fee arrangement."

3. On the subject of "non-mutual" arbitration clauses—where only one of the parties to the agreement is obligated to arbitrate—compare *Stevens/Leinweber/Sullens, Inc. v. Holm Development and Management, Inc.*, supra p. 102.

4. Note that the Supreme Court of California apparently assumed in *Armendariz* that it was *for a court—rather than for an arbitrator*—to determine whether the terms of the agreement were "unlawful" or "unconscionable." Cf. pp. 100–101 supra; see also Margaret M. Harding, The Redefinition of Arbitration By Those With Superior Bargaining Power, 1999 Utah L. Rev. 857, 922–23 ("The claim that an arbitration clause is invalid because it improperly restricts statutory remedies should be distinguished from the situation where the parties in the container contract exclude certain types of damages"; "a defense to arbitration based on public policy stemming * * * from the unsuitability of the particular arbitral scheme crafted for determining the claim does indeed challenge the validity of the arbitration agreement and the arbitrability of the dispute"). Do you agree?

Assume, though, that this is indeed a question for the court: Does it follow that a judicial finding of "unconscionability" necessarily means that *the arbitration agreement as a whole* "is tainted and cannot be enforced"? See Harding, supra at 944 (courts should "penalize parties who attempt to use the arbitral process for improper means"; [w]hen a party attempts to abuse the arbitral process and gets caught, that party should completely lose the privilege—gained only by its superior economic position—of requiring the weaker party to arbitrate). Do you agree? See also Coddington Enterprises, Inc. v. Werries, 54 F.Supp.2d 935 (W.D.Mo.1999), in which an arbitration clause, in an agreement between retail grocers and their wholesale supplier, provided that the arbitrators "will not award punitive, consequential or indirect damages." In the grocers' action for RICO violations, the court found the arbitration clause to be unenforceable: The quoted phrase amounts to "a limitation on the authority of arbitrators, something the parties can doubtless agree to—even if their agreement means that arbitration provides inadequate remedies and cannot be enforced." Cf. Wright v. Circuit City Stores, 82 F.Supp.2d 1279 (N.D.Ala. 2000), in which an employment agreement limited punitive damages "to the greater of the monetary awards rendered for back pay and/or front pay or $5000," and also provided that if any of the company's "Dispute Resolution Rules and Procedures" were held to be "in conflict with a mandatory provision of applicable law," it would be "modified." The employee sued for violations of Title VII and of 42 U.S.C. § 1981, but the court held that arbitration should be compelled; it relied both on the severability clause, and the employer's "good faith in devising the arbitration plan" as evidenced by the fact that employees were given an opportunity to "reject" Circuit City's arbitration proposal by opting out within 30 days following signature. The arbitration clause was, however, to be "modified * * * so that it allows for the full range of remedies that the Plaintiffs would be entitled to under § 1981."

5. Once it is clear that asserted violations of statutory rights may now be sent to arbitration, is it inevitable that a more intensive judicial scrutiny of arbitral awards will follow? See the *Mitsubishi* case, supra. One distinguished labor arbitrator has warned that "[w]hen arbitrators start interpreting statutes * * * there is no reason why their interpretations of the proper application of statutes should be given greater weight than that of the district courts. District courts' interpretations of statutes are constantly being reviewed by appellate courts.'' Feller, Arbitration and the External Law Revisited, 37 St. Louis U.L.J. 973, 980 (1993).

See, e.g., Halligan v. Piper Jaffray, Inc., 148 F.3d 197 (2d Cir.1998). Although a discharged employee had presented the arbitrators with ''overwhelming evidence'' of age-based discrimination, ''an NASD arbitration panel denied any relief in an award that 'did not contain any explanation or rationale for the result.' '' The Second Circuit held that the award should be vacated: ''In view of the strong evidence that Halligan was fired because of his age and the agreement of the parties that the arbitrators were correctly advised of the applicable legal principles, we are inclined to hold that they ignored the law or the evidence or both.'' The court stressed that in making this decision, the arbitrators' failure to explain their award ''can be taken into account.'' If the arbitrators had given as their rationale that they had simply believed the employer's witnesses rather than the employee's, ''on this record it would have been extremely hard to accept—but they did not do even that.'' The court disclaimed any holding that arbitrators must write reasoned awards in every case or ''even in most cases''—but it observed that ''where a reviewing court is inclined to find that arbitrators manifestly disregarded the law or the evidence and that an explanation, if given, would have strained credulity, the absence of explanation may reinforce the reviewing court's confidence that the arbitrators engaged in manifest disregard.''

Is it possible that too great an enthusiasm for arbitration in cases that touch on individual rights may create the danger of a ''backlash'' of hostility to the process generally?

6. The theoretical notion that an arbitration award could be overturned for ''manifestly disregarding the law'' has always been in considerable tension with a view of arbitration as a ''nonlegal'' process—a model in which arbitrators are ''free to ignore'' substantive rules of law in order to ''do justice as they see it,'' see pp. 15–17, 146–150 supra. The anomaly could be ignored as long as the doctrine of ''manifest disregard'' was largely moribund—see p. 150 supra and, for a very poor prophecy, Alan Rau, The New York Convention in American Courts, 7 Amer. Rev. of Int'l Arb. 213, 238 (1996)(''This will never happen in our lifetimes.''). Cases like *Halligan v. Piper Jaffray* seem, however, to represent efforts to breathe new life into the doctrine—for as disputes over statutory rights are increasingly swept into arbitration, courts naturally come under increasing pressure to ensure that these rights are being adequately addressed.

More recently, by contrast, the Seventh Circuit has attempted to put the doctrine of ''manifest disregard'' in its place—by essentially equating it with the review of awards on grounds of ''public policy,'' and suggesting that it is subject to the same limitations as ''public policy'' review. In George Watts & Son, Inc. v. Tiffany & Co., 248 F.3d 577 (7th Cir.2001), an arbitrator granted relief to a distributor under the state's ''Fair Dealership Law,'' but failed, allegedly in violation of the statute, to award attorneys' fees and costs. The court nevertheless upheld confirmation of the award: "Manifest disregard of the law," according to Judge Easterbrook, means simply that "an arbitrator may not direct the parties to violate the law." "The judiciary may step in when the arbitrator has commanded the parties to violate legal norms," but "judges may not deprive arbitrators of authority to reach compromise outcomes that legal norms leave within the discretion of the parties to the arbitration agreement." Here, the parties themselves could certainly have negotiated a settlement under which each side would bear its own fees and costs. And if there would be no legal objection to such an outcome, "what the parties may do, the arbitrator as their mutual agent may do." For a similar rationale in "public policy" cases, see *Eastern Associated Coal Corp. v. United Mine Workers,* supra pp. 166–167.

7. Another response to growing criticism of employment arbitration may be found in rules that have recently been approved by the AAA for the arbitration of employment disputes. These rules provide that the arbitrators must be "experienced in the field of employment law," and that "[t]he parties shall bear the same burdens of proof and * * of producing evidence as would apply if their claims * * * had been brought in court." The arbitrator has "the authority to order such discovery, by way of deposition, interrogatory, document production, or otherwise," as he considers necessary; he may grant any relief that he deems "just and equitable, including any remedy or relief that would have been available to the parties had the matter been heard in court." The arbitrator must also "provide the written reasons for the award unless the parties agree otherwise," and the resulting award (with the exception of the names of the parties and witnesses) "shall be publicly available, on a cost basis." AAA, National Rules for the Resolution of Employment Disputes (effective January 1, 2001), R. 7, R. 11(a), R. 22, R. 34(b), (c), (d). According to one attorney who helped draft them, by arbitrating under the new rules "you are getting something close to the type of hearing that you would have had, [in] a bench trial in state or federal court." Aquino, "Revamping Employment Arbitration," The Recorder, Aug. 4, 1994 at p. 1. Are these changes desirable?

8. Attorneys who represent management in employment matters have cautioned that there might be some dangers in using arbitration agreements: For example, arbitrators might "borrow from the experience of labor arbitrators" under collective bargaining agreements that require "just cause" for discharge, and thereby expand the rights of "at-will" employees. Piskorski & Ross, Private Arbitration as the Exclusive Means of Resolving Employment–Related Disputes, 19 Employee Relations L.J. 205, 210 (1993); see also Guidry & Huffman, Legal and Practical Aspects of Alternative Dispute Resolution in Non–Union Companies, 6 Lab.Law. 1, 25 (1990) (employer may be "hoist on its own petard"). Is this a serious risk? In PaineWebber, Inc. v. Agron, 49 F.3d 347 (8th Cir.1995), arbitrators found that a brokerage firm had "improperly fired" one of its vice-presidents. The employer objected that this award "manifestly disregarded" the state's employment-at-will doctrine, but the court disagreed. Even if a "manifest disregard of the law" standard applied, "the use of the arbitration procedure as a means of settling employment-related disputes

* * * necessarily alters the employment relationship from at-will to something else—some standard of discernable cause is inherently required in this context where an arbitration panel is called on to interpret the employment relationship." If the plaintiff's employment was purely at-will, "the arbitration procedure designed to interpret that employment relationship would serve no identifiable purpose."

9. The Supreme Court in *Gilmer* was "unpersuaded" by the employee's argument that compelling arbitration would "undermine" the role of the EEOC in enforcing statutes like the Age Discrimination in Employment Act: After all, it noted, a claimant subject to an arbitration agreement "will still be able to file a charge with the EEOC, even though [he] is not able to institute a private judicial action." And in any event, the EEOC's role in combating age discrimination is not dependent on the filing of a charge by a claimant—since the agency may receive information concerning alleged violations of the Act "from any source" and has independent authority to investigate discrimination. 500 U.S. at 28.

What possibilities then are open to the EEOC if it is convinced that Gilmer's employer had been violating the ADEA? It seems generally accepted (as the Supreme Court made clear in *Gilmer* itself) that "arbitration agreements will not preclude the EEOC from bringing actions seeking class-wide and equitable relief." The EEOC, however, is also empowered to seek monetary relief, such as back pay and damages, to "make whole" aggrieved employees: May it do so on behalf of employees like Gilmer who are bound to arbitrate their own claims?

The EEOC has asserted that it is allowed to seek such an order because it would not be "standing in the shoes" of the employees, but would rather be "suing in the public interest." The Sixth Circuit agreed with the EEOC in EEOC v. Frank's Nursery & Crafts, Inc., 177 F.3d 448 (6th Cir.1999)(EEOC and the employee "are not in privity, and [they] do not possess identical causes of action or interests"; the EEOC was granted by Congress "a right to represent an interest broader than that of a particular individual"; "[t]o empower a private individual to take away this congressional mandate, by entering into arbitration agreements or other contractual arrangements, would grant that individual the ability to govern whether and when the EEOC may protect the public interest * * * against employment discrimination"). It has even been suggested that in such cases the possibility of such EEOC actions "could slow the trend towards arbitration of employment-discrimination claims * * * by providing claimants with an end-run around *Gilmer*." See Negris, "Employment ADR: Sidestepping *Gilmer*," World Arb. & Med. Rep., March 1993 at 55. Other circuits, however, have disagreed, and the Supreme Court is likely to resolve the issue shortly. See EEOC v. Waffle House, Inc., 193 F.3d 805 (4th Cir.1999), *cert. granted*, ___ U.S. ___, 121 S.Ct. 1401, 149 L.Ed.2d 344 ("when the EEOC seeks 'make-whole' relief for [an employee], the federal policy favoring enforcement of private arbitration agreements outweighs the EEOC's right to proceed in federal court because in that circumstance, the EEOC's public interest is minimal"); see also EEOC v. Kidder, Peabody

& Co., Inc., 156 F.3d 298 (2d Cir.1998)("where an individual has freely contracted away, waived, or unsuccessfully litigated a claim, the public interest in a back pay award is minimal"). For an interesting contrast, see Olde Discount Corp. v. Tupman, supra p. 72.

10. The obstacles faced by an employee in pursuing an employment discrimination claim—whether through the EEOC's enforcement mechanism, or through a private suit—may be considerable. To seek relief on a federal statutory claim—under Title VII, the Age Discrimination in Employment Act, or the Americans with Disability Act—an individual must first file a charge of discrimination with the EEOC. If its investigation suggests the existence of a valid claim the EEOC must attempt conciliation, and may ultimately bring suit on behalf of the individual claimant. If for any reason the agency determines not to pursue the case, it must issue a "right to sue" notice informing the individual that she is free to initiate her own court action. In *each* of the years 1998 through 2000, between 77,000 and 80,000 charges of discrimination were filed by employees, former employees, or rejected job applicants; in these years the EEOC filed 366, 439, and 291 lawsuits respectively. The average processing time for a charge is "upwards of 300 days," and in some district offices is considerably higher. In discrimination lawsuits brought by individual employees, plaintiffs tend to receive a favorable jury verdict in fewer than half of litigated cases. More to the point, though, relatively few of these suits even reach a jury—since around 60% are disposed of by pre-trial motion, virtually always in favor of the defendant. In addition, a recent study indicates that employment discrimination plaintiffs who *do* win at trial see their judgments overturned on appeal in 43.6% of cases, while verdicts in favor of the employer are reversed in fewer than 6% of cases. See U.S. Commission on Civil Rights, Overcoming the Past, Focusing on the Future (Sept. 2000); U.S. Dept. of Justice, Bureau of Justice Statistics, Special Report: Civil Rights Complaints in U.S. District Courts, 1990–1998 (Jan. 2000); Gary R. Siniscalo, "Comparative Analysis of Jury Trials in Employment Cases," in Samuel Estreicher (ed.), Proceedings, New York University 49th Annual Conference on Labor 413 (1997); "Plaintiff Wins in Bias Cases Often Overturned: Study," Chicago Tribune, July 18, 2001 at p. 4.

In these circumstances, it is hardly surprising that employees may have some difficulty enlisting an attorney willing to pursue discrimination litigation on a contingent-fee basis: "Experienced litigators across the country tell me that the good plaintiffs' attorneys will accept on the average only about one in a hundred of the discrimination claimants who seek their help. One of the Detroit area's top employment specialists was more precise. His secretary kept an actual count; he took on one out of eighty-seven persons who contacted him for possible representation." Theodore J. St. Antoine, Mandatory Arbitration of Employment Discrimination Claims: Unmitigated Evil or Blessing in Disguise?, 15 T.M. Cooley L. Rev. 1 (1998)(arbitration "may well be the most realistic hope of the ordinary claimant"); see also Samuel Estreicher, Saturns for Rickshaws: The Stakes in the Debate over Predispute Employment Arbitration Agreements, 16 Ohio St. J. Disp. Resol. 559, 563 (2001)("the people who benefit under a litigation-based system are those whose salaries are high enough to warrant the costs and risks of a law suit undertaken by competent counsel"; "the system works well for high-end claimants and most plaintiff lawyers, and not very well for average claimants").

11. Professor Jerome Cohen once remarked, in a very different context, that the worst kind of Comparative Law thinking is that which compares "*our* theory" with "*their* reality"—and, inevitably, finds the latter deficient. Might the same thing be said about some of the literature critical of employment arbitration—redolent as it is with what has been termed "litigation romanticism"? See Carrie Menkel–Meadow, Mothers and Fathers of Invention: The Intellectual Founders of ADR, 16 Ohio St. J. on Disp. Resol. 1, 20 (2000).

12. There is very little reliable evidence that allows us to compare results in arbitration with those in *litigated* employment discrimination cases. One study of AAA employment arbitrations indicated that the total amount received by all plaintiffs in arbitration was 18% of the amount they had demanded, while all plaintiffs in litigation received only 10.4%, Lewis Maltby, Private Justice: Employment Arbitration and Civil Rights, in Paul Haagen (ed)., Arbitration Now 1, 18–19 (1999). Another comparison of litigated and arbitrated cases asserts that "an employee prevails with about the same frequency in each forum." The author did note that the average recovery in cases actually litigated through trial was "significantly greater than in arbitration." However, plaintiffs' lawyers typically required minimum provable damages of $60,000–$65,000, and a retainer of $3,000 to $3,600, before they would even accept a case—suggesting that "only the larger cases are litigated," William Howard, Arbitrating Claims of Employment Discrimination, Disp. Resol. J., Oct.-Dec. 1995, at pp. 40, 45. *But see* David Schwartz, Enforcing Small Print to Protect Big Business: Employee an Consumer Rights Claims in an Age of Compelled Arbitration, 1997 Wisc. L. Rev. 33, 64–66(while "evidence is admittedly sketchy, it does tend to support the perception * * * that regulated defendants systematically gain an advantage * * * at the expense of plaintiffs when they arbitrate rather than litigate their disputes"); Katherine Stone, Mandatory Arbitration of Individual Employment Rights: The Yellow Dog Contract of the 1990s, 73 Denv. U.L. Rev. 1017, 1040 (1996)(while "there is no comprehensive survey data on the subject * * * there is some anecdotal data that suggests that nonunion arbitration schemes tend to generate pro-employer outcomes"). Cf. Cole v. Burns Int'l Security Services, 105 F.3d 1465, 1485 n. 17 (D.C.Cir.1997)("It is hard to know what to make of these studies without assessing the relative *merits* of the cases in the surveys").

Assume, however, for the sake of argument, that employees can indeed be expected regularly to do better before a jury than before a panel of arbitrators: What do you think of the argument that "the lower arbitration awards are really the more fair assessments of redress"—since "the preconceived anti-employer sentiment of juries results in inflated court awards for plaintiffs"? David Sherwyn et al., In Defense of Mandatory Arbitration of Employment Disputes, 2 U. Pa. J. Lab. & Employment L. 73, 142–143

(1999). Aren't we still committed to the proposition that a jury verdict is necessarily the baseline for any notion of a "correct" result? Cf. William Glaberson, "Juries, Their Powers Under Siege, Find Their Role Is Being Eroded," N.Y. Times, March 2, 2001 at pp. A1, A15 (only 1.5% of federal civil cases are resolved by juries, down from 5.4% in 1962; in a survey of federal trial judges, 27.4% said "juries should decide fewer types of cases"); Kent Syverud, ADR and the Decline of the American Civil Jury, 44 U.C.L.A. L. Rev. 1935 (1997)("Other than the trial bar and an occasional exhilarated juror, is there anyone left in America whose impression of a civil jury trial is so positive that he or she is willing to pay for one?").

13. A job applicant signed an agreement to arbitrate. The agreement was included by the employer in its application packet and was made a condition of employment; it did not, however, run between the employer and the potential employee—it was instead between the employee and "Employment Dispute Services, Inc." EDSI agreed to provide an arbitration forum in exchange for the employee's agreement to submit to arbitration any dispute with his potential employer; the employer was purportedly a third-party beneficiary of the employee's agreement to arbitrate. The employee later filed suit against the employer for violations of the Americans with Disabilities Act, and the employer filed a motion to compel arbitration. The court held that the motion should be denied. The employee had argued that EDSI would be biased in favor of the employer "because it has a financial interest in maintaining its arbitration service contracts with employers." The court noted that it too had "serious reservations" as to whether the arbitral forum was "suitable for the resolution of statutory claims," in light of the "uncertain relationship" between the employer and EDSI: Although "the record does not clearly reflect whether EDSI, in contrast to the American Arbitration Association, operates on a non-profit basis," the court agreed that "the potential for bias exists." It did not, however, decide the case on that basis—finding an alternative rationale to make the arbitration agreement unenforceable. (Since EDSI had "unfettered discretion" to alter the arbitration rules and procedures without notice, its promise to provide an arbitration forum was "illusory" and thus "mutuality of obligation" was lacking.) Daniels v. Ryan's Family Steak Houses, Inc., 211 F.3d 306 (6th Cir.2000). See also Penn v. Ryan's Family Steakhouses, Inc., 95 F.Supp.2d 940 (N.D.Ind.2000)(since the employer is a "repeat" customer of EDSI, EDSI has an incentive to "load" its lists of arbitrators "with names that have sided with * * * any EDS customers/employers in the past"), aff'd, 269 F.3d 753 (7th Cir.2001) (but criticizing trial court for "plac[ing] too much weight on certain specifics of this system that * * * do not distinguish it from many others that have passed muster"); Geiger v. Ryan's Family Steak Houses, Inc., 134 F.Supp.2d 985 (S.D.Ind.2001)(EDSI "clearly has an incentive to maintain its contractual relationship" with the employer, while employees "have no leverage").

14. Another recent study of AAA employment arbitrations indicates that the process may give an advantage to employers who are "institutional repeat players": Employees who arbitrated with "repeat player employers"—that is, those who were in the case sample more than once—

prevailed around 16% of the time, while employees arbitrating with "one-time player" employers prevailed over 70% of the time. In cases involving non-repeat player employers, employees recovered an average of 48% of their demands, while against repeat player employers they recovered only 11%. Lisa Bingham, On Repeat Players, Adhesive Contracts, and the Use of Statistics in Judicial Review of Employment Arbitration Awards, 29 McGeorge L. Rev. 223 (1998).

Where, as in AAA arbitrations, arbitrators are chosen from a panel list submitted to the parties, only the institutional repeat player is likely to develop an "institutional memory": It is only the employer, and not the employee, who is likely to have the ability and incentive to invest in information about the arbitrator's background—and to monitor his past awards. Such asymmetry may suggest the need for some incremental reform of the arbitral process—perhaps in the form of tinkering with the institutional rules that are presented to the parties for adoption. The AAA's new National Rules for the Resolution of Employment Disputes—not yet in effect at the time of the Bingham study—now require that prospective arbitrators disclose their "service as a neutral in any past or pending case involving any of the parties and/or their representatives," Rule 11(b). Is this an adequate response? Cf. Alan Rau, Integrity in Private Judging, 38 So. Tex. L. Rev. 485, 526–27 (1997)("This must be of limited utility where information about the arbitrator's awards in analogous cases—involving, for example, other employers in employment disputes, or other insurance companies, or other repeat players faced with similar issues of contract interpretation—cannot be expected to be equally available to both parties. * * * [I]t is at least conceivable that the process of arbitrator selection could be structured so as to exclude *both* parties from any participation in naming their arbitrators").

c. LIMITATIONS ON REMEDIES IN ARBITRATION

Mastrobuono v. Shearson Lehman Hutton, Inc.

Supreme Court of the United States, 1995.
514 U.S. 52, 115 S.Ct. 1212, 131 L.Ed.2d 76.

■ JUSTICE STEVENS delivered the opinion of the Court.

New York law allows courts, but not arbitrators, to award punitive damages. In a dispute arising out of a standard-form contract that expressly provides that it "shall be governed by the laws of the State of New York," a panel of arbitrators awarded punitive damages. The District Court and Court of Appeals disallowed that award. The question presented is whether the arbitrators' award is consistent with the central purpose of the Federal Arbitration Act to ensure "that private agreements to arbitrate are enforced according to their terms." Volt Information Sciences, Inc. v. Board of Trustees of Leland Stanford Junior Univ., 489 U.S. 468, 479 (1989).

I

In 1985 petitioners, Antonio Mastrobuono, then an assistant professor of medieval literature, and his wife Diana Mastrobuono, an artist, opened a securities trading account with respondent Shearson Lehman Hutton, Inc. (Shearson), by executing Shearson's standard-form Client's Agreement. Respondent Nick DiMinico, a vice president of Shearson, managed the Mastrobuonos' account until they closed it in 1987. In 1989, petitioners filed this action in the United States District Court for the Northern District of Illinois, alleging that respondents had mishandled their account and claiming damages on a variety of state and federal law theories.

Paragraph 13 of the parties' agreement contains an arbitration provision and a choice-of-law provision. Relying on the arbitration provision and on §§ 3 and 4 of the Federal Arbitration Act (FAA), respondents filed a motion to stay the court proceedings and to compel arbitration pursuant to the rules of the National Association of Securities Dealers. The District Court granted that motion, and a panel of three arbitrators was convened. After conducting hearings in Illinois, the panel ruled in favor of petitioners.

In the arbitration proceedings, respondents argued that the arbitrators had no authority to award punitive damages. Nevertheless, the panel's award included punitive damages of $400,000, in addition to compensatory damages of $159,327. Respondents paid the compensatory portion of the award but filed a motion in the District Court to vacate the award of punitive damages. The District Court granted the motion, and the Court of Appeals for the Seventh Circuit affirmed. Both courts relied on the choice-of-law provision in Paragraph 13 of the parties' agreement, which specifies that the contract shall be governed by New York law. Because the New York Court of Appeals has decided that in New York the power to award punitive damages is limited to judicial tribunals and may not be exercised by arbitrators, Garrity v. Lyle Stuart, Inc., 353 N.E.2d 793 (N.Y.1976), the District Court and the Seventh Circuit held that the panel of arbitrators had no power to award punitive damages in this case.

We granted certiorari because the Courts of Appeals have expressed differing views on whether a contractual choice-of-law provision may preclude an arbitral award of punitive damages that otherwise would be proper. We now reverse.

II

* * *

[T]he Seventh Circuit interpreted the contract to incorporate New York law, including the *Garrity* rule that arbitrators may not award punitive damages. Petitioners ask us to hold that the FAA preempts New York's prohibition against arbitral awards of punitive damages because this state law is a vestige of the "ancient" judicial hostility to arbitration. Petitioners rely on Southland Corp. v. Keating and Perry v. Thomas, in which we held that the FAA preempted two California statutes that purported to require judicial resolution of certain disputes. In *Southland,* we explained that the FAA not only "declared a national policy favoring arbitration," but actually "withdrew the power of the states to require a judicial forum for the resolution of claims which the contracting parties agreed to resolve by arbitration."

Respondents answer that the choice-of-law provision in their contract evidences the parties' express agreement that punitive damages should not be awarded in the arbitration of any dispute arising under their contract. Thus, they claim, this case is distinguishable from *Southland* and *Perry,* in which the parties presumably desired unlimited arbitration but state law stood in their way. Regardless of whether the FAA preempts the *Garrity* decision in contracts not expressly incorporating New York law, respondents argue that the parties may themselves agree to be bound by *Garrity,* just as they may agree to forgo arbitration altogether. In other words, if the contract says "no punitive damages," that is the end of the matter, for courts are bound to interpret contracts in accordance with the expressed intentions of the parties—even if the effect of those intentions is to limit arbitration.

We have previously held that the FAA's pro-arbitration policy does not operate without regard to the wishes of the contracting parties. * * * Relying on our reasoning in *Volt* [Volt Information Sciences, Inc. v. Board of Trustees of the Leland Stanford Jr. Univ.], respondents thus argue that the parties to a contract may lawfully agree to limit the issues to be arbitrated by waiving any claim for punitive damages. On the other hand, we think our decisions in * * * *Southland* and *Perry* make clear that if contracting parties agree to include claims for punitive damages within the issues to be arbitrated, the FAA ensures that their agreement will be enforced according to its terms even if a rule of state law would otherwise exclude such claims from arbitration. Thus, the case before us comes down to what the contract has to say about the arbitrability of petitioners' claim for punitive damages.

III

Shearson's standard-form "Client Agreement," which petitioners executed, contains 18 paragraphs. The two relevant provisions of the agreement are found in Paragraph 13.[2] The first sentence of that paragraph

2. Paragraph 13 of the Client's Agreement provides:

> This agreement shall inure to the benefit of your [Shearson's] successors and assigns[,] shall be binding on the undersigned, my [petitioners'] heirs, executors, administrators and assigns, and shall be governed by the laws of the State of New York. Unless unenforceable due to federal or state law, any controversy arising out of or relating to [my] accounts, to transactions with you, your officers, directors, agents and/or employees for me or to this agreement or the breach thereof, shall be settled by arbitration in accordance with the rules then in effect, of the National Association of Securities Dealers, Inc. or the Boards of Directors of the New York Stock Exchange, Inc. and/or the American Stock Exchange Inc. as I may elect. If I do not make such election by registered mail addressed to you at your main office within 5 days after demand by you that I make such election, then you may make such election. Judgment upon any award rendered

provides, in part, that the entire agreement "shall be governed by the laws of the State of New York." The second sentence provides that "any controversy" arising out of the transactions between the parties "shall be settled by arbitration" in accordance with the rules of the National Association of Securities Dealers (NASD), or the Boards of Directors of the New York Stock Exchange and/or the American Stock Exchange. The agreement contains no express reference to claims for punitive damages. To ascertain whether Paragraph 13 expresses an intent to include or exclude such claims, we first address the impact of each of the two relevant provisions, considered separately. We then move on to the more important inquiry: the meaning of the two provisions taken together. See Restatement (Second) of Contracts § 202(2) (1979) ("A writing is interpreted as a whole").

The choice-of-law provision, when viewed in isolation, may reasonably be read as merely a substitute for the conflict-of-laws analysis that otherwise would determine what law to apply to disputes arising out of the contractual relationship. Thus, if a similar contract, without a choice-of-law provision, had been signed in New York and was to be performed in New York, presumably "the laws of the State of New York" would apply, even though the contract did not expressly so state. In such event, there would be nothing in the contract that could possibly constitute evidence of an intent to exclude punitive damages claims. Accordingly, punitive damages would be allowed because, in the absence of contractual intent to the contrary, the FAA would preempt the *Garrity* rule.

Even if the reference to "the laws of the State of New York" is more than a substitute for ordinary conflict-of-laws analysis and, as respondents urge, includes the caveat, "detached from otherwise-applicable federal law," the provision might not preclude the award of punitive damages because New York allows its courts, though not its arbitrators, to enter such awards. In other words, the provision might include only New York's substantive rights and obligations, and not the State's allocation of power between alternative tribunals. Respondents' argument is persuasive only if "New York law" means "New York decisional law, including that State's allocation of power between courts and arbitrators, notwithstanding otherwise-applicable federal law." But, as we have demonstrated, the provision need not be read so broadly. It is not, in itself, an unequivocal exclusion of punitive damages claims.[4]

by the arbitrators may be entered in any court having jurisdiction thereof. This agreement to arbitrate does not apply to future disputes arising under certain of the federal securities laws to the extent it has been determined as a matter of law that I cannot be compelled to arbitrate such claims.

4. The dissent makes much of the similarity between this choice-of-law clause and the one in *Volt,* which we took to incorporate a California statute allowing a court to stay arbitration pending resolution of related litigation. In *Volt,* however, we did not interpret the contract *de novo.* Instead, we deferred to the California court's construction of its own state's law. 489 U.S., at 474 ("the interpretation of private contracts is ordinarily a question of state law, which this Court does not sit to review"). In the present case, by contrast, we review a federal court's interpretation of this contract, and our interpretation accords with that of the only decision-maker

The arbitration provision (the second sentence of Paragraph 13) does not improve respondents' argument. On the contrary, when read separately this clause strongly implies that an arbitral award of punitive damages is appropriate. It explicitly authorizes arbitration in accordance with NASD rules; the panel of arbitrators in fact proceeded under that set of rules. The NASD's Code of Arbitration Procedure indicates that arbitrators may award "damages and other relief." NASD Code of Arbitration Procedure ¶ 3741(e) (1993). While not a clear authorization of punitive damages, this provision appears broad enough at least to contemplate such a remedy. Moreover, as the Seventh Circuit noted, a manual provided to NASD arbitrators contains this provision:

> "B. Punitive Damages. The issue of punitive damages may arise with great frequency in arbitrations. Parties to arbitration are informed that arbitrators can consider punitive damages as a remedy."

Thus, the text of the arbitration clause itself surely does not support—indeed, it contradicts—the conclusion that the parties agreed to foreclose claims for punitive damages.[7]

Although neither the choice-of-law clause nor the arbitration clause, separately considered, expresses an intent to preclude an award of punitive damages, respondents argue that a fair reading of the entire Paragraph 13 leads to that conclusion. On this theory, even if "New York law" is ambiguous, and even if "arbitration in accordance with NASD rules" indicates that punitive damages are permissible, the juxtaposition of the two clauses suggests that the contract incorporates "New York law relating to arbitration." We disagree. At most, the choice-of-law clause introduces an ambiguity into an arbitration agreement that would otherwise allow punitive damages awards. As we pointed out in *Volt,* when a court interprets such provisions in an agreement covered by the FAA, "due regard must be given to the federal policy favoring arbitration, and ambiguities as to the scope of the arbitration clause itself resolved in favor of arbitration."

Moreover, respondents cannot overcome the common-law rule of contract interpretation that a court should construe ambiguous language against the interest of the party that drafted it. Respondents drafted an ambiguous document, and they cannot now claim the benefit of the doubt. The reason for this rule is to protect the party who did not choose the

arguably entitled to deference—the arbitrator.

7. "Were we to confine our analysis to the plain language of the arbitration clause, we would have little trouble concluding that a contract clause which bound the parties to 'settle' 'all disputes' through arbitration conducted according to rules which allow any form of 'just and equitable' 'remedy of relief' was sufficiently broad to encompass the award of punitive damages. Inasmuch as agreements to arbitrate are 'generously construed,' it would seem sensible to interpret the 'all disputes' and 'any remedy or relief' phrases to indicate, at a minimum, an intention to resolve through arbitration any dispute that would otherwise be settled in a court, and to allow the chosen dispute resolvers to award the same varieties and forms of damages or relief as a court would be empowered to award. Since courts are empowered to award punitive damages with respect to certain types of claims, the Raytheon–Automated arbitrators would be equally empowered." Raytheon Co. v. Automated Business Systems, Inc., 882 F.2d 6, 10 (1st Cir.1989).

language from an unintended or unfair result.[10] That rationale is well-suited to the facts of this case. As a practical matter, it seems unlikely that petitioners were actually aware of New York's bifurcated approach to punitive damages, or that they had any idea that by signing a standard-form agreement to arbitrate disputes they might be giving up an important substantive right. In the face of such doubt, we are unwilling to impute this intent to petitioners.

Finally the respondents' reading of the two clauses violates another cardinal principle of contract construction: that a document should be read to give effect to all its provisions and to render them consistent with each other. We think the best way to harmonize the choice-of-law provision with the arbitration provision is to read "the laws of the State of New York" to encompass substantive principles that New York courts would apply, but not to include special rules limiting the authority of arbitrators. Thus, the choice-of-law provision covers the rights and duties of the parties, while the arbitration clause covers arbitration; neither sentence intrudes upon the other. In contrast, respondents' reading sets up the two clauses in conflict with one another: one foreclosing punitive damages, the other allowing them. This interpretation is untenable.

We hold that the Court of Appeals misinterpreted the parties' agreement. The arbitral award should have been enforced as within the scope of the contract. The judgment of the Court of Appeals is, therefore, reversed.

■ JUSTICE THOMAS, dissenting.

* * *

In this case, as in *Volt,* the parties agreed to mandatory arbitration of all disputes. As in *Volt,* the contract at issue here includes a choice-of-law clause. Indeed, the language of the two clauses is functionally equivalent: whereas the choice-of-law clause in *Volt* provided that "[t]he Contract shall be governed by the law of [the State of California]," the one before us today states, in Paragraph 13 of the Client's Agreement, that "[t]his agreement ... shall be governed by the laws of the State of New York." * * *

The majority claims that the incorporation of New York law "need not be read so broadly" as to include both substantive and procedural law, and that the choice of New York law "is not, in itself, an unequivocal exclusion of punitive damages claims." But we rejected these same arguments in *Volt,* and the *Garrity* rule is just the sort of "state rule[ ] governing the conduct of arbitration" that *Volt* requires federal courts to enforce. 489

10. The drafters of the Second Restatement justified the rule as follows:

> Where one party chooses the terms of a contract, he is likely to provide more carefully for the protection of his own interests than for those of the other party. He is also more likely than the other party to have reason to know of uncertainties of meaning. Indeed, he may leave meaning deliberately obscure, intending to decide at a later date what meaning to assert. In cases of doubt, therefore, so long as other factors are not decisive, there is substantial reason for preferring the meaning of the other party.

Restatement (Second) of Contracts § 206, Comment a (1979).

U.S. at 476. "Just as [the parties] may limit by contract the issues which they will arbitrate, so too may they specify by contract the rules under which that arbitration will be conducted." *Id.* at 479. To be sure, the majority might be correct that *Garrity* is a rule concerning the State's allocation of power between "alternative tribunals," although *Garrity* appears to describe itself as substantive New York law.[2] Nonetheless, *Volt* makes no distinction between rules that serve only to distribute authority between courts and arbitrators (which the majority finds unenforceable) and other types of rules (which the majority finds enforceable). Indeed, the California rule in *Volt* could be considered to be one that allocates authority between arbitrators and courts, for it permits California courts to stay arbitration pending resolution of related litigation.

* * *

Thankfully, the import of the majority's decision is limited and narrow. This case amounts to nothing more than a federal court applying Illinois and New York contract law to an agreement between parties in Illinois. Much like a federal court applying a state rule of decision to a case when sitting in diversity, the majority's interpretation of the contract represents only the understanding of a single federal court regarding the requirements imposed by state law. As such, the majority's opinion has applicability only to this specific contract and to no other. But because the majority reaches an erroneous result on even this narrow question, I respectfully dissent.

NOTES AND QUESTIONS

1. Even before *Mastrobuono,* federal courts regularly asserted that under the FAA arbitrators had the power to award punitive damages. It would readily be presumed that the parties had been willing to grant such power to the arbitrators, especially where the arbitration clause was broadly phrased so as to make "all disputes" arbitrable, or to give the arbitrators power to award "any remedy or relief which is just and equitable." See Raytheon Co. v. Automated Business Systems, Inc., 882 F.2d 6 (1st Cir. 1989) (agreement to arbitrate under AAA rules); Kelley v. Michaels, 830 F.Supp. 577 (N.D.Okl.1993) (NASD Code of Arbitration; agreement to arbitrate "any dispute, claim or controversy" includes a claim for punitive damages). In such cases it would take a "clear and express exclusion" in the agreement to deprive the arbitrator of the power to award punitive damages. And if authorized by the parties' agreement, an award of punitive damages by arbitrators was not considered by these courts to be against any "public policy." "[A]n arbitrator steeped in the practice of a given trade is often better equipped than a judge not only to decide what behavior so transgresses the limits of acceptable commercial practice in

2. The New York Court of Appeals rested its holding on the principle that punitive damages are exemplary social remedies intended to punish, rather than to compensate. Because the power to punish can rest only in the hands of the State, the Court found that private arbitrators could not wield the authority to impose such damages. *Garrity,* 353 N.E.2d, at 796–797.

that trade as to warrant a punitive award, but also to determine the amount of punitive damages needed to (1) adequately deter others in the trade from engaging in similar misconduct, and (2) punish the particular defendant in accordance with the magnitude of his misdeed." Willoughby Roofing & Supply Co., Inc. v. Kajima Int'l, Inc., 598 F.Supp. 353 (N.D.Ala. 1984), aff'd, 776 F.2d 269 (11th Cir.1985).

Can the *Mastrobuono* decision be taken as an approval of these federal cases? See note 7 to the Supreme Court's opinion.

2. As the Court notes, however, a number of states (notably New York) have taken the position that arbitrators may *not* award punitive damages. In these states, an arbitral award of punitive damages is against "public policy" even though the parties had granted the arbitrators the power to award such damages—and even though on a similar cause of action a court or jury could impose them. The leading case is Garrity v. Lyle Stuart, Inc., 40 N.Y.2d 354, 386 N.Y.S.2d 831, 353 N.E.2d 793 (1976), in which the court vacated an award of punitive damages to an author for his publisher's "malicious withholding of royalties":

> If arbitrators were allowed to impose punitive damages, the usefulness of arbitration would be destroyed. It would become a trap for the unwary given the eminently desirable freedom from judicial overview of law and facts. It would mean that the scope of determination by arbitrators, by the license to award punitive damages, would be both unpredictable and uncontrollable. * * *
>
> In imposing penal sanctions in private arrangements, a tradition of the rule of law in organized society is violated. One purpose of the rule of law is to require that the use of coercion be controlled by the State. In a highly developed commercial and economic society the use of private force is not the danger, but the uncontrolled use of coercive economic sanctions in private arrangements. For centuries the power to punish has been a monopoly of the State, and not that of any private individual. The day is long past since barbaric man achieved redress by private punitive measures.

What is the practical result of the New York rule? The lower courts in *Mastrobuono* assumed that the plaintiff, merely by agreeing to arbitration, should be deemed to have "waived" any potential right to receive punitive damages at all. In other cases, however, it is apparently envisaged that the plaintiff would have to institute a separate judicial proceeding in order to assert a claim for punitive damages—at best a wasteful exercise undermining many of the advantages of arbitration. E.g., DiCrisci v. Lyndon Guaranty Bank of New York, 807 F.Supp. 947, 953 (W.D.N.Y.1992).

3. The Oregon Constitution prohibited judicial review of jury awards of punitive damages "unless the court can affirmatively say there is no evidence to support the verdict." In Honda Motor Co., Ltd. v. Oberg, 512 U.S. 415, 114 S.Ct. 2331, 129 L.Ed.2d 336 (1994), the Supreme Court held that this violated the due process clause of the 14th Amendment:

> "Punitive damages pose an acute danger of arbitrary deprivation of property. Jury instructions typically leave the jury with wide discretion in choosing amounts, and the presentation of evidence of a defendant's net worth creates the potential that juries will use their verdicts to express biases against big businesses, particularly those without strong local presences. Judicial review of the amount awarded was one of the few procedural safeguards which the common law provided against that danger."

By contrast, Oregon apparently permitted judicial review to ensure only "that there is evidence to support *some* punitive damages, not that there is evidence to support the amount actually awarded. * * * What we are concerned with is the possibility that a guilty defendant may be unjustly punished; evidence of guilt warranting some punishment is not a substitute for evidence providing at least a rational basis for the particular deprivation of property imposed by the State to deter future wrongdoing."

Is *Honda Motor Co.* at all relevant to the problems in these notes?

4. The *Volt* case in 1989 created considerable confusion as to the continuing validity of state law in cases otherwise governed by the FAA. See, e.g., Barbier v. Shearson Lehman Hutton Inc., 948 F.2d 117 (2d Cir.1991), holding that a New York choice of law clause captured that state's bar on punitive damages in arbitration: "It is apparent from the inclusion of the choice-of-law provision that the parties intended to be bound by *Garrity,* and as with any other contract, the parties' intentions control." Has the Supreme Court clarified this question? See note 4 to the Court's opinion.

For a while, New York courts were ready to indulge in the grossest forms of wishful thinking—believing that they still remained free independently to construe choice-of-law clauses differently from the Supreme Court in *Mastrobuono,* and that, should they do so, federal courts would have to defer to their reading even where the result would be to exclude punitive damage awards. See Dean Witter Reynolds, Inc. v. Trimble, 166 Misc.2d 40, 631 N.Y.S.2d 215, 217 n. 4 (Sup. Ct. 1995)("the interpretation of contracts is a matter of state law"). This, however, failed to take very seriously that "liberal federal policy favoring arbitration agreements" which has been the subject of a relentless Supreme Court jurisprudence. In more recent cases the New York courts seem, at last, to have sensibly capitulated—and they now appear to consider themselves bound by *Mastrobuono*'s reading of choice-of-law clauses to permit arbitral awards of punitive damages. See Olde Discount Corp. v. Dartley, N.Y.L.J., Dec. 12, 1997, at pp. 26–27 (Sup. Ct.)(under the FAA, "a reference to the substantive law of a particular State, without more, is simply insufficient to bar arbitrators from considering the question of punitive damages"); Americorp Securities, Inc. v. Sager, 239 A.D.2d 115, 656 N.Y.S.2d 762 (App.Div.1997)(petitioner's reliance on New York rule "was unjustified in light of the judicial recognition of the FAA's preemptive effect in *Mastrobuono*").

Is there, then, anything left of the opinion in *Volt*? What does it mean to say that the case can be "limited to its own facts"? See NOS Communications, Inc. v. Robertson, 936 F.Supp. 761, 765 n. 1 (D.Colo.1996).

5. After *Mastrobuono,* would you expect that potential defendants will now begin to draft arbitration clauses that contain an "unequivocal exclusion of punitive damages claims"? The National Association of Securities Dealers has warned its members that attempts in customer agreements to limit the arbitrators' power to award punitive damages—either directly or "indirectly by the use of a so-called 'governing law clause' "—would violate NASD rules and could result in disciplinary action. NASD NTM no. 95–16 (1995 NASD LEXIS 28) (March 1995).

6. Strictures against arbitral "punishment" (such as those in *Garrity*) may as a practical matter turn out to be meaningless unless the arbitrator is ingenuous enough to label his award as punitive. As all first-year law students quickly learn, calculating "compensatory" damages in contract cases is hardly an exact science. In addition, arbitrators may find in particular cases that remedies other than the traditional award of damages are warranted; for example they may think it appropriate, on a theory of unjust enrichment, to require the defendant to "disgorge" the benefits he has made from breach. Cf. International Union of Operating Engineers v. Mid–Valley, Inc., 347 F.Supp. 1104 (S.D.Tex.1972). In the absence of a reasoned opinion or a transcript, it will be difficult to say that the arbitrator has in fashioning appropriate remedies gone beyond permitted "flexibility" to forbidden "punishment."

7. Staklinski was hired as an executive. His contract provided that should he become "permanently disabled" he would receive reduced compensation for the next three years, and then the contract would end. Several years later the company's Board determined that Staklinski had become permanently disabled; he disagreed with this finding and the dispute was submitted to arbitration. The arbitrator found in favor of Staklinski and ordered the corporation to reinstate him. The court confirmed the award: "The power of an arbitrator to order specific performance in an appropriate case has been recognized from early times. * * * Whether a court of equity could issue a specific performance decree in a case like this is beside the point." In the Matter of the Arbitration Between Staklinski and Pyramid Electric Co., 6 N.Y.2d 159, 188 N.Y.S.2d 541, 160 N.E.2d 78 (1959). See also Coopertex, Inc. v. Rue De Reves, Inc., 1990 WL 6548 (S.D.N.Y.) (specific performance of a contract for the sale of goods; "[w]hether or not a court would have awarded specific performance in this case is not the issue").

8. As the preceding note suggests, arbitrators are usually assumed to have broad discretion in fashioning a remedy for the particular circumstances of the case. An important recent decision is Advanced Micro Devices, Inc. v. Intel Corp., 9 Cal.4th 362, 885 P.2d 994, 36 Cal.Rptr.2d 581 (1994). AMD and Intel had entered into a contract under which each company could acquire the right to manufacture under license semiconductor products initially developed by the other. After an arbitration that lasted almost five years, an arbitrator found that Intel had "breached the implied covenant of good faith and fair dealing" under this contract. The arbitrator found that Intel's breach had prevented AMD from acquiring the right to manufacture Intel's highly successful "386" computer chip, and had also delayed AMD's efforts to independently develop its own competitive product by "reverse engineering" Intel's chip. AMD's actual damages were found to be "immeasurable." So the arbitrator gave AMD a permanent, royalty-free license to any of Intel's intellectual property that was embodied in AMD's competing chip—thereby providing AMD with "a complete and dispositive defense" against "legal harassment by Intel over AMD's alleged use of Intel intellectual property," notably in patent and copyright infringement claims that were being pressed by Intel in separate litigation. In confirming the award, the California Supreme Court rejected the proposition that arbitrators could not award a party "benefits different from those the party could have acquired through performance of the contract." The court also rejected any rule by which the remedial power of arbitrators would be limited to remedies "that a court could award on the same claim." "The choice of remedy * * * may at times call on any decision maker's flexibility, creativity and sense of fairness."

The dissenting judges protested that "the majority has greatly increased the risks and uncertainty of arbitration," and that the decision "will make businesses think twice about whether they should agree to resolve disputes by arbitration." They acknowledged that a number of reasons might contribute to granting wide remedial powers to *labor* arbitrators—such as the impossibility of reducing all aspects of a labor-management relationship to writing, and the need for "an ongoing process during the life of a collective bargaining agreement that adjusts and modifies the agreement to meet the changing conditions of the workplace." By contrast, in *commercial* arbitration the "possibility of unlimited and unpredictable forms of relief is not one of the advantages that a party normally expects to receive from choosing to arbitrate." Under the majority test, the dissent wrote, "it is theoretically possible for an arbitrator to order the losing party to be placed in the stocks or the pillory, or to direct that the contractual relationship be repaired by ordering the marriage of the parties' first-born children."

See also Alan Rau, Resolving Disputes Over Attorneys' Fees: The Role of ADR, 46 S.M.U.L.Rev. 2005, 2071 (1993) (in fee dispute between attorney and client, an arbitrator awarded the attorney $356 "to be paid with no more than 12 hairstylings"; "[i]f the client was in fact a hairstylist, this is surely an efficient settlement, reducing the cost of settlement 'with the same net gain to plaintiff at a lower cost to the defendant' "); David Co. v. Jim W. Miller Construction, Inc., 444 N.W.2d 836 (Minn.1989) (developer sought monetary damages against contractor who had built defective townhouses; arbitrators fashioned an "innovative and unique remedy" ordering the builder—who was himself a real estate developer—to purchase from the plaintiff the townhouses and the land on which they were built).

D. THE ARBITRATION PROCEEDING

"Within broad limits * * * private parties who submit an existing dispute to arbitration may write their own ticket about the terms of submission, if they can agree to a ticket. [The authors refer to an old story about a person who, in a dream, was threatened by an ominous character and who asked, tremulously, 'Wh-what are you going to do now?'—only to receive the answer, 'How do I know? This is *your* dream.'] The arbitration of an existing dispute is the parties' dream, and they can make it what they want it to be.

The trouble is that it takes time and money to draft elaborate private laws * * *. Only in the most exceptional circumstances can a private disputant stop to negotiate and draft a complete constitution, together with a substantive and procedural code, for the governance of his private court.[1]"

It is quite common to find leading members of the ADR community willing to question whether arbitration is "really" an "ADR process" at all—who may suggest, for example, that it is somehow inappropriate to include a discussion of the arbitration process in a conference or law school course devoted primarily to "the gentler arts of reconciliation and accommodation."[2] We gather that this is true because, paradoxically, arbitration "matters"—that is, that it is merely "adjudication."[3] Nevertheless it should be obvious enough that what the arbitration process is in fact all about is private ordering and self-determination. "In the run-of-the-mill case, the task of planning for dispute resolution necessarily requires a high level of party participation. Choosing a dispute resolution process, designing its structure, and selecting the decisionmaker, all proceed through negotiation and agreement—and giving thought to such matters may thus make the same calls on the parties' creativity and imagination as do more openly 'empowering' ADR processes."[4]

Rather than draft their own "procedural code," however, parties to arbitration agreements commonly prefer to incorporate by reference the standard rules for the conduct of arbitration proceedings prepared by institutions like the AAA. This allows them to avoid having to reinvent the wheel through lengthy negotiation and drafting—especially at a time when there may not be much incentive for cooperation—and instead to build upon the experience of others. In the materials that follow, frequent reference will be made to the practice of the AAA and particularly to its Commercial Arbitration Rules. But it must be remembered that arbitration

1. Henry Hart & Albert Sacks, The Legal Process 310 (1994).

2. Derek Bok, A Flawed System of Law Practice and Training, 33 J. Legal Educ. 570, 582–83 (1983).

3. See, e.g., Jean Sternlight, Is Binding Arbitration A Form of ADR?: An Argument That the Term "ADR" Has Begun to Outlive its Usefulness, 2000 J. of Disp. Resol. 97, 102 (discussing the agenda at annual conferences of the Society of Professionals in Dispute Resolution), 103–04 ("Where is the empowerment?"), 106 ("It makes no more sense to group all these techniques together than it would to group together contracts, torts, property, UCC, etc. in a single three credit course called 'private law' "); William Howard, Arbitrating Employment Discrimination Claims: Do You Really Have To? Do You Really Want To?, 43 Drake L. Rev. 255, 279–80 (1994)(since arbitration is "nonconsensual," it "has nothing in common with the other ADR techniques beyond not being a state institution").

4. See Alan Rau, Integrity in Private Judging, 38 So. Tex. L. Rev. 485, 486 (1997).

remains ultimately "the parties' dream." It is always necessary to consider carefully the special features of each individual transaction, with a view to adding to the pre-existing structure or adapting it in light of the parties' particular circumstances.

1. THE DECISION-MAKERS

a. SELECTION OF ARBITRATORS

Selecting the arbitrators is obviously a critical aspect of the arbitration process. After all, the ability to have a dispute decided by "judges" of one's own choosing is perhaps the most distinctive characteristic of this dispute resolution mechanism. How to provide for arbitrator selection is therefore an essential question for the parties in their planning.

The parties may, of course, simply try to agree by name on the individuals who will arbitrate their dispute. The arbitrator might, for example, be named in the original agreement. Or selection of the arbitrator might be left for later agreement on an ad hoc basis after a dispute arises. The choice of the "appropriate" arbitrator may in fact often be a function of the nature of the dispute which has arisen, or of the issues which happen to be in contention. In labor arbitration, for example, the parties may prefer lawyers as arbitrators when the issue is one of arbitrability, but may well prefer economists for wage disputes in "interest" arbitration, and industrial engineers for disputes over job evaluation.[5]

However, reliance on this method of arbitrator selection carries obvious dangers. When the arbitrator is named in advance, he may have become unwilling or unable to serve by the time a dispute later arises. This may then open up a challenge to the whole process; one party may argue that his agreement to arbitration was not unconditional but dependent on the personal choice of this "known and trusted expert," and that therefore arbitration should not proceed in his absence.[6] Such an argument will rarely be found persuasive, but in any event a means must be found to select a replacement.

On the other hand, where the agreement contemplates only that the parties will select their arbitrator *after* a dispute arises, there is an obvious

5. See Retzer and Petersen, Strategies of Arbitrator Selection, 70 Lab.Arb. 1307, 1319 (1978).

6. See Uniform Commercial Code § 2–305, Comment 4; Ballas v. Mann, 3 Misc.2d 445, 82 N.Y.S.2d 426 (Sup.Ct.1948) (was intention to arbitrate "the dominant intention, the personality of the arbitrator being an auxiliary incident rather than the essence"?). Similar questions arise when the arbitration forum agreed on by the parties declines jurisdiction over the case, see In re Salomon Inc. Shareholders' Derivative Litigation, 68 F.3d 554, 559 (2d Cir.1995) ("[b]ecause the parties had contractually agreed that only the NYSE could arbitrate any disputes between them, [the lower court] properly declined to appoint substitute arbitrators and compel arbitration in another forum"), or is simply nonexistent, see Stinson v. America's Home Place, Inc., 108 F.Supp.2d 1278 (M.D.Ala.2000)(the "National Academy of Conciliators, the arbitrator designated in the contract for resolution of disputes, was not in existence at the time the contract was formed or at any time thereafter").

potential for a recalcitrant party to drag his feet. The larger the stakes in the transaction, the more likely it is that the parties will wish to retain at least a veto over the identity of the decision-maker. Consider for example the agonizingly prolonged contract dispute between the Hunt brothers of Texas and the major oil-producing companies, a complex case arising out of various interests in Libyan oil concessions and involving sixteen parties and a welter of legal issues. The arbitration extended over a period of seven years; more than *two years* were consumed by the process of screening arbitrators, "as arbitrators proposed by one party were rejected by one or more of the other parties." The complexity of the issues in the case made the search for the requisite "arbitrators of unusual legal qualifications and broad experience in complicated transactions" particularly difficult. The court, however, made it clear that much of the delay was due to the tactics of the Hunts and their "campaign of obstruction to impede and defeat the arbitration." [7]

Under AAA rules, as soon as a demand for arbitration is made the AAA distributes to the parties a short list of potential arbitrators. It chooses these from its extensive panel of arbitrators, trying to match the names to the nature of the dispute and the industry involved. It may, for example, suggest arbitrators who have had experience in solar heating or landscape architecture if the dispute centers on practice in those trades. The parties may in their agreement have already specified the background or qualification of their arbitrators. In maritime arbitration, for example, it is the usual practice to stipulate that the arbitrators "shall be commercial men"—a phrase not meant to exclude women, but definitely meant to exclude lawyers.[8] Unless the parties have ruled out the possibility, however, it is customary to have at least one attorney on the list. Lawyers in fact play a dominant part in many AAA arbitrations. In 1999, for example, almost half of the names on the AAA's construction arbitration panel were attorneys—almost twice as many as the next largest professional category, engineers. And a recent survey of labor arbitrators indicates that almost 60% of them have law degrees.[9]

The information that the parties are given about a potential arbitrator is not extensive; it usually contains summary biographical information indicating the arbitrator's profession, present and past employment, education, and areas in which he claims expertise. There is no mechanism analogous to voir dire in which the parties have the opportunity to examine potential arbitrators prior to selection—although in large cases they have

7. See Hunt v. Mobil Oil Corp., 654 F.Supp. 1487 (S.D.N.Y.1987).

8. In W.K. Webster & Co. v. American President Lines, Ltd., 32 F.3d 665 (2d Cir. 1994), the Society of Maritime Arbitrators took the position (as *amicus curiae*) that a person cannot be a "commercial man" and a practicing attorney at one and the same time. The court disagreed, however, and upheld the appointment of an attorney who "had substantial practical experience on the commercial side of the maritime industry"—it noted that the attorney had not obtained his experience "*solely* as [a] practicing" attorney.

9. Bognanno & Smith, The Demographic and Professional Characteristics of Arbitrators in North America, Proceedings, 41st Annual Meeting, Nat'l Academy of Arbitrators 266, 270 (1988).

an obvious incentive to do some research on their own. Under AAA procedure, each party is allowed to cross off the list any names he finds unacceptable. Each then ranks the remaining names in order of preference, and from these the AAA is supposed to appoint an arbitrator "in accordance with the designated order of mutual preference." (The British refer to this method as "knocking the brains out of the panel.")[10] In the (unusual) event that every name turns out to be objectionable to one or both of the parties, the AAA may at that point simply choose another name from its panel without submitting any further lists; barring disqualification for cause, this selection is final.

Arbitration can proceed before any number of arbitrators—it is, again, "the parties' dream." But the most common pattern is to use either a single individual or three arbitrators. Under AAA rules, a single arbitrator is to be used unless the parties specify otherwise or unless the AAA "in its discretion" selects a larger number. In the year 2000, 25% of the AAA's commercial and construction cases involved claims of $75,000 or less and were administered under its "Expedited Procedures," where a single arbitrator is always used. However, in complex cases, or cases where the stakes are large, it is common to use three neutral arbitrators; current AAA policy is to prefer three arbitrators where the amount in controversy exceeds $300,000. (The ICC's rule of thumb is that only a single arbitrator is warranted in cases involving less than $1 million). With three arbitrators, of course, far more time is consumed in selection, in scheduling the hearings, and, probably, in hearing time; the fees paid to the arbitrators are also likely to be higher.

What do parties look for in selecting arbitrators? In labor cases, where a large cadre of professional arbitrators has developed, it is often observed that parties have a strong preference for only the most experienced and active arbitrators. A recent survey submitted a sample case to a selected number of union and management representatives and asked for their preferences as to whom they wanted to hear the case: 47.6% of the management representatives and 61.5% of the union representatives chose a decision-maker whose primary occupation was as a "full-time arbitrator."[11] Some union and management representatives, in responding to another survey, indicated that they would require a potential arbitrator to have a case load of at least fifty arbitrations in one year.[12] The fact that many labor arbitration opinions are published not only helps the parties in doing "research" on potential arbitrators; it also serves to focus even greater attention on the well-known "name" arbitrators whose cases appear regularly in the reports.

10. Bernstein, Nudging and Shoving All Parties to a Jurisdictional Dispute Into Arbitration: The Dubious Procedure of *National Steel,* 78 Harv.L.Rev. 784, 790–91 (1965).

11. See Nelson, The Selection of Arbitrators, Lab.L.J., October 1986, at 703, 711.

12. Rezler and Petersen, Strategies of Arbitrator Selection, 70 Lab.Arb. 1307, 1308 (1978).

This leads to a classic "Catch–22." Without experience, it is difficult for an arbitrator to be chosen to hear a labor case—and difficult therefore to develop the experience and reputation that will enable her to be chosen to hear *future* cases. One survey's estimate of the number of labor arbitrators "willing and able to practice" in 1986 was 3,669. Only 16% of these practiced full-time as arbitrators. Part-timers worked an average of four days per month as arbitrators—although 30% of them would have wanted to work full-time. And approximately 22% of the entire group did not work at all as arbitrators during the year, largely because no assignments were offered to them.[13] So "a small percentage of arbitrators do most of the business."[14]

The natural result of this selective demand is that there are often lengthy delays before the chosen arbitrator will have the time to hear and dispose of a given case; the most experienced arbitrators may not be available for a hearing within several months after being asked to serve. While this is not perhaps a long time in comparison with some crowded judicial dockets, it is still troubling for a supposedly "expeditious" dispute resolution process—particularly in cases where an employee has been discharged, and the employer is facing potential liability for back pay.

The profession of "labor arbitrator" is made possible by the often substantial fees that arbitrators are regularly paid for their services in labor cases. According to internal reports compiled by the Federal Mediation and Conciliation Service, the average per diem fee in the year 2000 for private arbitrators on the Service's roster was $672—although individual fees could of course range considerably higher. We have already noted the possible effects of such a prospect on the decision patterns of professional arbitrators. See, e.g., p. 44 supra. Commercial arbitrators, in contrast, rarely hear more than a few cases a year; the supply of acceptable arbitrators here is relatively more elastic. For many years, the AAA's Commercial Arbitration Rules provided that commercial arbitrators were expected to serve without compensation for the first day of hearing—presumably as a form of public service. Under the current rules, however, arbitrators are paid beginning with the first day of hearing where a claim exceeds $10,000;[15] arbitrators may also be paid for "study time" prior to the hearing. Arbitrators are free to state their own rate of compensation, and a $2000 per diem fee has been termed not "excessively high" or "far beyond the applicable standard for such services."[16] This is in addition to

13. Bognanno & Smith, The Demographic and Professional Characteristics of Arbitrators in North America, Proceedings, 41st Annual Meeting, Nat'l Academy of Arbitrators 266, 269, 277–79 (1988).

14. Mario Bognanno & Charles Coleman, Labor Arbitration in America: The Profession and Practice 89 (1992). See also The Chronicle (Journal of the Nat'l Academy of Arbitrators), May 1988 at p. 3 (11.9% of all active arbitrators handled 60 or more cases in 1986, representing 50.5% of the total grievance arbitration case load).

15. AAA, Commercial Arbitration Rules, R. 53(a),(b).

16. Polin v. Kellwood Co., 103 F.Supp.2d 238, 257 n. 27 (S.D.N.Y.2000).

In California, arbitrators in patient-HMO disputes "typically charge $250 to $400 per hour," Nieto & Hosel, Arbitration in California Managed Health Care Systems 2 (Cal-

the administrative fee, based on the amount of the claim, which is paid to institutions like the AAA and the ICC for their services in supervising the arbitration.

NOTES AND QUESTIONS

1. Another traditional pattern in arbitration is a "tripartite" panel, in which each party is allowed to select one arbitrator and a third, "neutral" chairman is chosen by the other two (or in the absence of agreement, by an institution like the AAA).

What effects might this kind of panel have on the decision-making process? The AAA's Commercial Arbitration Rules provide that where there is a panel of more than one arbitrator, decision is to be by *majority vote* unless the agreement provides otherwise. To the same effect is § 4 of the Uniform Arbitration Act, which has been enacted by most states. Where the party-appointed arbitrators agree on a particular result, may the neutral be led to acquiesce in what is in reality a negotiated settlement being given the prestige of an arbitral award? And where the other two arbitrators *disagree,* may the neutral be forced to trim or compromise his own views in order to obtain a majority? Consider In re Publishers' Ass'n of N.Y. and N.Y. Typographical Union, 36 Lab.Arb. 706 (1961). The neutral arbitrator here voted with the employer to discharge a worker but wrote, in an unusually candid opinion, that this penalty had been "forced upon" him. While he would have preferred a lesser penalty such as a disciplinary suspension, his most "patient and painstaking efforts" had convinced him that "there was no possibility whatever of an award issuing which would reflect a view intermediate to the polar position of my colleagues." He therefore saw no choice other than to join in the position which was *closest* to the one he preferred!

Would it have been possible or appropriate for the neutral in *Publishers' Association* to have acted differently? To avoid placing such a burden on the neutral, would it not be better simply to stipulate that in the absence of a majority decision the final decision is to be made by the neutral alone—or even that the function of the party-appointed arbitrators is always to be merely advisory? This is in fact commonly provided in collective bargaining agreements. And in that case, is any purpose ever served by having a tripartite board at all? Can you think of any countervailing advantages to using a tripartite board with party-named representatives? See Zack, Tripartite Panels: Asset or Hindrance in Dispute Settlement?, Proceedings, 34th Annual Meeting, Nat'l Academy of Arbitrators 273, 279 (1982) (deliberations between neutral and party-appointed arbitrators can help clarify technical issues, provide assurance that the neutral fully understands the issues and background of the case, and allow discussion and review of the possible implications of the neutral's written opinion); Lowenfeld, The Party–Appointed Arbitrator in International Con-

ifornia Research Bureau 2000). JAMS/Endispute arbitrators charge an average of $400 per hour, although "fees of $500 or $600 per hour are not uncommon," Cole v. Burns Int'l Security Services, 105 F.3d 1465, 1480 n. 8 (D.C.Cir.1997).

troversies: Some Reflections, 30 Tex.Int'l L.J. 59, 65–67 (1995) (in international disputes a party-appointed arbitrator can help in the "translation of legal culture * * * when matters that are self-evident to lawyers from one country are puzzling to lawyers from another"; such an arbitrator also gives some "confidence that at least one member of the tribunal is listening, and listening sympathetically, to the submission of counsel").

2. Where the parties are unable to agree on an arbitrator and the proceeding is not being administered by an institution like the AAA, modern statutes empower a court to make the choice. See FAA, § 5.

A contract for the delivery of rice provided that any disputes "shall be resolved by means of the judgment of arbitrators appointed by mutual agreement. This could be in Nicaragua or the Rice Millers' Association [RMA] in the United States." When a dispute arose over the condition of the rice, the buyer made a demand for arbitration with the RMA. Under RMA rules, the RMA arbitration committee appoints the arbitrators; the panel appointed by this committee proceeded to arbitrate the dispute and awarded the buyer $1.3 million. The court vacated the award, holding that the seller was instead "entitled" to an arbitration before arbitrators chosen by mutual agreement of the parties. "The arbitration clause does not set forth how this choice of arbitrators by the parties should be conducted." The district court was therefore instructed to require that arbitration "be conducted under the standard method, where both parties choose an arbitrator and these arbitrators select a third arbitrator"; if the two party-appointed arbitrators cannot agree, then the third arbitrator would be appointed by the court under § 5 of the FAA. Cargill Rice, Inc. v. Empresa Nicaraguense Dealimentos Basicos, 25 F.3d 223 (4th Cir.1994). Does this make any sense at all?

3. Where an arbitration clause calls for "tripartite" arbitration, one of the parties may be tempted to delay or frustrate the proceedings by simply refusing to name "its" arbitrator. To deal with this problem, contracts frequently provide that should one party fail to appoint an arbitrator, "the one arbitrator nominated may act as sole arbitrator"—or alternatively, that the party who has named one arbitrator should also have the right to appoint the second arbitrator himself. Either method should speed things along considerably.

In one case, a respondent refused to arbitrate, and the claimant moved for an order under § 4 of the FAA to compel arbitration. The court denied the motion, because the arbitration clause allowed the claimant to name a second arbitrator if the respondent refused to do so. Since "the very purpose of such a self-executing mechanism in an arbitration clause is to avoid the time and expense of Federal Court motion practice," the claimant was simply not a party "aggrieved" within the meaning of § 4 by the respondent's refusal to arbitrate. Waterspring, S.A. v. Trans Marketing Houston Inc., 717 F.Supp. 181 (S.D.N.Y.1989). Do you agree with this result? Does it matter that if the respondent should later successfully challenge the existence of a binding arbitration agreement, the claimant would then find that the arbitration had turned out to be nothing more than a useless gesture?

4. Three members of a family were parties to a partnership agreement: Charles, Albert (Charles' son), and Isidore (Charles' brother). The agreement provided for arbitration in which Charles and Albert would jointly name one arbitrator, Isidore would name another, and the two arbitrators would select a third.

However, the drafting of this clause proved to be inept. There was a change of alignment in the partnership not originally contemplated; Isidore and Charles, complaining about Albert's lack of concern for the partnership, sought arbitration. Charles and Albert could not jointly agree on an arbitrator; Albert insisted that he be permitted to select an arbitrator independently since the interests of the other two parties were identical and adverse to his. On application to the court to name an arbitrator, what result? See Lipschutz v. Gutwirth, 304 N.Y. 58, 106 N.E.2d 8 (1952).

5. One study of party preferences in labor arbitration suggests that employers tend to prefer economists over lawyers as arbitrators, while unions on the other hand "prefer arbitrators with legal training and dislike economists." Why might this be true? The authors speculate that this result may be explained by "the fact that economists are likely to be heavily influenced by efficiency considerations, whereas lawyers are more likely to place greater emphasis on equity." Bloom & Cavanagh, An Analysis of the Selection of Arbitrators, 76 Am.Econ.Rev. 408, 418, 421 (1986).

6. A "routine contract suit" was assigned to a magistrate judge. "Protracted efforts at settlement ensued but were unsuccessful. Then the lawyers had a brainstorm: appoint [the magistrate judge] the arbitrator of their dispute." An order, drafted by the lawyers and signed by the judge, provided that an independent auditor selected by the parties would determine the actual losses sustained, and "the Court will retain jurisdiction to act as the arbitrator * * * and shall make a decision binding upon the parties." The auditor submitted a report; the magistrate judge then held two hearings to consider the parties' objections and issued a document, captioned "judgment," calling for the defendant to pay $125,000.

The Seventh Circuit (in an opinion by Judge Posner) affirmed this "judgment"—"if that is what it is"—but seemed puzzled by just what it was that the parties and the magistrate judge had done. Had the judge issued an award as arbitrator, and then judicially confirmed his own award? If so, his order would clearly be void: "[A]rbitration is not in the job description of a federal judge"; "since 'alternative dispute resolution' is all the rage these days * * * the day may not be distant when federal judges will be recommissioned (or issued supplementary commissions) as arbitrators. But it has not arrived." However, there was an alternative characterization of what the parties had done that was "slightly more plausible": Perhaps they had simply "stipulated to an abbreviated, informal procedure for [the magistrate judge's] deciding the case in his judicial capacity. * * * [T]hey agreed that the judge would make a decision on a record consisting of the auditor's report plus the parties' objections, * * * and that they would not appeal the decision. So viewed, the procedure was not improper." By "talking the language of arbitration" the parties had essentially intended to limit judicial review of the magistrate judge's decision. DDI Seamless Cylinder Int'l, Inc. v. General Fire Extinguisher Corp., 14 F.3d 1163 (7th Cir.1994).

b. ARBITRAL IMPARTIALITY

Commonwealth Coatings Corp. v. Continental Casualty Co.

Supreme Court of the United States, 1968.
393 U.S. 145, 89 S.Ct. 337, 21 L.Ed.2d 301.

MR. JUSTICE BLACK delivered the opinion of the Court.

At issue in this case is the question whether elementary requirements of impartiality taken for granted in every judicial proceeding are suspended when the parties agree to resolve a dispute through arbitration.

[Having read this far, what do you think the answer is going to be?—Eds.]

The petitioner, Commonwealth Coatings Corp., a subcontractor, sued the sureties on the prime contractor's bond to recover money alleged to be due for a painting job. The contract for painting contained an agreement to arbitrate such controversies. Pursuant to this agreement petitioner appointed one arbitrator, the prime contractor appointed a second, and these two together selected the third arbitrator. This third arbitrator, the supposedly neutral member of the panel, conducted a large business in Puerto Rico, in which he served as an engineering consultant for various people in connection with building construction projects. One of his regular customers in this business was the prime contractor that petitioner sued in this case. This relationship with the prime contractor was in a sense sporadic in that the arbitrator's services were used only from time to time at irregular intervals, and there had been no dealings between them for about a year immediately preceding the arbitration. Nevertheless, the prime contractor's patronage was repeated and significant, involving fees of about $12,000 over a period of four or five years, and the relationship even went so far as to include the rendering of services on the very projects involved in this lawsuit. An arbitration was held, but the facts concerning the close business connections between the third arbitrator and the prime contractor were unknown to petitioner and were never revealed to it by this arbitrator, by the prime contractor, or by anyone else until after an award had been made. Petitioner challenged the award on this ground, among others, but the District Court refused to set aside the award. The Court of Appeals affirmed.

* * * [B]oth sides here assume that [the FAA] governs this case. Section 10 sets out the conditions upon which awards can be vacated. The two courts below held, however, that § 10 could not be construed in such a

way as to justify vacating the award in this case. We disagree and reverse. Section 10 does authorize vacation of an award where it was "procured by corruption, fraud, or undue means" or "[w]here there was evident partiality * * * in the arbitrators." These provisions show a desire of Congress to provide not merely for *any* arbitration but for an impartial one. It is true that petitioner does not charge before us that the third arbitrator was actually guilty of fraud or bias in deciding this case, and we have no reason, apart from the undisclosed business relationship, to suspect him of any improper motives. But neither this arbitrator nor the prime contractor gave to petitioner even an intimation of the close financial relations that had existed between them for a period of years. We have no doubt that if a litigant could show that a foreman of a jury or a judge in a court of justice had, unknown to the litigant, any such relationship, the judgment would be subject to challenge. This is shown beyond doubt by Tumey v. State of Ohio, 273 U.S. 510 (1927), where this Court held that a conviction could not stand because a small part of the judge's income consisted of court fees collected from convicted defendants. Although in *Tumey* it appeared the amount of the judge's compensation actually depended on whether he decided for one side or the other, that is too small a distinction to allow this manifest violation of the strict morality and fairness Congress would have expected on the part of the arbitrator and the other party in this case. Nor should it be at all relevant, as the Court of Appeals apparently thought it was here, that "[t]he payments received were a very small part of [the arbitrator's] income * * *." For in *Tumey* the Court held that a decision should be set aside where there is "the slightest pecuniary interest" on the part of the judge, and specifically rejected the State's contention that the compensation involved there was "so small that it is not to be regarded as likely to influence improperly a judicial officer in the discharge of his duty * * *." Since in the case of courts this is a *constitutional* principle, we can see no basis for refusing to find the same concept in the broad statutory language that governs arbitration proceedings and provides that an award can be set aside on the basis of "evident partiality" or the use of "undue means." It is true that arbitrators cannot sever all their ties with the business world, since they are not expected to get all their income from their work deciding cases, but we should, if anything, be even more scrupulous to safeguard the impartiality of arbitrators than judges, since the former have completely free rein to decide the law as well as the facts and are not subject to appellate review. We can perceive no way in which the effectiveness of the arbitration process will be hampered by the simple requirement that arbitrators disclose to the parties any dealings that might create an impression of possible bias.

[Justice Black then referred to the AAA rules of procedure which, "while not controlling in this case," called on an arbitrator "to disclose any circumstances likely to create a presumption of bias or which he believes might disqualify him as an impartial Arbitrator."]

[B]ased on the same principle as this Arbitration Association rule is that part of the 33d Canon of Judicial Ethics which provides:

33. Social Relations

* * * [A judge] should, however, in pending or prospective litigation before him be particularly careful to avoid such action as may reasonably tend to awaken the suspicion that his social or business relations or friendships, constitute an element in influencing his judicial conduct.

This rule of arbitration and this canon of judicial ethics rest on the premise that any tribunal permitted by law to try cases and controversies not only must be unbiased but also must avoid even the appearance of bias. We cannot believe that it was the purpose of Congress to authorize litigants to submit their cases and controversies to arbitration boards that might reasonably be thought biased against one litigant and favorable to another.

Reversed.

MR. JUSTICE WHITE, with whom MR. JUSTICE MARSHALL joins, concurring.

While I am glad to join my Brother Black's opinion in this case, I desire to make these additional remarks. The Court does not decide today that arbitrators are to be held to the standards of judicial decorum of Article III judges, or indeed of any judges. It is often because they are men of affairs, not apart from but of the marketplace, that they are effective in their adjudicatory function. This does not mean the judiciary must overlook outright chicanery in giving effect to their awards; that would be an abdication of our responsibility. But it does mean that arbitrators are not automatically disqualified by a business relationship with the parties before them if both parties are informed of the relationship in advance, or if they are unaware of the facts but the relationship is trivial. I see no reason automatically to disqualify the best informed and most capable potential arbitrators.

The arbitration process functions best when an amicable and trusting atmosphere is preserved and there is voluntary compliance with the decree, without need for judicial enforcement. This end is best served by establishing an atmosphere of frankness at the outset, through disclosure by the arbitrator of any financial transactions which he has had or is negotiating with either of the parties. In many cases the arbitrator might believe the business relationship to be so insubstantial that to make a point of revealing it would suggest he is indeed easily swayed, and perhaps a partisan of that party.* But if the law requires the disclosure, no such imputation can arise. And it is far better that the relationship be disclosed at the outset, when the parties are free to reject the arbitrator or accept him with knowledge of the relationship and continuing faith in his objectivity, than to have the relationship come to light after the arbitration, when a suspicious or disgruntled party can seize on it as a pretext for invalidating the award. The judiciary should minimize its role in arbitration as judge of the arbitrator's impartiality. That role is best consigned to the parties, who are the architects of their own arbitration process, and are far better

* In fact, the District Court found—on the basis of the record and petitioner's admissions—that the arbitrator in this case was entirely fair and impartial. I do not read the majority opinion as questioning this finding in any way.

informed of the prevailing ethical standards and reputations within their business.

Of course, an arbitrator's business relationships may be diverse indeed, involving more or less remote commercial connections with great numbers of people. He cannot be expected to provide the parties with his complete and unexpurgated business biography. But it is enough for present purposes to hold, as the Court does, that where the arbitrator has a substantial interest in a firm which has done more than trivial business with a party, that fact must be disclosed. If arbitrators err on the side of disclosure, as they should, it will not be difficult for courts to identify those undisclosed relationships which are too insubstantial to warrant vacating an award.

MR. JUSTICE FORTAS, with whom MR. JUSTICE HARLAN and MR. JUSTICE STEWART join, dissenting.

I dissent and would affirm the judgment.

The facts in this case do not lend themselves to the Court's ruling. The Court sets aside the arbitration award despite the fact that the award is unanimous and no claim is made of actual partiality, unfairness, bias, or fraud.

* * *

Both courts below held, and petitioner concedes, that the third arbitrator was innocent of any actual partiality, or bias, or improper motive. There is no suggestion of concealment as distinguished from the innocent failure to volunteer information.

The third arbitrator is a leading and respected consulting engineer who has performed services for "most of the contractors in Puerto Rico." He was well known to petitioner's counsel and they were personal friends. Petitioner's counsel candidly admitted that if he had been told about the arbitrator's prior relationship "I don't think I would have objected because I know Mr. Capacete [the arbitrator]."

Clearly, the District Judge's conclusion, affirmed by the Court of Appeals for the First Circuit, was correct, that "the arbitrators conducted fair, impartial hearings; that they reached a proper determination of the issues before them, and that plaintiff's objections represent a 'situation where the losing party to an arbitration is now clutching at straws in an attempt to avoid the results of the arbitration to which it became a party.' "

* * *

Arbitration is essentially consensual and practical. The United States Arbitration Act is obviously designed to protect the integrity of the process with a minimum of insistence upon set formulae and rules. The Court applies to this process rules applicable to judges and not to a system characterized by dealing on faith and reputation for reliability. Such formalism is not contemplated by the Act nor is it warranted in a case where no claim is made of partiality, of unfairness, or of misconduct in any degree.

NOTES AND QUESTIONS

1. Did Justice White really "join" in Justice Black's opinion? Note that the votes of Justices White and Marshall were essential to a majority in *Commonwealth Coatings.*

2. The current version of the AAA's Commercial Arbitration Rules requires "any person appointed as a neutral arbitrator" to "disclose to the AAA any circumstance likely to affect impartiality or independence, including any bias or any financial or personal interest in the result of the arbitration or any past or present relationship with the parties or their representatives." The AAA communicates this information to the parties and if any of them objects, "the AAA shall determine whether the arbitrator should be disqualified and shall inform the parties of its decision, which shall be conclusive." (Rule 19). A "Code of Ethics for Arbitrators in Commercial Disputes" has also been adopted by the AAA and by the American Bar Association. Canon II of this Code provides that "An Arbitrator should disclose any interest or relationship likely to affect impartiality or which might create an appearance of partiality or bias":

> A. Persons Who Are Requested To Serve As Arbitrators Should, Before Accepting, Disclose:
>
> (1) Any direct or indirect financial or personal interest in the outcome of the arbitration;
>
> (2) Any existing or past financial, business, professional, family or social relationships which are likely to affect impartiality or which might reasonably create an appearance of partiality or bias. Persons requested to serve as arbitrators should disclose any such relationships which they personally have with any party or its lawyer, or with any individual whom they have been told will be a witness. They should also disclose any such relationships involving members of their families or their current employers, partners or business associates.
>
> E. In The Event That An Arbitrator Is Requested By All Parties To Withdraw, The Arbitrator Should Do So. In The Event That An Arbitrator Is Requested To Withdraw By Less Than All Of The Parties Because Of Alleged Partiality Or Bias, The Arbitrator Should Withdraw Unless Either Of The Following Circumstances Exists:
>
> (1) If an agreement of the parties, or arbitration rules agreed to by the parties, establishes procedures for determining challenges to arbitrators, then those procedures should be followed; or
>
> (2) If the arbitrator, after carefully considering the matter, determines that the reason for the challenge is not substantial, and that he or she can nevertheless act and decide the case impartially and fairly, and that withdrawal would cause unfair delay or expense to another party or would be contrary to the ends of justice.

Notes to this "Canon" make clear that it is

> intended to be applied realistically so that the burden of detailed disclosure does not become so great that it is impractical for persons in the business world to be arbitrators, thereby depriving parties of the services of those who might be best informed and qualified to decide particular types of cases.

3. What use can be made of the AAA Rules and Canons in a judicial proceeding to vacate an arbitral award? Judge Posner has written that:

> [E]ven if the failure to disclose was a material violation of the ethical standards applicable to arbitration proceedings, it does not follow that the arbitration award may be nullified judicially. * * * The arbitration rules and code do not have the force of law. If [a party] is to get the arbitration award set aside it must bring itself within the statute * * *.
>
> The American Arbitration Association is in competition not only with other private arbitration services but with the courts in providing—in the case of the private services, selling—an attractive form of dispute settlement. It may set its standards as high or as low as it thinks its customers want. The [FAA] has a different purpose—to make arbitration effective by putting the coercive force of the federal courts behind arbitration decrees that affect interstate commerce or are otherwise of federal concern. * * * The standards for judicial intervention are therefore narrowly drawn to assure the basic integrity of the arbitration process without meddling in it. Section 10 is full of words like corruption and misbehavior and fraud. The standards it sets are minimum ones. * * * The fact that the AAA went beyond the statutory standards in drafting its own code of ethics does not lower the threshold for judicial intervention.

Merit Ins. Co. v. Leatherby Ins. Co., 714 F.2d 673 (7th Cir.1983).

Do you agree?

4. The arbitration statutes of some states impose additional and more explicit requirements of disclosure on potential arbitrators. For example, a recent California statute provides that any potential arbitrator shall disclose the "names of any prior or pending cases involving any party to the arbitration agreement or the lawyer for a party" for whom she "served or is serving as a neutral arbitrator, and the results of each case arbitrated to conclusion * * * and the amount of monetary damages awarded, if any." The proposed appointee "shall be disqualified as a neutral arbitrator on the basis of the disclosure statement" after any of the party objects to her serving on the panel. Cal.Code Civ.Pro. § 1281.9.

5. If courts held arbitrators to the same standards of isolation and purity to which they hold Article III judges, an adverse decision might invariably become the occasion for frantic research by the losing party into possible links between his adversary and the arbitrator. The obvious dangers to the arbitral process have led courts to be unreceptive to such attempts.

In their reluctance to set aside awards on these grounds courts have also been sensitive to the need for decision-makers with extensive professional experience and knowledge, and to what Judge Posner has called the necessary "tradeoff between impartiality and expertise." *Merit Ins. Co.,* 714 F.2d at 679. A good example is presented by International Produce, Inc. v. A/S Rosshavet, 638 F.2d 548 (2d Cir.1981). This was a maritime arbitration in which the neutral arbitrator was the Vice–President of a management firm retained by owners of various commercial vessels. After the hearings had begun, this arbitrator's firm became involved in an unrelated arbitration involving another vessel. It happened that the law firms representing the parties in the second arbitration were the same firms that were handling the *International Produce* arbitration; in this second proceeding the arbitrator appeared as a non-party witness, prepared in his testimony by one of the law firms and cross-examined by the other. Although requested to withdraw, the arbitrator refused to do so, and his award was successfully challenged in district court. The Second Circuit held that the award should not have been vacated:

> It is not unusual that those who are selected as arbitrators in maritime arbitrations have had numerous prior dealings with one or more of the parties or their counsel. * * * Arbitrator Klosty aptly analogized New York's maritime-arbitration community to a busy harbor, where the wakes of the members often cross.
>
> The most sought-after arbitrators are those who are prominent and experienced members of the specific business community in which the dispute to be arbitrated arose. Since they are chosen precisely because of their involvement in that community, some degree of overlapping representation and interest inevitably results. Those chosen as arbitrators in important shipping arbitrations have typically participated in a great number of prior maritime disputes, not only as arbitrators but also as parties and witnesses. They have therefore almost inevitably come into contact with a significant proportion of the relatively few lawyers who make up the New York admiralty bar. Under these circumstances, a decision on our part to vacate arbitration awards whenever a mere appearance of bias can be made out would seriously disrupt the salutary process of settling maritime disputes through arbitration.

Of course, the alleged conflict of interest in *International Produce* was immediately known to both of the parties in the case as soon as it arose. Would the matter be different—should a higher standard be imposed—if one party is claiming that the arbitrator failed before the hearing to disclose facts about his relationship with the other?

6. A labor arbitrator issued an award sustaining a grievance by the United Mine Workers against a coal company. The employer moved to vacate the award, alleging that the arbitrator had failed to disclose that his brother was employed by the UMW. The court suggested that the standard of FAA § 10(a)(2)—which permits a court to vacate an award for "evident partiality" in the arbitrators—should also apply to awards arising out of collective bargaining agreements. "To demonstrate evident partiality under the FAA, the party seeking vacation has the burden of proving that a reasonable person would have to conclude that an arbitrator was partial to the other party to the arbitration." Under this standard, the court declined to vacate the award. Neither the arbitrator nor his brother "had any discernible interest in the outcome of the proceeding." In addition, the court stressed that the coal industry decisions that this arbitrator had made in the past underlined the absence of "evident partiality." He had served as a "coal industry arbitrator" for three years under procedures adopted by the UMW and the Bituminous Coal Operators Association; of his 66 awards, the Union had "won 30, lost 29, split 5, and settled 2 before a hearing." Consolidation Coal Co. v. Local 1643, United Mine Workers of Amer., 48 F.3d 125 (4th Cir.1995). See also pp. 44–46 supra ("Compromise Decisions").

7. There are at least some cases in which one can recognize "evident partiality" without a great deal of trouble. In one major insurance arbitration, the claimant was awarded $92 million by a "tripartite" panel. After the award was rendered—but before confirmation by a court—the losing attorneys surreptitiously made videotapes indicating that the claimant's lawyer and the panel's "neutral" arbitrator had spent several nights together in the lawyer's hotel room. "She says he spent the two nights in question in a separate room in her suite, one night because she was sick and another night because he didn't have a room of his own." (A full account appears in Schmitt, "Suite Sharing: Arbitrator's Friendship With Winning Lawyer Imperils Huge Victory," Wall St. J., Feb. 14, 1990, p. 1.) We understand that the award was later vacated by stipulation of the parties.

8. Are party-appointed representatives on "tripartite" boards held to the same standards as other arbitrators? Section 23(a)(2) of the Revised Uniform Arbitration Act permits a court to vacate an award where there was "corruption by an arbitrator," "misconduct by an arbitrator prejudicing the rights of a party," or "evident partiality by an arbitrator *appointed as a neutral*." What do the italicized words add? The AAA/ABA "Code of Ethics for Arbitrators in Commercial Disputes" presumes that party-appointed arbitrators "should be considered non-neutrals" unless the parties have specified otherwise. Under the Code, they "may be predisposed toward the party who appointed them." With respect to Canon II concerning disclosure, the Code provides that non-neutral party-appointed arbitrators "need not include as detailed information as is expected from persons appointed as neutral arbitrators"; in addition, they "are not obliged to withdraw if requested to do so by the party who did not appoint them."

This different treatment of party-appointed arbitrators is reflected in most of the cases, which "implicitly recognize it is not necessarily unfair or unconscionable to create an effectively neutral tribunal by building in presumably offsetting biases." Tate v. Saratoga Savings & Loan Ass'n, 216 Cal.App.3d 843, 265 Cal.Rptr. 440, 445 (1989). In one case an arbitrator, after being appointed, assisted the party that had named him "in preparing its case by attending and participating in meetings with [its] witnesses [and suggesting] lines or areas of testimony." The court found this conduct "not only unobjectionable, but commonplace," Sunkist Soft Drinks, Inc. v. Sunkist Growers, Inc., 10 F.3d 753 (11th Cir.1993). But for the view that this sort of behavior might constitute "overt misconduct" that exceeds even the partisanship expected of party-appointed arbitrators, see Metropolitan Property & Casualty Ins. Co. v. J.C. Penney Casualty Ins. Co., 780 F.Supp. 885 (D.Conn.1991).

Assuming that proper disclosure is made, can a party appoint a member of its Board of Directors as "its" arbitrator on a tripartite board? See In the Matter of the Arbitration between the Astoria Medical Group v. Health Ins. Plan of Greater N.Y., 11 N.Y.2d 128, 227 N.Y.S.2d 401, 182 N.E.2d 85 (1962) (yes; the right to appoint "one's own arbitrator" "becomes a valued right, which parties will bargain for * * * only if it involves a choice of one believed to be sympathetic to his position or favorably disposed to him"). Does it follow, then, that an individual party can *itself* sit as its own arbitrator? See Edmund E. Garrison, Inc. v. International Union of Operating Engineers, 283 F.Supp. 771 (S.D.N.Y.1968). Can the claimant in an arbitration agree to compensate "its" arbitrator on the basis of a percentage of the award? See Aetna Casualty & Surety Co. v. Grabbert, 590 A.2d 88 (R.I.1991).

9. In international commercial arbitrations, the "tripartite" model is in fact a norm which will be surrendered only with difficulty—to many, indeed, the right to choose one member of the panel is the very essence of arbitration. And in such arbitrations the general understanding calls for a rule that is nominally different from our domestic practice: Arbitrators on international panels are expected to be both independent of the party appointing them and impartial. Apparently there is "no room for debate" that a party-appointed arbitrator may be partisan, and ICC practice, for example, is to refuse confirmation to an arbitrator where there exists a professional or financial relationship with any of the parties.

Cf. Rau, On Integrity in Private Judging, 14 Arb. Int'l 115, 230–31 (1998):

> Nevertheless it is usually conceded that without violating in any way this theoretical obligation of independence, the arbitrator may quite acceptably share the nationality, or political or economic philosophy, or "legal culture" of the party who has nominated him—and may therefore be supposed from the very beginning to be "sympathetic" to that party's contentions, or "favorably disposed" to its position. * * *
>
> I would think it very doubtful that this could possibly be considered an improvement over the practice in our domestic commercial arbitrations. Even in the best of circumstances an official rhetoric of "independence" and a tolerated latent "sympathy" must exist in an uneasy tension. Indeed one occasionally comes across the argument that codes of ethics mandating impartiality are useful precisely in that they give arbitrators who "wish to behave entirely impartially" some sort of "moral protection" against pressure to rule in favor of the party

naming them—an argument that itself illustrates nicely the sort of dynamic that must often arise.

When the Continental jurist writes that a party-appointed arbitrator must be impartial—but can be impartial "in his own fashion"—the echo of Cole Porter is undoubtedly inadvertent. But in such circumstances the potential for ambiguity, uncertainty and confusion seems obvious. Even the arbitrator himself may be unaware of the extent to which his identification with the party who has appointed him may be affecting his view of a given procedural or substantive issue—and what is more important, this may be appreciated still less by his two colleagues, particularly the chairman. A mythology that promotes the belief that international arbitrators can be relied on not to allow their sympathy "to override their conscience and professional judgment"—regardless of whether this is taken as empirical description or as a mere aspiration—seems calculated only to increase these dangers of self-deception and sandbagging.

It is true of course that too visible an advocacy is likely to be simply counterproductive. Once he is perceived as little more than an agent for the party appointing him, an arbitrator may well lose all his clout with the rest of the panel and all his ability to influence the course of the proceedings. But these are counsels of prudence and discreet self-presentation, not of impartiality. In the course of discussions aimed at selecting party-appointed arbitrators in international cases, the highest praise one can give, apparently—one actually hears this said—is that the potential arbitrator "knows just how far he can go in advocacy" without losing all credibility with his colleagues. By contrast, to recognize quite openly the inevitability of partisanship once party-appointed arbitrators are used might instead * * * be "the only intellectually honest approach to the situation".

10. Westinghouse entered into a contract with the New York City Transit Authority (NYCTA) for the delivery of equipment for the New York subway system. Numerous disputes arose between the parties; NYCTA declared Westinghouse in default, and Westinghouse submitted a claim for additional compensation. Under the contract, disputes were to be submitted to the Superintendent of the NYCTA—who was an NYCTA employee and its Chief Electrical Officer; judicial review was to be limited to the question whether the Superintendent's decision was "arbitrary, capricious, or grossly erroneous to evidence bad faith." Westinghouse later challenged an adverse determination by the Superintendent, arguing that the contract "imposes a procedure for dispute resolution by a functionary inseparable from one of the parties to the dispute and, thus, fosters a predisposed adjudication process" contrary to public policy. The court, however, rejected this argument: "Westinghouse chose, with its business eyes open, to accept the terms, specifications and risk" of the contract; this was "part of the calculated business risk it undertook." Private contractors are "often economic giants in their own right," and the fact that municipalities may enjoy a "virtual monopolistic-kind of power" on their public works jobs "does not make these contracts adhesion agreements. * * * [W]here, as here, the parties are dealing at arm's length with relative equality of bargaining power, they ought to be left to themselves." The court found its conclusion buttressed by the fact that the contract "allows broader review than the usual and stricter standards" of judicial review of arbitration awards. Westinghouse Electric Corp. v. New York City Transit Authority, 82 N.Y.2d 47, 603 N.Y.S.2d 404, 623 N.E.2d 531 (1993). Compare Graham v. Scissor–Tail, Inc., supra p. 108. ("Contracts of Adhesion and Unconscionability").

11. The CPR Institute for Dispute Resolution has published a set of rules for "non-administered arbitration"—rules "that could be used by sophisticated users who didn't need a babysitter," see 18 Alternatives 149, 151–52 (Sept. 2000). A recent revision of these rules provides for an optional "screened" selection of party-appointed arbitrators—designed "in such a manner so that the arbitrators wouldn't know who picked them." Under the new rules, parties wishing to follow this procedure are given a copy of the CPR "Panel of Distinguished Neutrals," and each party is to designate three candidates, in order of preference, "as candidates for its party-designated arbitrator." A party may object to any appointment "on independent and impartial grounds by written and reasoned notice to CPR," which is to make a final decision with respect to any objection. "Neither CPR nor the parties shall advise or otherwise provide any information or indication to any arbitrator candidate or arbitrator as to which party selected either of the party-designated arbitrators." Rule 5.4(d).

What do you think of this solution?

12. On occasion a losing party, claiming that the arbitrator did not decide fairly or that he proceeded in violation of the rules, will bring a suit directly against the arbitrator or the administering institution. Such claims are usually rebuffed with an invocation of "arbitral immunity." Just as with judges, it is thought that "the independence necessary for principled and fearless decision-making can best be preserved by protecting these persons from bias or intimidation caused by the fear of a lawsuit arising out of the exercise of official functions within their jurisdiction." Corey v. New York Stock Exchange, 691 F.2d 1205 (6th Cir.1982). This "federal policy" dictates that the only remedy for a disgruntled party is under § 10 and § 11 of FAA and not by means of collateral attacks on the award. A similar interest in protecting arbitrators also means that when a court *does* hear a motion under § 10 or § 11, it is unlikely to permit depositions or examination of the arbitrators themselves aimed at developing a factual basis for impeaching the award. See, e.g., Portland Gen. Elec. Co. v. U.S. Bank Trust Nat'l Ass'n, 38 F.Supp.2d 1202 (D.Or.1999)("discovery in the challenge of an arbitral award is tightly circumscribed and available only upon 'clear evidence of impropriety' ").

The Revised Uniform Arbitration Act also provides that "an arbitrator or an arbitration organization acting in such capacity is immune from civil liability to the same extent as a judge of a court of this State acting in a judicial capacity"; where a suit against an arbitrator or an arbitral institution is dismissed on the ground of immunity, the defendants are entitled to recover "reasonable attorney's fees and other reasonable expenses of litigation." § 14(a),(e).

13. Who is acting as an "arbitrator" for purposes of "arbitral immunity"? Can former New York City mayor Edward Koch, who presided over a televised episode of "The People's Court," be liable for allegedly defamatory statements made in the course of the hearing? See Kabia v. Koch, 186 Misc.2d 363, 713 N.Y.S.2d 250 (City Ct.2000)(no; this is "arbitration" under state law even though any award is to be paid by the producers of the television program and not by the losing party; "arbitrators in contractually agreed upon arbitration proceedings are absolutely immune from liability for all acts within the scope of the arbitral process").

Should immunity be extended to an architect, employed and paid by the owner of a construction project and charged with interpreting the contract documents and deciding whether the contractor has substantially performed? See Lundgren v. Freeman, 307 F.2d 104, 116–19 (9th Cir.1962) (granting immunity when architect was acting as "quasi-arbitrator"). What about an accountant who is hired by both parties to a contract for the sale of stock to determine the earnings of the company? See Wasyl, Inc. v. First Boston Corp., 813 F.2d 1579 (9th Cir.1987) (claim of breach of contract and gross negligence by defendant in appraisal of value of partnership interest; immunity granted, relying on state arbitration statute that expressly "includes * * * valuations [and] appraisals"); contra, Comins v. Sharkansky, 38 Mass.App.Ct. 37, 644 N.E.2d 646 (1995) (defendant-accountant "is neither an arbitrator exercising 'quasi-judicial' functions nor an expert rendering expert services to the court"; "[w]hile an arbitration may be less formal than court proceedings, the parties contemplate that an arbitrator will hold hearings and will take evidence in the presence of the parties"). Cf. Arenson v. Casson Beckman Rutley & Co., [1975] 3 All E.R. 901 (H.L.) (Lord Kilbrandon) ("It would be absurd if the situation were that, when an expert is asked by one customer to value a picture, he is liable in damages if he is shown to have done so negligently, but that if two customers had jointly asked him to value the same picture he would have been immune from suit").

Do the reasons justifying arbitral immunity extend to protecting an arbitrator from a lawsuit that alleges he is liable for "breach of contract" for simply failing to render any award at all? See Baar v. Tigerman, 140 Cal.App.3d 979, 189 Cal.Rptr. 834 (1983) (arbitrator did not meet deadline imposed for decision under AAA rules; cases granting immunity were distinguished because here the arbitrators were not "acting in a quasi-judicial capacity" and plaintiffs had not alleged "misconduct in arriving at a decision").

2. Conduct of the Proceeding

a. INTRODUCTION

In any discussion of arbitration it is almost mandatory to mention the supposed "informality" of the process: "Submission of disputes to arbitration always risks an accumulation of procedural and evidentiary shortcuts that would properly frustrate counsel in a formal trial."[1] However, there is not merely one form of procedure for arbitration in the United States, but an almost infinite variety:

> At one extreme, we have what is practically courtroom procedure, with carefully drawn submissions, formal procedures, emphasis upon technicalities, formal opening and closing statements, arguments as to the admissibility and relevance of evidence, qualifications of witnesses, and the burden of proof, and briefs, rebuttal briefs, and sur-rebuttal briefs. At the other extreme, we have an atmosphere which is barely distinguishable from a mediation proceeding; the issue is vague and ill-defined, everybody talks at the same time, says irrelevant things, no standards of evidence appear, and the arbitrator seems to be working chiefly at the task of securing agreement between the disputants. Between the extremes are innumerable shadings and variations.[2]

The personality and the professional background of the arbitrator, the attitudes and the relationship of the parties, the issues in contention—all will influence the way the arbitration proceeds.

We should not be surprised to find a considerable amount of procedural innovation in the practice of arbitration—stemming, first, from the unbounded ability of the parties to "write their own ticket," and, second, from the traditionally broad discretion of arbitrators in structuring the proceedings. "Indeed, short of authorizing trial by battle or ordeal or, more doubtfully, by a panel of three monkeys, parties can stipulate to whatever procedures they want to govern the arbitration of their disputes."[3] In one large and complex antitrust dispute, for example, the parties had selected as their arbitrator a noted antitrust scholar and law professor:

> Based on his reading of briefs and affidavits, [the arbitrator] advised counsel which witnesses he wanted to have at the hearing. Rather than putting on the plaintiff's case in full, followed by defendant's case in full, [the arbitrator] proceeded by topic or category of witness; and in several instances, he put corresponding witnesses for the two sides on the stand at the same time. In so doing, he was able to let both parties' witnesses respond in succession to the same question and then engage in dialogue to explore differences of opinion. Throughout the proceeding, [he] peppered counsel with questions to explore the bases for and merits of various legal theories.

This technique avoided both the rigidity of traditional direct and cross-examination, and the usual "ships-passing-in-the-night" quality of most competing expert testimony. In fact most of the questioning at the hearing was done by the arbitrator, and only "limited follow-up questioning" was

1. Forsythe Int'l, S.A. v. Gibbs Oil Co. of Texas, 915 F.2d 1017, 1022 (5th Cir.1990).

2. Stein, The Selection of Arbitrators, N.Y.U. Eighth Annual Conference on Labor 291, 293 (1955).

3. Baravati v. Josephthal, Lyon & Ross, Inc., 28 F.3d 704, 709 (7th Cir.1994)(Posner, C.J.).

conducted by counsel. In addition, the parties agreed that the arbitrator would write a reasoned opinion that "could be published because of its potential value to other parties who might be faced with similar issues."[4]

b. THE ROLE OF LAWYERS

"[E]ven in the most informal of proceedings certain minimum requirements of 'due process' must be met if the award is to be legally binding."[5] State and federal statutes governing arbitration mandate certain elements supposed to be essential to a fair hearing. Under the Revised Uniform Arbitration Act, "the parties to the arbitration proceeding are entitled to be heard, to present evidence material to the controversy and to cross-examine witnesses appearing at the hearing." § 15(d). The parties also have the right to be represented by an attorney, and any waiver of that right "before a controversy arises" subject to the arbitration agreement is ineffective. §§ 4(b)(4), 16.

Attorneys can play a useful role in arbitration. In framing and focusing the issues, and in eliciting and marshalling the evidence, the attorney can help create a more coherent and rational process. However, the use of attorneys—along with the adversarial proceedings that seem to be envisaged by the arbitration statutes—may be responsible for some of the vociferous complaints about the growing "legalization" of the arbitration process. These complaints seem to be heard most loudly in the self-contained enclave of labor arbitration. One observer, for example, has written:

> In the past two decades, a change in orientation of labor arbitrators and a rise in the use of attorneys as advocates have accelerated the introduction into labor arbitration of procedures that approximate those of the courts. * * *
>
> [The former president of the National Academy of Arbitrators has written that]
>
> * * * The ratio of hard fought, legalistic arbitration presentations to problem-solving presentations is increasing. I now have more long, drawn-out cases in which employers and unions present prehearing briefs, spend endless hours haggling over the language of the submitted issue, have stenographic records made of the hearings and insist upon briefs, reply briefs, and sometimes, reply briefs to the reply briefs. * * *
>
> Legalism adds to the complexity of arbitration, and correspondingly to the confusion of an employee. The impersonality that legalism brings to the process undermines its credibility. Employees who have

4. Baker, Alexander, Cohan & Heike, "The First Texas–Pulse Arbitration: A Case Study," reprinted in John Murray, Alan Rau, and Edward Sherman, Dispute Resolution: Materials for Continuing Legal Education IV–136, IV–141 (NIDR 1991).

5. Smith, Merrifield & Rothschild, Collective Bargaining and Labor Arbitration 212 (1970).

been assisted in their grievances by union representatives who may have known them for years may be represented at the arbitration by attorneys whom they have seen for the first time on the day of the arbitration. When these attorneys, competent though they may be, neglect to raise questions that the grievants feel are important, which they feel would have been asked by union representatives, the grievants feel cheated.[6]

In this debate, however, as in most others, where one ends up may well depend upon one's starting point. The author of the preceding excerpt is a "Professor of Human Resource Development" in a College of Business. A lawyer, by contrast, is far more likely to be using a judicial yardstick when he evaluates arbitration. He may be struck most forcibly by the way in which the process *falls short* of the ritual trappings and judicial solemnity of the model with which he is most comfortable.

Commercial arbitrations are somewhat more likely even than labor cases to involve lawyers (acting either as arbitrators or as advocates), and to look like "loose approximations of judicial proceedings."[7] This is a tendency that may be accelerating. More than half a century ago, Lon Fuller could advise advocates that the commercial arbitrator, "who will usually be a layman, * * * will be unimpressed by arguments resting upon the abstract 'rights' of the parties. The arbitrator will chiefly want to know whether the parties conducted themselves honorably and fairly and made a genuine effort to settle their differences by negotiation."[8] Given the remedial flexibility and freedom from the constraint of legal rules that typify arbitration, there remains much truth in this counsel. On the other hand, pressures by lawyers "always to guarantee as much due process as possible" may be creating subtle changes in the appearance of arbitration—and might well cause it "over time by accretion" to become almost "indistinguishable from the system you were trying to get away from."[9] When important questions of external law are routinely entrusted to arbitrators—and when the paradigm arbitration case increasingly becomes, not a dispute over the quality of goods delivered but over alleged violations of the Sherman Act or Title VII—then the attention to legal rules, and the accompanying level of procedural formality, may be expected to be much higher.

The attorney can still however expect in all forms of arbitration to encounter an environment that is noticeably different from that of litiga-

6. Raffaele, Lawyers in Labor Arbitration, 37 Arb.J. No. 3 (Sept. 1982). See also Alleyne, Delawyerizing Labor Arbitration, 50 Ohio St. L.J. 93 (1989)("creeping formalism took sway with the commonly held notion that representation by a lawyer in an adversary proceeding, even a labor arbitration hearing, enhances the possibility of a successful outcome").

7. Shell, ERISA and Other Federal Employment Statutes: When Is Commercial Arbitration an "Adequate Substitute" for the Courts?, 68 Tex.L.Rev. 509, 534 (1990).

8. Lon Fuller, Basic Contract Law 713 (1947).

9. McKeen, "Med–Mal Arbitration in California: Murky Results," Legal Times, Sept. 13, 1993, at pp. 10, 13 (quoting the general counsel for the Association for California Tort Reform).

tion. Lawyers who are unfamiliar with the process may at first find it difficult to adapt themselves to the different quality of advocacy expected in arbitration, and must struggle to adjust their behavior to the different style and atmosphere of an arbitration proceeding. Such a mainstay of a litigator's life as pre-"trial" motion practice is for all practical purposes absent from arbitration. And a forensic style carefully honed for courtroom use may be totally out of place in an arbitration proceeding, where the parties and the arbitrators are all seated together around a conference-room table. In this more relaxed setting a non-theatrical, even conversational style is likely to be much more effective. A less confrontational and less argumentative approach may be hardest to pull off in the cross-examination of the opponent's witnesses—although this may be all the more important if the arbitrators are prone to identify closely with witnesses from the industry involved in the dispute.

c. EVIDENCE

The classic illustration of the relative "informality" of the arbitration process is the usual absence of the rules of evidence, which play such a dominant role in any courtroom. Under the AAA's Commercial Arbitration Rules, "[c]onformity to legal rules of evidence shall not be necessary"; "[t]he arbitrator shall determine the admissibility, relevance, and materiality of the evidence offered and may exclude evidence deemed by the arbitrator to be cumulative or irrelevant." (Rule 33). It is not unusual for evidence to be presented in the form of affidavits rather than live testimony, despite the absence of any possibility for cross-examination. See Commercial Arbitration Rules, Rule 34 (but it shall be given "only such weight as the arbitrator deems it entitled to after consideration of any objection made to its admission"); Pierre v. General Accident Ins., 100 A.D.2d 705, 474 N.Y.S.2d 622 (App.Div.1984) (widow's claim for death benefit under automobile insurance policy was denied; arbitrator accepted "an unsworn report, in the form of a letter, from respondent's expert cardiologist, who did not testify or make himself available for cross-examination").

An arbitrator is in fact more likely to get into trouble by following the rules of evidence than by ignoring them—and far more likely to get into trouble by excluding evidence than by admitting it. Section 10(a)(3) of the FAA allows a court to vacate an award where the arbitrator was "guilty of misconduct" "in refusing to hear evidence pertinent and material to the controversy." There are many cases in which an arbitrator's disregard of testimony in reliance on rules of evidence has caused his award to be vacated, on the ground that a party has been denied a "fair hearing." See, e.g., Harvey Alum. v. United Steelworkers of America, 263 F.Supp. 488 (C.D.Cal.1967). Perhaps as a consequence, the common tendency of arbitrators seems to be to admit most proffered evidence and to consider it "for whatever it may be worth." "I am prepared to listen to just about anything a party wants me to hear."[10]

10. McDermott, An Exercise in Dialectic: Should Arbitration Behave As Does Liti-

A good example of how this can work in practice is provided by one lawyer's account of his service on an arbitration panel. In this construction case a contractor who had built a building for a private school submitted a substantial claim for "extras," work done but supposedly not covered by the contract price:

> In his opening statement to the panel, the lawyer for the school asserted that even without the extras, the contractor had made a profit. He then gave the arbitrators an affidavit from the school's controller. It stated that the school, which enjoyed an excellent reputation in the community, would have to raise each student's tuition at least $1,300 a year just to pay the interest on the amount sought by the contractor. The affidavit also stated that the school had granted scholarships to at least 28 students, who might have to withdraw if the contractor obtained the award he was seeking.
>
> [Over an objection by the contractor's lawyer that the affidavit was "incompetent, irrelevant, hearsay, prejudicial, and not probative on any issue in dispute," the panel (which also included an architect and an engineer) received it in evidence. The arbitration lasted for weeks, with copious, and confusing, evidence offered on each of the contractor's claims:]
>
> Among the few facts which retained their persuasive power throughout the arbitration were the points the school lawyer had made at the outset. Almost every day, in private conversations over lunch or over an early evening drink, or during any one of the several recesses taken during the day, one or more of the arbitrators mentioned that the contractor had already made a profit and that granting the claim would injure the school and hurt innocent scholarship students.

The ultimate decision was in favor of the school.[11]

NOTES AND QUESTIONS

1. The lowering of barriers to the admission of evidence in arbitration is often the subject of serious criticism, particularly on the part of lawyers, who are likely to find it chaotic, sloppy—and worse. For example, one prominent attorney and arbitrator has written:

> [T]he common arbitration practice often admits costly immaterial and/or prejudicial evidence. * * * The arbitrators do that out of [a desire] to appear to be fair and * * * [t]hereby they become unfair by receiving prejudicial evidence or making parties spend effort and money responding to immaterial evidence. * * * It is fairly common knowledge that uncross-examined affidavit evidence is *extremely* unreliable. Lawyers hear a narrative, draft a preliminary affidavit proposal with many voids filled in out of their own imagination, send it to the affiant perhaps "to check and execute if it is OK." * * * The wildest

gation?, Proceedings, 33rd Annual Meeting, Nat'l Academy of Arbitrators 1, 14 (1981).

11. Roth, When to Ignore the Rules of Evidence in Arbitration, 9 Litigation 20 (Winter 1983).

> hearsay upon hearsay is often pretended to be "personal knowledge." A party ought not [to] have to fight such irresponsible evidence presented by the adversary.

Arnold & Hubert, Focus Points in Arbitration Practice 51–52 (1992, unpublished), quoted in Rau & Sherman, Tradition and Innovation in International Arbitration Procedure, 30 Tex.Int'l L.J. 89, 95, 101 (1995).

In many cases such criticism is undoubtedly well-founded. In some kinds of cases, however, may criticisms of this sort overlook some of the premises of arbitration? The opportunity to present evidence that is not particularly relevant or even particularly reliable by the usual standards of the courtroom may nevertheless provide arbitrators with an insight into the "total situation" of the parties not afforded by a narrower scope of inquiry. (This may be true of the school construction arbitration discussed above.) And when the parties are engaged in a continuing relationship, such an opportunity can permit a useful "ventilation" of a grievance; as in mediation, when the parties are given a sense that they have had a full opportunity to "have their say" on points that are personally important to them, the process is legitimated and their confidence in it increased: "This is therapy evidence." Jones, Evidentiary Concepts in Labor Arbitration: Some Modern Variations on Ancient Legal Themes, 13 U.C.L.A.L.Rev. 1241, 1254 (1966). In addition, it is far from clear that generosity in admitting evidence will necessarily prolong the hearings: Laying a proper "foundation" for evidence and qualifying witnesses, making a series of witnesses personally available for the purposes of cross-examination—and resolving the inevitable attorney wranglings over admissibility—all may consume at least as much if not more time than does the present practice.

2. On the tendency of labor arbitrators to admit evidence "for what it is worth," see W. Daniel Boone, A Debate: Should Labor Arbitrators Receive Evidence "For What It's Worth"?: The Union Perspective, Proceedings, 51st Annual Meeting, Nat'l Academy of Arbitrators 89, 92 (1999):

> Within the arbitrator community in Northern California, I take this to mean, "this evidence is not worth anything, but I'll let it in anyway." I understand the arbitrator to be saying (1) the evidence is neither relevant nor probative, (2) it has no persuasive impact, (3) it will not assist in making a decision, (4) the opposing party need not respond with evidence or argument, and (5) the proponent may proceed only if a truly short amount of time is taken.

3. Although it is well known that arbitrators are not bound by "rules of evidence," it is nevertheless quite common to find lawyers objecting in arbitration to the introduction of what, in litigation, would be "inadmissible" evidence. The goal here, obviously, is not so much to keep the evidence out—as it is to emphasize its unreliability, and to reduce the weight it might have for the arbitrator.

4. In none of the statutes governing arbitration is there any mention of improperly *admitting* evidence as a form of arbitral "misconduct." Can an award ever be vacated on such grounds? It is quite common for arbitrators to hear testimony in the form of what would be "hearsay" in a court of law, and this clearly is not a ground for overturning an award. Farkas v. Receivable Financing Corp., 806 F.Supp. 84 (E.D.Va.1992). See also In the Matter of the Arbitration between Norma Brill and Muller Brothers, Inc., 40 Misc.2d 683, 243 N.Y.S.2d 905 (Sup. Ct. 1962), in which the arbitrator received in evidence a detective agency report consisting of a "dime-novel series of stories about the petitioner and her behavior, said to be gathered from her former neighbors" and "detailing specific acts of alleged avarice, malice and chicanery." The trial court, calling this "hearsay on hearsay" and "thoroughly unfair evidence," "inflammatory and prejudicial to the highest degree," vacated the award. Higher courts, however, reversed, 17 A.D.2d 804, 232 N.Y.S.2d 806 (App.Div.1962), aff'd, 13 N.Y.2d 776, 242 N.Y.S.2d 69, 192 N.E.2d 34 (1963).

5. In a Better Business Bureau arbitration between General Motors and a car owner, the owner requested that GM be made to buy back the car; he had bought it second-hand, and had replaced the engine after driving it for an additional 23,000 miles. "The arbitrator awarded the owner half the cost of the second engine, or $875. The rationale was that, during mediation, the manufacturer had indicated a willingness to assume half the cost of the engine * * *." This anecdote is reported without comment in Note, Virginia's Lemon Law: The Best Treatment for Car Owner's Canker?, 19 U.Rich.L.Rev. 405, 421 (1985).

See Bowles Financial Group, Inc. v. Stifel, Nicolaus & Co., Inc., 22 F.3d 1010 (10th Cir.1994). In this case the attorney for the claimant had "deliberately, intentionally, affirmatively and repeatedly communicated to the arbitrators an offer of settlement" from the respondent, arguing that the settlement offer "evidenced [the respondent's] admission of liability." "Counsel also indicated he routinely submitted settlement offers to the arbitrators in the cases where he represented clients in arbitration." The arbitrators, "after receiving the settlement offer, commented they would not consider it," but they subsequently made an award to the claimant that exceeded the offer. The court held that the respondent "has not proven it was subjected to a fundamentally unfair hearing":

> Had [the claimant's] counsel done before a court of law what he did before the arbitrators, significant sanctions would have been imposed and a mistrial ordered. But however well-established may be the judicial rules of evidence, they legitimately did not apply to this arbitration.

See Rule 408 of the Federal Rules of Evidence concerning the inadmissibility at trial of offers made during settlement negotiations.

6. Should the arbitrator be expected to make a decision based solely on the evidence received at the hearing? After all, one of the premises of arbitration is that the arbitrator may himself be an "expert," chosen to bring to the process his own knowledge and familiarity with the subject matter. It seems clear that an arbitrator, unlike a judge, is free to draw on this background. In one commercial dispute, for example, the arbitrators awarded the buyer money damages for non-delivery even though no evidence as to the market price of the goods had been introduced. Judge Learned Hand dismissed the seller's argument that this constituted arbitral "misconduct," remarking that if the arbitrators "were of the trade, they were justified in resorting to their personal acquaintance with its prices." When the parties have chosen arbitration, he added, "they must be content with its informalities; they may not hedge it about with those procedural limitations which it is precisely its purpose to avoid." American Almond Prods. Co. v. Consolidated Pecan Sales Co., 144 F.2d 448, 450–51 (2d Cir.1944). See also In the Matter of the Arbitration between Oinoussian Steamship Corp. of Panama and Sabre Shipping Corp., 224 F.Supp. 807 (S.D.N.Y.1963) (arbitrators allegedly relied on trade custom not mentioned at hearing; "it would be carrying coals to Newcastle to require presentation of evidence to experts in the field").

However, the arbitrator's relative freedom in supplementing the evidence introduced by the parties is hardly a license to make his own independent investigation into the facts of the dispute. Where the quality of goods is in dispute, an arbitrator who gives samples of the goods to his own salesmen for the purpose of obtaining an opinion as to "merchantability" is inviting a court to vacate his award for "misconduct.". See Stefano Berizzi Co. v. Krausz, 239 N.Y. 315, 146 N.E. 436 (1925) (Cardozo, J.) ("The plaintiff, knowing nothing of the evidence, had no opportunity to rebut or even to explain it."). So is the arbitrator who in attempting to fix the rental value of real estate asks the opinion of real estate brokers as to the value of similar property. See 290 Park Ave. v. Fergus Motors, 275 A.D. 565, 90 N.Y.S.2d 613 (App.Div.1949).

7. The conduct of an international arbitration is naturally likely to be influenced by the legal background and nationality of the arbitrators, and particularly of the chairman. Arbitrators from civil-law jurisdictions may share the preference of judges in those systems for the submission and exchange of documentary evidence and written witness statements, de-emphasizing oral testimony. Written statements "may entirely replace oral testimony," as "the entire testimony of some witnesses and much of the testimony of others often goes unchallenged." See W. Laurence Craig, William Park, & Jan Paulsson, International Chamber of Commerce Arbitration § 24.05 (3rd ed. 2000); id. at § 26.02 (practice of taking depositions outside the presence of the arbitrators to be submitted to panel as part of documentary evidence). See also the International Bar Association's "Supplementary Rules Governing the Presentation and Reception of Evidence in International Commercial Arbitration," which contain detailed ground rules for the production of documents and witness statements. Under these rules each party would be required to provide in advance a witness statement containing "a full statement of the evidence it is desired by that party to present through the testimony of that Witness." A witness may only give oral evidence if all parties agree or if the Arbitrator himself "in his discretion" orders that oral evidence be given; the testimony of all other witnesses "shall be taken by means of his Witness Statement only." See Alan Redfern & Martin Hunter, The Law and Practice of International Commercial Arbitration 704 (2d ed. 1991).

Arbitrators with a civil-law background are also likely to share the propensity of civil-law judges to take a more active role in the development of the facts. They may themselves routinely call—and examine—witnesses, obtain the assistance of experts, or order inspections or site visits, all on their own initiative. See generally Craig et al., supra at 415–434; Lowenfeld, The Two–Way Mirror: International Arbitration as Comparative Procedure, 7 Mich. Yrbk. of Int'l Legal Studies 163 (1985); Rau & Sherman, Tradition and Innovation in International Arbitration Procedure, 30 Tex. Int'l L.J. 89 (1995).

d. DISCOVERY

Another illustration of the relative informality of arbitration is the sharply limited availability of discovery, both "pre-trial" and at the hearing itself.

A starting point is a common statutory provision such as § 7 of the Uniform Arbitration Act:

> (a) The arbitrators may issue subpoenas for the attendance of witnesses and for the production of books, records, documents and other evidence, and shall have the power to administer oaths. * * *
>
> (b) On application of a party and for use as evidence, the arbitrators may permit a deposition to be taken, in the manner and upon the terms designated by the arbitrators, of a witness who cannot be subpoenaed or is unable to attend the hearing.

See also § 7 of the FAA.

Issuance or enforcement of a subpoena is, however, rarely necessary; an informal request for information by the arbitrator at a hearing usually suffices. At least where it is a *party* who has been requested to produce evidence, he will be reluctant to antagonize the arbitrator by refusing. Most importantly, the party will be aware that should he decline to produce relevant evidence within his control, the arbitrator is likely to draw the inference that it would have been unfavorable to him.[12] And so in most cases "an informal indication that such an inference will or may be drawn is sufficient to extract the document."[13]

The provisions of § 7 leave it to the discretion of the arbitrator to decide what materials he feels he needs to resolve the dispute; a party has no "right" to the issuance of a subpoena.[14] Exercise of this discretion is likely to be limited to demands for documents that can be "described with

12. See In re U.S. Dept. of Labor and American Federation of Govt. Employees, 98 Lab.Arb. 1129 (1992) (sexual harassment case; "I draw an adverse inference against Management from its failure to produce [the supervisor alleged to have harassed the grievant] to testify at the hearing to deny that he conducted himself as grievant testified or to otherwise explain his behavior").

13. Lowenfeld, The *Mitsubishi* Case: Another View, 2 Arb.Int'l 178, 184 (1986).

14. See National Broadcasting Co., Inc. v. Bear Stearns & Co., Inc., 165 F.3d 184, 187 (2d Cir.1999)("§ 7 explicitly confers authority only upon *arbitrators*; by necessary implication, the *parties* to an arbitration may not employ this provision to subpoena documents or witnesses").

specificity (for example, if they are internally referenced in documents put into evidence by one side'').[15] It is conceivable that an arbitrator's refusal to order the production of evidence might lead to a successful challenge to the award: In one maritime case, for example, the arbitrators had refused to order the shipowner to produce the ship's logs during the proceeding; a court indicated that this could constitute a violation of § 10(a)(3) of the FAA where the charterer of the ship could "show prejudice as a result." The court noted that the ship's logs are "perhaps the most important items of documentary evidence in any maritime controversy," and failure to supply them before the hearing's end could prejudice the ability of a party "not only in cross examination of witnesses, but in the preparation of its own case."[16] Such judicial action is, however, extremely rare.

True "discovery" in the litigation sense—for example, interrogatories and depositions taken before "trial" for the purposes of "trial" preparation—is even more limited. Provisions such as § 7 of the Uniform Arbitration Act assume, of course, that the arbitrators have already been named. Even where the arbitration panel is in place, the power of arbitrators to order pre-hearing discovery—at least in the absence of an agreement between the parties—is uncertain. An arbitrator's authority to order the production of documents in advance of a hearing has been upheld;[17] in some other jurisdictions, however, even this authority has been denied.[18] In any event the full range of discovery provided by the Federal Rules of Civil Procedure will not be available: While the Rules apply to motions made under the FAA (for example, motions to compel arbitration or to confirm an award), it is clear that they do not apply *to the conduct of the actual proceedings* before the arbitrators.

There are, however, some state statutes that do envisage more extensive arbitral discovery. For example, the Texas version of the Uniform Arbitration Act adds to § 7 that the arbitrators "may authorize a deposition of an adverse witness for discovery or evidentiary purposes, such depositions to be taken in the manner provided by law for depositions in a

15. Tupman, "Discovery and Evidence in U.S. Arbitration: The Prevailing Views," 44 Arb.J. (March 1989) at pp. 27, 32. Cf. Hunt v. Mobil Oil Corp., 654 F.Supp. 1487, 1512 (S.D.N.Y.1987) (arbitrators refused to issue a "broadcast subpoena" demanding "all documents" of various kinds; such a request "is not uncommon in litigation [but] is precisely the type of production demand that is the exception rather than the rule in arbitration").

16. In the Matter of the Arbitration between Chevron Transport Corp. and Astro Vencedor Compania Naviera, S.A., 300 F.Supp. 179 (S.D.N.Y.1969).

17. Meadows Indemnity Co., Ltd. v. Nutmeg Ins. Co., 157 F.R.D. 42 (M.D.Tenn. 1994) (given "the sheer number of documents," it would be "quite fantastic and practically unreasonable" for the arbitrators to require a witness to bring them all to the hearing; their power to compel production of documents for the purposes of a hearing "implicitly authorizes the lesser power to compel such documents for arbitration purposes prior to a hearing"); Security Life Ins. Co. of Amer. v. Duncanson & Holt, Inc., 228 F.3d 865 (8th Cir.2000)("interest in efficiency" is "furthered by permitting a party to review and digest relevant documentary evidence prior to the arbitration hearing").

18. North American Foreign Trading Corp. v. Rosen, 58 A.D.2d 527, 395 N.Y.S.2d 194 (App.Div.1977) (arbitration panel "exceed[ed] its authority by directing pre-arbitration disclosure").

civil action pending in a district court." Tex.Civ.Prac. & Rem.Code § 171.007(b). The recent Revised Uniform Arbitration Act adds that an arbitrator may "permit such discovery as the arbitrator decides is appropriate in the circumstances, taking into account the needs of the parties to the arbitration proceeding and other affected persons and the desirability of making the proceeding fair, expeditious, and cost effective." § 17(c). See also Cal.Code Civ.Pro. §§ 1283.05, 1283.1 ("right to take depositions and to obtain discovery" in arbitration of personal injury claims).

The reluctance to make pre-hearing discovery more widely available in arbitration may reflect the concern that this would be inconsistent with the goal of rapid and inexpensive dispute resolution. Looming over the debate is likely to be the specter of the "abuse" of the discovery process—"unfocused, unthoughtful, often massive, and always expensive"—which many observers blame for the delay and excessive cost characterizing complex federal litigation.[19] The fear is expressed that the use of pre-hearing discovery would add one further layer of complexity and "legalism" to a process which in the eyes of some observers has already come too much to resemble formal adjudication. In addition, there is a concern that judicial supervision and administration of the discovery process might interfere with the functions of the arbitrators chosen by the parties, and "preshape" the issues presented to them for decision. The point is also frequently made that by choosing arbitration, the parties have voluntarily accepted the risk that pre-hearing discovery and the other "procedural niceties which are normally associated with a formal trial" would not be available to them.[20]

The general unavailability of pre-hearing discovery in arbitration often leads parties to an arbitrable dispute to seek discovery ordered and supervised by a *court*. A fairly liberal attitude towards allowing discovery is exemplified by Bigge Crane & Rigging Co. v. Docutel Corp., 371 F.Supp. 240 (E.D.N.Y.1973). In *Bigge*, a subcontractor brought suit against a general contractor for payments due under a construction contract. The plaintiff, asserting that it had been given "no explanation" of the reasons it had not been paid for the work performed, then sought to take depositions of the defendant's employees and to obtain inspection of job records, contracts, and other documents. The defendant moved for a stay of the action under § 3 of the FAA and for an order compelling arbitration. The court granted the motion and stayed the trial pending completion of arbitration—"without prejudice," however, "to the rights of [the parties] to utilize the pretrial discovery procedures of the Federal Rules of Civil Procedure in a manner which does not delay the course of the arbitration":

> In this case there will have been considerable delay by the time the elaborate proceedings of the American Arbitration Association for the

19. See Lundquist, In Search of Discovery Reform, 66 A.B.A.J. 1071 (1980). Cf. Mullenix, Discovery in Disarray: The Pervasive Myth of Pervasive Discovery Abuse and the Consequences for Unfounded Rulemaking, 46 Stan.L.Rev. 1393 (1994) (the notion of discovery abuse "is based on questionable social science, 'cosmic anecdote,' and pervasive, media-perpetuated myths").

20. Burton v. Bush, 614 F.2d 389, 390 (4th Cir.1980).

> selection of arbitrators have been completed; and the arbitrators, selected for this particular case, may be under some pressure to complete their task promptly. On the other hand, discovery proceedings in the court action can go forward while the selection of arbitrators and scheduling of a hearing is under way.
>
> * * *
>
> Arbitration is not a separate proceeding independent of the courts, as was sometimes thought. The courts are brigaded with the arbitral tribunal in proceedings to compel arbitration or stay judicial trials, proceedings to enforce or quash subpoenas issued by arbitrators and proceedings to enforce or set aside arbitral awards. * * * [T]he court believes that it should exercise discretion to permit discovery in this case because (1) discovery is particularly necessary in a case where the claim is for payment for work done and virtually completed, and the nature of any defense is unknown; (2) the amounts involved are so substantial that any expense in taking depositions is relatively small; [and] (3) the action has proceeded to such a point that the taking of depositions can probably be accomplished without delaying the arbitration.

Most cases, however, are considerably more restrictive than *Bigge*. There is a tendency to require that pre-arbitration discovery be "necessary" to a party to allow him to "present a proper case to the arbitrators," or even that "extraordinary circumstances" be present, before a court may order it.[21] Cf. Deiulemar Compagnia Di Navigazione S.p.A. v. M/V Allegra, 198 F.3d 473 (4th Cir.1999). Here an agreement for a time charter specified that the vessel would maintain a guaranteed speed of 12–13 knots; the agreement also provided for arbitration in London. When the vessel reached its final destination at Baltimore, the charterer claimed that the promised performance specifications had not been met, and tried to inspect the vessel in order to gather and preserve evidence to support its claim. The owner refused, and argued that all of the information sought "could be requested through the arbitration process" in London. The trial court granted the charterer's request for discovery under Rule 27 of the Federal Rules Civil Procedure, and the Fourth Circuit affirmed: Since the ship's engine was scheduled for repair, "the circumstances and conditions extant today can never be recreated"; since the vessel was scheduled to leave the territorial waters of the United States immediately following repairs, the charterer "was in danger of losing access to any evidence of the ship's condition." "Given the time sensitive nature of [the charterer's] request and the evanescent nature of the evidence sought, we do not believe that the district court abused its discretion" in accepting the charterer's representation that it could not obtain "emergency discovery" from the London arbitrator "in time to preserve the rapidly changing condition of the ship."

21. See In re the Application of Moock, 99 A.D.2d 1003, 473 N.Y.S.2d 793 (App. Div. 1984); International Components Corp. v. Klaiber, 54 A.D.2d 550, 387 N.Y.S.2d 253 (App.Div.1976) ("absolutely necessary").

The sealed evidence gathered from the vessel was to be transferred to the pending arbitration in London: "The arbitrator does not have to admit the evidence; nor does he have to suppress it; that choice is left entirely to the arbitrator."

NOTES AND QUESTIONS

1. "[I]n the large, complex case, discovery is almost inevitable." Gorske, An Arbitrator Looks at Expediting the Large, Complex Case, 5 Ohio St.J.Disp.Res. 381, 394 (1990). In an increasing number of such disputes, procedures are being introduced aimed at insuring that both parties in arbitration will have available to them all the information they need for the full presentation of their cases. Experiments in this area usually arise out of some combination of arbitrator initiative and party cooperation.

In one large construction case—involving claims of almost $800 million and requiring more than 2½ years to complete—the arbitrators "proposed, and the parties agreed upon, a format similar to that used by numerous regulatory agencies whereby direct testimony and exhibits would be pre-filed in written form two weeks before each hearing session in order to reduce hearing time and to facilitate preparation for cross-examination." Discovery depositions of each sides' witnesses "were conducted by agreement of the parties or at the suggestion of the [panel] in order to reduce the likelihood that hearing time would be used for discovery" and as "the most efficient way for each side to prepare for cross-examination." This discovery was "closely supervised" by the arbitrators, who would often pass on any objections raised by one of the parties "within hours of their submission." Gorske, supra at 383–85; see also Hedlund & Paskin, Another View of Expediting the Large, Complex Case, 6 Ohio St.J.Disp.Res. 61 (1990); Gorske, A Reply, 6 id. 77 (1990).

As such devices have become more familiar, they have also become the subject of institutional rules that attempt to create a formal framework for information exchange prior to the actual hearings. For example, the AAA has recently published its "Optional Procedures for Large, Complex Commercial Disputes." These procedures—obviously influenced by the "case-management" role of federal judges—call for a preliminary hearing shortly after the selection of the arbitrators. The preliminary hearing provides an opportunity to draw up a detailed statement of claims, damages, and defenses and "a statement of the issues asserted by each party," to stipulate to uncontested facts, to "exchange * * * those documents which each party believes may be offered at the hearing," and to identify witnesses and their expected testimony. The "Procedures" also provide:

> 5(b) Parties shall cooperate in the exchange of documents, exhibits and information within such party's control if the arbitrator(s) consider such production to be consistent with the goal of achieving a just, speedy and cost-effective resolution of a Large, Complex Commercial Case.

(c) The parties may conduct such document discovery as may be agreed to by all the parties provided, however, that the arbitrator(s) may place such limitations on the conduct of such discovery as the arbitrator(s) shall deem appropriate. If the parties cannot agree on document discovery, the arbitrator(s) for good cause shown and consistent with the expedited nature of arbitration, may establish the extent of same.

(d) The arbitrator(s) upon good cause shown may order the conduct of the deposition of, or the propounding of interrogatories to, such persons who may possess information determined by the arbitrator(s) to be necessary to a determination of a Large, Complex Commercial Case.

2. If depositions of adverse witnesses have not been taken prior to the hearing, attorneys may feel compelled at the hearing itself to engage in protracted cross-examination that can become "a 'fishing expedition'—in effect, a deposition with the arbitrators looking on." Stipanowich, Rethinking American Arbitration, 63 Indiana L.J. 425, 451 (1988). See also Wilkinson, "Streamlining Arbitration of the Complex Case," Disp. Res. J., Aug.-Oct. 2000 at pp. 8, 11 ("I have witnessed many cross-examinations at arbitration hearings that plod down one dead-end street after another, while the questioner endlessly gropes for any testimony that might be of help"). Alternatively, an arbitration proceeding may readily be adjourned or continued at the arbitrator's discretion, to allow a party to study and respond to information revealed as a result of testimony or document production—it is in this respect unlike a trial which once begun is likely to proceed more or less continuously. "If [the arbitrators] wish to allow the questioner further opportunity to investigate after receiving the answers they will do so. What more is there to an examination before trial?" Motor Vehicle Accident Indemnification Corp. v. McCabe, 19 A.D.2d 349, 243 N.Y.S.2d 495 (App.Div.1963). See also Thomson, Arbitration Theory and Practice: A Survey of AAA Construction Arbitrators, 23 Hofstra L.Rev. 137, 147–48 (1994) (survey indicates that 51% of construction arbitrators would grant a request for a continuance during the hearing on the ground that evidence is being "seen for the first time").

3. One study suggests that there is a "striking difference" between the settlement rate of cases that are litigated and those that are arbitrated: "Only about 5 percent of court cases are fully adjudicated, compared to over 50 percent of AAA arbitration cases." Kritzer & Anderson, The Arbitration Alternative, 8 Justice System J. 6, 11 (1983). Might the lower settlement rate of cases in arbitration be attributable to the relative unavailability of discovery? Is settlement less likely in part because the parties have not been led to clarify or narrow the issues in dispute, or to focus on the relative strengths and weaknesses of their cases and that of their opponents? Stipanowich, Rethinking American Arbitration, 63 Indiana L.J. 425, 444 & n. 110 (1988). Cf. Henry H. Perritt, "And the Whole Earth Was of One Language": A Broad View of Dispute Resolution, 29 Villanova L. Rev. 1221, 1269 n.161 (1984)("The greater likelihood of an arbitration award that both parties can live with also reduces the incentives for negotiated settlement"). Or might there be other explanations as well? See, e.g., p. 294 infra ("Final Offer Arbitration").

4. May an arbitrator issue a subpoena to a *non-party* to the arbitration, directing him to appear for a pre-hearing deposition? See Integrity Ins. Co. v. American Centennial Ins. Co., 885 F.Supp. 69 (S.D.N.Y.1995) (no); see also COMSAT Corp. v. National Science Foundation, 190 F.3d 269 (4th Cir.1999)(FAA "does not authorize an arbitrator to subpoena third parties during prehearing discovery, absent a showing of special need or hardship"; in addition, if non-party recipient of a subpoena is a governmental agency, "principles of sovereign immunity" apply and the decision whether to provide documents or employee testimony "is committed to agency discretion"). What about an order to a non-party to produce documents prior to the hearing, for inspection by a party? See Integrity Ins. Co., supra, 885 F. Supp. at 73 ("Documents are only produced once, whether it is at the arbitration or prior to it. Common sense encourages the production of documents prior to the hearing so that the parties can familiarize themselves with the contents of the documents"). See also Brazell v. American Color Graphics, Inc., 2000 WL 364997 (S.D.N.Y.)(arbitrators have authority to provide for pre-hearing production of documents from third parties).

5. Are there any territorial limits to the power of arbitrators to issue subpoenas under FAA § 7? See Fed. R. Civ. P. R. 45. *Compare* Amgen Inc. v. Kidney Center of Delaware County, Ltd., 879 F.Supp. 878 (N.D.Ill.1995) ("the statute is specific in stating that the arbitrator may summon any person," and so "there is no territorial limitation on that ability"), *with* Commercial Solvents Corp. v. Louisiana Liquid Fertilizer Co., 20 F.R.D. 359 (S.D.N.Y.1957) (arbitrators "could not perhaps" compel the attendance of witnesses on whom service of subpoenas could not be made within the territorial limits of Fed. R. Civ. P. R.45). Cf. In re Security Life Ins. Co. of America, 228 F.3d 865 (8th Cir.2000)("whether or not [respondent] is correct in insisting that a subpoena for witness testimony must comply with Rule 45, we do not believe an order for the production of documents requires compliance with Rule 45(b)(2)'s territorial limit. This is because the burden of producing documents need not increase appreciably with an increase in the distance those documents must travel").

In the unusual event that the arbitrator's subpoena is not honored, a petition to enforce it must under § 7 be brought before *the district court where the arbitration is to take place*—and the power of that court is undoubtedly limited, under Fed. R. Civ. P. R.45(b)(2), to enforcement within its own district or within 100 miles of the place of the hearing (*Amgen,* supra, 879 F.Supp. at 882: "Although the Act allows the arbitrator to subpoena anyone, it also provides that this court may enforce the arbitrator's subpoena only in the same manner that it would compel attendance before the court"). Rather than conclude that there is a gap in the law, however, the *Amgen* court "direct[ed]" the party's attorney himself to issue a subpoena under Fed. R. Civ. P. R. 45 (a)(3)(B)—with the understanding that this subpoena could then be enforced by the district court where the production of documents was to take place.

6. At an arbitration hearing the arbitrator orders the plaintiff to produce certain documents; the plaintiff refuses to comply, asserting that this material consists of the confidential communication of information to his attorney and is thus exempt from subpoena on the basis of the attorney-client privilege. The arbitrator then announces that following his usual practice, he will conclude that the evidence if produced would have been unfavorable to the plaintiff; his award is in favor of the defendant. On the plaintiff's motion to vacate the award, what result?

The California Evidence Code makes the testimonial privileges applicable in all "proceedings," a term defined to include arbitration and any other hearing "in which, pursuant to law, testimony can be compelled to be given." Cal.Evidence Code §§ 901, 910. Section 913 further provides that if a privilege is exercised not to testify or disclose information, "the trier of fact may not draw any inference therefrom as to the credibility of the witness or as to any matter at issue in the proceeding."

7. A party to a collective bargaining agreement frequently needs information to help him decide whether to carry a grievance to arbitration in the first place. For example, the agreement may state a general policy against the subcontracting of work, and provide that where equipment is moved to another plant, employees who are laid off as a result may transfer to the new location. If machinery is moved out of the plant, the union will need to know where it has gone and what it is being used for. See NLRB v. Acme Industrial Co., 385 U.S. 432, 87 S.Ct. 565, 17 L.Ed.2d 495 (1967). To obtain such information in advance of arbitration, the Union may appeal to the National Labor Relations Board. In *Acme,* the Board found that the employer's refusal to furnish information about the removed equipment was in violation of the statutory duty to "bargain in good faith" because the information was "necessary in order to enable the Union to evaluate intelligently the grievances filed." The employer was therefore ordered to furnish the information to the union prior to any arbitration hearing. The Supreme Court held that this order should be enforced; Justice Stewart wrote that:

> Far from intruding upon the preserve of the arbitrator, the Board's action was in aid of the arbitral process. Arbitration can function properly only if the grievance procedures leading to it can sift out unmeritorious claims. For if all claims originally initiated as grievances had to be processed through to arbitration, the system would be woefully overburdened. Yet, that is precisely what the respondent's restrictive view would require. It would force the union to take a grievance all the way through to arbitration without providing the opportunity to evaluate the merits of the claim. The expense of arbitration might be placed upon the union only for it to learn that the machines had been relegated to the junk heap.

Invoking the Board's enforcement machinery can, however, be a slow and cumbersome process. See Laura Cooper et al., ADR in the Workplace 226

(2000) ("a party seeking a legally-enforceable order to disclose information may have to wait for years").

8. Consider the following provision in an arbitration clause:

> In no case shall the arbitrators order or permit any party to obtain from any other party documents, testimony, or any other evidence relating in any way to a transaction or occurrence other than the specific transaction or occurrence which is the subject of the arbitration proceeding.

Such a clause, it has been suggested, can ensure that "pattern and practice discovery"—which "permits plaintiffs' lawyers to rifle through company files looking for potential new clients and discovering potentially inflammatory fact situations which are analogous to their own cases"—"can be eliminated almost entirely in arbitration." Russel Myles & Kelly Reese, Arbitration: Avoiding the Runaway Jury, 22 Am. J. Trial Advoc. 129, 140 (1999). (This article was originally presented at a seminar for insurance executives and corporate counsel).

e. INTERIM MEASURES

Teradyne, Inc. v. Mostek Corp.

United States Court of Appeals, First Circuit, 1986.
797 F.2d 43.

[Mostek manufactured and marketed semiconductor components for use in computers and telecommunications equipment. Virtually all of Mostek's supply of laser systems and memory testers, which were essential to its manufacturing operations, were provided by Teradyne. Mostek always bought from Teradyne pursuant to the terms of a Quantity Purchase Agreement (QPA), which provided that Mostek would get price discounts on Teradyne equipment if it ordered certain minimum quantities, and that Mostek would be liable for cancellation and rescheduling charges if it cancelled an order.

[In early 1985 a dispute arose between the parties over cancellation charges claimed by Teradyne. At that time the 1984 QPA had expired; Mostek had held off entering into a QPA for 1985 because it was experiencing financial difficulties. As consideration for waiving the claimed charges, Teradyne demanded that Mostek place an order for twenty memory testers; Teradyne also supposedly "insisted" that before it would fill earlier orders placed by Mostek at the quoted prices, Mostek had to enter into a new QPA for 1985. In March 1985, Mostek did agree to enter into a QPA for 1985 and to place an order for twenty memory testers.

[Later that year, Mostek cancelled its orders; it refused to pay the cancellation charges demanded by Teradyne, assessed at 70% of the original purchase price. In September Teradyne requested arbitration, claiming approximately $3,500,000 for cancellation charges, goods and services invoiced, and incidental and consequential damages. In October Mostek's parent company announced that Mostek would cease operations; in November, substantially all of Mostek's assets were sold for approximately $71 million in cash. The proceeds of the sale were deposited in a separate bank account in Mostek's name and dedicated to the payment of the claims of its creditors. Teradyne then brought an action seeking an injunction ordering Mostek to set aside sufficient funds to satisfy a judgment pending the outcome of arbitration. The district court enjoined Mostek from disposing of or encumbering $4,000,000 of its assets and directed it to set that amount aside in an interest-bearing account to satisfy any arbitration award obtained by Teradyne.

[The First Circuit first held that the district court's "interlocutory order which has the attributes of both an attachment and an injunction" should be treated as a preliminary injunction, and was therefore appealable.

[The court then addressed Mostek's contention "that the policy of the Arbitration Act precludes the grant of preliminary injunctive relief in an arbitrable dispute."]

The Arbitration Act does not address this issue specifically and it has not previously been ruled upon by this circuit. Other circuits, however, have examined the issue in some detail. The Second, Fourth and Seventh Circuits all take the view that a court can, and should, grant a preliminary injunction in an arbitrable dispute whenever an injunction is necessary to preserve the status quo pending arbitration.

* * *

The Fourth Circuit's examination of this issue, in Merrill Lynch, Pierce, Fenner & Smith, Inc. v. Bradley, 756 F.2d 1048 (4th Cir.1985), focused on the effect of § 3 of the Arbitration Act on the court's power to issue preliminary injunctive relief. * * * Merrill Lynch sued Bradley, a former account executive, for damages for alleged breach of contract, and sought injunctive relief to prevent Bradley from using its records and soliciting its clients. The district court granted Merrill Lynch a preliminary injunction * * * and ordered expedited arbitration, both parties having agreed that the dispute was arbitrable. Bradley appealed, claiming that the injunction was an abuse of discretion because § 3 of the Arbitration Act precluded a court from considering the merits of an arbitrable dispute. The Fourth Circuit rejected this argument, holding that nothing in § 3 abrogated the equitable power of district courts to enter preliminary injunctions to preserve the status quo pending arbitration. The court also stated that it thought its decision would further rather than frustrate the policies underlying the Arbitration Act by ensuring that the dispute resolution would be a meaningful process.

* * *

Running counter to the approach taken by the Second, Fourth and Seventh Circuits is that taken by the Eighth Circuit in Merrill Lynch, Pierce, Fenner & Smith, Inc. v. Hovey, 726 F.2d 1286 (8th Cir.1984) * * *.

Hovey involved a petition by Merrill Lynch for an injunction against five former employees to prevent them from using Merrill Lynch's records and from soliciting Merrill Lynch clients. The employees counterclaimed, seeking to compel arbitration pursuant to New York Stock Exchange rules regulating dispute resolution procedures. The district court granted Merrill Lynch a preliminary injunction and refused to submit the dispute to arbitration. The employees appealed, claiming that the dispute was arbitrable. The Eighth Circuit held that the dispute was arbitrable and that issuing a preliminary injunction was, therefore, precluded by § 3 of the Arbitration Act. The court took the view that granting preliminary injunctive relief in an arbitrable dispute ran counter to the "unmistakably clear congressional purpose that the arbitration procedure, when selected by the parties to a contract, be speedy and not subject to delay and obstruction in the courts." (quoting *Prima Paint Corp.*).

* * *

[W]e are persuaded that the approach taken by the Second, Fourth and Seventh Circuits should be followed. We hold, therefore, that a district court can grant injunctive relief in an arbitrable dispute pending arbitration, provided the prerequisites for injunctive relief are satisfied. * * * We believe that the congressional desire to enforce arbitration agreements would frequently be frustrated if the courts were precluded from issuing preliminary injunctive relief to preserve the status quo pending arbitration and, ipso facto, the meaningfulness of the arbitration process. Accordingly, we hold that it was not error for the district court to issue the preliminary injunction before ruling on the arbitrability of this dispute. We next consider whether Teradyne established the prerequisites for such relief.

[The court then turned to the question whether the criteria for preliminary injunctive relief were satisfied. In the First Circuit, a court must find: "that plaintiff will suffer irreparable injury if the injunction is not granted"; "that such injury outweighs any harm which granting injunctive relief would inflict on the defendant"; and "that plaintiff has exhibited a likelihood of success on the merits."]

The district court here clearly articulated its reasons for finding that Teradyne had satisfied the prerequisites for injunctive relief. It held that Mostek's freedom to dispose of its assets created a substantial risk of irreparable harm to Teradyne, given that Mostek was in the process of winding down after selling the bulk of its assets, that it had failed to provide adequate assurances to alleviate Teradyne's concerns, and that it could at any time make itself judgment proof. Further, the court found that the affidavits submitted to it showed a likelihood that Teradyne would succeed on its contractual claims, and that the balance of hardships was in Teradyne's favor. The court dismissed Mostek's claims that the injunction would create a ripple effect whereby the creditors would rush to court seeking similar relief, noting that the injunction would have no precedential effect on other disputed claims, and that Mostek could pay undisputed claims and thereby avoid any possible ripple effect on them.

* * *

Although Mostek realized assets far exceeding Teradyne's claims when the sale of its assets occurred, the record shows that those assets were being used to pay off creditors' claims and wind down expenses in what Mostek itself described as an "orderly liquidation process." Further, the amount Mostek received for its assets was stated to be subject to a number of unspecified offsets and debits and no assurances were given that Mostek would be able to pay a Teradyne judgment.

* * * Under these circumstances, we affirm the district court's conclusion that the possible hardship to Teradyne of having a $3–4 million judgment prove worthless, outweighed the inchoate hardship to Mostek of having $4 million of its assets tied up in an interest bearing account pending judgment.

[The court then turned to the trial court's conclusion that Teradyne had a "reasonable likelihood of success on the merits." Mostek had argued that the 1985 QPA and the order for the twenty memory testers were "void for duress"; it asserted "that Teradyne took advantage of Mostek's weak financial condition and used its position, as Mostek's only source of supply, to force Mostek to sign the QPA and to place the new order."]

Mostek's allegations of undue pressure exerted on it by Teradyne are rebutted to some extent by Teradyne's account of the facts which indicates that Mostek entered the 1985 QPA voluntarily in order to obtain discounts on its 1984 orders and that it ordered the twenty memory testers of its own accord. But, even if the facts were as Mostek alleges, it is not clear that it has made out a prima facie case of economic duress.

It is well established that not all economic pressure constitutes duress. * * * [Under Massachusetts law,] "[m]erely taking advantage of another's financial difficulty is not duress," * * * the person alleging financial difficulty must allege that it was "contributed to or caused by the one accused of coercion," and the assertion of duress "must be proved by evidence that the duress resulted from defendant's wrongful and oppressive conduct and not by plaintiff's necessities." There is no indication here that Teradyne caused or contributed to Mostek's financial difficulties. Indeed, Mostek itself concedes that its difficulties came about as a result of a downturn in the semiconductor industry. Accordingly, we see no abuse of discretion in the trial court's conclusion that Teradyne had shown a likelihood of success on the merits.

Affirmed.

NOTES AND QUESTIONS

1. Will the arbitrator be bound by the views of the First Circuit as to the "merits" of the controversy? Is he likely to be influenced by them? Might this "threaten the independence of the arbitrator's ultimate determination"? Cf. The Guinness–Harp Corp. v. Jos. Schlitz Brewing Co., 613 F.2d 468, 471 n. 1 (2d Cir.1980).

2. Provisional relief granted by an arbitrator will not, of course, always be an adequate substitute for the sort of judicial order approved in *Teradyne.* (Why not?) Nevertheless such relief, if backed by the courts, can often be an effective way of preserving the status quo pending a final decision. See, e.g., Sperry Int'l Trade, Inc. v. Government of Israel, 532 F.Supp. 901 (S.D.N.Y.1982), in which arbitrators required the parties to place the proceeds of a letter of credit in a joint escrow account, pending a later decision on the merits of the underlying claim. The district court temporarily enjoined one of the parties from taking any action to collect the proceeds and confirmed the arbitrators' order within two weeks. It rejected the argument that the order was not "final" within the meaning of § 10(a)(4) of the FAA. See also Yasuda Fire & Marine Ins. Co. of Europe, Ltd. v. Continental Casualty Co., 37 F.3d 345 (7th Cir.1994) (at preliminary hearing, arbitration panel ordered respondent to post a $2.5 million interim letter of credit "against a possible future arbitration award"; award confirmed).

3. Should the interim relief granted by a court in a case like *Teradyne* remain in effect until the award is handed down? Or should a party only be entitled to judicial preservation of the status quo until the arbitrators *themselves* can decide whether interim relief should be granted, and how it should be structured—so that the court order would "expire when the issue of preserving the status quo is presented to and considered by the arbitration panel"? The latter solution was adopted in Merrill Lynch, Pierce, Fenner & Smith, Inc. v. Dutton, 844 F.2d 726 (10th Cir.1988) (preliminary injunction preventing former employee from removing customer lists and soliciting former clients). See also Performance Unlimited, Inc. v. Questar Publishers, Inc., 52 F.3d 1373 (6th Cir.1995) (license agreement; court should issue preliminary injunction requiring licensee "to pay only that amount of royalties necessary to ensure that [licensor] is not driven out of business prior to the time the arbitration proceeds"; "once the arbitration begins, it is for the arbitrators to decide how to maintain the status quo during the pendency of the arbitration process").

4. The AAA's Commercial Arbitration Rules provide (at Rule 36) that

> The arbitrator may take whatever interim measures he or she deems necessary, including injunctive relief and measures for the protection or conservation of property and disposition of perishable goods.

In addition, the AAA has promulgated a separate set of "Optional Rules for Emergency Measures of Protection" which provides for the possibility of interim relief "prior to the constitution of the panel": If the parties have adopted these rules in their arbitration clause or by special agreement, the AAA will appoint within one business day "a single emergency arbitrator from a special AAA panel of emergency arbitrators designated to rule on emergency applications"; this arbitrator may enter an interim award if he is satisfied "that immediate and irreparable loss or damage will result in the absence of emergency relief."

5. Under the New York Convention, each contracting state is required to "recognize" written agreements to arbitrate controversies; the courts of each nation, when seized of an arbitrable matter, "shall, at the request of one of the parties, refer the parties to arbitration * * *." (Art. II(3)). Curiously enough, it has been held that this language prohibits a court "from acting in any capacity except to order arbitration"; on this view they would have no power to take any interim measures in aid of international arbitrations to which the Convention applies. Cooper v. Ateliers de la Motobecane, S.A., 57 N.Y.2d 408, 456 N.Y.S.2d 728, 442 N.E.2d 1239 (1982). In this case the New York Court of Appeals, in denying an order of attachment, wrote:

> It is open to dispute whether attachment is even necessary in the arbitration context. Arbitration, as part of the contracting process, is subject to the same implicit assumptions of good faith and honesty that permeate the entire relationship. Voluntary compliance with arbitral awards may be as high as 85%. Moreover, parties are free to include security clauses (e.g., performance bonds or creating escrow accounts) in their agreements to arbitrate.
>
> * * *
>
> The essence of arbitration is resolving disputes without the interference of the judicial process and its strictures. When international trade is involved, this essence is enhanced by the desire to avoid unfamiliar foreign law.

Is this convincing? Does the language of the New York Convention require this result? Might it not be argued—given the complexity, delays, and risks inherent in international commercial disputes—that judicial intervention is *particularly* appropriate to insure that an arbitration award will ultimately be meaningful? It has been said that the United States "stands alone" among all the signatories to the New York Convention in having case law to the effect that pre-arbitration attachment is incompatible with the treaty. W. Laurence Craig, William Park & Jan Paulsson, International Chamber of Commerce Arbitration § 27.04 at 483–484 (3rd ed. 2000); see also Ebb, Flight of Assets from the Jurisdiction "In the Twinkling of a Telex": Pre–and Post–Award Conservatory Relief in International Commercial Arbitrations, 7 J.Int'l Arb. 9 (1990).

6. The California International Commercial Arbitration and Conciliation Act makes it clear that:

> It is not incompatible with an arbitration agreement for a party to request from a superior court, before or during arbitral proceedings, an interim measure of protection, or for the court to grant such a measure.
>
> Measures which the court may grant in connection with a pending arbitration include, but are not limited to:
>
> (a) An order of attachment issued to assure that the award to which applicant may be entitled is not rendered ineffectual by the dissipation of party assets.

(b) A preliminary injunction granted in order to protect trade secrets or to conserve goods which are the subject matter of the arbitral dispute.

The statute also authorizes the arbitral tribunal itself to "order a party to take any interim measure of protection as the arbitral tribunal may consider necessary in respect of the subject matter of the dispute," and a court may enforce such an interim award. See Cal.Code Civ.Pro. §§ 1297.91, 1297.92, 1297.93, 1297.171.

7. The Eighth Circuit continues to adhere to the restrictive view that "injunctive relief is inappropriate in a case involving arbitrable issues unless the contract terms contemplate such relief and it can be granted without addressing the merits." In Manion v. Nagin, 255 F.3d 535 (8th Cir.2001), the district court had denied the request by a dismissed employee for interim relief in aid of arbitration; the arbitration clause stipulated that the agreement to arbitrate was "without prejudice to the right of a party under applicable law to request interim relief from any court * * *." The court of appeals affirmed: "The provision allowing a party to *request* interim relief has been fulfilled since [the employee] filed a motion for a preliminary injunction and it was ruled on by the district court."

E. VARIATIONS ON A THEME

1. COMPULSORY ARBITRATION

John Allison, The Context, Properties, and Constitutionality of Nonconsensual Arbitration

1990 Journal of Dispute Resolution 1, 6, 15.

Most ADR mechanisms have been and continue to be completely voluntary. Alongside the evolution of volitional alternatives, however, we recently have witnessed the accelerating use of nonconsensual ADR mechanisms in both the private claims and administrative contexts. [The author refers to arbitration as "nonconsensual" "when its selection as a dispute resolution mechanism is driven primarily by governmental power rather than by the volition of contracting parties."] Although several forms of nonconsensual ADR have been attempted for the resolution of private disputes,[25] the most ambitious and well-known is the "court-annexed arbitration" now found in a substantial number of states and federal districts.

Several important instances of nonconsensual ADR have been adopted within the administrative-regulatory realm, as well. When a nontraditional form of conflict resolution is imposed without the full consent of the parties in the administrative arena, arbitration appears so far to be the procedure

25. Medical malpractice prescreening and early neutral evaluation are two common examples. [See p. 49 supra.—Eds.].

of choice. Examples include * * * commodity futures customer-broker disputes, and data compensation disputes under the federal pesticide law. Use of nonconsensual ADR will probably become much more common in this setting than in the resolution of purely private claims, because in the former case (a) a substantial degree of government coercion is already established and expected and (b) the constitutional barriers to nonconsensual ADR will be easier to surmount. Perhaps the most unusual form of nonconsensual administrative ADR to date is the data compensation arbitration program of the Federal Insecticide, Fungicide, and Rodenticide Act (FIFRA).

Note: Data Compensation Disputes Under "FIFRA"

Pesticide manufacturers are required to register their products with the Environmental Protection Agency (EPA), and must submit research and test data to the EPA concerning the product's health, safety, and environmental effects. The development of a potential commercial pesticide may require the expenditure of millions of dollars annually over a period of several years. Frequently, after one product has been registered, *another* applicant may wish to register the same or a similar product. Can the EPA consider, in support of this second application, data already in its files that had been submitted by the previous registrant? By avoiding some duplication of test data, this would presumably result in lower costs and increased competition. (Such later registrations are colloquially known as "me too" or "follow on" registrations.)

The Federal Insecticide, Fungicide, and Rodenticide Act (FIFRA) allows the EPA to consider such data (after a 10-year period of exclusive use), but "only if the applicant has made an offer to compensate the original data submitter." 7 U.S.C.A. § 136a(c)(1)(F)(ii). "In effect, the provision instituted a mandatory data-licensing scheme." See Ruckelshaus v. Monsanto Co., 467 U.S. 986, 992, 104 S.Ct. 2862, 81 L.Ed.2d 815 (1984). If the original data submitter and the second applicant fail to agree on the terms of compensation, then either may ask for binding arbitration.

The statute entrusts the arbitration program to the Federal Mediation and Conciliation Service (FMCS)—a federal agency whose primary function is to provide mediators and arbitrators to aid in the resolution of labor disputes. Since the FMCS "rarely arranges or conducts arbitration of commercial disputes," the Service has delegated its administrative functions to the AAA: The FMCS decided "to adopt and use the Commercial Arbitration Roster of the AAA as its roster and to adopt the AAA's rules of commercial arbitration as its rules of procedure for disputes arising under FIFRA." 45 Fed.Reg. 55,395 (1980). Under the statute, the award of the arbitrators is "final and conclusive," with no judicial review "except for fraud, misrepresentation, or other misconduct by one of the parties to the arbitration or the arbitrator." If the original data submitter fails to participate in an arbitration proceeding, he forfeits any right to compensation for the use of his data; if a "follow-on" applicant fails to participate, his application is denied.

A number of large firms engaged in the development and marketing of pesticides challenged this arbitration scheme, claiming that Article III of the Constitution bars Congress from requiring arbitration of disputes concerning compensation "without also affording substantial review by tenured judges of the arbitrator's decision." A unanimous Supreme Court upheld the FIFRA arbitration scheme in Thomas v. Union Carbide Agricultural Prods. Co., 473 U.S. 568, 105 S.Ct. 3325, 87 L.Ed.2d 409 (1985).

In an earlier case, the Supreme Court had suggested that Congress could not establish Article I "legislative courts" to adjudicate "private rights" disputes. Such disputes, involving "the liability of one individual to another under the law as defined," "lie at the core of the historically recognized judicial power." Northern Pipeline Construction Co. v. Marathon Pipe Line Co., 458 U.S. 50, 102 S.Ct. 2858, 73 L.Ed.2d 598 (1982). Justice O'Connor, writing for the Court in *Thomas,* found that the situation presented by FIFRA was different:

> [T]he right created by FIFRA is not a purely "private" right, but bears many of the characteristics of a "public" right. Use of a registrant's data to support a follow-on registration serves a public purpose as an integral part of a program safeguarding the public health. Congress has the power, under Article I, to authorize an agency administering a complex regulatory scheme to allocate costs and benefits among voluntary participants in the program without providing an Article III adjudication. It also has the power to condition issuance of registrations or licenses on compliance with agency procedures. Article III is not so inflexible that it bars Congress from shifting the task of data valuation from the agency to the interested parties.
>
> * * * Congress, without implicating Article III, could have authorized EPA to charge follow-on registrants fees to cover the cost of data and could have directly subsidized FIFRA data submitters for their contributions of needed data. Instead, it selected a framework that collapses these two steps into one, and permits the parties to fix the amount of compensation, with binding arbitration to resolve intractable disputes. Removing the task of valuation from agency personnel to civilian arbitrators, selected by agreement of the parties or appointed on a case-by-case basis by an independent federal agency, surely does not diminish the likelihood of impartial decisionmaking, free from political influence.
>
> * * *
>
> The danger of Congress or the Executive encroaching on the Article III judicial powers is at a minimum when no unwilling defendant is subjected to judicial enforcement power as a result of the agency "adjudication." See, e.g., L. Jaffe, Judicial Control of Administrative Action 385 (1965) (historically judicial review of agency decisionmaking

has been required only when it results in the use of judicial process to enforce an obligation upon an unwilling defendant).

We need not decide in this case whether a private party could initiate an action in court to enforce a FIFRA arbitration. But cf. 29 CFR pt. 1440, App. § 37(c) (1984) (under rules of American Arbitration Association, parties to arbitration are deemed to consent to entry of judgment). FIFRA contains no provision explicitly authorizing a party to invoke judicial process to compel arbitration or enforce an award. In any event, under FIFRA, the only potential object of judicial enforcement power is the follow-on registrant who explicitly consents to have his rights determined by arbitration.

* * *

Our holding is limited to the proposition that Congress, acting for a valid legislative purpose pursuant to its constitutional powers under Article I, may create a seemingly "private" right that is so closely integrated into a public regulatory scheme as to be a matter appropriate for agency resolution with limited involvement by the Article III judiciary. To hold otherwise would be to erect a rigid and formalistic restraint on the ability of Congress to adopt innovative measures such as negotiation and arbitration with respect to rights created by a regulatory scheme.

Justice Brennan, joined by Justices Marshall and Blackmun, wrote in concurrence:

Congress has decided that effectuation of the public policies of FIFRA demands not only a requirement of compensation from follow-on registrants in return for mandatory access to data but also an administrative process—mandatory negotiation followed by binding arbitration—to ensure that unresolved compensation disputes do not delay public distribution of needed products. * * * Although a compensation dispute under FIFRA ultimately involves a determination of the duty owed one private party by another, at its heart the dispute involves the exercise of authority by a federal government arbitrator in the course of administration of FIFRA's comprehensive regulatory scheme. As such it partakes of the character of a standard agency adjudication.

NOTES AND QUESTIONS

1. In one FIFRA case arbitrators awarded Stauffer (the original registrant) one-half of its direct testing cost for a chemical, plus a royalty on all sales of the product by PPG (the second applicant) between 1983 and 1992. PPG asked the court to vacate this award; it argued that the arbitrators were limited to compensating Stauffer for the actual cost of producing the test data and could not make an award based on the value to PPG of earlier market entry. The court granted Stauffer's motion to dismiss, concluding that "Congress intentionally left to the arbitrators the choice of what formula to use in determining compensation." PPG Industries, Inc. v. Stauffer Chemical Co., 637 F.Supp. 85 (D.D.C.1986).

FIFRA had originally provided that in the absence of an agreement between the parties as to compensation, the figure was to be determined by the EPA. However, the court noted that "[t]he EPA found this task to be beyond its means":

> Congress concluded that the EPA lacked the requisite expertise in determining compensation, and Congress and the EPA agreed that a determination of compensation did not require "active government involvement." Consequently, Congress removed all suggestion of a standard from the statute and replaced EPA with binding arbitration as the mechanism for determining what compensation was proper. It seems quite reasonable to this Court that Congress intentionally obliterated all suggestion of a standard in view of the fact that not even the EPA could identify a formula which would adequately compensate a data submitter in every case. Congress determined to leave the matter to arbitrators who had more expertise and could evaluate each case individually.

The court also rejected the argument that such "standardless delegation" to private arbitrators was an unconstitutional delegation of legislative authority:

> [T]he concern with delegation to private parties has to do with the private party's interest in the industry being regulated. See, e.g., [A.L.A. Schechter Poultry Corp. v. United States, 295 U.S. 495, 55 S.Ct. 837, 79 L.Ed. 1570 (1935)] (holding unconstitutional a statute delegating power to institute penal provisions to a body comprised of members of the industry involved). The private parties involved here are not members of the pesticide industry, but rather disinterested arbitrators appointed by the FMCS, which adopted the roster of the American Arbitration Association.

Is it important in FIFRA cases to develop a body of "common law" concerning the measure of compensation, in order to provide guidance for the future conduct of registrants and later applicants? Will a series of arbitration awards be likely to provide such standards and criteria of decision? See "Data Compensation Decision Seen as Victory by Both Sides in a Lengthy FIFRA Dispute," Pesticide & Toxic Chemical News, October 8, 1998 (arbitrators added a 25% "enhancement" to respondent's share of compensable costs "to reflect [its] early entry into the market by means of citations of claimants' data"; this was "the first time since the award in [*PPG Industries*] that an arbitration award has been based on the value of early entry"). How is the "expertise" of the individual arbitrators likely to aid in resolving the disagreement in *PPG* as to the choice of the appropriate standard of compensation?

2. The Supreme Court supported its decision in *Thomas* by stressing that FIFRA "does not preclude review of the arbitration proceeding by an Article III court." The judicial review provided by the statute "preserves the appropriate exercise of the judicial function," said the Court, since it "protects against arbitrators who abuse or exceed their powers or willfully misconstrue their mandate under the governing law." 473 U.S. at 592. What does this mean?

3. The Commodity Futures Trading Commission (CFTC) is an independent agency established by Congress. The CFTC requires members of commodity exchanges like the Chicago Board of Trade (CBOT) to submit disputes with customers to arbitration if their customers request it; at CFTC insistence, this requirement is incorporated into the rules of the exchanges. Geldermann, a member of the CBOT, refused to arbitrate a customer-initiated claim, and brought suit challenging the arbitration requirement. The court held that "by virtue of its continued membership in the CBOT," Geldermann had "consented to arbitration, and thus waived any right he may have possessed to a full trial before an Article III court." The court also rejected Geldermann's claim that the mandatory arbitration scheme violated its right to a jury trial: Since "Geldermann is not entitled to an Article III forum, the Seventh Amendment is not implicated." That Geldermann "had no choice but to accept the CBOT's rules" if it were to continue in business was irrelevant. Geldermann, Inc. v. CFTC, 836 F.2d 310 (7th Cir.1987).

The statute creating the CFTC also provides an alternative "reparations procedure" by which the agency itself may hear complaints brought by aggrieved customers of commodity brokers. In one such CFTC proceeding, the broker asserted a counterclaim for the balance owed by the investor on his account—a "traditional" state-law action for debt. The investor invoked Article III to challenge the CFTC's authority to hear the counterclaim, but the Supreme Court rejected this challenge: "[I]t seems self-evident that just as Congress may encourage parties to settle a dispute out of court or resort to arbitration without impermissible incursions on the separation of powers, Congress may make available a quasi-judicial mechanism through which willing parties may, at their option, elect to resolve their differences." CFTC v. Schor, 478 U.S. 833, 106 S.Ct. 3245, 92 L.Ed.2d 675 (1986).

Is arbitration under FIFRA similarly limited to "willing parties"? Consider the Court's characterization in *Thomas* of the pesticide registration scheme as "voluntary," and its reliance on the fact that the follow-on registrant "explicitly consents to have his rights determined by arbitration."

4. We have already come across a number of cases in which the state has chosen to require arbitration as a dispute resolution mechanism. Recall, for example, the statutory schemes making "lemon law" arbitration under AAA auspices mandatory on automobile manufacturers at the initiative of the consumer; consider also the states in which arbitration of fee disputes is made mandatory for attorneys at the initiative of the client. See pp. 55–56 supra. There are many other instances. See, e.g., Nev.Rev.Stat. § 689A.0403 ("Each policy of health insurance must include a procedure for binding arbitration to resolve disputes concerning independent medical evaluations pursuant to the rules of the [AAA]"); N.J.Stat. § 39:6A–5 (required coverage for personal injury protection in automobile policy; all insurers "shall provide any claimant with the option of submitting a dispute * * * to binding arbitration" administered by AAA). The Amateur Sports Act of 1978 requires every amateur sports organization that wishes to be recognized as the national governing body for a particular sport to submit disputes over the rights of athletes to participate in competition—for example, disputes over alleged drug use—to arbitration; the arbitration is to be "conducted in accordance with the commercial rules of the [AAA]." See 36 U.S.C.A. §§ 371, 391(b)(3).

"Mandatory arbitration may indeed not benefit from the dynamic of self-government that often makes labor and commercial arbitration an extension of the parties' own negotiations. It may indeed lack the legitimacy of processes founded on consent, in which an arbitrator chosen and paid by the parties is charged with interpreting substantive standards laid down by them in their agreement, in accordance with procedures to which they have also consented. Mandatory arbitration is, instead, simply a form of economic or professional regulation." Alan Rau, Resolving Disputes Over Attorneys' Fees: The Role of ADR, 46 S.M.U.L.Rev. 2005, 2032–33 (1993).

5. Are there plausible claims that constitutional rights have been violated when a binding arbitration process is imposed on private parties? In GTFM, LLC v. TKN Sales, Inc., 2000 WL 364871 (S.D.N.Y.), a Minnesota distributor alleged that it had been wrongfully terminated in violation of the Minnesota Sales Representative Act, and brought suit against the manufacturer not only for violations of the Act, but also for failure to pay commissions and for breach of contract. There was no arbitration agreement between the parties—but the Act provided that a sales representative had the right to submit any such claims to "final and binding" arbitration. The court held that the MSRA's "mandatory and binding arbitration system operates to deny [the manufacturer] its right to a jury trial" guaranteed by the Seventh Amendment: Claims under the Act for wrongful termination were "analogous to actions at common law," for the Act "provides a specialized remedy for a breach of contract claim involving sales representatives and supplies additional terms to sales representative agreements regarding notice and grounds for termination."

Compare Motor Vehicle Manufacturers Ass'n of the U.S. v. New York, 75 N.Y.2d 175, 551 N.Y.S.2d 470, 550 N.E.2d 919 (1990), in which New York's "lemon law" arbitration statute was upheld against a claim that it deprived manufacturers of their right to a trial by jury. The statutory remedies—replacement of the vehicle or refund of the purchase price—were found analogous to claims for specific performance and restitution; since such remedies were "equitable in nature" they would not in any event "have been triable by jury under the common law." Nor did the law deprive them of their right to "have a court or public officer adjudicate their disputes" with consumers by "delegating sovereign judicial power to private arbitrators": The court reasoned that the legislature had "merely created a new limited class of disputes and provided a procedure for resolving them, much in the same way it removed automobile claims from judicial cognizance by the No–Fault Insurance Law." In addition, since "arbitrators are selected pursuant to detailed standards, the procedures they must follow are specified, the grounds for relief defined and their determinations are subject to judicial review," it followed that "the arbitration proceeding remains within the judicial domain." See also Lyeth v. Chrysler Corp., 929 F.2d 891 (2d Cir.1991) ("the compulsory alternative arbitration mechanism affords the basic procedural safeguards required by due process").

6. The Florida "lemon law" provides that an aggrieved consumer may apply for arbitration before the "New Motor Vehicle Arbitration Board"—whose members are appointed by the Attorney General—and that the consumer *must* submit to arbitration before filing a civil suit under the law. By contrast with the New York statute, either the consumer or the manufacturer in Florida is entitled to a trial de novo after completion of this "mandatory alternative dispute resolution procedure"; at such a trial the decision of the arbitration board is admissible in evidence.

In Chrysler Corp. v. Pitsirelos, 721 So.2d 710 (Fla.1998), the consumer prevailed before the arbitration board, and the trial judge instructed the jury that the board's decision was "presumed to be correct." The state supreme court held, however, that the statute should not be interpreted in this way—indeed, that such a presumption would raise serious constitutional issues, since it "would diminish the right to have the ultimate decision in a case made by a court." The board's decision should be treated "only as evidence with its weight to be determined by the fact-finder." Nevertheless the court held that the manufacturer now had the burden of persuasion in establishing why the board's decision was erroneous: To require the consumer to bear the burden of proof "as if no previous proceeding had been held" would "relegate the mandatory arbitration to simply being a procedural impediment to the consumer." Does *Pitsirelos* appear to you to be a coherent decision?

7. The state's traditional supervisory authority over the legal profession has provided strong constitutional support for any requirement that attorneys submit to binding arbitration of fee disputes. See Rau, supra note 4, at 2036–40. Some courts have in addition found more fanciful justifications: Does an attorney somehow "waive" her right to a jury trial merely by engaging in the profession? See Kelley Drye & Warren v. Murray Indust., Inc., 623 F.Supp. 522 (D.N.J.1985) (New Jersey's mandatory arbitration program; "by taking advantage of the opportunity to practice law in New Jersey" the firm had "voluntarily given up its right to a trial of any kind" and had agreed to arbitration).

Note: Mandatory Arbitration in Public Employment

A number of statutes require the arbitration of "interest" disputes concerning the terms of a new collective bargaining agreement between a state or local government, and a union representing its employees. Fairly typical examples of the growing number of such statutes are Rhode Island's

Fire Fighter's Arbitration Act and Policemen's Arbitration Act.[1] In recognition of "the necessity to provide some alternative method of settling disputes where employees must, as a matter of public policy, be denied the usual right to strike," the legislation requires that where a city and a union cannot reach agreement, "any and all unresolved issues" shall be submitted to arbitration. The arbitration panel is to be tripartite—one arbitrator being named by each of the parties and the third, in the absence of agreement, is selected under the rules of the AAA. The legislation attempts to enumerate the "factors" which the panel must take into account—including the "interest and welfare of the public," the "community's ability to pay," and a comparison of wage rates and employment conditions with prevailing local conditions "of skilled employees of the building trades and industry" and with police or fire departments in cities of comparable size.

It is obvious that "interest" disputes in public sector employment are intimately connected to the political process. Many public services, such as police protection and education, raise questions that are "politically, socially, or ideologically sensitive."[2] A number of such sensitive issues have in fact been held to be "non-bargainable"—despite their obvious impact on the working conditions of public employees—and thus outside the permissible scope of "interest" arbitration. Such "non-negotiable matters of governmental policy" might in public education include questions of curriculum or of class size; in police services, questions of the manpower level of the force or a civilian review board for police discipline. See, e.g., San Jose Peace Officer's Ass'n v. City of San Jose, 78 Cal.App.3d 935, 144 Cal.Rptr. 638 (1978) (police policy governing when officer is allowed to fire weapon; "The forum of the bargaining table with its postures, strategies, trade-offs, modifications and compromises is no place for the 'delicate balancing of different interests: the protection of society from criminals, the protection of police officers' safety, and the preservation of all human life, if possible.' ").

In a more general sense, however, the resolution of *all* disputes over the terms of public employment—even disputes over nuts and bolts issues like wages—is inescapably "political." To resolve a wage dispute by applying the "factors" set out in the Rhode Island legislation requires an accommodation of the competing interests of employees, taxpayers, and the users of public services. The arbitrator will inevitably be led to determine priorities among various public programs, the level of public services, or the need and feasibility of increased public revenue. Such exercises of judgment are necessarily political compromises. Should such issues be resolved "in an arbitrator's conference room as an alternative to facing up to vexing problems in the halls of state and local legislatures"?[3] It has been suggested in fact that "interest" arbitration of public-sector disputes may be inconsistent with the democratic premise that governmental priorities are to be

1. R.I.Stat. § 28–9.1–1; R.I.Stat. § 28–9.2–1.

2. Harry Wellington & Ralph K. Winter, Jr., The Unions and the Cities 23 (1971).

3. Dearborn Fire Fighters Union v. City of Dearborn, 394 Mich. 229, 231 N.W.2d 226 (1975).

fixed by elected representatives, responsible to all the competing interest groups and responsive to the play of political forces. Resolving public sector "interest" disputes, it is asserted, is not an exercise in neutral, "objective" adjudication but rather one in "legislative" policymaking:

> The size of the budget, the taxes to be levied, the purposes for which tax money is to be used, the kinds and levels of governmental services to be enjoyed, and the level of indebtedness are issues that should be decided by officials who are politically responsible to those who pay the taxes and seek the services. The notion that we can or should insulate public employee bargaining from the political process either by arbitration or with some magic formula is a delusion of reality and a denigration of democratic government.[4]

It should not be surprising, then, that the constitutionality of compulsory interest arbitration in the public sector has repeatedly been challenged. Successful challenges have been rare.[5] Nevertheless, it is clear that there are real tensions here with the values traditionally underlying the arbitration process. It seems hard to justify compulsory "interest" arbitration on the usual rationale that the process is merely an extension of the parties' own bargaining, an application of "self-government" in the workplace. In the final analysis, how does compulsory "interest" arbitration in public-sector employment differ from decisions made directly by a governmental agency? How different really is Rhode Island's compulsory arbitration statute from the Nebraska scheme—which entrusts the settlement of public-sector "interest" disputes to a state "Commission of Industrial Relations" consisting of five "judges" named for six-year terms by the Governor with the advice and consent of the legislature?[6]

Some years ago the Rhode Island Supreme Court rebuffed a constitutional attack on that state's compulsory arbitration statutes by the simple device of characterizing the arbitrators as "public officers" rather than as mere "private persons": The arbitration panel *must* be considered "an administrative or governmental agency," reasoned the court; after all, the arbitrators had been granted "a portion of the sovereign and legislative power of the government"![7] But such a semantic tour de force obviously does not resolve the problem. If the arbitrators are appointed on an ad hoc basis, with no continuing legislative or administrative oversight, there may be no real accountability to the electorate; these are "hit and run" decision-

4. Summers, Public Sector Bargaining: Problems of Governmental Decisionmaking, 44 U.Cinn.L.Rev. 669, 672 (1975). See also Grodin, Political Aspects of Public Sector Interest Arbitration, 64 Cal.L.Rev. 678 (1976).

5. See, e.g., Salt Lake City v. International Ass'n of Firefighters, 563 P.2d 786 (Utah 1977) (the "legislature may not surrender its legislative authority to a body wherein the public interest is subjected to the interest of a group which may be antagonistic to the public interest").

6. Neb.Rev.Stat. § 48–801; see also id. § 48–805 (the "judges" of the Commission "shall not be appointed because they are representatives of either capital or labor, but * * * because of their experience and knowledge in legal, financial, labor and industrial matters").

7. City of Warwick v. Warwick Regular Firemen's Ass'n, 106 R.I. 109, 256 A.2d 206 (1969).

makers.[8] If, in contrast, the arbitrators are *not* to be private decision-makers and are instead made politically responsible, may not the neutrality of the entire process be called into question? Does the arbitrator not then become merely "an agent of government involved primarily in implementing public policy"?[9] Isn't it implicit in the very notion of an "impartial" or "neutral" arbitrator that the decision-maker is *not* to be responsive to political intervention, or to be held accountable for his decision by any constituency? Or might the personal "accountability" of private arbitrators be affected in any event by the well-known need of those in the profession to maintain their acceptability for future employment?

NOTES AND QUESTIONS

1. Is the same judicial deference traditionally accorded arbitral awards appropriate in the case of compulsory "interest" arbitration in the public sector? In many states with such statutes, the arbitration panel is in fact treated for purposes of review much like an administrative agency. A record of the proceedings and a written decision are commonly required, and courts may examine the result to see whether it is "supported by substantial credible evidence present in the record." See Hillsdale PBA Local 207 v. Borough of Hillsdale, 263 N.J.Super. 163, 622 A.2d 872 (App.Div.1993).

What is it that justifies a more extensive standard of judicial review here? Is it primarily the fact that "interest" rather than grievance arbitration is involved? See Craver, The Judicial Enforcement of Public Sector Interest Arbitration, 21 B.C.L.Rev. 557, 572 (1980) (deference to arbitral determinations gives rise to the "possibility of catastrophic consequences resulting from an entirely intemperate award"). Is it the fact that public-sector arbitration is more likely to involve "governmental" decisions—so that any delegation to arbitrators necessarily calls for a closer scrutiny of their assessment of the "interest and welfare of the public"? Or might it simply be the fact that the arbitration process has been imposed on the parties and does not arise out of their consent? Cf. General Accident Ins. Co. v. Poller, 321 N.J.Super. 252, 728 A.2d 845 (1999)(in automobile insurance policy for personal injury protection, arbitration is mandatory for the carrier under state law at the election of the insured; however, "the carrier's participation in this market, circumscribed as it is by state law, is nevertheless voluntary," and so "no different standard" of judicial review from that familiar in private voluntary arbitration is warranted).

2. A "Model Termination of Employment Act" was approved by the National Conference of Commissioners on Uniform State Laws in 1991. Under this Act, an employee who has worked for the same employer for at least one year may not be fired without "good cause"—a term defined to include both the employee's misconduct and job performance, and the employer's good faith "exercise of business judgment" concerning the goals

8. Dearborn Fire Fighters Union v. City of Dearborn, 394 Mich. 229, 231 N.W.2d 226, 243 (1975) (Kavanagh, C.J., concurring).

9. Grodin, supra n. 4, 64 Cal.L.Rev. at 693–94.

and organization of his operations and the size and composition of his work force. An employee who has been wrongfully terminated under the Act may be entitled to reinstatement or, alternatively, up to three years of severance pay, along with attorneys' fees. "[D]ecisionmaking by professional arbitrators is the preferred method of enforcing the Act"—although states that are concerned about "the possible extra expense of outside arbitrators" may instead choose hearing officers who are full-time civil service personnel, while states concerned "about possible constitutional problems" may leave enforcement in the hands of the courts. In addition to all the usual procedural grounds for overturning awards that are found in modern arbitration statutes, the arbitrator's decision may be vacated for "a prejudicial error of law." This standard of review was apparently thought necessary because "individual statutory rights are the issue, and arbitration as the enforcement method has been imposed upon, not agreed to by, the parties." Model Employment Termination Act, prefatory note, § 8 & cmt.

Note: Mandatory Arbitration and Public Regulation

Nursing homes, and care facilities for the mentally retarded, must in Texas be licensed by the Texas Department of Human Services. As the state agency responsible for their regulation, the Department is required to inspect these facilities periodically to see if they are meeting state health and safety standards; if a facility is not in compliance with the state's standards, the Department may initiate enforcement action and may seek remedies such as the suspension or revocation of a license, or "administrative penalties." (In determining the amount of such a penalty, the Department is to consider "the seriousness of the violation, including the * * * hazard or potential hazard * * * to the health or safety of the public," and "deterrence of future violations." Tex. Health & Safety Code § 242.066.)

However, a 1995 statute now permits either the Department, or the nursing home or care facility itself, to "elect binding arbitration" of any such dispute; such arbitration "is an alternative to a contested case hearing" brought by the Department seeking suspension or revocation of a license or the imposition of a penalty. The arbitrator "must be on an approved list of a nationally recognized association that performs arbitrations" or be otherwise qualified under rules promulgated by the State Office of Administrative Hearings; he may be paid up to $500 per day for his services. The arbitrator's decision may be vacated by a court if it was "arbitrary or capricious and against the weight of the evidence." Tex. Health & Safety Code §§ 242.252, 242.253, 242.254, 242.267.

The sponsor of this legislation claimed that it gives the state "a new tool to enforce the rules regulating nursing homes. If this tool is properly used, nursing homes who do not comply with basic standards of health and safety will face the quick collection of the appropriate fines and penalties." Austin American–Statesman, Dec. 20, 1995, at A14. Is this claim completely disingenuous? Is this statutory use of ADR appropriate? Is it consistent with the historical goals of alternative processes?

2. FINAL-OFFER ARBITRATION

For almost 100 years professional baseball players were bound to their teams for life by the sport's infamous "reserve clause." In consequence, most players had little choice but to accept the salary their team was willing to pay them. In recent years, however, collective bargaining between the clubs and the players' union has replaced the old "reserve clause" with a system that considerably enhances player mobility between teams. At the same time, it has introduced a novel form of "interest" arbitration to fix salaries where player and team cannot agree.

Under the collective bargaining agreement between the teams and the players' union, players who have been in the major leagues for at least six years can choose to become "free agents"; they can thus have their salaries determined through negotiation in the free market with other teams that might be interested in them.[10] Players with fewer than six years in the majors are still not free to look elsewhere, but are tied to their original team unless they are traded or released. However, those with at least *three* years service do have the right to submit the question of their salary to binding arbitration.[11]

Salary disputes are submitted to arbitration in February. The collective bargaining agreement specifies a number of criteria which the "interest" arbitrators must consider in determining salaries for the coming season—for example, the player's contribution to the team during the past season (including his "overall performance, special qualities of leadership, and public appeal"), "the length and consistency of his career contribution," and "comparative baseball salaries" (which may include salaries paid to free agents). They are instructed *not* to consider salary offers made by either party prior to arbitration, salaries in other sports or occupations, or the financial situation of the player or the team. The hearing is to be private and informal. Unless extended by the arbitrators, each party is limited to one hour for an initial presentation and one-half hour for rebuttal; awards are to be handed down by the arbitrators, without explanation, within 24 hours following the hearing.

The most distinctive feature of this arbitration scheme is the limits it places on the discretion of the arbitrators. The arbitrators are not free to choose whatever salary figure they think is appropriate. Instead, the player and the club each submits a "final offer" on salary for the coming season (these "final offers" need not be the figures offered during prior negotiations). The arbitrators may then award "only one or the other of the two figures submitted."

10. At least in theory. In a number of grievance arbitrations between 1987 and 1990, arbitrators found that the owners of baseball teams had been acting in concert to restrain salaries by refraining from bidding competitively on "free agents." See Andrew Zimbalist, Baseball and Billions 24–26 (1992).

11. In addition, 17% of the players with at least two, but less than three, years of experience are also eligible for salary arbitration. See generally Roger Abrams, The Money Pitch: Baseball Free Agency and Salary Arbitration (2000).

What is the rationale behind this final-offer arbitration? As we have seen, in conventional arbitration it is often assumed that arbitrators will have a tendency to compromise and "split the difference" between the parties in an effort to maintain their future acceptability. Being aware of this, the parties at the bargaining stage are likely to hold back concessions that they would otherwise be willing to make, in order to avoid giving the game away. "If the parties view conventional arbitration as a procedure for securing compromise, bargaining tactics dictate that each party preserve a position *from* which the arbitrator can move to a compromise."[12] Indeed, the party which stakes out the *most extreme* initial position may hope to gain the most from an eventual arbitral compromise, and this is often said to have a "chilling effect" on good-faith bargaining.[13] On the other hand, the constraints imposed by "final-offer arbitration" should have the opposite effect on the parties' negotiating behavior. Where the arbitrators may not compromise, each party may fear that if its offer is perceived as extreme or "unreasonable," the arbitrators will choose the offer of the *other* party. This may impel each party to adjust his bargaining position to make it more "reasonable"—and thus more likely to be chosen—than his opponent's. There is thus set up a movement of each party towards the other, narrowing the difference between them and at best making any arbitration award unnecessary. Ideally, "final-offer arbitration" operates as a "doomsday weapon that invariably induces negotiated settlement."[14]

To some extent this dynamic can be observed in major league baseball. Typically, more than 80% of cases will settle after players have filed for arbitration and hearings have been scheduled.[15] Only a handful of cases actually go through the arbitration process—in the years between 1995 and 2001, an average of around 9 cases per year. "For most players, filing for arbitration and submitting salary proposals are stages of an ultimately successful bargaining process."[16] There are, of course, many other reasons for a high settlement rate in "baseball" arbitration. An arbitration hearing at which a player sits and listens to management's presentation of his many faults and shortcomings must inevitably strain the relationship between him and the club. And if the parties settle, they "can be creative in designing a compensation package, including bonuses, for example, or a no-trade clause," or a multi-year deal;[17] the product of salary arbitration, on the other hand, is merely a standard player contract (contained in the "Uniform Player's Contract" that is made part of the collective bargaining agreement) for a single year at a defined salary.

Final-offer arbitration is also frequently used to resolve "interest" disputes in public-sector employment. In contrast to arbitration in major-

12. Chelius & Dworkin, An Economic Analysis of Final–Offer Arbitration as a Conflict Resolution Device, 24 J.Conflict Res. 293, 294 (1980).

13. See Feuille, Final Offer Arbitration and the Chilling Effect, 14 Ind.Rel. 302 (1975).

14. Id. at 307.

15. Abrams, supra n.11 at 147, 152.

16. Faurot & McAllister, Salary Arbitration and Pre–Arbitration Negotiation in Major League Baseball, 45 Ind. & Lab.Rel. Rev. 697, 701 (1992).

17. Abrams, supra n.11 at 124–25, 149.

league baseball, however, public-sector "interest" arbitrators are frequently charged with determining a wide range of bargainable issues in addition to salary—all going to make up the terms of employment in the new agreement. In some states, the statutory scheme calls for each party to present to the arbitrators a "package" including a position on *all* the bargainable issues not yet agreed on. The arbitrators must then choose what they consider to be the more reasonable of the two "packages." In other states, in contrast, the arbitrators are allowed to consider each issue separately and to choose between the positions of the parties on an issue-by-issue basis. This variation enables the arbitrators to develop their own compromise "package" by balancing the parties' positions on the various issues. See, e.g., Mich.Comp.Laws § 423.238 (arbitration panel shall adopt "last offer of settlement" "as to each economic issue," while disputes over "non-economic" issues are resolved by conventional arbitration).

NOTES AND QUESTIONS

1. How might the strategy and bargaining behavior of the parties differ depending on whether the final-offer arbitration is to be on an "issue-by-issue" or "package" basis?

2. It should be obvious that all forms of final-offer arbitration have the greatest impact on the party who is the more risk-averse. In determining its final offer, each party is faced with a trade-off. It must weigh the loss involved in making a particular concession (say, a reduction in salary demands) against the greater probability of having its offer chosen by the arbitrator should an award become necessary. The more risk-averse party will be likely to move further in adjusting his demand downwards, in the direction of "reasonableness," in order to reduce the chances of an unfavorable result. This is particularly likely where arbitration is on a "package" basis. There is some evidence that unions nominally "win" public-sector "interest" arbitrations more frequently than public employers, and this would seem to support the proposition that the unions are more likely than the employer to be risk-averse. See Farber, An Analysis of Final–Offer Arbitration, 24 J.Conflict Res. 683 (1980); Bloom, Collective Bargaining, Compulsory Arbitration, and Salary Settlements in the Public Sector, 2 J.Lab.Res. 369 (1981); Schwochau & Feuille, Interest Arbitrators and Their Decision Behavior, 27 Ind.Rel. 37, 53–54 (1988) (union demands are much larger under conventional arbitration than under final offer arbitration, while offers by employers "show no significant differences").

See also Howard Raiffa, The Art and Science of Negotiation 118 (1982):

> [I]t seems that the proportion of cases going to final-offer arbitration is smaller than the proportion going to conventional arbitration. This is often cited as an advantage of final-offer arbitration. Of course, the logic is marred a bit because conventional arbitration preceded by a round of Russian roulette would still do better.

3. The concern is often expressed that final-offer arbitration on a "package" basis may lead to results that are unworkable or inequitable. Consider, for example, the dilemma of the arbitrator in an "interest" dispute between a city and a firefighter's union. The union submits a proposal on salary and benefits which the arbitrators find preferable to the city's. However, the union has also included a "zinger," in the form of a demand for mandatory manning levels at certain fire stations—an unusual proposal that the arbitrators find objectionable. (Perhaps union negotiators slipped in this demand hoping that it would be carried along by the force of their "irresistible" economic package; perhaps they were forced to include it for reasons of internal union politics.) In such circumstances, arbitrators often express frustration at being limited to choosing one package or the other. Cf. In re Monroe County, 113 Lab. Arb. 933 (1999)("If I had the authority to decide this on an issue by issue basis, I would adopt the [union's] wage proposal and the [employer's] vacation proposal. Unfortunately, I do not possess that authority. It is all or nothing").

Is it a sufficient answer to such concerns to say that the *whole point* of final-offer arbitration is to discourage actual arbitration, and that "if the case reaches the arbitrator, the parties both deserve whatever they get"? Zack, Final Offer Selection—Panacea or Pandora's Box, 19 N.Y.L.F. 567, 585 (1974). Consider the following proposal for an alternative system of final-offer arbitration by "package": Each side is to submit *three* different final offers. The arbitrator chooses one of the six packages presented to him but does not reveal his choice to the parties; instead, he merely announces *which side* has made the better offer. The *losing party* is then allowed to choose one of the three packages submitted by the winning party, and this becomes the final award. See Donn, Games Final–Offer Arbitrators Might Play, 16 Ind.Rel. 306, 312 (1977). What might be the advantages of such a system?

4. Consider this variation of final-offer arbitration: The arbitrator first draws up a proposed award without having seen the respective final offers of the parties. The final offer that was "closest" to this proposed settlement by the arbitrator then becomes the actual award binding on the parties. This is sometimes referred to as "night baseball." What are the possible advantages of this variant?

5. Under some statutes governing public-sector employment, "interest" disputes may be submitted to a neutral "fact-finder," who after hearing evidence from the parties makes a "recommendation." The term "fact-finder" may be chosen to lend an air of precision and inevitability to the process—but the fact-finder, in issuing his recommendations, is still likely to make the same sorts of value judgments and show the same concern for the acceptability of his conclusions to the parties as is typical of the "interest" arbitrator. The fact-finder's recommendations are usually made public, in the hope that the resulting public scrutiny and pressure of "public opinion" may make it more difficult for the parties to reject them. See, e.g., Ore.Rev.Stat. § 243.722(3), (4) (fact-finder's recommendations shall be "publicized" unless parties agree to accept them or agree to submit the dispute to final and binding arbitration). In all but the most exceptional cases, however, there is room for considerable skepticism as to the extent of any public awareness of or concern for the reports of public-sector fact-finders.

In some states, fact-finding is the final prescribed stage in the resolution of public-sector "interest" disputes. In others, both mediation and then fact-finding are imposed as preliminary steps before mandatory arbitration. Such arbitration is often of the "final-offer" variety. See, e.g., N.J.Stat. § 34:13A–16 (police and fire departments). Iowa's version adds further flexibility to the process: The arbitrators are allowed to choose not only one of the parties' last offers, but also—as a third option—the recommendation of the fact-finder on "each impasse item." Iowa Code §§ 20.21, 20.22. As might be expected this recommendation usually turns out to be a compromise, an intermediate position between the positions taken by the parties. And in those cases where an award proves necessary, the arbitrators tend overwhelmingly to choose the recommendation of the fact-finder. Even in jurisdictions where this option is not given to the arbitrator, the fact-finder's recommendation will often simply be incorporated into the final offer of one of the parties; the arbitration may then become a "show cause" hearing as to why this offer should not be accepted. "For those disputes that are not going to get resolved at the bargaining table, fact-finding is where the concrete for the foundation of an arbitration award is first poured." Holden, Final Offer Arbitration in Massachusetts, 31 Arb.J. 26, 28–29 (1976).

What might be the advantages and disadvantages of combining fact-finding and arbitration in this way? Might this two-step process tend to dilute the supposed benefits of final-offer arbitration? See generally Bierman, Factfinding: Finding the Public Interest, 9 Rutgers–Camden L.J. 667 (1978).

3. "MED-ARB"

There are many different styles of arbitration. One arbitrator may see himself chiefly as a passive adjudicator, presiding over the confrontation of adversaries. At the other extreme may be found the arbitrator who intervenes actively, in an effort to help the parties reach their own mutually agreeable settlement without the need for an imposed award.

Combining the roles of mediator and adjudicator poses a unique challenge to an arbitrator's skill: "When you sit there with the parties, separately or together—listening, persuading, cajoling, looking dour or relieved—your responsibility is a heavy one. Every lift of your eyebrow can be interpreted as a signal to the parties as to how you might eventually decide an issue if agreement is not reached."[18] This style of arbitration is seen most frequently in public-sector "interest" disputes. In fact, one

18. Bairstow, The Canadian Experience, Proceedings, 34th Annual Meeting, Nat'l Academy of Arbitrators 93 (1982).

survey estimates that arbitrators with experience in such disputes first attempt to mediate in at least 30 to 40 percent of their cases.[19]

Frequently, the statutory procedure for the settlement of public-sector disputes encourages and even institutionalizes "med-arb." For example, Michigan's form of final-offer arbitration permits the parties to revise their offers as the hearing progresses; in addition the arbitrators, after hearing evidence, may remand the dispute to the parties for further negotiations before the ultimate "final" offers must be submitted. In the course of the hearing, the arbitrator may indicate that on a particular issue he is "leaning towards" the position of one party. It does not require much imagination to see how this may influence the settlement process, and may force an adjustment in the position taken by the *other* party. In addition, use in public-sector "interest" disputes of a tripartite panel may also encourage resort to mediation techniques. In the executive session following the hearing, the neutral arbitrator has the opportunity to consult with his "partisan" colleagues. He may be expected to make efforts to reduce the area of disagreement between them, and can certainly draw on them in order to put together a coherent package reflecting the parties' true priorities.

The New Jersey statute is even more explicit, expressly mandating that in the "interest" disputes of police and firefighters, "[t]hroughout formal arbitration proceedings [the arbitrators] may mediate or assist the parties in reaching a mutually agreeable settlement."[20] Arbitrators under this statute are often quite outspoken in inducing settlement by advising parties of the unacceptability of their positions. This is what has often been termed "mediation with a club." One arbitrator explained that "I beat up on the parties. I believe that scaring them helps them to settle their own dispute."[21]

Lon Fuller, Collective Bargaining And The Arbitrator

Proceedings, Fifteenth Annual Meeting, National Academy of Arbitrators 8, 29–33, 37–48 (1962).

There remains the difficult problem of mediation by the arbitrator, where instead of issuing an award, he undertakes to persuade the parties to reach a settlement, perhaps reinforcing his persuasiveness with "the gentle threat" of a decision. Again, there is waiting a too-easy answer: "Judges do it." Of course, judges sometimes mediate or at least bring pressure on the parties for a voluntary settlement. Sometimes this is done usefully and sometimes in ways that involve an abuse of office. In any event the judiciary has evolved no uniform code with respect to this problem that the arbitrator can take over ready-made. Judicial practice varies over a wide

19. James L. Stern et al., Final–Offer Arbitration: The Effects on Public Safety Employee Bargaining 140 (1975).

20. N.J.Stat. § 34: 13A–16f(3).

21. Weitzman & Stochaj, Attitudes of Arbitrators toward Final–Offer Arbitration in New Jersey, 35 Arb.J. 25, 30 (1980).

range. If the arbitrator were to pattern his conduct after the worst practices of the bench, arbitration would be in a sad way.

Analysis of the problem as it confronts the arbitrator should begin with a recognition that mediation or conciliation—the terms being largely interchangeable—has an important role to play in the settlement of labor disputes. There is much to justify a system whereby it is a prerequisite to arbitration that an attempt first be made by a skilled mediator to bring about a voluntary settlement. This requirement has at times been imposed in a variety of contexts. Under such systems the mediator is, I believe, invariably someone other than the arbitrator. This is as it should be.

Mediation and arbitration have distinct purposes and hence distinct moralities. The morality of mediation lies in optimum settlement, a settlement in which each party gives up what he values less, in return for what he values more. The morality of arbitration lies in a decision according to the law of the contract. The procedures appropriate for mediation are those most likely to uncover that pattern of adjustment which will most nearly meet the interests of both parties. The procedures appropriate for arbitration are those which most securely guarantee each of the parties a meaningful chance to present arguments and proofs for a decision in his favor. Thus, private consultations with the parties, generally wholly improper on the part of an arbitrator, are an indispensable tool of mediation.

Not only are the appropriate procedures different in the two cases, but the facts sought by those procedures are different. There is no way to define "the essential facts" of a situation except by reference to some objective. Since the objective of reaching an optimum settlement is different from that of rendering an award according to the contract, the facts relevant in the two cases are different, or, when they seem the same, are viewed in different aspects. If a person who has mediated unsuccessfully attempts to assume the role of arbitrator, he must endeavor to view the facts of the case in a completely new light, as if he had previously known nothing about them. This is a difficult thing to do. It will be hard for him to listen to proofs and arguments with an open mind. If he fails in this attempt, the integrity of adjudication is impaired.

These are the considerations that seem to me to apply where the arbitrator attempts to mediate before hearing the case at all. This practice is quite uncommon, and would largely be confined to situations where a huge backlog of grievances seemed to demand drastic measures toward an Augean clean-up. I want now to pass to consideration of the case where the arbitrator postpones his mediative efforts until after the proofs are in and the arguments have been heard. * * *

One might ask of mediation first undertaken after the hearing is over, what is the point of it? If the parties do not like the award, they are at liberty to change it. If there is some settlement that will effect a more apt adjustment of their interests, their power to contract for that settlement is the same after, as it is before, the award is rendered. One answer would be to say that if the arbitrator undertakes mediation after the hearing but before the award, he can use "the gentle threat" of a decision to induce settlement, keeping it uncertain as to just what the decision will be. Indeed, if he has a sufficiently Machiavellian instinct, he may darkly hint that the decision will contain unpleasant surprises for both parties. Conduct of this sort would, however, be most unusual. Unless the role thus assumed were played with consummate skill, the procedure would be likely to explode in the arbitrator's face.

There is, however, a more convincing argument for mediative efforts after the hearing and before the award. This lies in the peculiar fact—itself a striking tribute to the moral force of the whole institution of adjudication—that an award tends to resist change by agreement. Once rendered it seems to have a kind of moral inertia that puts a heavy onus on the party who proposes any modification by mutual consent. Hence if there exists the possibility of a voluntary settlement that will suit both parties better than the award, the last chance to obtain it may occur after the hearing and before the award is rendered. This may in fact be an especially propitious moment for a settlement. Before the hearing it is quite usual for each of the parties to underestimate grossly the strength of his adversary's case. The hearing not uncommonly "softens up" both parties for settlement.

What, then, are the objections to an arbitrator's undertaking mediative efforts after the hearing and before rendering the award, this being often so advantageous a time for settlement? Again, the objection lies essentially in the confusion of role that results. In seeking a settlement the arbitrator turned mediator quite properly learns things that should have no bearing on his decision as an arbitrator. For example, suppose a discharge case in which the arbitrator is virtually certain that he will decide for reinstatement, though he is striving to keep his mind open until he has a chance to reflect on the case in the quiet of his study. In the course of exploring the possibilities of a settlement he learns that, contrary to the position taken by the union at the hearing, respectable elements in the union would like to see the discharge upheld. Though they concede that the employee was probably innocent of the charges made by the company, they regard him as an ambitious troublemaker the union would be well rid of. If the arbitrator fails to mediate a settlement, can he block this information out when he comes to render his award?

It is important that an arbitrator not only respect the limits of his office in fact, but that he also appear to respect them. The parties to an arbitration expect of the arbitrator that he will decide the dispute, not according to what pleases the parties, but by what accords with the contract. Yet as a mediator he must explore the parties' interests and seek to find out what would please them. He cannot be a good mediator unless he does. But if he has then to surrender his role as mediator to resume that of adjudicator, can his award ever be fully free from the suspicion that it was influenced by a desire to please one or both of the parties?

* * *

These, then, are the arguments against the arbitrator's undertaking the task of mediation. They can all be summed up in the phrase, "confusion of role.'' Why, then, should any arbitrator be tempted to depart from his proper role as adjudicator? In what follows I shall try to analyze the considerations that sometimes press him toward a departure from a purely judicial role.

* * *

[Fuller then discusses ''polycentric'' (that is, ''many-centered'') problems—the type of problem exemplified by the testator who in her will left a varied collection of paintings to two museums ''in equal shares.'' See p. 22 supra.].

[P]robably the nearest counterpart to Mrs. Timken's will is the following case: Union and management agree that the internal wage structure of the plant is out of balance—some jobs are paid too little in comparison with others, some too much. A kind of wage fund (say, equal to a general increase of five cents an hour) is set up. Out of this fund are to be allotted, in varying amounts, increases for the various jobs that will bring them into better balance. In case the parties cannot agree, the matter shall go to arbitration. Precisely because the task is polycentric, it is extremely unlikely that the parties will be able to agree on most of the jobs, leaving for arbitration only a few on which agreement proved impossible. Since in the allotment every job is pitted against every other, any tentative agreements reached as to particular jobs will have to lapse if the parties fail in the end to reach an agreement on the reorganization of the wage structure as a whole. In short, the arbitrator will usually have to start from scratch and do the whole job himself.

Confronted with such a task the arbitrator intent on preserving judicial proprieties faces a quandary much like that of a judge forced to carry out Mrs. Timken's ''equal'' division through adjudicative procedures. * * *

What modifications of his role will enable the arbitrator to discharge this task satisfactorily? The obvious expedient is a resort to mediation. After securing a general education in the problems involved in reordering the wage scale, the arbitrator might propose to each side in turn a tentative solution, inviting comments and criticisms. Through successive modifications a reasonably acceptable reordering of rates might be achieved, which would then be incorporated in an award. Here the dangers involved in the mediative role are probably at a minimum, precisely because the need for that role seems so obvious. Those dangers are not, however, absent. There is always the possibility that mediative efforts may meet shipwreck. Prolonged involvement in an attempt to work out a settlement agreeable to both parties obscures the arbitrator's function as a judge and makes it difficult to reassume that role. Furthermore, a considerable taint of the ''rigged'' award will in any event almost always attach to the final solution. The very fact that this solution must involve a compromise of interests within the union itself makes this virtually certain.

* * *

There is one general consideration that may incline the arbitrator to resolve any doubts presented by particular cases in favor of assuming a mediative role. This lies in a conviction—to be sure, not expressed in the terms I am about to employ—that all labor arbitrations involve to some extent polycentric elements. The relations within a plant form a seamless web; pluck it here, and a complex pattern of adjustments may run through the whole structure. A case involving a single individual, say a reclassification case, may set a precedent with implications unknown to the arbitrator, who cannot see how his decision may cut into a whole body of practice that is unknown to him. The arbitrator can never be sure what aspects of the case post-hearing consultations may bring to his attention that he would otherwise have missed.

That there is much truth in this observation would be foolish to deny. The integrity of the adjudicative process can never be maintained without some loss, without running some calculated risk. Any adjudicator—whether he be called judge, hearing officer, arbitrator, or umpire—who depends upon proofs and arguments adduced before him in open court, with each party confronting the other, is certain to make occasional mistakes he would not make if he could abandon the restraints of his role. The question is, how vital is that role for the maintenance of the government—in this case a system of industrial self-government—of which he is a part?

In facing that question as it arises in his practice, the arbitrator ought to divest himself, insofar as human nature permits, of any motive that might be called personal. It has been said that surgeons who have perfected some highly specialized operation tend strongly to favor a diagnosis of the patient's condition that will enable them to display their special skills. Can the arbitrator be sure he is immune from a similar desire to demonstrate virtuosity in his calling? It is well known in arbitrational circles that combining the roles of arbitrator and mediator is a tricky business. The amateur who tries it is almost certain to get in trouble. The veteran, on the other hand, takes an understandable pride in his ability to play this difficult dual role. He would be less than human if he did not seek out occasions for a display of his special talents, even to the point of discerning a need for them in situations demanding nothing more than a patient, conscientious judge, about to put a sensible meaning on the words of the contract.

* * *

Sometimes judgment on the issues here under discussion is influenced by a kind of slogan to the effect that an agreed settlement is always better than an imposed one. As applied to disputes before they have gone to arbitration, this slogan has some merit. When the case is in the hands of the arbitrator, however, I can see little merit in it, except in the special cases I have tried previously to analyze. After all, successful industrial self-government requires not only the capacity to reach and abide by agreements, but also the willingness to accept and conform to disliked awards. It is well that neither propensity be lost through disuse. Furthermore, there is something slightly morbid about the thought that an agreement coerced by the threat of decision is somehow more wholesome than an outright decision. It suggests a little the father who wants his children to obey him, but who, in order to still doubts that he may be too domineering, not only demands that they obey but insists that they do so with a smile. After having had his day in court, a man may with dignity bend his will to a judgment of which he disapproves. That dignity is lost if he is compelled to pretend that he agreed to it.

NOTES AND QUESTIONS

1. One arbitrator has noted that,

> [y]ou have to recognize the danger is there even by the mere overture to the arbitrator to step outside and "Let's have a look at this." It could be nothing more than one side broadly indicating, "Yes, we are ready to compromise this," and the other side saying, "Under no circumstances. We think we have a solid case." Back we go into the room, and you have to decide. It is conceivable that that conversation is going to influence the arbitrator. * * * I just don't think you can say even in the most cautious way that there won't be some prejudice.

Panel Discussion (Valtin), Proceedings, 33rd Annual Meeting, National Academy of Arbitrators 232 (1981).

Is it fair to suggest, then, that the "med-arb" process may often serve as an invitation to the parties to be candid—an invitation which only the more inexperienced or ingenuous of the two is likely to accept?

2. A recent survey of litigators indicated that the overwhelming majority preferred judges in settlement conferences to "actively offer suggestions and observations" for the settlement of the case: "They want the judge's opinions. They want the judge's suggestions. They want the perspective of the experienced neutral." See Wayne Brazil, Settling Civil Disputes 44–46 (1985). Does this affect in any way your view of Fuller's criticisms respecting arbitrators who depart from the proper "judicial role"?

3. Where in other legal cultures arbitrators routinely engage in efforts to induce a negotiated settlement, they do not seem overly troubled by Fuller's concern with respect to a possible "confusion of role." See pp. 34–35 supra. "As the Chinese put it: who better to be the arbitrator than the failed conciliator"? Kaplan, Hong Kong and the UNCITRAL Model Law, 4 Arb.Int'l 173, 176 (1988). See also Marriott, The Role of ADR in the Settlement of Commercial Disputes, 3 Asia Pacific L.Rev. 1, 15 (1994) ("the Chinese concept of * * * a rolling arbitration, whereby the arbitrator could become a conciliator and then revert to an adjudicatory role if the search for compromise and consensus proved in vain"). Attempts by arbitrators to facilitate compromise, suggest formulas for settlement, and induce agreement are not only seen in the Far East; such activity is also apparently quite common in Northern European arbitration. See, e.g., Trappe, Conciliation in the Far East, 5 Arb.Int'l 173 (1989) (approach of "concilio-arbitration," combining arbitration and mediation, "makes German practice, at least to a certain extent, similar to the Chinese"); cf. Peter, Med–Arb in International Arbitration, 8 Amer. Rev. Int'l Arb. 83 (1997)(referring to a "low-intensity form of mediation" used in Swiss and German arbitrations; "there is minimal, if any, intervention in the negotiation process," and "confidential private caucusing is not commonly used.").

4. The Hong Kong Arbitration Ordinance provides expressly that the arbitrator "may act as a conciliator," and in so doing may meet with the parties "collectively or separately." Where the parties fail to reach an agreement, the arbitrators may then "resume" the arbitration process. But in such a case, how should the arbitrators treat the confidential information that they were bound to receive in the course of their earlier efforts? The Ordinance requires the arbitrator to "disclose to all other parties * * * as much of [the confidential] information as he considers is material to the arbitration proceedings." § 2B. What do you think of this solution?

5. Nine union members were laid off by their employer, but were nevertheless told to report for work the next day—to perform substantially the same duties, but in the nominal capacity of "temporary" workers. The union brought a grievance; after an initial arbitration hearing was held, "the parties invited the arbitrator to attempt mediation." However, mediation was not successful and the arbitration resumed. The arbitrator ultimately issued an award in favor of the union; in calculating the award, she relied in part on answers that the laid-off employees had given to questions in a questionnaire that the parties had developed jointly during their efforts at mediation. The employer's motion to vacate the award was denied: "None of the information that was used in calculating the award came from [the employer]," whose participation "was in no way necessary to the Union's gathering of this information from its own members." "Had the parties not developed the questionnaire jointly during mediation, the same information still would have been required during the remedy phase," and the union could have collected it alone. WWOR–TV, Inc. v. Local 209, NABET–CWA, 166 F.3d 1203 (2d Cir.1998).

6. The AAA is now offering a program it refers to as "MEDALOA"—mediation combined with last-offer arbitration. Under this program, parties mediate their dispute under the AAA's Commercial Mediation Rules; if they are unable to reach a settlement, they agree that a neutral appointed by the AAA—or the mediator himself if the parties choose—will select between their final negotiated positions, that selection being binding on them. "During the mediation phase each party has made concessions and has developed some sort of feel for the other party's concessions and views. * * * Often the offers come so close together that the arbitrator's choice is of no real importance—you get what in effect is a mediated compromise." It has even been claimed that this "little-known-little used process * * * is the process of choice in the vast majority of commercial cases." Arnold, A Vocabulary of ADR Procedures, in PLI, 1 Patent Litigation 1994 at pp. 287, 330–31.

7. Consider a process by which the arbitrator *first* hears evidence and reaches a decision in the traditional manner; an award is written and placed in a sealed envelope without having been revealed to the parties. Only *then* does she attempt to bring the parties to a consensual agreement through mediation; if she is successful in doing so, the award is simply destroyed. (This in effect is "arb-med.") What might be the advantages of such a process?

8. Some schemes of "med-arb" provide for the different functions of mediation and arbitration to be performed by different individuals. If mediation fails, the dispute is then entrusted to a separate arbitrator who has the power to make a binding award. See Iowa Code §§ 20.20–20.22; Goldberg, The Mediation of Grievances Under a Collective Bargaining Contract: An Alternative to Arbitration, 77 Nw.U.L.Rev. 270 (1982).

In some cases, however, the mediator is charged also with making a *recommendation* to the ultimate decision-maker as to how the dispute should be resolved. This is true, for example, under California's mandatory mediation scheme, where the mediator may make a recommendation to the court as to child custody and visitation matters. See Cal.Fam.Code, §§ 3170, 3183. How might the possibility of such a recommendation by the mediator affect the mediation process? See Jay Folberg & Alison Taylor, Mediation 277–78 (1984):

> The consensus among mediators appears to confirm that the trust and candor required in mediation are unlikely to exist if the participants know the mediator may be formulating an opinion or recommendation that will be communicated to a judge or tribunal. The recommendation of the mediator, particularly in a child custody and visitation case, would generally be given such great weight that the mediator, in effect, would be switching roles from decision facilitator to decision maker. The confusion and suspicion created by this crossover role taint the validity, effectiveness, and integrity of the mediation process.
>
> The participants may, in some circumstances, agree or contract for the mediator to decide the matter if they are unable to do so or to testify as to a recommendation. Using the informal, consensual process of mediation with no evidentiary or procedural rules as the basis for an imposed decision does, however, create a considerable risk that the more clever or sophisticated participant may distort or manipulate the mediation in order to influence the mediator's opinion.

4. "RENT A JUDGE"

A California statute provides that "upon the agreement of the parties," a court may "refer" a pending action to any person or persons whom the parties themselves may choose. The court may also "refer" an action where the parties had previously entered into a written contract calling for a referee to hear controversies that might arise in the future. Referees may be asked:

> to try any or all of the issues in an action or proceeding, whether of fact or of law, and to report a statement of decision thereon; [or] to

ascertain a fact necessary to enable the court to determine an action or proceeding.

Cal.Code Civ.Pro. §§ 638, 640.

After hearing the case, the referees are to report their decision to the court within twenty days after the close of testimony; judgment must then be entered on the referees' decision "in the same manner as if the action had been tried by the court." Cal.Code Civ.Pro. §§ 643, 644.

Barlow F. Christensen, Private Justice: California's General Reference Procedure

1982 American Bar Foundation Research J. 79, 81–82, 103.

The statute says nothing at all about the qualifications of referees. Presumably, the parties might agree to have a case referred to almost anyone—to another lawyer, perhaps, or even to a layman. But parties using this statutory procedure are seeking judicial determination of their causes, and so references are made to retired judges selected by the parties. The reasons are obvious. A retired judge who would be acceptable to both parties would almost surely possess acknowledged judicial skills and, in many instances, expertise in the particular kind of case at issue, thus ensuring a trial that is both expeditious and fair.

The statute is also silent about the time and place of trials by referees. As a consequence, the parties and the referee are free to select the times and places that will be most convenient. This has obvious advantages with respect to such things as securing the presence of witnesses, and it means that trials can be scheduled at times that will be most advantageous to counsel. Moreover, because the procedure is most often used by parties who want to get to trial promptly, both sides know that when they do go to trial both parties will be ready, thus avoiding the continuances and postponements that are often so frustrating in the course of regular trials in courts.

Trials by referees are conducted as proper judicial trials, following the traditional rules of procedure and evidence. Transcripts are made of the proceedings, and the judgment of the referee becomes the judgment of the court. It is thus enforceable and appealable, as any other judgment would be. One lawyer who uses the reference procedure suggests that parties might agree to submit disputes to retired judges for decision independently, without any court order, but that they use the statutory procedure to preserve their rights of enforcement and appeal. * * *

In theory, almost any kind of case might be referred to a referee for trial. The consensual portion of the statute imposes no restrictions. In practice, however, the procedure has been used primarily in technical and complex business litigation involving substantial amounts of money. The case in which the procedure was first used, for instance, was a complicated dispute between a medical billing company and two attorneys who had acquired interests in the company. Other examples have been a suit by major oil companies against a California governmental agency over air pollution control standards, a contract dispute between a nationally known television entertainer and his broadcasting company employer, and an action between a giant motor vehicle manufacturer and one of its suppliers over the quality of parts supplied.

The compensation of a retired judge appointed to try a case as a referee is also the subject of agreement between the parties, and the cost is borne equally by the parties.

NOTES AND QUESTIONS

1. A survey of private ADR firms and independent neutrals offering dispute resolution services in Los Angeles is reported in Elizabeth Rolph et al., Escaping the Courthouse: Private Alternative Dispute Resolution in Los Angeles, 1996 J. Disp. Resol. 277. According to this study, the total "private ADR caseload" in Los Angeles grew at an average rate of 15% per year between 1988 and 1993—while during that period, the *public* court caseload declined an average of about 0.5%; private ADR, however, still represented only 5% of the total dispute "caseload" filed both in private fora and in the public courts (small claims, municipal, and superior courts) combined. Claims involving amounts in controversy greater than $25,000 accounted for between 60–70% of the private caseload, as compared to only 14% of the public court caseload.

This private ADR market was dominated by arbitration (58% of disputes) and by mediation (22%): Only 5% of private forum disputes were handled in "private judging" proceedings under the California statute (including discovery matters that courts often refer to private judges even without the consent of the parties, see Cal. Code Civ. Pro. Sec. 639 (e)). About 91 former judges are now offering their services in Los Angeles as neutrals in private ADR; most of these retired from the bench following 20 years of service, and "therefore cannot be characterized as leaving the bench 'prematurely.' " Of those neutrals who were characterized as "heavy hitters"—each handling 100 or more disputes in a year—almost half came from the bench. Unsurprisingly, while attorneys tended to dominate the provision of arbitration services, "former judges provide voluntary settlement conferences and private judging much more often than do attorneys."

2. The California statute appears to be the most often-used, and is certainly the most highly-publicized, in the country. However, comparable procedures exist in some other states. In some cases, the "referee" is *required* to be a retired judge. Under the Texas statute, for example, a "special judge" must be a retired or former district, county, or appellate judge with at least four years service, who has "developed substantial experience in his area of specialty" and who each year completes five days of continuing legal education courses. Here too, however, the parties are free to select their own "special judge" and to agree with him on the fee that he is to be paid. See Texas Trial by Special Judge Act, Tex.Civ.Prac. & Rem.Code § 151.001 et seq.

3. How does the California or Texas reference procedure differ from arbitration? Are there reasons why parties might prefer to utilize the reference procedure rather than to submit an existing dispute to arbitration?

Consider the following provisions of the Texas statute:

Sec. 151.005. Rules and statutes relating to procedure and evidence in district court apply to a trial under this chapter.

Sec. 151.006. (a) A special judge shall conduct the trial in the same manner as a court trying an issue without a jury.

(b) While serving as a special judge, the judge has the powers of a district court judge except that he may not hold a person in contempt of court unless the person is a witness before him.

Sec. 151.011. The special judge's verdict must comply with the requirements for a verdict by the court. The verdict stands as a verdict of the district court. * * *

Sec. 151.013. The right to appeal is preserved. * * *

4. In response to a number of criticisms of the "rent-a-judge" system, the Judicial Council of California approved new rules in February 1993 to govern trials by privately compensated judges. What objections were these rules intended to address—and how adequately do they deal with the perceived problems?

Rule 532.1. Reference by agreement

(b) * * * The referee shall disclose as soon as practicable any facts that might be grounds for disqualification. A referee who has been privately compensated in any other proceeding in the past 18 months as a judge, referee, arbitrator, mediator, or settlement facilitator by a party, attorney, or law firm in the instant case shall disclose the number and nature of other proceedings before the first hearing. Any objection to the appointment of a person as a referee shall be in writing and shall be filed and served upon all parties and the referee.

(c) A party who has elected to use the services of a privately compensated referee * * * is deemed to have elected to proceed outside the courthouse; therefore, court facilities and court personnel shall not be used, except upon a finding by the presiding judge that the use would further the interests of justice. * * *

(d) The presiding judge or supervising judge, on request of any person or on the judge's own motion, may order that a case before a privately compensated referee must be heard at a site easily accessible to the public and appropriate for seating those who have made known their plan to attend hearings. * * * The order may require that notice of trial or of other proceedings be given to the requesting party directly. * * *

(e) * * * A motion to seal records in a cause before a privately compensated referee shall be served and filed and shall be heard by the

> presiding judge or a judge designated by the presiding judge. The moving party shall mail or deliver a copy of the motion to the referee and to any person or organization who has requested that the case take place at an appropriate hearing site.
>
> A motion for leave to file a complaint for intervention in a cause before a privately compensated referee shall be served and filed, and shall be assigned for hearing as a law and motion matter. The party seeking intervention shall mail or deliver a copy of the motion to the referee. If intervention is allowed, the case shall be returned to the trial court docket unless all parties stipulate * * * to proceed before the referee.

See also Tex.Civ.Prac. & Rem.Code § 151.009(c) ("The state or a unit of local government may not pay any costs related to a trial under this chapter"); § 151.010 ("A trial under this chapter may not be held in a public courtroom, and a public employee may not be involved in the trial during regular working hours").

5. The following excerpts from a student-written note raise a number of objections to the California reference procedure. In light of everything that you have read in this chapter on arbitration, how do you assess these criticisms?

> While the comparatively affluent can realize the cost and time savings of hiring a referee, other litigants may not. Those appearing pro se, for example, or who are represented by Legal Aid or by attorneys appearing pro bono or on a contingency fee basis, may be able to afford little or no out-of-pocket expenditure prior to entry of a judgment and hence will be unable to hire a referee. The use of referees paid by the parties, then, in effect creates two classes of litigants: wealthy litigants, who can afford the price of a referee, and poorer litigants, who cannot. The former group obtains all of the advantages of reference, while the latter must endure all the systemic disadvantages that led wealthy litigants to seek reference in the first place.
>
> Such a system of reference is clearly unfair to the poorer litigant and may even run against the best interests of society. It would allow, in the extreme case, an utterly frivolous suit to obtain a speedy trial solely because the litigants were wealthy, while forcing a suit involving issues important to society and vital to the parties to languish for a considerable time awaiting trial. Even if the suits are similar, the bias against the poor is still striking. If, for example, the poor litigant is in court because he needs to protect a valuable property interest affected by the dispute, his interest is kept in jeopardy for a longer period of time than that of a similarly situated litigant using the referee system. The state's action in according the wealthy the privilege of using a faster form of procedure gives them an additional property right, the right to be more secure in their ownership.
>
> * * *
>
> A due process problem may arise when referees are privately paid, particularly if overloading in the regular court system has driven some

> parties to a reference procedure they otherwise might not have chosen. As early as 1215, Magna Charta declared that it was wrong for the government to sell justice or to delay or deny it to anyone. In a private reference system, the state does not sell justice, but it does sanction the payment of private adjudicators to act in its place. The ultimate product purchased by these payments is a judgment that is entered on the court rolls and enforced by state authority. To whom the payments ultimately go is not nearly so important as the fact that they are made, with the sanction of the state, in order to obtain a state-monopolized enforceable order.

Note, The California Rent–A–Judge Experiment: Constitutional and Policy Considerations of Pay–As–You–Go Courts, 94 Harv.L.Rev. 1592, 1601–02, 1607–08 (1981). Similar arguments are advanced in Note, Rent–A–Judges and the Cost of Selling Justice, 44 Duke L.J. 166 (1994) ("The rent-a-judge system is an unconstitutional, elitist institution that unfairly grants privileges to the wealthy").

Further References

Websites:

www. adr.org (American Arbitration Association)

www.naarb.org (National Academy of Arbitrators)

www.arbitrators.org (Chartered Institute)

www.lcia-arbitration.com (LCIA)

www.jamsadr.com (JAMS)

www.iccwbo.org (ICC)

www.cpradr.org (CPR Institute of Dispute Resolution)

www.asser.nl (T.M.C. Asser Institute)

Books:

Born, Gary, International Commercial Arbitration in the United States (1994).

___, International Arbitration and Forum Selection Agreements: Planning, Drafting, and Enforcing (1999).

Bühring-Uhle, Christian, Arbitration and Mediation in International Business: Designing Procedures for Effective Conflict Management (1996).

Carbonneau, Tom, Cases and Materials on Commercial Arbitration (1997).

Cooper, Laura J., Dennis R. Nolan, & Richard A. Bales, ADR in the Workplace (2000).

Craig, W. Laurence, William W. Park & Jan Paulsson, International Chamber of Commerce Arbitration (3d ed. 2000).

___, Craig, Park, & Paulsson's Annotated Guide to the 1998 ICC Arbitration Rules: with Commentary (1998).

Dezalay, Yves & Bryant G. Garth, Dealing in Virtue: International Commercial Arbitration and the Construction of a Transnational Legal Order (1996).

Derains, Yves & Eric A. Schwartz, A Guide to the New ICC Rules of Arbitration (1998).

Domke, Martin, Commercial Arbitration (Rev. ed.).

Elkouri, Frank, & Edna A. Elkouri, How Arbitration Works (5th ed. 1997) (labor arbitration).

Fox, William F., Jr., International Commercial Agreements: A Primer on Drafting, Negotiating, and Resolving Disputes (3d ed. 1998).

Fouchard, Philippe, Emmanuel Gaillard, & Berthold Goldman, International Commercial Arbitration (1999).

Frommel, Stefan N. & Barry A. K. Rider (eds.), Conflicting Legal Cultures in Commercial Arbitration: Old Issues and New Trends (1999).

Haagen, Paul, Arbitration Now: Opportunities for Fairness, Process Renewal and Invigoration (1999).

Hill, Marvin F. Jr., & Sinicropi, Anthony V., Remedies in Arbitration, (2d ed. 1991) (labor arbitration).

Lookofsky, Joseph, M., Transnational Litigation and Commercial Arbitration: A Comparative Analysis of American, European and International Law (1992).

Macneil, Ian R., American Arbitration Law: Reformation, Nationalization, Internationalization (1992).

___, Richard E. Speidel, & Thomas J. Stipanowich, Federal Arbitration Law: Agreements, Awards, and Remedies Under the Federal Arbitration Act (1994).

Redfern, Alan, & Martin Hunter, Law and Practice of International Commercial Arbitration (3d ed. 1999).

Reisman, W. Michael, W. Lawrence Craig, William Park & Jan Paulsson, International Commercial Arbitration (1997).

Samuel, Adam, Jurisdictional Problems in International Commercial Arbitration (1989).

Schoonhoven, Ray J. (ed.), Fairweather's Practice and Procedure in Labor Arbitration (3d ed. 1991).

Várady, Tibor, John J. Barceló, III, & Arthur T. von Mehren, International Commercial Arbitration (1999).

Zack, Arnold M. (ed.), Arbitration in Practice (1984) (labor arbitration).

___, Grievance Arbitration: Issues on the Merits in Discipline, Discharge, and Contract Interpretation (1989).

Zimny, Max, William F. Dolson, & Christopher A. Barreca, Labor Arbitration: A Practical Guide For Advocates (ABA 1990).

Articles:

Allison, John R., The Context, Properties and Constitutionality of Non–Consensual Arbitration, 1990 J.Disp.Resol. 1 (1990).

Bruff, Harold H., Public Programs, Private Deciders: The Constitutionality of Arbitration in Federal Programs, 67 Tex.L.Rev. 441 (1989).

Brunet, Edward, Arbitration and Constitutional Rights, 71 N.C.L.Rev. 81(1992).

___, Replacing Folklore Arbitration with a Contract Model of Arbitration, 74 Tulane L.Rev. 39 (1999).

Carbonneau, Thomas E., Arbitral Justice: The Demise of Due Process in American Law, 70 Tul. L. Rev. 1945 (1996).

Carrington, Paul D. & Paul H. Haagen, Contract and Jurisdiction, 1996 Sup. Ct. Rev. 331 (1997).

Cole, Sarah Rudolph, Managerial Litigants? The Overlooked Problem of Party Autonomy in Dispute Resolution, 51 Hastings L.J. 1199 (2000).

Dezalay, Yves, & Bryant Garth, Merchants of Law as Moral Entrepreneurs: Constructing International Justice from the Competition for Transnational Business Disputes, 29 Law & Society Rev. 27 (1995).

Drahozal, Christopher R., Privatizing Civil Justice: Commercial Arbitration and the Civil Justice System, 9 Kan. J.L. & Pub. Pol'y 578 (2000).

___, Commercial Norms, Commercial Codes, and International Commercial Arbitration, 33 Vanderbilt J. of Transnational L. 79 (2000).

___, "Unfair" Arbitration Clauses, 2001 U. of Illinois L. Rev. 695.

Getman, Julius G., Labor Arbitration and Dispute Resolution, 88 Yale L.J. 916 (1979).

Heilbron, David M., The Arbitration Clause, the Preliminary Conference, and the Big Case, 45 Arb.J. 38 (1990).

Hill, Marvin F., Jr., Interest Criteria in Fact–Finding and Arbitration: Evidentiary and Substantive Considerations, 74 Marq.L.Rev. 399 (1991).

Kerr, Justice, International Arbitration vs. Litigation, J.Bus.L. 164 (May, 1980).

Mehtschikoff, Soia, Commercial Arbitration, 61 Colum.L.Rev. 846 (1961).

___, The Significance of Arbitration–A Preliminary Inquiry, 17 Law & Contemp.Probs. 698 (1952).

Morgan, Edward M., Contract Theory and the Sources of Rights: An Approach to the Arbitrability Question, 60 S.Cal.L.Rev. 1059 (1987).

Park, William W., Duty and Discretion in International Arbitration, 93 Am. J. Int'l L. 805 (1999).

___, Arbitration's Discontents: Of Elephants and Pornography, 17 Arb. Int'l 263 (2001).

Peter, James T., Med–Arb in International Arbitration, 8 Amer. Rev. Int'l Arb. 83 (1997).

Rau, Alan Scott, Resolving Disputes Over Attorneys' Fees: The Role of ADR, 46 SMU L.Rev. 2005 (1993).

___, The UNCITRAL Model Law in State and Federal Courts: The Case of "Waiver," 6 Am. Rev. Int'l Arb. 223 (1995).

___, The New York Convention in American Courts, 7 Am. Rev. Int'l Arb. 213 (1996).

___, "The Arbitrability Question Itself," 10 Am. Rev. of Int'l Arb. 287 (1999).

Speidel, Richard E., Arbitration of Statutory Rights Under the Federal Arbitration Act: The Case for Reform, 4 Ohio St.J. on Disp.Res. 157(1989).

Sternlight, Jean R., As Mandatory Binding Arbitration Meets the Class Action, Will the Class Action Survive?, 42 William & Mary L. Rev. 1 (2000).

___, Rethinking the Constitutionality of the Supreme Court's Preference for Binding Arbitration: A Fresh Assessment of Jury Trial, Separation of Powers, and Due Process Concerns, 72 Tulane L. Rev. 1 (1997).

___, Mandatory Binding Arbitration and the Demise of the Seventh Amendment Right to a Jury Trial, 16 Ohio St. J. on Disp. Res. 669 (2001).

Stipanowich, Thomas J., Rethinking American Arbitration, 63 Ind.L.J. 425(1988).

___, Punitive Damages and the Consumerization of Arbitration, 92 Northwestern U. L. Rev. 1 (1997).

Symposium on International Commercial Arbitration, 30 Tex.Int'l.L.J. No. 1 (Winter 1995).

Symposium, Commercial Arbitration: A Discussion of Recent Developments and Trends, 31 Wake Forest L. Rev. No. 1 (1996).

Appendix A

Federal Arbitration Act 9 U.S.C. § 1 (1925)

CHAPTER 1. GENERAL PROVISIONS

§ 1. "Maritime Transactions," and "Commerce" Defined; Exceptions to Operation of Title

"Maritime transactions," as herein defined, means charter parties, bills of lading of water carriers, agreements relating to wharfage, supplies furnished vessels or repairs of vessels, collisions, or any other matters in foreign commerce which, if the subject of controversy, would be embraced within admiralty jurisdiction; "commerce," as herein defined, means commerce among the several States or with foreign nations, or in any Territory of the United States or in the District of Columbia, or between any such Territory and another, or between any such Territory and any State or foreign nation, or between the District of Columbia and any State or Territory or foreign nation, but nothing herein contained shall apply to contracts of employment of seamen, railroad employees, or any other class of workers engaged in foreign or interstate commerce.

§ 2. Validity, Irrevocability, and Enforcement of Agreements to Arbitrate

A written provision in any maritime transaction or a contract evidencing a transaction involving commerce to settle by arbitration a controversy thereafter arising out of such contract or transaction, or the refusal to perform the whole or any part thereof, or an agreement in writing to submit to arbitration an existing controversy arising out of such a contract, transaction, or refusal, shall be valid, irrevocable, and enforceable, save upon such grounds as exist at law or in equity for the revocation of any contract.

§ 3. Stay of Proceedings Where Issue Therein Referable to Arbitration

If any suit or proceeding be brought in any of the courts of the United States upon any issue referable to arbitration under an agreement in writing for such arbitration, the court in which such suit is pending, upon being satisfied that the issue involved in such suit or proceeding is referable to arbitration under such an agreement, shall on application of one of the parties stay the trial of the action until such arbitration has been had in accordance with the terms of the agreement, providing the applicant for the stay is not in default in proceeding with such arbitration.

§ 4. Failure to Arbitrate Under Agreement; Petition to United States Court Having Jurisdiction for Order to Compel Arbitration; Notice and Service Thereof; Hearing and Determination

A party aggrieved by the alleged failure, neglect, or refusal of another to arbitrate under a written agreement for arbitration may petition any United States district court which, save for such agreement, would have jurisdiction under Title 28, in a civil action or in admiralty of the subject matter of a suit arising out of the controversy between the parties, for an order directing that such arbitration proceed in the manner provided for in such agreement. Five days' notice in writing of such application shall be served upon the party in default. Service thereof shall be made in the manner provided by the Federal Rules of Civil Procedure. The court shall hear the parties, and upon being satisfied that the making of the agreement for arbitration or the failure to comply therewith is not in issue, the court shall make an order directing the parties to proceed to arbitration in accordance with the terms of the agreement. The hearing and proceedings, under such agreement, shall be within the district in which the petition for an order directing such arbitration is filed. If the making of the arbitration agreement or the failure, neglect, or refusal to perform the same be in issue, the court shall proceed summarily to the trial thereof. If no jury trial be demanded by the party alleged to be in default, or in the matter in dispute is within admiralty jurisdiction, the court shall hear and determine such issue. Where such an issue is raised, the party alleged to be in default may, except in cases of admiralty, on or before the return day of the notice of application, demand a jury trial of such issue, and upon such demand the court shall make an order referring the issue or issues to a jury in the manner provided by the Federal Rules of Civil Procedure, or may specially call a jury for that purpose. If the jury find that no agreement in writing for arbitration was made or that there is no default in proceeding thereunder, the proceeding shall be dismissed. If the jury find that an agreement for arbitration was made in writing and that there is a default in proceeding thereunder, the court shall make an order summarily directing the parties to proceed with the arbitration in accordance with the terms thereof.

§ 5. Appointment of Arbitrators or Umpire

If in the agreement provision be made for a method of naming or appointing an arbitrator or arbitrators or an umpire, such method shall be followed; but if no method be provided therein, or if a method be provided and any party thereto shall fail to avail himself of such method, or if for any other reason there shall be a lapse in the naming of an arbitrator or arbitrators or umpire, or in filling a vacancy, then upon the application of either party to the controversy the court shall designate and appoint an arbitrator or arbitrators or umpire, as the case may require, who shall act under the said agreement with the same force and effect as if he or they had been specifically named therein; and unless otherwise provided in the agreement the arbitration shall be by a single arbitrator.

§ 6. Application Heard as Motion

Any application to the court hereunder shall be made and heard in the manner provided by law for making and hearing of motions, except as otherwise herein expressly provided.

§ 7. Witnesses Before Arbitrators; Fees; Compelling Attendance

The arbitrators selected either as prescribed in this title or otherwise, or a majority of them, may summon in writing any person to attend before them or any of them as a witness and in a proper case to bring with him or them any book, record, document, or paper which may be deemed material as evidence in the case. The fees for such attendance shall be the same as the fees of witnesses before masters of the United States Courts. Said summons shall issue in the name of the arbitrator or arbitrators, or a majority of them, and shall be signed by the arbitrators, or a majority of them, and shall be directed to the said person and shall be served in all the same manner as subpoenas to appear and testify before the court; if any person or persons so summoned to testify shall refuse or neglect to obey said summons, upon petition the United States court in and for the district in which such arbitrators or a majority of them, are sitting may compel the attendance of such person or persons before said arbitrator or arbitrators, or punish said person or persons for contempt in the same manner provided on February 12, 1925, for securing the attendance of witnesses or their punishment for neglect or refusal to attend in the courts of the United States.

§ 8. Proceedings Begun by Libel in Admiralty and Seizure of Vessel or Property

If the basis of jurisdiction be a cause of action otherwise justiciable in admiralty, then, notwithstanding anything herein to the contrary, the party claiming to be aggrieved may begin his proceeding hereunder by libel and seizure of the vessel or other property of the other party according to the usual course of admiralty proceedings, and the court shall then have jurisdiction to direct the parties to proceed with the arbitration and shall retain jurisdiction to enter its decree upon the award.

§ 9. Award of Arbitrators; Confirmation; Jurisdiction; Procedure

If the parties in their agreement have agreed that a judgment of the court shall be entered upon the award made pursuant to the arbitration, and shall specify the court, then at any time within one year after the award is made any party to the arbitration may apply to the court so specified for an order confirming the award, and thereupon the court must grant such an order unless the award is vacated, modified, or corrected as prescribed in sections 10 and 11 of this title. If no court is specified in the agreement of the parties, then such application may be made to the United

States court in and for the district within which such award was made. Notice of the application shall be served upon the adverse party, and thereupon the court shall have jurisdiction of such party as though he had appeared generally in the proceeding. If the adverse party is a resident of the district within which the award was made, such service shall be made upon the adverse party or his attorney as prescribed by law for service of notice of motion in an action in the same court.

§ 10. Same; Vacation; Grounds; Rehearing

(a) In any of the following cases the United States court in and for the district wherein the award was made may make an order vacating the award upon the application of any party to the arbitration?

(1) Where the award was procured by corruption, fraud, or undue means.

(2) Where there was evident partiality or corruption in the arbitrators, or either of them.

(3) Where the arbitrators were guilty of misconduct in refusing to postpone the hearing, upon sufficient cause shown, or in refusing to hear evidence pertinent and material to the controversy; or of any other misbehavior by which the rights of any party have been prejudiced.

(4) Where the arbitrators exceeded their powers, or so imperfectly executed them that a mutual, final, and definite award upon the subject matter submitted was not made.

(5) Where an award is vacated and the time within which the agreement required the award to be made has not expired the court may, in its discretion, direct a rehearing by the arbitrators.

(b) The United States district court for the district wherein an award was made that was issued pursuant to section 580 of title 5 may make an order vacating the award upon the application of a person, other than a party to the arbitration, who is adversely affected or aggrieved by the award, if the use of arbitration or the award is clearly inconsistent with the factors set forth in section 572 of title 5.

§ 11. Same; Modification or Correction; Grounds; Order

In either of the following cases the United States court in and for the district wherein the award was made may make an order modifying or correcting the award upon the application of any party to the arbitration?

(a) Where there was an evident material miscalculation of figures or an evident material mistake in the description of any person, thing, or property referred to in the award.

(b) Where the arbitrators have awarded upon a matter not submitted to them, unless it is a matter not affecting the merits of the decision upon the matter submitted.

(c) Where the award is imperfect in matter of form not affecting the merits of the controversy.

The order may modify and correct the award, so as to effect the intent thereof and promote justice between the parties.

§ 12. Notice of Motions to Vacate or Modify; Service; Stay of Proceedings

Notice of a motion to vacate, modify, or correct an award must be served upon the adverse party or his attorney within three months after the award is filed or delivered. If the adverse party is a resident of the district within which the award was made, such service shall be made upon the adverse party or his attorney as prescribed by law for service of notice of motion in an action in the same court. If the adverse party shall be a nonresident then the notice of the application shall be served by the marshal of any district within which the adverse party may be found in like manner as other process of the court. For the purposes of the motion any judge who might make an order to stay the proceedings in an action brought in the same court may make an order, to be served with the notice of motion, staying the proceedings of the adverse party to enforce the award.

§ 13. Papers Filed with Order on Motions; Judgment; Docketing; Force and Effect; Enforcement

The party moving for an order confirming, modifying, or correcting an award shall, at the time such order is filed with the clerk for the entry of judgment thereon, also file the following papers with the clerk:

(a) The agreement: the selection or appointment, if any, of an additional arbitrator or umpire; and each written extension of the time, if any, within which to make the award.

(b) The award.

(c) Each notice, affidavit, or other paper used upon an application to confirm, modify, or correct the award, and a copy of each order of the court upon such an application.

The judgment shall be docketed as if it was rendered in an action.

The judgment so entered shall have the same force and effect, in all respects, as, and be subject to all the provisions of law relating to, a judgment in an action; and it may be enforced as if it had been rendered in an action in the court in which it is entered.

§ 14. Contracts Not Affected

This title shall not apply to contracts made prior to January 1, 1926.

§ 15. Inapplicability of the Act of State Doctrine

Enforcement of arbitral agreements, confirmation of arbitral awards, and execution upon judgments based on orders confirming such awards shall not be refused on the basis of the Act of State doctrine.

§ 16. Appeals

(a) An appeal may be taken from

(1) an order

(A) refusing a stay of any action under section 3 of this title,

(B) denying a petition under section 4 of this title to order arbitration to proceed,

(C) denying an application under section 206 of this title to compel arbitration,

(D) confirming or denying confirmation of an award or partial award, or

(E) modifying, correcting, or vacating an award;

(2) an interlocutory order granting, continuing, or modifying an injunction against an arbitration that is subject to this title; or

(3) a final decision with respect to an arbitration that is subject to this title.

(b) Except as otherwise provided in section 1292(b) of title 28, an appeal may not be taken from an interlocutory order

(1) granting a stay of any action under section 3 of this title;

(2) directing arbitration to proceed under section 4 of this title;

(3) compelling arbitration under section 206 of this title; or

(4) refusing to enjoin an arbitration that is subject to this title.

CHAPTER 2. CONVENTION ON THE RECOGNITION AND ENFORCEMENT OF FOREIGN ARBITRAL AWARDS

§ 201. Enforcement of Convention

The Convention on the Recognition and Enforcement of Foreign Arbitral Awards of June 10, 1958, shall be enforced in United States courts in accordance with this chapter.

§ 202. Agreement or Award Falling Under the Convention

An arbitration agreement or arbitral award arising out of a legal relationship, whether contractual or not, which is considered as commercial, including a transaction, contract, or agreement described in section 2 of this title, falls under the Convention. An agreement or award arising out of such relationship which is entirely between citizens of the United States shall be deemed not to fall under the Convention unless that relationship involves property located abroad, envisages performance or enforcement abroad, or has some other reasonable relation with one or more foreign states. For the purpose of this section a corporation is a citizen of the United States if it is incorporated or has its principal place of business in the United States.

§ 203. Jurisdiction; Amount in Controversy

An action or proceeding falling under the Convention shall be deemed to arise under the laws and treaties of the United States. The district courts of the United States (including the courts enumerated in section 460 of title 28) shall have original jurisdiction over such an action or proceeding, regardless of the amount in controversy.

§ 204. Venue

An action or proceeding over which the district courts have jurisdiction pursuant to section 203 of this title may be brought in any such court in which save for the arbitration agreement an action or proceeding with respect to the controversy between the parties could be brought, or in such court for the district and division which embraces the place designated in the agreement as the place of arbitration if such place is within the United States.

§ 205. Removal of Cases From State Courts

Where the subject matter of an action or proceeding pending in a State court relates to an arbitration agreement or award falling under the Convention, the defendant or the defendants may, at any time before the trial thereof, remove such action or proceeding to the district court of the United States for the district and division embracing the place where the action or proceeding is pending. The procedure for removal of causes otherwise provided by law shall apply, except that the ground for removal provided in this section need not appear on the face of the complaint but may be shown in the petition for removal. For the purposes of Chapter 1 of this title any action or proceeding removed under this section shall be deemed to have been brought in the district court to which it is removed.

§ 206. Order to Compel Arbitration; Appointment of Arbitrators

A court having jurisdiction under this chapter may direct that arbitration be held in accordance with the agreement at any place therein provided for, whether that place is within or without the United States. Such court may also appoint arbitrators in accordance with the provisions of the agreement.

§ 207. Award of Arbitrators; Confirmation; Jurisdiction; Proceeding

Within three years after an arbitral award falling under the Convention is made, any party to the arbitration may apply to any court having jurisdiction under this chapter for an order confirming the award as against any other party to the arbitration. The court shall confirm the award unless it finds one of the grounds for refusal or deferral of recognition or enforcement of the award specified in the said Convention.

§ 208. Chapter 1; Residual Applications

Chapter 1 applies to actions and proceedings brought under this chapter to the extent that chapter is not in conflict with this chapter or the Convention as ratified by the United States.

CHAPTER 3. INTER–AMERICAN CONVENTION ON INTERNATIONAL COMMERCIAL ARBITRATION

§ 301. Enforcement of Convention

The Inter–American Convention on International Commercial Arbitration of January 30, 1975, shall be enforced in United States courts in accordance with this chapter.

§ 302. Incorporation by Reference

Sections 202, 203, 204, 205, and 207 of this title shall apply to this chapter as if specifically set forth herein, except that for the purposes of this chapter "the Convention" shall mean the Inter–American Convention.

§ 303. Order to Compel Arbitration; Appointment of Arbitrators; Locale

(a) A court having jurisdiction under this chapter may direct that arbitration be held in accordance with the agreement at any place therein provided for, whether that place is within or without the United States. The court may also appoint arbitrators in accordance with the provisions of the agreement.

(b) In the event the agreement does not make provision for the place of arbitration or the appointment of arbitrators, the court shall direct that the arbitration shall be held and the arbitrators be appointed in accordance with Article 3 of the Inter–American Convention.

§ 304. Recognition and Enforcement of Foreign Arbitral Decisions and Awards; Reciprocity

Arbitral decision or awards made in the territory of a foreign State shall, on the basis of reciprocity, be recognized and enforced under this chapter only if that State has ratified or acceded to the Inter–American Convention.

§ 305. Relationship Between the Inter–American Convention and the Convention on the Recognition and Enforcement of Foreign Arbitral Awards of June 10, 1958

When the requirements for application of both the Inter–American Convention and the Convention on the Recognition and Enforcement of Foreign Arbitral Awards of June 10, 1958, are met, determination as to which Convention applies shall, unless otherwise expressly agreed, be made as follows:

(1) If a majority of the parties to the arbitration agreement are citizens of a State or States that have ratified or acceded to the Inter–American Convention and are member States of the Organization of American States, the Inter–American Convention shall apply.

(2) In all other cases the Convention on the Recognition and Enforcement of Foreign Arbitral Awards of June 10, 1958, shall apply.

§ 306. Applicable Rules of Inter–American Commercial Arbitration Commission

(a) For the purposes of this chapter the rules of procedure of the Inter–American Commercial Arbitration Commission referred to in Article 3 of the Inter–American Convention shall, subject to subsection (b) of this section, be those rules as promulgated by the Commission on July 1, 1988.

(b) In the event the rules of procedure of the Inter–American Commercial Arbitration Commission are modified or amended in accordance with the procedures for amendment of the rules of that Commission, the Secretary of State, by regulation in accordance with section 553 of title 5, consistent with the aims and purposes of this Convention, may prescribe that such modifications or amendments shall be effective for purposes of this chapter.

§ 307. Chapter 1; Residual Application

Chapter 1 applies to actions and proceedings brought under this chapter to the extent chapter 1 is not in conflict with this chapter or the Inter–American Convention as ratified by the United States.

APPENDIX B

United Nations Convention on the Recognition and Enforcement of Foreign Arbitral Awards

[The New York Convention]

June 10, 1958

Article I

1. This Convention shall apply to the recognition and enforcement of arbitral awards made in the territory of a State other than the State where the recognition and enforcement of such awards are sought, and arising out of differences between persons, whether physical or legal. It shall also apply to arbitral awards not considered as domestic awards in the State where their recognition and enforcement are sought.

2. The term "arbitral awards" shall include not only awards made by arbitrators appointed for each case but also those made by permanent arbitral bodies to which the parties have submitted.

3. When signing, ratifying or acceding to this Convention, or notifying extension under article X hereof, any State may on the basis of reciprocity declare that it will apply the Convention to the recognition and enforcement of awards made only in the territory of another Contracting State. It may also declare that it will apply the Convention only to differences arising out of legal relationships whether contractual or not, which are considered as commercial under the national law of the State making such declaration.

Article II

1. Each Contracting State shall recognize an agreement in writing under which the parties undertake to submit to arbitration all or any differences which have arisen or which may arise between them in respect of a defined legal relationship, whether contractual or not, concerning a subject matter capable of settlement by arbitration.

2. The term "agreement in writing" shall include an arbitral clause in a contract or an arbitration agreement, signed by the parties or contained in an exchange of letters or telegrams.

3. The court of a Contracting State, when seized of an action in a matter in respect of which the parties have made an agreement within the meaning of this article, shall, at the request of one of the parties, refer the parties to arbitration, unless it finds that the said agreement is null and void, inoperative or incapable of being performed.

Article III

Each Contracting State shall recognize arbitral awards as binding and enforce them in accordance with the rules of procedure of the territory where the award is relied upon, under the conditions laid down in the following articles. There shall not be imposed substantially more onerous conditions or higher fees or charges on the recognition or enforcement of arbitral awards to which this Convention applies than are imposed on the recognition or enforcement of domestic arbitral awards.

Article IV

1. To obtain the recognition and enforcement mentioned in the preceding article, the party applying for recognition and enforcement shall, at the time of the application, supply:

(a) the duly authenticated original award or a duly certified copy thereof;

(b) the original agreement referred to in article II or a duly certified copy thereof.

2. If the said award or agreement is not made in an official language of the country in which the award is relied upon, the party applying for recognition and enforcement of the award shall produce a translation of these documents into such language. The translation shall be certified by an official or sworn translator or by a diplomatic or consular agent.

Article V

1. Recognition and enforcement of the award may be refused, at the request of the party against whom it is invoked, only if that party furnishes to the competent authority where the recognition and enforcement is sought, proof that:

(a) the parties to the agreement referred to in article II were, under the law applicable to them, under some incapacity, or the said agreement is not valid under the law to which the parties have subjected it or, failing any indication thereon, under the law of the country where the award was made; or

(b) the party against whom the award is invoked was not given proper notice of the appointment of the arbitrator or of the arbitration proceedings or was otherwise unable to present his case; or

(c) the award deals with a difference not contemplated by or not falling within the terms of the submission to arbitration, or it contains decisions on matters beyond the scope of the submission to arbitration, provided that, if the decisions on matters submitted to arbitration can be separated from those not so submitted, that part of the award which contains decisions on matters submitted to arbitration may be recognized and enforced; or

(d) the composition of the arbitral authority or the arbitral procedure was not in accordance with the agreement of the parties, or, failing such agreement, was not in accordance with the law of the country where the arbitration took place; or

(e) the award has not yet become binding on the parties, or has been set aside or suspended by a competent authority of the country in which, or under the law of which, that award was made.

2. Recognition and enforcement of an arbitral award may also be refused if the competent authority in the country where recognition and enforcement is sought finds that:

(a) the subject matter of the difference is not capable of settlement by arbitration under the law of that country; or

(b) the recognition or enforcement of the award would be contrary to the public policy of that country.

Article VI

If an application for the setting aside or suspension of the award has been made to a competent authority referred to in Article V paragraph (1)(e), the authority before which the award is sought to be relied upon may, if it considers it proper, adjourn the decision on the enforcement of the award and may also, on the application of the party claiming enforcement of the award, order the other party to give suitable security.

Article VII

1. The provisions of the present Convention shall not affect the validity of multilateral or bilateral agreements concerning the recognition and enforcement of arbitral awards entered into by the Contracting States nor deprive any interested party of any right he may have to avail himself of an arbitral award in the manner and to the extent allowed by the law or the treaties of the country where such award is sought to be relied upon.

2. The Geneva Protocol on Arbitration Clauses of 1923 and the Geneva Convention on the Execution of Foreign Arbitral Awards of 1927 shall cease to have effect between Contracting States on their becoming bound and to the extent that they become bound, by this Convention.

Article VIII

1. This Convention shall be open until 31 December 1958 for signature on behalf of any Member of the United Nations and also on behalf of any other State which is or hereafter becomes a member of any specialized

agency of the United Nations, or which is or hereafter becomes a party to the Statute of the International Court of Justice, or any other State to which an invitation has been addressed by the General Assembly of the United Nations.

2. This Convention shall be ratified and the instrument of ratification shall be deposited with the Secretary–General of the United Nations.

Article IX

1. This Convention shall be open for accession to all States referred to in article VIII.

2. Accession shall be effected by the deposit of an instrument of accession with the Secretary–General of the United Nations.

Article X

1. Any State may, at the time of signature, ratification or accession, declare that this Convention shall extend to all or any of the territories for the international relations of which it is responsible. Such a declaration shall take effect when the Convention enters into force for the State concerned.

2. At any time thereafter any such extension shall be made by notification addressed to the Secretary–General of the United Nations and shall take effect as from the ninetieth day after the day of receipt by the Secretary–General of the United Nations of this notification, or as from the date of entry into force of the Convention for the State concerned, whichever is the later.

3. With respect to those territories to which this Convention is not extended at the time of signature, ratification or accession, each State concerned shall consider the possibility of taking the necessary steps in order to extend the application of this Convention to such territories, subject, where necessary for constitutional reasons, to the consent of the Governments of such territories.

Article XI

1. In the case of a federal or non-unitary State, the following provisions shall apply:

(a) With respect to those articles of this Convention that come within the legislative jurisdiction of the federal authority, the obligations of the federal Government shall to this extent be the same as those of Contracting States which are not federal States;

(b) With respect to those articles of this Convention that come within the legislative jurisdiction of constituent states or provinces which are not, under the constitutional system of the federation, bound to take legislative action, the federal Government shall bring such articles with a favourable recommendation to the notice of the appropriate authorities of constituent states or provinces at the earliest possible moment;

(c) A federal State party to this Convention shall, at the request of any other Contracting State transmitted through the Secretary–General of the United Nations, supply a statement of the law and practice of the federation and its constituent units in regard to any particular provision of this Convention, showing the extent to which effect has been given to that provision by legislative or other action.

Article XII

1. This Convention shall come into force on the ninetieth day following the date of deposit of the third instrument of ratification or accession.

2. For each State ratifying or acceding to this Convention after the deposit of the third instrument of ratification or accession, this Convention shall enter into force on the ninetieth day after deposit by such State of its instrument of ratification or accession.

Article XIII

1. Any Contracting State may denounce this Convention by a written notification to the Secretary–General of the United Nations. Denunciation shall take effect one year after the date of receipt of the notification by the Secretary–General.

2. Any State which has made a declaration or notification under article X may, at any time thereafter, by notification to the Secretary–General of the United Nations, declare that this Convention shall cease to extend to the territory concerned one year after the date of the receipt of the notification by the Secretary–General.

3. This Convention shall continue to be applicable to arbitral awards in respect of which recognition or enforcement proceedings have been instituted before the denunciation takes effect.

Article XIV

A Contracting State shall not be entitled to avail itself of the present Convention against other Contracting States except to the extent that it is itself bound to apply the Convention.

Article XV

The Secretary–General of the United Nations shall notify the States contemplated in article VIII of the following:

(a) Signature and ratifications in accordance with article VIII;

(b) Accessions in accordance with article IX;

(c) Declarations and notifications under articles I, X and XI;

(d) The date upon which this Convention enters into force in accordance with article XII;

(e) Denunciations and notifications in accordance with article XIII.

Article XVI

1. This Convention, of which the Chinese, English, French, Russian and Spanish texts shall be equally authentic, shall be deposited in the archives of the United Nations.

2. The Secretary–General of the United Nations shall transmit a certified copy of this Convention to the States contemplated in article VIII.

Note:

The United States became a party to the New York Convention in 1970. As of December 15, 1999, 124 nations—including most major commercial states—had ratified the Convention. (In addition, Pakistan had signed but not yet ratified the Convention.) At the present time, Brazil and Taiwan are perhaps the only states of any commercial importance that have not yet acceded to the Convention.

The United States ratified the Convention with the reservation that it would be applied, "on the basis of reciprocity, to the recognition and enforcement of only those awards made in the territory of another Contracting State." A total of 68 contracting states have ratified with this reservation of "reciprocity"—those that have ratified *without* making this reservation have the obligation to enforce *all* foreign awards, wherever rendered. See art. I(3). The United States also ratified the Convention with the reservation that it would be applied "only to differences arising out of legal relationships, whether contractual or not, which are considered as commercial under the national law of the United States." See art. I (3); FAA sec. 202. A total of 40 states have ratified with this reservation.

APPENDIX C

Inter–American Convention on International Commercial Arbitration

[The Panama Convention]

January 30, 1975

PREAMBLE

The Governments of the Member States of the Organization of American States, desirous of concluding a convention on international commercial arbitration, have agreed as follows:

Article 1

An agreement in which the parties undertake to submit to arbitral decision any differences that may arise or have arisen between them with respect to a commercial transaction is valid. The agreement shall be set forth in an instrument signed by the parties, or in the form of an exchange of letters, telegrams, or telex communications.

Article 2

Arbitrators shall be appointed in the manner agreed upon by the parties. Their appointment may be delegated to a third party, whether a natural or juridical person. Arbitrators may be nationals or foreigners.

Article 3

In the absence of an express agreement between the parties, the arbitration shall be conducted in accordance with the rules of procedure of the Inter–American Commercial Arbitration Commission.

Article 4

An arbitral decision or award that is not appealable under the applicable law or procedural rules shall have the force of a final judicial judgment. Its execution or recognition may be ordered in the same manner as that of decisions handed down by national or foreign ordinary courts, in accordance with the procedural laws of the country where it is to be executed and the provisions of international treaties.

Article 5

1. The recognition and execution of the decision may be refused, at the request of the party against which it is made, only if such party is able to prove to the competent authority of the State in which recognition and execution are requested:

a. That the parties to the agreement were subject to some incapacity under the applicable law or that the agreement is not valid under the law to which the parties have submitted it , or, if such law is not specified under the law of the State in which the decision was made; or

b. That the party against which the arbitral decision has been made was not duly notified of the appointment of the arbitrator or of the arbitration procedure to be followed, or was unable, for any other reason, to present his defense; or

c. That the decision concerns a dispute not envisaged in the agreement between the parties to submit to arbitration; nevertheless, if the provisions of the decision that refer to issues submitted to arbitration can be separated from those not submitted to arbitration, the former may be recognized and executed; or

d. That the constitution of the arbitral tribunal or the arbitration procedure has not been carried out in accordance with the terms of the agreement signed by the parties or, in the absence of such agreement, that the constitution of the arbitral tribunal or the arbitration procedure has not been carried out in accordance with the law of the State where the arbitration took place; or

e. That the decision is not yet binding on the parties or has been annulled or suspended by competent authority of the State in which, or according to the law of which, the decision has been made.

2. The recognition and execution of an arbitral decision may also be refused if the competent authority of the State in which the recognition and execution is requested finds:

a. That the subject of the dispute cannot be settled by arbitration under the law of the State; or

b. That the recognition or execution of the decision would be contrary to the public policy ("ordre public") of that State.

Article 6

If the competent authority mentioned in Article 5.1.e has been requested to annul or suspend the arbitral decision, the authority before which such decision is invoked may, if it deems it appropriate, postpone a decision on the execution of the arbitral decision and, at the request of the party requesting execution, may also instruct the other party to provide appropriate guaranties.

Article 7

This Convention shall be open for signature by the Member States of the Organization of American States.

Article 8

This Convention is subject to ratification. The instruments of ratification shall be deposited with the General Secretariat of the Organization of American States.

Article 9

This Convention shall remain open for accession by any other State. The instruments of accession shall be deposited with the General Secretariat of the Organization of American States.

Article 10

This Convention shall enter into force on the thirtieth day following the date of deposit of the second instrument of ratification.

For each State ratifying or acceding to the Convention after the deposit of the second instrument of ratification, the Convention shall enter into force on the thirtieth day after deposit by such State of its instrument of ratification or accession.

Article 11

If a State Party has two or more territorial units in which different systems of law apply in relation to the matters dealt with in this Convention, it may, at the time of signature, ratification or accession, declare that this Convention shall extend to all its territorial units or only to one or more of them.

Such declaration may be modified by subsequent declarations, which shall expressly indicate the territorial unit or units to which the Convention applies. Such subsequent declarations shall be transmitted to the General Secretariat of the Organization of American States, and shall become effective thirty days after the date of their receipt.

Article 12

This Convention shall remain in force indefinitely, but any of the States Parties may denounce it. The instrument of denunciation shall be deposited with the General Secretariat of the Organization of American States. After one year from the date of deposit of the instrument of denunciation, the Convention shall no longer be in effect for the denouncing State, but shall remain in effect for the other States Parties.

Article 13

The original instrument of this Convention, the English, French, Portuguese and Spanish texts of which are equally authentic, shall be deposited with the General Secretariat of the Organization of American

States. The Secretariat shall notify the Member States of the Organization of American States and the States that have acceded to the Convention of the signatures, deposits of instruments or ratification, accession, and denunciation as well as of reservations, if any. It shall also transmit the declarations referred to in Article 11 of this Convention.

Note:

As of December 15, 1999, 17 nations had ratified the Panama Convention. (In addition, the Dominican Republic and Nicaragua had signed but not yet ratified the Convention). Of these states, four—Brazil, the Dominican Republic, Honduras, and Nicaragua—were not parties to the New York Convention.

The United States became a party to the Panama Convention effective October 27, 1990. In ratifying the Convention, the Government of the United States made the following reservations:

"1. Unless there is an express agreement among the parties to an arbitration agreement to the contrary, where the requirements for application of both the Inter–American Convention on International Commercial Arbitration and the Convention on the Recognition and Enforcement of Foreign Arbitral Awards are met, if a majority of such parties are citizens of a state or states that have ratified or acceded to the Inter–American Convention and are member states of the Organization of American States, the Inter–American Convention shall apply. In all other cases, the Convention on the Recognition and Enforcement of Foreign Arbitral Awards shall apply.

"2. The United States of America will apply the rules of procedure of the Inter–American Commercial Arbitration Commission which are in effect on the date that the United States of America deposits its instrument of ratification, unless the United States of America makes a later official determination to adopt and apply subsequent amendments to such rules.

"3. The United States of America will apply the Convention, on the basis of reciprocity, to the recognition and enforcement of only those awards made in the territory of another Contracting State."

†